Girls®

Girls®

Gen Z and the Commodification of Everything

FREYA INDIA

Swift

SWIFT PRESS
First published in Great Britain by Swift Press 2026

1 3 5 7 9 8 6 4 2

Copyright © Freya India 2026

All rights reserved

The right of Freya India to be identified as the Author of this Work has been asserted in accordance with the Copyright, Designs and Patents Act 1988.

Typeset by Tetragon, London
Printed and bound in Great Britain by CPI Group (UK) Ltd, Croydon, CR0 4YY

A CIP catalogue record for this book is available from the British Library.

We make every effort to make sure our products are safe for the purpose for which they are intended. Our authorised representative in the EU for product safety is Easy Access System Europe, Mustamäe tee 50, 10621 Tallinn, Estonia gpsr.requests@easproject.com

ISBN: 9781800754706
eISBN: 9781800754713

To Evan,
who showed me I was worth more.

Contents

Introduction	1
Filtered	21
Diagnosed	57
Documented	93
Disconnected	127
Detached	157
'Empowered'	195
Conclusion	227
Acknowledgements	255
Notes	257
Index	335

Introduction

This is not the story of a generation falling apart. This is the story of a generation being remade, from people into products, from girls into GIRLS®.

We did fall apart, long ago. We were pulled apart from the pressure. But then we were remade, the fragments of us forged into products on display, objects to be optimised, things without feelings.

For a long time I thought the problem was me. Growing up, I felt disconnected from the modern world. I have always been shy and reserved; I'm sensitive, I overthink things, and I spent most of my childhood hiding out in my own head, observing, thinking, feeling too much.

For me, every experience of girlhood – insecurity about my appearance, changes to my body, talking to boys, trying to fit in and make friends – felt excruciating. I hated how young I looked, desperate to be older but also terrified of growing up. I hated how shy I was, how I would finally find my way into a friendship group only to sit in silence, afraid to say anything, then wonder why I didn't belong. I hated how I was seen as frigid and insecure, being the last girl in my friend group to kiss a boy, and go on a date. These were things I spent most of my adolescence punishing myself for.

In the early 2010s, when my friends and I were 10 or 11, social media apps arrived, and everything got worse. All the girls

I knew joined Instagram, and the face and body I hated suddenly had to be offered up to the market, ranked and reviewed. Now I had all these girls on my phone to compare myself to, not just from my school but from every school, always there to measure myself against. Sleepovers I hadn't been invited to now had to be scrolled through. Boys I liked were now rating me in front of everyone. My worth was made public, measured in likes and followers. I had constant reminders of how lonely and left out I was, but knew that feeling would only get worse if I removed myself from it all. The very thing hurting me became my lifeline.

The only word I can think of to describe it is *disconnected*. I felt disconnected from everyone, from everything. The friendships I had felt shallow and superficial, more about getting selfies together than anything else. The only community I had was online, the closest thing I had to neighbours the influencers I watched every night. And it wasn't only social media making me feel this way. My family had fallen apart when I was three and I was devastated, completely crushed by it, and I carried that feeling with me all through my teens and twenties. Much of my childhood was spent being exchanged between my mum and dad on their doorsteps, before sitting alone in my bedroom, messaging my friends on a screen.

For years I accepted that something was wrong with me. I wasn't cut out for the modern world; everyone else could cope but I couldn't. I needed more to get through life, more guidance and guard rails, more stability and security, something, anything, solid to hold on to.

All the while, adults around me insisted that these feelings were nothing new. Over and over again, I was reminded that adolescent

INTRODUCTION

girls always worry about their appearance, about fitting in, about finding their place in the world. They grow out of it eventually.

But God, things didn't feel *right*. They felt unmanageable. I was so unhappy with how I looked that I felt worthless and defective. I was so shy that I wanted to withdraw from everyone, even my own family. I was desperate to connect but also desperate to be left alone. I wanted to hide from the world but also obsessed over how I was performing, tracking my online reviews like I was some sort of product. I began to wonder if I had an anxiety disorder, then got even more trapped in my head going over signs and symptoms. Back then I had no words to describe what I was feeling; I wouldn't have known where to begin.

Over the years, though, I started sensing that other girls felt this way too. Friends were opening up to me, admitting that they suffered from anxiety and depression. Others were starving themselves, or showing up to school with cuts on their arms. Even extroverted, popular girls who seemed to have it together on the outside were beginning to fall apart on the inside.

Gradually I found girls talking online about this feeling. Some posted about crippling anxiety; others confessed to always feeling alone. Some felt so disconnected that they described observing themselves from the outside, as though they were inanimate objects. They felt detached from their bodies, from their sex, from their real selves, describing feelings of what would now be called dysphoria, dysmorphia and disassociation. Some girls suffered from social anxiety so severe they couldn't leave their homes, while others had panic attacks so extreme they needed emergency care. This was nothing new? Really?

At 18 I left for university in London, still feeling this way but shoving it down. I distracted myself however I could, but it was always there, simmering away. Life became about pretending to be this secure, confident young woman on the outside while feeling like a helpless girl on the inside. I stopped eating enough, I worked all the time, I withdrew from my friends, and while I didn't fall apart as dramatically as some other girls did, I carried this thing, this weight, this feeling of disconnection, everywhere.

Then, in 2020, as I was about to graduate, the pandemic hit. I moved back home, started watching my lectures and seminars online, and finally had time to think about why I felt this way. I started pitching to magazines and newspapers, trying to put into words how I felt about social media, about dating apps, about family breakdown, about how girlhood *felt* in the modern world. Eventually I found a job in a cafe and started a Substack called *GIRLS*, somewhere I could finally articulate all this. I wrote obsessively, scrawling ideas on receipts behind the till, writing notes on my hand between coffees, then rushing home to pour it all into essays. And as I wrote, it was as if the words flowed through my fingertips. I began to notice threads running through it all: the pain girls and young women felt, the industries profiting from this, the commodification of everything including our very selves, the lies we were being told. I realised I had so much to say about modern life – about the rapid rate of change, the complete lack of direction and guidance, the collapse of any real community – and about the industries dedicated to intensifying and profiting from our anxiety. I wrote about social media algorithms stripping girls of their unique personalities. I wrote about loneliness becoming a lucrative industry. I wrote about why so many of us were in therapy and on antidepressants. I wrote about the loss of religion and what it felt like to live without it. I wrote about everything that confused and angered me in the modern world but had

INTRODUCTION

somehow become normal: romance reduced to swiping and sliding into DMs, girls watching influencers live their lives instead of living their own, young women advertising themselves online like products on display.

And the more I put into words, the more I paid attention to the problem, the more I realised this was not 'nothing new'.

Everything I was feeling, everything young women were sharing with me and admitting online, was normal in a sense – but it was all unfolding against a backdrop that was unbelievably *abnormal*. We were the first generation to learn to flirt on Instagram, to try to find teenage love by swiping. We were the first to have our faces and bodies ranked and reviewed on social media before we had even reached puberty, the first to document our adolescence for an online audience. Our problems were painfully familiar and yet agonisingly different. I realised that the same adults telling me this was nothing new had no advice to give. Our world was moving too fast for them to know where to begin.

By this time, in my early twenties, I was also hearing about Gen Z's 'mental health crisis' everywhere: in headlines, bestselling books, surveys and studies. Suddenly there were reams of statistics about our rising rates of anxiety, depression, eating disorders, self-harm and suicide. And not only was I reading about it, I was *seeing* it, more and more: cousins, family friends, girls and young women I worked with at the cafe, all dealing with some sort of crisis, from panic attacks to social anxiety to eating disorders.

But we were all trying to hide it, one way or another. When I went out with friends we talked about hating the way we looked, ruminating on everything that was wrong with us, before rushing to take selfies. We complained about how shallow and fake it all felt, we wondered what had happened to real love and romance, before swiping on dating apps. We acted like we were strong and independent women, before battling over who had to order in restaurants. We opened up about our feelings, before insisting that we didn't have any. Beneath the laughter, behind the detachment, there was something else, a quiet despair. We talked about the world as though it was over, as though our time was already up, as though there was no hope for the future, no chance of achieving anything real or lasting. We would joke about our medication, our therapy sessions, our anxiety and attachment issues, about how unwell and unhappy we were. I was finding it harder and harder to believe we were all broken. Something else had to be happening.

I had sunk inward in my early teens, but by now I was seeing girls withdrawing at 12, 11, 10. Now my friends' sisters were falling apart. The feelings they were describing, no matter how familiar they sounded, were hitting them so hard and with such intensity that they just could not cope. Even everyday things like answering the phone, showing up to school or eating enough were too much to manage. Every adolescent experience, from hanging out with their friends to going on first dates to getting their first jobs, now came with such fear and rumination they would rather avoid it entirely and stay inside. How had girls become this anxious? This disconnected? Maybe I could accept that there was something wrong with me, but this many of us?

The truth, I came to realise, is that girls haven't changed. The world has. While we wrestle with the same age-old anxieties and insecurities as generations of young women before us, they are now being amplified, and commodified, like never before. Girls have always felt anxious, insecure and unsure of who they are, but never has this feeling been so intense. And never has it been so profitable.

INTRODUCTION

WHAT HAPPENED?

Before we begin, it's important to acknowledge that *some* of these struggles are nothing new. Adolescence has always been a time of angst and inner turmoil, especially for girls. Studies show that women are, on average, more ruminative, risk-averse and prone to anxiety than men.[1] Generally, girls and young women are more sensitive to negative stimuli than boys and men, but this gap becomes especially pronounced during puberty, when girls seem to experience a sudden drop in confidence, which falls below that of boys and never fully catches up.[2] At this age every emotion feels very intense, and girls become particularly vulnerable to social pressure.

But this is more than that.

What girls and young women are going through today *is* something new. We see this most clearly in the complete collapse of their mental health. Since the early 2010s, Generation Z (those of us born between roughly 1996 and 2011) has been falling apart, with adolescent girls hit hardest. And the generation after that, Gen Alpha (born between 2012 and 2025), is heading in the same direction.

The symptoms are everywhere. Rates of anxiety disorders, depression, self-harm and eating disorders among adolescent girls have soared since the early 2010s.[3] Across the Anglosphere, girls' self-harm and suicide rates have also reached record highs.[4] In the US, nearly one in three teenage girls seriously considered suicide in 2021, up from 19% a decade earlier, and double the rate for boys.[5] Suicide rates for girls as young as ten have also risen in recent years, along with emergency room visits for suicide attempts.[6]

There are countless theories for this crisis, but I still don't believe we have the full story. Yes, the mass adoption of smartphones, the rise of social media platforms and the advance of algorithms and online advertising had a huge impact in the early 2010s. But these were simply the mechanism, the machinery, for what I believe is the bigger story: the mass commodification of girls. Over the past 15 years, my generation has not only been broken but reassembled into something consumable, sellable, inanimate.

This book will attempt to tell that bigger story. *GIRLS®* will trace memories of my girlhood, from 2010 (when I was ten, just about to start secondary school) to 2025, to track where my generation, the older cohort of Gen Z, has ended up. I was born in 1999, given my first smartphone at 11, and came of age on social media. By thinking back through my memories I hope not only to make some sense of Gen Z's mental health crisis but also to answer other important questions along the way. How, for example, has the generation raised on self-love and body positivity become so insecure, and so convinced they need cosmetic surgery? How has a generation of girls and young women given more power and opportunities than ever before ended up so fragile and risk-averse? Why, despite all the mental health awareness, anti-stigma campaigns and a culture fluent in therapy-speak, are girls so anxious and depressed? And how is it possible that a generation of women promised the freedom to be whoever we want, with more ways to express ourselves than any before, is falling apart?

What happened?

My basic argument is simple. Modern digital technology amplifies the age-old anxieties adolescent girls have always felt. Throughout history, girls and young women have always worried about their appearance, their emotions, their social status, their friendships and families, their romantic relationships and their futures. But today these anxieties are being magnified to such an extreme that they have become unmanageable.

The problem, though, is more sinister than that. Not only does the modern world magnify these age-old anxieties, it ruthlessly exploits and profits from them. Corporations capitalise on our fears and vulnerabilities to constantly sell us products and services. The worse our mental health gets, the more 'solutions' we can be sold: a continuous conveyor belt of apps, products, services, pills and procedures promising happiness and fulfilment yet trapping us in a cycle of introspection, consumption, dependency and dissatisfaction.

Girls have always worried about their appearance, for example. But today they have to handle these insecurities in a world of Augmented Reality beauty filters, TikTok plastic surgeons pushing lip fillers and rhinoplasties, and an endless stream of edited, surgically enhanced Instagram influencers flooding their feeds.

It's also normal for girls to feel anxious and unsure about their emotions, confused about what's healthy and unhealthy. But now they are trying to make sense of all that in a world of therapy apps insisting they need professional help and intervention, TikTok influencers sharing vague symptoms of disorders and diagnoses for views, and ads for ADHD medication that can be delivered to their door.

It's normal, too, for girls and young women to worry about dating, relationships and their sexuality. But try dealing with all of that in a world where you feel you have to advertise yourself like a product on dating apps, where you watch violent videos on porn sites before you reach puberty, where casual sex and self-commodification are sold as female empowerment. And if you feel uncomfortable with any of this you are made to feel uptight, frigid and childlike, as if something is wrong with you.

Of course, there is nothing new about industries profiting from women's vulnerabilities. Over the past decade, though – with the rise of social media platforms, digital advertising and artificial intelligence (AI) – corporations have learned how to commodify not only girls' and young women's faces and bodies, but every part of our personal lives.

Corporations now have more immediate and intimate access to us than ever before. Smartphones and social media allow industries and influencers to reach girls all the time, day and night. Tech giants like Google, TikTok and Meta (the owner of Facebook, WhatsApp and Instagram) can also track every girl's move online, collecting and storing massive amounts of data on her activity. This data is then sold to advertisers who target her constantly through customised ads, delivered by algorithms on feeds designed to be as addictive as possible. Every worry a girl has can be monitored, categorised and monetised: from hating the shape of her nose, to fearing she might have a mental health disorder, to distrusting her boyfriend. This is aside from the rise of beauty, mental health and dating influencers who pretend to be her best friend while preying on her insecurities. The scale and sophistication of this exploitation is unprecedented.

But *GIRLS®* is not just another book about social media. It is about a vast, interconnected web of industries, each profiting from our experiences and anxieties. It is about how these industries influence everything from how we look to how we feel, from how we love to how we treat other people. It is about an entire commercial ecosystem that uses our emotions as raw material: a beauty industry that thrives on our self-loathing; a wellness industry that relies on our stress and anxiety; a pharmaceutical industry that needs

INTRODUCTION

our distress and diagnoses; a dating industry that depends on our dissatisfaction and continuous swiping; a porn industry that profits from our objectification; a consumer culture that cashes in on our search for identity and belonging. Our despair and disempowerment are worth billions.

And today we are not merely *sold* commodities like previous generations were. We *are* the commodity. We market and sell ourselves all the time. Girls and young women are packaging up their personal lives for Instagram, advertising themselves like products on dating apps and transforming themselves into professional brands to be monitored and managed. Since the rise of social media, girls have grown up seeing themselves as nothing but objects in a marketplace. Our happiness and self-worth now depend on how sellable we are.

'GIRLS®' is how I think of what girls have become in the modern world: products on display, things to be sold. I hope this term can capture how every experience of girlhood, every anxiety of adolescence, has been commodified. How we package it all up and perform it for an online audience. How we measure its worth, *our* worth, by public reviews and ratings. And how these ratings influence who we are, how we look, how we feel, how we act, and how we make sense of life. What has happened over the past decade is a radical transformation of girlhood. We are no longer girls but GIRLS®. This is why so many of us feel disconnected from ourselves, and from the world around us.

All the while, we have been led to believe that happiness and empowerment lie in our own commodification. A vast machinery of corporations and advertisers mines our confidence, self-worth and sense of belonging, only to sell it back to us at a profit. These industries turn our pain and struggles into sales strategies, positioning themselves as perfect solutions. They promise us better faces, better bodies, better personalities, better substitutes for human connection. But these 'solutions' only deepen that feeling of disconnection. And the cycle never ends, because a generation of girls who have had it drilled into them during their most formative and vulnerable years that they are not enough – while plied with empty promises of beauty, of love, of belonging, and an ever-expanding list of purchases to 'fix' them – are a generation of perfect consumers.

We are both the consumers and the consumed. What girls and young women are experiencing is an entirely new way of existing. Now we have been fashioned into things, we live to tweak, optimise and upgrade ourselves so we can sell better.

But for something to be remade, first it has to fall apart. Or, more accurately, first it has to be broken.

ABOUT THIS BOOK

GIRLS® is made up of six chapters: Filtered, Diagnosed, Documented, Disconnected, Detached and 'Empowered'. Each chapter covers an age-old anxiety with which I believe most girls and young women will be intimately familiar. Filtered focuses on anxiety about our faces and bodies; Diagnosed on our feelings and emotions; Documented on our social status and popularity; Disconnected on our friendships and family; Detached on our romantic relationships; and 'Empowered' on our sense of purpose and fulfilment.

Each chapter traces what has changed from the early 2010s to the present. These changes are not only technological but also cultural, from the evolving language of feminism to the expansion

INTRODUCTION

of therapy culture to the emergence of new progressive norms. Together these cultural, technological and commercial forces collide and intersect, intensifying insecurities like never before.

I have three main audiences in mind for this book.

The first is young women in their twenties, like me, who remember the timeline of how we became GIRLS®: technological changes like the launch of Instagram, the first selfie-editing apps like Facetune, and their first time swiping on Tinder, along with cultural changes like the rise of therapy-speak, the new demands of social justice activism, the language of self-love and finding our authentic selves. These readers will probably look back on all of this with both nostalgia and unease, as I do. I'm out of my girlhood now, but as I think back to those years, I'm beginning to realise I never really had one. My teenage memories, many that I have reflected on for the first time while writing this book, are much bleaker than I ever realised before, and hard to make sense of now.

To those readers, I hope this doesn't feel like a lecture. This is not a book written by someone who has never used Snapchat filters, or edited herself on Facetune, or swiped on dating apps, someone who saw through it all from the start. I wrestled with all these things. I tried to keep up with every trend and technology mentioned in this book, and felt anxious about it for years. I still do. Everything written here, and on my Substack, *GIRLS*, is a note to myself, a reminder of what matters in life, to try to keep myself on track. I don't pretend to have the entire explanation, or all the answers.

My second audience is younger girls: those who have never known another world than this one. For you, I want to show how drastically life has changed in the last 15 years, and that things weren't always this way. I want to show how we got here, how rapidly this new world came into being, and, crucially, who benefits from it. Because it certainly isn't you.

By the end of this book, I hope both girls and young women will see that their struggles make sense, and will stop punishing themselves for feeling unhappy. I want them to see the truth: that many of us have been misled, manipulated and exploited in our most vulnerable and formative years, and that the companies behind this do not care about our empowerment or well-being or connection; they care about profit. My goal is for girls to finish this book feeling angry that their girlhoods were stolen, determined to take back their dignity, and empowered to make a change – not anxious about what's wrong with them.

Lastly, this book is for older readers: parents, grandparents, aunts, uncles, carers, teachers, anybody who has a girl or young woman in their life. My hope for you is to get across the sheer pace and scale of the change. I want to show how radically different this world is from the one you grew up in, how the very concepts of friendship, family, community and falling in love have been ripped apart and redefined, and how, as these foundations have crumbled, girls have fallen apart with them.

To these readers, I hope you will relate to the age-old anxieties and adolescent experiences I describe in this book. That you will think back to your first crush, that need for belonging and acceptance you felt as a teenager, along with the insecurity, anxiety and jealousy that likely came with it. But I also want to convey the vastly different context in which girls today are trying to handle these feelings. My goal is to inspire some empathy, and a little more grace. When I was a teenager, there was a tendency to mock, trivialise and dismiss Gen Z's distress as ordinary adolescence, to

INTRODUCTION

call any concern a moral panic. But the pain is too real now. That time is over.

Before we begin, let me briefly explain what this book isn't.

WHAT THIS BOOK ISN'T

There are a few things to clarify. First, I am aware that not all girls and young women feel the same way I do. We are all different, and when I talk about 'Gen Z' or 'girls and young women' in the book, I am of course generalising. Plenty of girls couldn't care less about keeping up with Instagram beauty trends; many easily manage their emotions without overthinking or self-diagnosing; some don't feel any anxiety from dating apps. And while young women in their twenties might remember some of the trends and technological changes I mention in the book, they might not relate to how they made me *feel* – maybe Instagram never made them insecure, maybe they did maintain deep friendships, maybe they do feel empowered by mainstream feminism. I have friends who feel this way. I also have many who are falling apart.

So no, not all girls and young women will relate. But I am speaking for and to those wrestling with the modern world and themselves; those, who, like me, are always overthinking, over-analysing and obsessing over what is wrong with them. Those who feel alone and ashamed for hurting this way. After years of trying to articulate these feelings, I know these girls and young women exist, and that there are more of us than I ever thought. I wish someone had told me when I was younger that they felt the same way, that they couldn't cope either. That is why this book exists.

Most readers will likely relate to some chapters and not others. Some parts will resonate, others might not. Some readers might struggle with the mental health industry but not with dating apps. Others might feel anxious about romantic relationships but unbothered by hustle culture. Personally I have felt all these pressures at once, and I suspect many girls will relate to that too. I hope I can do justice to the intensity of that feeling.

GIRLS®, then, is not an exhaustive list of every challenge girls and young women face in the modern world. It is a reflection on my own experiences and memories of girlhood, and a starting point, I hope, for more young women to think and talk about theirs. I am attempting to capture a snapshot of the world we live in now, and to make some sense of the past decade, both for the benefit of young women today and to help the next generation of girls avoid the traps so many of us fell into.

I also want to make it clear that this book does not argue that girls are suffering more than boys. Boys and young men are struggling too, with rising rates of depression, loneliness, hopelessness and suicide.[7] By objective measures of education and employment, young men are often doing worse than young women.[8] This is a huge cause for concern, and deserves our attention.

My focus here is on girls though, and this is for a few reasons. First, what is alarming about the mental health crisis among girls is the speed and scale of the change. Both boys and girls began struggling with their mental health in the early 2010s, but the rise in self-harm and eating disorders has been especially steep for girls.[9]

Second, I focus on girls because I feel I can speak with what little authority I have. I am not an expert or an academic; I am a woman in her twenties. It's safe to say there aren't many topics I can write about with confidence. But over the past three years I have devoted almost all my time to understanding what is happening to girls: researching and writing for my own Substack, pitching articles to publications, speaking with dozens of parents and daughters. Along the way I became a staff writer for Jonathan Haidt's Substack, *After Babel*, where I spent month after month thinking about what smartphones and social media are doing to us. And I know these struggles intimately. Many young women have suffered far worse than I have, but what I can sincerely say is this: I have felt that anxiety, that loneliness, that disconnection and detachment. I will try my best to articulate it, both for my own sanity and hopefully for some of yours.

Finally, I acknowledge that this is not the worst world to grow up in. I understand that much of this book could be dismissed as 'first-world problems'. And throughout, I am mostly talking about girls and young women in the developed Western world. Of course there are girls in these countries who don't have the luxury of worrying about TikTok mental health trends or Instagram beauty standards, but many of the girls struggling with what may seem like superficial things are now barely hanging on. When this many girls and young women are harming themselves, starving themselves and *killing* themselves, the time for trivialising these problems has passed.

There is also much to be grateful for in the modern world. But while our world may be more materially comfortable, while we might have it easier in many ways, it is *psychologically* demanding in ways we have never seen before. Our challenges are so novel we can barely comprehend them, let alone combat them. And while our material needs may be met, deeper human needs – for connection, for meaning, for love, for face-to-face contact – have been neglected. We have better technologies, but we have nowhere to belong. We have more free time, but we kill it with our devices. We have constant online connection, but we often feel alone. There is no imminent threat to our lives, but there is little meaning to them either.

We are also relentlessly reminded how good we have it. My generation is always being told how lucky we are to have all of this cutting-edge technology, to have access to so much mental health advice, to have the world at our fingertips. So when girls feel the way I did, they can't make sense of it. They think something is wrong with *them*, not with the world in which they are growing up.

That is why we need to go back.

GOING BACK

It's time we hear the other side of the story. This book is about where modern culture is hurtling in the wrong direction, and what new constraints and pressures girls have been put under, having been liberated from older ones. For previous generations of women, the biggest battles may have been the stigma around mental health, having to hide parts of themselves, and, in some cases, complete dependence on men. But these are not the most pressing problems any more – at least not for the girls and young women I'm talking about.

For us, the issue is no longer stigma but the pathologising of normal human emotions and experiences, and relying on experts to explain how we feel. Instead of totally depending on men, many of us now fear and resent *all* men, are anxious and risk-averse about dating, and are terrified to trust anyone. What began as having no sense of self and few opportunities for self-expression has now veered into an obsession with ourselves, into vanity and narcissism. And while previous generations of women were once bound by their communities, held back by responsibilities and expectations,

INTRODUCTION

we now live with almost no obligations to anyone, face a complete loss of community, and can't even look our neighbours in the eye. Girls are being lied to about the real problems, and it's time to start telling the truth.

The only way to understand the world I'm talking about is to go back. Back to the early 2010s, as I was hitting puberty, as the first social media apps like Instagram and Snapchat were launching, as everything was beginning to change. This is the story of how we became GIRLS®, and how we can find our way back again.

Filtered

'Beautiful is easier than ever.'
Facetune[1]

FACETUNE

'For today's video,' says James Charles, an American beauty influencer with more than 24 million subscribers on YouTube, 'I tweeted asking you babes to send me your unedited make-up selfies and something that you want fixed.'

The YouTube video I'm watching, 'FACETUNING MY FOLLOWERS SELFIES', is from 2018 and has over 11 million views. 'EVERYONE edits their photos, whether they want to admit it or not,' the caption reads, 'and I love openly talking about it because I love photo editing.'

I watch as James scrolls through a series of selfies sent in by his young fans. 'Fix my nose, please and thanks,' a young girl named Zoe asks him on Twitter, attaching a selfie. She looks like a teenager. 'Wow, a sister looks beautiful and snatched.' James grins. 'Let's go ahead and snatch this nose up just a little bit more.'

He loads her selfie into Facetune and starts smoothing her skin, giving viewers tips on how to keep edits subtle. 'There's nothing wrong with fixing any insecurities,' James assures us as he sketches in a 'new nose bridge', drawing two dark lines down Zoe's nose using the paint tool, before blending them out using the smooth tool. By the end, her nose is half the size.

'Literally so good,' James giggles, toggling between the before and after. 'It looks like she can barely even breathe.' He smirks at the camera and snaps his fingers: 'I just fixed up Zoe's nose nice and good ... that is how you get a rhinoplasty with Facetune.'

James then moves on to another girl who wants a 'different feature fixed'. The next young woman has sent in a selfie but forgotten to mention which feature she wants edited. James decides it's her skin. 'She does have a few blemishes right here on the cheek that we can definitely get rid of super easily.'

Before we continue, I have to be clear: I'm watching this against my will. I'm researching the selfie-editing app Facetune and its rise since the early 2010s. I expect the comments to be combative – after all, this is a man 'fixing' girls' faces for entertainment. But instead I find the opposite. The video is flooded with praise; the most popular comments include 'this is so educational wtf I am learning so much', 'this is a better way to learn i feel like school is so stressful this is kinda relaxing', and 'james seems like such a good person to be friends with, like i swearrrr. we all need someone like him'. As I scroll through them, wondering where the outrage is, I hear James end his video with an empowering message: 'It is so important that you guys love yourselves, love your bodies, and love the person that you are.'[2]

I have so many questions. The first is: how the hell did we get here?

Facetune is a photo and video editing app created by the software company Lightricks. When it launched in 2013, Instagram had already been around for almost three years. Back then, though, it felt relatively innocent. Girls mostly posted scenic sunsets, funny selfies with friends and pictures of their breakfasts, with only a few filters to choose from: 'Nashville' added a soft pink tint; '1977' applied a faded, retro effect; 'Inkwell' was monochrome; 'Toaster' gave a warm glow. We could filter our pictures with other apps too, like CamWow and websites like Webcam Toy, but these were mostly playful: we could swirl our features, add a thermal effect or turn ourselves into cartoons. Girls also had basic editing apps like Perfect365 which would apply virtual make-up to our selfies, like fake eyelashes or glittery eyeshadow.

But Facetune went further. Suddenly we could *reshape* our features, with precise tools to slim noses, sculpt cheekbones and smooth skin. 'Very bad acne days?' the company asked in 2017. 'Facetune is going to be your next best friend.'[3] And they were right.

Facetune dominated the market. Within a year of release, the editing app was the most popular paid photo and video app across more than 120 countries.[4] By 2019, Facetune and its free follow-up app, Facetune2, had more than 55 million combined users.[5]

The pressure for girls to Facetune themselves grew fast. Soon, so many Instagram selfies were edited that unedited ones felt invisible. As James Charles put it while Facetuning his fans, 'Posting an unedited photo online these days is very very very brave.'[6]

By the late 2010s, editing apps had become not only accepted but *celebrated*. Celebrities admitted to using and loving Facetune. In 2018, when popular influencer Tana Mongeau was asked about her skincare routine on X (formerly Twitter), she replied, 'people keep asking, so, my skin care routine !!!!!! it's facetune. that's it. that's my skin care routine' to 58,000 likes.[7]

Soon the conversation turned from whether it was acceptable for girls to Facetune themselves to whether it was okay to Facetune other people. 'get u a girl who will Facetune u both,' American model Chrissy Teigen tweeted in 2020 after an American diplomat was called out for Facetuning herself in a photo while leaving her husband unedited.[8] In 2022, *VICE* published 'The Complicated Ethics of Facetuning Your Friends', asking whether it was fair to only edit yourself or if you should extend the courtesy. As one influencer put it in the article, 'It's selfish when someone edits themselves without offering the same to everyone else in the picture.'[9] (Maybe not *everyone* though: in 2018 Khloé Kardashian was accused of Facetuning her five-month-old baby for Instagram…[10])

As a teenager I went from watching make-up tutorials on YouTube to watching Facetune tutorials. Girls my age stopped cringing at catfishing – pretending to look completely different online – and started following step-by-step tutorials like 'HOW TO FACETUNE LIKE A PRO' and 'how to ACTUALLY catfish people (makeup tutorial + beauty secrets)' (1.4 million views).[11]

In 2017, for example, James Charles posted a YouTube video called 'HOW TO TAKE YOUR SELFIES FROM DRAB TO FAB! FACETUNE TUTORIAL', which has over 2 million views. James begins by making it clear he is only going to make small changes, before changing his eye colour from brown to blue. 'Unfortunately I cannot afford plastic surgery and I also legally cannot get plastic surgery because I'm underage,' James jokes while sharpening his jawline, 'so this is the next best thing we got up in here.' He goes to edit the other side of his face, but – after insisting earlier that there is nothing shameful about selfie-editing – pauses before continuing, 'I'm not going to do anything here just because my jawline lines up with the corner of this wall and if I move it around, it's gonna look very very distorted and weird. Not trying to get called out for editing today!' (Wait – which is it? If there's nothing wrong with fixing insecurities, why is getting caught embarrassing?) 'My nose is the thing that I'm most insecure about, so I do like to edit it,' James continues as he makes his nose smaller. 'If you don't want to edit your nose like this, don't fricking do it! It's really not that serious.' But then he ends the video by encouraging everyone to try out his tips and tricks.[12]

By 2020, one UK survey found that only 29% of respondents would post a picture of themselves without retouching it first. Among those who edited their photos, 71% of them used Facetune.[13] By 2021, Facetune had ranked among Apple's top five paid apps every year since 2015, a record unmatched by any other app on the list.[14] By 2023, apps developed by Lightricks had been downloaded over 730 million times, with the company valued at around $1.8 billion.[15]

Facetune kept evolving. Facetune2, released in 2016, added a 'one-tap fix' feature, allowing users to apply all their edits with a single click. In 2020, Facetune introduced its most anticipated feature yet: *video* editing. Girls could now pause a video of themselves, edit a single frame to narrow their waist, make their bum bigger and whiten their teeth, and the app would seamlessly apply these changes across the whole video. They could walk, dance, talk, and their new face and body would stay intact. 'That's right,' said Facetune's website, 'a Kylie Jenner pout can be yours – live on video, no Botox required.'[16]

Now the app also has an instant AI enhancer ('your one-stop solution for all your natural and instant retouching needs') and even an 'AI personal assistant' (your 'new photo editing bestie').[17] Simply ask for smoother skin, a sharper jawline or a curvier body, and the chatbot will give you 'exactly what you need'.[18] As Facetune puts it: 'Let's be real – we've all been there, tapping through endless tools trying to get that perfect look. But what if you could just say what you want, like you're chatting with a friend?'[19]

Today, girls and young women can fix their insecurities whenever they want, with more options than ever before. Other editing apps include BeautyPlus, FaceApp and PrettyUp, which calls itself an 'AI Body Editor Video' and is rated for ages 13 and up.[20] Perfect365, the app I used in my pre-teens to apply cartoon eyelashes and neon eyeshadow, has also become an 'AI Makeup App', promising girls that 'With just a few taps, you can change your entire appearance'.[21]

This all feels normal now. But when Facetune first launched, what it gave girls like me was something entirely new. For the first time, those age-old insecurities had an instant, portable fix. Forget the painful process of accepting yourself, of coming to terms with your flaws or even learning to love them; none of that was necessary any more. Childhoods were spent chiselling cheeks. Twelve-year-olds taught themselves to perform virtual rhinoplasties. I spent my teenage years following a routine for correcting my face and body: upload photo, shrink nose, sculpt jaw, cinch waist, contour cheeks, bronze skin. *Retouch, Refine, Resize.* Delete the original before anyone could see it. Sometimes I would accidentally hit the *undo* button, see the real me flash up, and feel repulsed. My face and body were unbearable, in ways I had never even noticed before but now could not unsee.

Back then, the only real downside to Facetune was the time it took. Before AI and one-tap fixes, teenage girls like me spent hours meticulously reshaping and resizing, trying to find the balance between looking perfect and not getting caught. So when Snapchat introduced filters in 2015, everything changed.

FILTERS

Snapchat launched its Augmented Reality (AR) filters, known as 'Lenses', in September 2015, having acquired the technology from a start-up called Looksery in a $150 million deal.[22] Using facial recognition, AR filters could overlay effects on our faces in real time, adjusting to our movements. When we smiled, frowned or opened our mouths, the filter moved along with us, or played an animation.

At first, filters were fun and playful. 'Dog Filter' gave us floppy puppy ears and a dog nose; 'Flower Crown' gave us a crown of pastel flowers; 'Puking Rainbows' enlarged our eyes and simulated us vomiting a rainbow when we opened our mouths; 'Face Swap' let us switch faces with friends. 'They are very silly,' a *Vox* video put it in 2016, 'but the engineering behind them is serious.'[23]

Snapchat filters became a fixation. Filtered selfies, screenshotted from the app, filled our Instagram and Facebook feeds. The selection of filters rotated daily, so girls at my school would check the home page every morning to see what was new. We were obsessed with the puppy ears and flower crown filters, partly because they were cute and funny, but mostly because they subtly changed our faces. They smoothed our skin, widened our eyes and narrowed our noses, distracting us with dog ears and fun animations. We loved how we looked with them, but we weren't sure why. All we knew was that we couldn't stand to see our faces without them. I remember girls cropping out the cartoon parts – the sparkles, butterflies and flower crowns – to post their filtered faces on Instagram, keeping the glowing skin and longer lashes. Snapchat soon seemed to realise that their most popular filters were the ones that made girls look better, and they doubled down.

In 2017, Snap Inc., the parent company of Snapchat, introduced Lens Studio, a desktop app where both users and brands could create custom AR filters. Instagram followed in 2018, launching its own AR filters and allowing users to design their own. Beauty filters became less playful and more realistic. Instagram soon filled with filters that smoothed skin, applied precise virtual make-up and made tiny tweaks to our features that were difficult to detect. The Instagram filter 'Paris' made skin look poreless; 'Shiny Fox' subtly changed our eye shape and tucked in our chin; 'Belle' gave us the perfect natural nose job.

But TikTok took things even further. In 2021, it introduced its first AR filters, followed in 2022 by Effect House, a platform allowing users and brands to create their own filters. Filters rapidly advanced. By 2023, TikTok had launched AI-powered effects that could plump lips, add smiles and alter faces in real time.[24] These new filters don't simply overlay cartoon graphics on our faces but use machine learning to blend our real features with virtual ones. 'It's a competition between the camera's view of your face and the style TikTok wants to morph you into,' *The Verge* explained in 2023. These filters compare our features to a vast dataset of images – of cheeks, eyebrows, lips and eyes – and reconstruct our faces in real time, combining the two. Trained on a huge database of human faces and expressions, AI filters are disturbingly precise, always learning how to better adjust to different faces, movements and expressions.[25]

Now AI-powered filters are so seamless, so realistic, they are almost undetectable. The Snapchat filters I used as a teenager would often lag or glitch if I moved too fast. Now, girls can cover their features, turn their heads or wave their hands across their faces, and the filters stay perfectly intact.

'Bold Glamour', for example, launched on TikTok in 2023. This beauty filter scans and reshapes faces in real time: it contours cheeks, lifts brows, slims noses, fills lips, smooths skin, reshapes eyes and applies heavy make-up with smoky eyeshadow, winged eyeliner and thick eyelashes, all while looking so realistic that you would never know it was on. 'Today I learned that this new viral beauty filter was created using machine learning,' TikToker @zhangsta explains in a viral video. 'Unlike traditional beauty filters that use an augmented 3D face mesh that is overlaid on top of your face, filters like "Bold Glamour" and "Teenage Look" use a machine deep-learning tech called GAN [generative adversarial networks], meaning every pixel on your face is regenerated and then outputted after referencing another dataset of images – which is why the filter looks so realistic.'[26]

Within a month of release on TikTok, 'Bold Glamour' had more than 400 million views.[27] The filter is so realistic and alters your appearance so dramatically that beauty brand Dove launched the campaign #TurnYourBack, urging girls and young women not to use it.[28] And this was not the first time beauty filters had caused controversy. In 2019, Instagram banned filters replicating or promoting cosmetic surgery, after growing concerns about girls' mental health.[29] Only a year later, though, the decision was reversed and Meta once more allowed distortion filters, banning only those that 'directly promote cosmetic surgery'.[30] 'Bold Glamour', meanwhile, remains available on TikTok.

Today, girls and young women have access to every type of beauty filter imaginable. TikTok's 'Teenage Look' seamlessly erases all signs of ageing; 'Hourglass' cinches waists and exaggerates curves live on video. Until 2019, Instagram even had a filter called 'FixMe' (created by developer Daniel Mooney, who invites users to 'come live your plastic surgery fantasy'[31]) which covers girls' faces with bruises, surgical markings and the words 'FIX ME'. TikTok has body modification filters too, which can lengthen legs, add curves and slim waists on video. And filter after filter is designed to reveal to girls flaws they would never have noticed otherwise: 'Symmetry' analyses how symmetrical their faces are; 'Inverted Filter' flips their face to show them how others see them; 'Golden Ratio' overlays a grid onto their faces which measures their facial proportions against a perfect mathematical ideal. Some filters even morph users' features to match it.

By 2022, Snapchat had over 300,000 active Lens creators who had made more than 3 million custom AR Lenses.[32] By 2024, over 350 million Snapchat users were using AR filters daily.[33] (According to Snapchat, over 90% of young people in the UK, US and France use the company's AR products.)[34] In 2020, Facebook reported that 400,000 creators from 190 countries had published over a million AR filters on its platform and Instagram.[35] More than 600 million people had used at least one AR effect, with beauty filters among the most popular.[36]

Filters have become so addictive that girls and young women are now trying to replicate them in real life. Beauty influencers post make-up tutorials on how to look like the edited version of ourselves ('HOW TO LOOK FACETUNED IN REAL LIFE!!') and mimic beauty filters with make-up ('The Viral 'BOLD GLAMOUR' Filter Tutorial'), while cosmetic brands like L'Oréal promote products to recreate filters ('3 SNAPCHAT FILTER-INSPIRED MAKEUP LOOKS').[37]

By 2020, almost half of girls aged 11 to 16 in the UK said they regularly used apps or filters to look better online.[38] By 2021, 85% of girls had altered their appearance online by the age of 13.[39] Even for those who choose not to use filters, they are becoming harder to avoid. TikTok's built-in Retouch feature lets users edit their faces for live videos,[40] and some have even complained it was switched on by default. Several young women describe opening the app only to find their teeth whitened, under-eyes smoothed and nose thinned, without even selecting a filter.[41] Meanwhile Snapchat's front-facing camera is believed to soften features before filters are applied, and Zoom has a 'Touch Up My Appearance' option that smooths skin during video calls.[42]

The more girls use these filters, the more distorted their view of themselves seems to become. They forget what humans look like. They punish themselves for not having skin as smooth as 'Teenage Look', faces as chiselled as 'Bold Glamour' and body proportions like 'Hourglass Body'.

In the early 2010s, filters gave girls like me instant confidence. Immediate relief from insecurity. Don't like your skin? Hate your nose? Look too young without make-up? We could apply a filter and kill any discomfort. But filters gave us a fragile confidence, the kind that spikes when your crush views your flower-crown Snapchat Story or you get hundreds of likes on your puppy-ear selfie, only to crash when you catch your reflection in the mirror.

And at the same time, something else was coming for our confidence. Social media platforms began placing us on what I can only describe as conveyor belts. If you wanted to avoid filtered selfies, or beauty trends that made you feel insecure, it became almost impossible. We were attached to algorithms, ready to transport us to dark and extreme places.

ALGORITHMS AND ADVERTISING

In the early 2010s Instagram used a chronological feed, with users seeing posts in the order they were uploaded. But in 2016, it switched to an algorithmic feed, where posts appeared based on what the app calculated we wanted to see. The goal was to make our feeds more personalised, and more addictive, so we would keep scrolling for longer. That way, Instagram could show us more ads, and make more money.

This changed everything. Algorithms, essentially mechanisms for sorting and prioritising information, were already being used by platforms like Facebook and Instagram. But early algorithms targeted users based on basic demographic data like age, sex and location.

As data analytics and machine learning advanced, so did the algorithms. Soon they could categorise us based on specific behaviour patterns – tracking what posts we liked, saved, commented on and lingered over – and even our emotional states.[43] And this wasn't only happening on Instagram. In 2016, Twitter also introduced an algorithmic feed, and Snapchat followed in 2017, sorting Stories by relevance rather than when they were posted. Across social media, users began to complain that they no longer saw posts from their friends, just reels of recommendations showing them what they should buy, who they should look like, and finding them strangers to follow.

Fast forward to the 2020s, and algorithms have more intimate access to girls' inner lives than ever before. Few are as powerful as TikTok's 'For You' page, the default home screen for anyone opening the app. Even if you don't follow a single account, 'For You' delivers an infinite stream of videos, adapting instantly based on your every move: how long you watch a video, whether you like it, share it, save it, watch it all the way through.⁴⁴ The algorithm adjusts so fast that girls' feeds can change within seconds of showing interest in, or being insecure about, something. Some feel as though TikTok is reading their mind, or knows them better than they know themselves.

Algorithms can also recommend *new* insecurities. During the pandemic, for example, a fear of ageing started trending on TikTok. Skincare videos flooded 'For You' pages, promoting procedures like Baby Botox (preventative Botox injections for teenagers and twenty-somethings) and an endless parade of essential new purchases: retinols, peptide creams, chemical exfoliants, LED light masks, even pillows shaped like electrical plugs to stop us getting wrinkles. One popular TikToker started teaching girls how to train their 'facial muscles to stop working' to prevent smile lines, reminding us to avoid the sun, stick silicone patches over our faces while we sleep, and rehearse a new, wrinkle-free smile in the mirror.⁴⁵ Other influencers insisted that girls apply sun cream every two hours, even indoors. One even suggested sleeping in it.⁴⁶

Beauty trends have always changed, and fast. But now the pace feels like it is giving us whiplash. Girls no longer need to read beauty magazines or follow brands to know what is trending. Trends change every week, every day. Now we have 'micro trends' (better known as 'micro insecurities'), viral beauty fads that blow up on apps like TikTok and vanish just as fast. Had your lips filled? Now everyone is dissolving them. One week everyone wants a curvy body and a Brazilian Butt Lift; the next, being skinny is back. Then it's all about 'hip dips' (tiny curves between our hips and thighs) and how to get rid of them, before girls are worrying whether they have the right eye shape (do you have doe eyes? Fox eyes? Siren eyes? Are you 'girl pretty' or 'boy pretty'?). Fox-eye surgery, a procedure that lifts the corners of the eyes for a catlike look, is in and then forgotten, replaced by buccal fat removal, which extracts fat from the cheeks to sculpt the face. Overcome one insecurity only to be hit with the next, from 'bad facial harmony' to 'septum arms' to 'double lip lines' to 'cortisol face' to 'myofascial imbalances' (who knows?!).[47]

But algorithms aren't just experts at reminding girls what to worry about. They also recommend exactly what to buy to fix it.

Instagram introduced ads in 2013, starting with sponsored posts and videos in our feeds. As the app grew, reaching around 600 million monthly users by 2016, so did opportunities for advertisers.[48] With a chronological feed, though, it was hard to reach the right people at the right time.

That all changed with algorithms. Social media platforms could soon target us not only by age or location, but also by emotions and vulnerabilities. According to the daily newspaper *The Australian*, by 2017 Facebook was allegedly telling advertisers that it could tap into 'moments of psychological vulnerability' by tracking words like 'worthless', 'insecure', 'stressed', 'anxious', 'stupid', 'useless' and 'like a failure'.[49] Former Facebook executive Sarah Wynn-Williams said that the company even tracked when teenage girls deleted selfies, to serve them beauty ads at that exact moment.[50]

Then there are facial filters, many of which collect biometric data for advertisers. Young women my age have been using these filters for about a decade now, since we were pre-teens, unknowingly feeding platforms data about our faces and insecurities. What seemed like harmless fun has helped apps guess our age, gender and vulnerabilities to better target ads. In 2020, for example, TikTok was accused of illegally collecting biometric data about users' facial features, age, ethnicity and sex, to improve ads. Eventually the $92 million claim was settled out of court.[51]

Editing apps are no exception. Perfect365, which has over 100 million users, openly admits to analysing biometric data like facial features, and collecting personal information including full names and locations. Privacy analysts say this data is then sold to third parties, often without clear consent.[52] In 2024, Lightricks faced a class action lawsuit for also collecting and storing biometric data without permission. The company agreed to a settlement of nearly $4.5 million.[53]

Imagine you are a 14-year-old girl today who hates her lips. Before social media, you might have seen the occasional billboard or magazine ad for lip-plumping serums. By the mid 2010s, when I was a teenager, you might have stumbled across Kylie Jenner and thought about buying her lip kit. But now? Now the algorithm knows about your insecurity. It has been tracking how long you linger on lip filler videos, how often you pause on influencers like Kylie, and when you try on filters that give you bigger lips. One day you cave and search for lip fillers, and within minutes your feed transforms into a torrent of ads and influencers: *Look at this lip filler transformation! Come with me to get lip filler! Lip fillers 50% off!* Hate your nose too? *Nose jobs near you! Try the full 'Kylie Package': lips, cheeks, jawline, nose and chin fillers for £599!*[54] And on and on it goes: plastic surgery transformations, before and after pictures, recovery diaries, links to buy products. While previous generations of girls and young women might have opened up to their friends and family about their insecurities, and been reassured they are beautiful as they are, today girls turn to TikTok, which is designed to never let them forget.

These insecurities are now worth billions too. TikTok's global ad revenue is predicted to reach around $33 billion in 2025, up more than 40% from the year before.[55] In 2024, on TikTok's in-app marketplace TikTok Shop, over 79% of US sales were health and beauty products.[56] Over the course of the same year, Instagram's global ad revenue reached around $70.9 billion.[57] In the US alone, Instagram's ad revenue is predicted to make up over 11% of all US digital ad spending by 2026.[58]

Back in the early 2010s, though, it wasn't only algorithms that forever changed advertising. When I was a teenage girl, beauty ads on YouTube or Instagram might have made me feel insecure, but it was easy to see through them. Nobody really believed Facetune was their 'best friend', and big beauty brands were obviously trying to sell us something.

But soon things began to change. Companies realised they were too corporate, too impersonal. Girls didn't stay loyal to brands when better ones came along. Who we responded to were women – beautiful, friendly, *influential* women. Women we wanted to become. That's when things started to get much more personal.

BEAUTY INFLUENCERS

Beauty influencers were among the first to find fame on social media. By the early 2010s, when I was a pre-teen, a group of young YouTube personalities had already gained millions of subscribers by sharing beauty advice. One of my favourites was Zoe Sugg, better known as Zoella. By her early twenties, she had around 3 million subscribers, posting videos like 'How To: My Quick and Easy Hairstyles', 'Back To School Beauty' and 'Boyfriend Does My Makeup'.[59] Most influencers back then weren't trying to make money, so it felt like Zoella was telling us tips, rather than selling us things.

But over time, beauty influencers became bigger and bigger. Companies caught on and started sending YouTubers like Zoella free products to review and promote, realising this came with two major advantages. First, influencers were the perfect targeted ads: they already had dedicated audiences of teens and pre-teens, ready to buy whatever they recommended. And second, influencers were trusted much more than brands. Girls had grown up watching them. We felt as though we knew them through intimate Q&A videos and vlogs of their daily lives. Zoella didn't feel like some distant celebrity; she felt like a friend. So when she smiled and said she was obsessed with something, it sold.

Over the years, YouTube introduced more ways for influencers to monetise their content. Brands began offering discount codes, affiliate links and sponsorships, allowing creators to earn commissions on sales. Soon ads didn't just appear between YouTube videos; influencers interrupted their own content with sponsored segments.

This wasn't only happening on YouTube. Soon all our feeds were filled with ads: Snapchat Stories turned into reels of recommendations; our Instagram 'Explore' pages became billboards. On Instagram, Kim Kardashian promoted everything from waist trainers ('#ad I'm really obsessed with waist training! Thank you @premadonna87 for my new waist shapers!' #whatsawaist) to weight-loss lollipops ('You guys... @flattummyco just dropped a new product. They're Appetite Suppressant Lollipops and they're literally unreal. They're giving the first 500 people on their website 15% OFF so if you want to get your hands on some... you need to do it quick! #suckit').[60] Girls like me grew up getting discount codes for teeth whiteners, contour sticks, flat stomach teas, hair vitamins and body-sculpting shapewear before we had even hit puberty (and all this was from the Kardashian family alone…).

Now a vast network of agencies connects companies with influencers. For beauty brands, these partnerships have become central to their marketing. Since 2020, the global influencer market has more than tripled in size and was worth around $24 billion by 2024.[61] And just under 80% of Gen Z women now say influencers are their most trusted source of beauty recommendations.[62]

We trust them because they pretend to be our friends. Beauty influencers call their viewers their *family*, their *babies*, their *besties*; James Charles calls his subscribers his sisters while fixing their faces. They try to be as open, relatable and friendly as possible. They spill their secrets during make-up tutorials. They open up about their mental health problems and smoothly transition into selling self-care products. 'Storytime' videos are especially popular, where influencers divulge everything from break-ups with boyfriends to arguments with friends to stories about their stalkers, all while getting ready for the day. Videos with titles like 'GRWM [Get Ready with Me]… like we're besties on facetime… *this might all be TMI*' and 'GRWM while I overshare about my life because I broke up with my boyfriend' are watched by millions.[63] By being vulnerable with their 'besties', influencers rack up views. By encouraging comments from their 'friends', they boost engagement. And by sharing solutions and discount codes with their 'family', they earn commissions.

This has been happening for years now. Some women my age have been watching the same influencers since our pre-teens, following every life update, every relationship, every break-up. Already by 2016, 70% of teenage YouTube subscribers said they related more to influencers they watched than traditional celebrities. And

40% of millennial subscribers felt that their favourite influencer understood them better than their own friends.[64]

But back then, beauty influencers weren't just influencing what girls bought. They were changing how we looked. By the mid 2010s, girls as young as 13 and 14 were wearing more and more make-up. We were contouring our cheeks, wearing fake eyelashes for school and overlining our lips to look as though we had fillers. Girls started looking the same. We were being sold the same things, and we were being funnelled toward the same face.

As the influencer economy exploded, an American reality show called *Keeping Up with the Kardashians* was also on the rise. Premiering in 2007, it followed the personal and professional lives of the Kardashian-Jenner family, who rose to fame after Kim's sex tape leaked online. I had never seen the show, but I couldn't escape Kim and Kylie on Instagram.

Kylie started becoming popular on the platform in the early 2010s. Back then she was much more relatable, posting unfiltered selfies and candid pictures with her friends. But over the years she became more and more distinctive: her skin tone darkened; her lips became fuller; her face more sculpted. Her sister Kim was already known for having the perfect face – chiselled cheekbones, big Bratz-doll lips and airbrushed skin – and Kylie was starting to look like her.

By the mid 2010s, scrolling through Instagram meant seeing that same face over and over again, mass-produced versions of Kim and Kylie. Not only did the sisters start to look like each other, but they began to resemble something more like virtual avatars. Their faces were flawless, almost inanimate. In a 2019 *New Yorker* essay, Jia Tolentino referred to the 2010s as 'The Age of Instagram Face', when young women everywhere wanted this 'single, cyborgian look'.⁶⁵

Girls desperately tried to replicate Instagram Face: online with Facetune and Snapchat filters, offline with make-up, fillers and injectables. And as algorithms rewarded the most clickable content, beauty tutorials became more extreme. Our contours got harsher, our eyebrows thicker, our fake tan darker.

As a teenage girl I stopped watching Zoella and started following Kim Kardashian's contouring tutorials (like her viral 2017 YouTube video 'Kim Does Her Own Makeup', which has had more than 15 million views) and influencers like NikkieTutorials, who posted step-by-step guides to dramatic transformations (like 'The Power of MAKEUP!' which has more than 43 million views).⁶⁶ Influencers taught me 'How to look like Kylie Jenner !!!' (3.8 million views) and filmed videos like 'spending $1000 to be an instagram baddie | transformation challenge' (4.9 million views).⁶⁷ Suddenly, pre-teens had access to professional contouring techniques, supermodel lighting tips and tricks, and portable airbrushing apps. Not only did girls start to look the same, but we looked older too. Teenagers seemed like they were in their twenties.

And more and more, we applied make-up to look good in *selfies*. As a teenager I started noticing a new genre of YouTube videos with titles like 'MY GO TO EVERYDAY MAKEUP FOR INSTAGRAM' and 'GET READY WITH ME TO TAKE A SELFIE! (lol)'.⁶⁸ It began to feel as though doing our hair and make-up was pointless unless we got a good Instagram post out of it. Young women were suddenly transforming their faces – even getting them injected, filled and re-designed – not for anyone they actually knew, but for strangers online.

At the same time, beauty influencers were getting rich and famous. Girls moved on from watching relatable young women reviewing affordable beauty products to influencers casually vlogging their lip filler appointments and cosmetic surgeries, sometimes as sponsored ads. Popular influencer Tana Mongeau, for example, started documenting her procedures on YouTube, posting videos like 'GET A FACE FULL OF FILLER WITH ME' (2.9 million views), 'I GOT A NOSE JOB?' (2.8. million views) and 'i got Kylie Jenner butt shots... oops (needle warning)' (3 million views).[69] Cosmetic surgeries became more accessible, more affordable, and presented as a standard part of a beauty routine.

It's hard to overstate the hold beauty influencers had over us. Kylie for a long time denied having had lip filler, claiming a lip liner pencil had transformed her look. But finally, in 2015, on an episode of *Keeping Up with the Kardashians*, she admitted to getting lip injections. 'It's just an insecurity of mine,' she confessed, 'and it's what I wanted to do.'[70] After the episode aired, one UK clinic reported a 70% rise in lip filler enquiries overnight.[71]

Around the same time, the #KylieJennerChallenge went viral worldwide. To copy Kylie's lip fillers, young girls used shot glasses or small containers to create suction over their mouths and cause their lips to swell, before posting the results online. Some ended up with severe bruising, broken blood vessels and, in some cases, they even needed stitches. Doctors publicly warned teenagers about the dangers of the trend, and Kylie herself responded – although she didn't exactly tell girls to stop, instead tweeting 'I'm not here to encourage people/young girls to look like me or to think this is the way they should look,' followed by, 'I want to encourage people/young girls like me to be YOURSELF & not be afraid to experiment w your look.'[72]

That same year, Kylie launched her own beauty brand, Kylie Cosmetics, starting with the 'Kylie Lip Kit', a liquid lipstick and matching liner promising fuller-looking lips. The kits sold out instantly, crashing the website. Fifteen thousand units were gone in less than 60 seconds.[73]

By 2018, Kylie Cosmetics had generated around $125 million in sales.[74] The following year, at the age of 21, Kylie was named by *Forbes* as the world's youngest 'self-made' billionaire – though this was later disputed after an investigation found her earnings had been exaggerated.[75] Still, whatever her worth, nobody could deny her influence. In 2018, for example, after Snapchat redesigned its app, Kylie tweeted, 'sooo does anyone else not open Snapchat anymore? Or is it just me… ugh this is so sad.' The next day, Snapchat's stock market value plunged by around $1.3 billion.[76]

Today Kylie has one of the biggest social media followings in the world, with over 392 million followers on Instagram alone. By 2018, she was allegedly earning around $1 million per sponsored post on Instagram; some estimates now put it closer to $2.4 million.[77] Her face is everywhere.

But since the early 2010s, as the influencer economy has exploded and diversified, so have beauty trends. Instagram Face is no longer the only ideal; countless beauty influencers and subcultures now compete for our attention. Some girls get into 'glow-ups' and transformations, watching TikTok plastic surgeons share shocking before and after results, influencers insist 'This is your sign to get a nose job!', and vlogs titled 'GRWM for a BBL [Brazilian Butt Lift] consultation'![78] Others spiral into skincare influencers, scrolling through 20-step nighttime routines, anti-ageing experts recommending Baby Botox with 'the earlier you start, the less you need later!'[79] and young women selling them anti-wrinkle drinking straws so they can sip without ever having to purse their lips.

And now anyone can become a beauty influencer. Take pre-teen sisters Koti and Haven Garza, who post beauty and skincare videos to 5 million followers on TikTok. In one viral video with over 4 million views, seven-year-old Koti, missing her front teeth, sits in front of rows of serums and sprays. 'We're Gen Alpha influencers, of course we are obsessed with skincare,' Koti says to the camera. Haven adds: 'We're Gen Alpha influencers, of course our favourite stores are Sephora and Ulta.' Back to Koti: 'We're Gen Alpha influencers, of course we wear a headband when we're doing our get ready with mes.' And finally, from Haven: 'We're Gen Alpha influencers, of course we don't have toys,' as she throws her toys aside.[80]

Listening to all these friendly influencers, it's easy to forget what they are. They are advertisers. They are always selling something – a product, a procedure, themselves. They are not our friends. Sometimes I step back from all this and think about Kim Kardashian shilling appetite suppressant lollipops, or smiling TikTokers promoting anti-wrinkle straws to teenage girls, and I wonder how they get away with it. Why isn't there a bigger backlash? And the truth is, to sell us all these products and procedures, to make all of this work, they also had to sell us lies.

SELF-LOVE

Back in the late 1990s and early 2000s, there was a backlash against beauty magazines Photoshopping images of women by reshaping their bodies, lengthening their legs and airbrushing their skin. In 2004, for example, Dove launched its 'Real Beauty' campaign, featuring women of different sizes, ethnicities and ages, to remind girls what real bodies look like.[81] The message was clear: beauty standards shouldn't feel impossible.

But by the mid 2010s, everything had changed. By 2016, reality TV star Khloé Kardashian was on a Netflix show calling Facetune 'the best thing to bring to the table', 'life-changing' and 'the only way to live'.[82] By 2017 James Charles was celebrating Facetune as 'one of my all-time favourite used apps'.[83] By 2018, influencer Tana Mongeau was posing on Instagram in a T-shirt that said 'Facetuned'.[84] And by 2020, on the popular podcast *Call Her Daddy*, which averages around 5 million weekly listeners, Tana and host Alex Cooper were joking about Facetuning themselves, laughing as Tana called herself a 'beached whale' and admitted to editing a picture of her at the beach beyond recognition: 'The hair, the nails, face, titty, booty and toes… I facetuned it all.'[85]

As technology advanced on one side, urging us to edit and upgrade ourselves, conversations around female empowerment were evolving on the other. Throughout the 2010s it felt as if feminism was turning inwards, from fighting for women as a whole to fighting battles within ourselves. Now it was all about our identities, insecurities and self-expression. Young women were celebrated for making their own choices, whatever those choices were. This was the era of liberal feminism, where every decision was empowering so long as it was our own.

Soon it became a convenient sales strategy. What was labelled as empowering became less about women's interests and more about commercial interests. Empowerment became a product, a service, a procedure. Empowerment was whatever we were being sold.

'Celebrate #InternationalWomensDay – reclaim the way you look at selfie editing, a habit which can actually be a powerful form of #selfexpression,' Facetune tweeted in 2018, linking to an article declaring that '#NoFilter Is Dead and Selfie Editing Empowers You'.[86] By 2020, plastic surgery clinics were describing cosmetic procedures as a form of self-love, insisting that having our breasts cut open and filled with silicone was giving ourselves 'the present of improved self-esteem'.[87] Even the Brazilian Butt Lift, the deadliest cosmetic surgery of all, was being sold as a way for women to 'celebrate the bodies they live in'.[88]

For beauty influencers and celebrities, liberal feminism was especially convenient. Now they could use the language of self-love and empowerment while promoting cosmetic products and defending their own procedures. In 2023, for example, Madonna appeared almost unrecognisable at the Grammys, her face seemingly transformed by fillers and surgery. After she was mocked online, she blamed the backlash on 'ageism and misogyny', declaring she looked forward to 'many more years of subversive behaviour', 'pushing boundaries' and 'standing up to the patriarchy'.[89]

The contradictions are now impossible to ignore. In 2021, Khloé Kardashian made headlines when her team scrambled to erase her unedited bikini picture from the internet after it was accidentally posted by an assistant. Reports claimed Khloé 'completely lost it' when she realised, demanding the photo be taken down 'as soon as possible.'[90] Her team reportedly issued legal threats to those sharing it online.

But it was too late; the image went viral. Khloé later addressed the incident on Instagram, writing: 'I am not perfect but I promise you that I try every day to live my life as honestly as possible and with empathy and kindness. It doesn't mean that I have not made mistakes. But I'm not going to lie. It's almost unbearable trying to live up to the impossible standards that the public have all set for me.' (What happened to selfie-editing being empowering?) Later in the same post, Khloé defended her right to edit herself: 'My body, my image, and how I choose to look and what I want to share is my choice. It's not for anyone to decide or judge what is acceptable or not any more.'[91]

Khloé isn't the only Kardashian feeling the pressure. In 2024, Kylie broke down on *The Kardashians* after being mocked for her overfilled face, saying she wished people would stop caring so much about how she looked: 'It's a miracle I still have confidence and can still look in the mirror and still think I'm pretty.'[92] And despite all the treatments she has had, Kim Kardashian said in 2022 that she might 'eat poop every single day' if it would make her look younger.[93] She later admitted she felt she only had about 'ten years left' of looking good before she would have to take time off.[94] These influencers are now buckling under the beauty standards they helped set. Everything they sold to girls as confidence and self-love causes them pain and anxiety, and even they can't keep up. How can the average 14-year-old girl expect to feel empowered by any of this?

And girls my age weren't just told that it was empowering. These products and procedures were also sold as good for our mental health. Beauty routines became self-care. Cosmetic surgeries became a path to self-discovery and self-actualisation. Fixing ourselves became therapeutic.

'Oh my god, I'm so excited,' squeals Nikkie de Jager, the face of NikkieTutorials. She announces that she is teaming up with a company she loves. 'I have a routine… where I really know what works for my face, for my body,' she says, as if describing a new diet or workout plan.

She's talking, of course, about Facetune.

The video, uploaded in 2020 – 'My Facetune SECRETS Exposed!' – is sponsored by Lightricks and has more than 1.3 million views.

I watch as Nikkie whitens her eyes, and – after a heartfelt speech about how she has been through 'years of self-love and growth to kind of accept that my face looks the way it looks' – shrinks her forehead, jaw and chin. 'Honestly, to me Facetuning is so therapeutic. Whenever I'm like stressed out or I need to get my thoughts in order, I just go Facetuning because it makes me so zen that it's like therapy to me,' she gushes. 'It makes me so happy, it makes me so happy, oh my god.'[95]

Throughout the early 2010s there was a growing cultural emphasis on mental health. Conversations about opening up and raising awareness trended online, and there seemed to be a widespread focus on self-care and self-love. And much like the language of feminism, these therapeutic terms soon became convenient for beauty brands and influencers. Twenty-five-step beauty routines were framed as self-care rituals, editing apps were described as therapeutic, even cosmetic procedures were sold as essential to emotional well-being.

The concept of an 'authentic self' was also becoming more mainstream. There was a growing belief that we each had a real, inner self buried beneath our flaws and imperfections, which didn't always match what we saw in the mirror. But now, with the help of ever-evolving technologies, products and procedures, we could finally reveal it. It was as if the virtual version of ourselves, the avatar we created with filters and editing apps, was the actual us, and now girls could make that a reality. Coming of age came to feel like a search for one thing only: finding our true selves – or, more accurately, buying them.

Beauty treatments and surgeries are now part of our journey to self-actualisation. 'A comprehensive breast makeover is about more than resculpting your figure,' says one Beverly Hills surgeon.

'It's about resculpting your confidence with a body that *finally* resonates with your true self.'[96] Consultations for breast implants and BBLs can now be booked on a website called 'RealSelf'.[97] Even butt-enlarging gummies are promoted on Instagram as a way to 'let your authentic self shine!'[98] Beauty interventions aren't only about looking good any more; they are about becoming who we were always meant to be.

And so NikkieTutorials can lecture girls about self-love while redesigning her face. Facetune can claim it 'empowers' us to bring out our best selves and that it boosts our confidence.[99] TikTok can pretend its filters are about users being true to themselves.[100] And James Charles can get away with fixing the faces of teenage girls without backlash. His video even features on Facetune's official website with the caption: 'James believes photo editing is an art form, and after viewing this video, there's no way you won't agree. Watch as he shares the love for his artistry with some awesome Tunes of some of his loyal followers' selfies.'[101]

Our world is one with more platitudes about accepting and loving ourselves than ever before. But this is beginning to feel like a front for a much sadder reality. Because as far as I can see, the more we try to look perfect on the outside, the more insecure we feel on the inside.

INSECURE

One of the clearest signs that girls and young women feel insecure today is how they see themselves and their bodies. As the lies about self-love, body positivity and empowerment grow louder, the statistics only become bleaker. The better we can look online, the more distress we seem to feel offline.

Body image issues, for example, are affecting girls more than ever. In 2016, young people in the UK aged 16 to 25 were already ranking body image as the third biggest challenge they faced.[102] That same year, a global review found that children as young as *six* felt dissatisfied with their bodies.[103] By 2019, 35% of teenagers said they worried about how their bodies looked often or every day; four in ten said social media images made this worse.[104] By 2023, three out of four children as young as 12 said they disliked their bodies and felt embarrassed by the way they looked, rising to eight in ten among 18- to 21-year-olds.[105]

Some girls are even developing Body Dysmorphic Disorder (BDD), a condition where obsessing over perceived flaws can completely distort how they see themselves. Some confess to looking in mirrors for hours at a time every day, needing constant reassurance, and feeling 'practically housebound' from the anxiety.[106] Many hide behind filters and editing apps; some turn to cosmetic surgery; others end up in psychiatric hospitals. In one study, the risk of suicide among those with BDD was around 45 times higher than the average population.[107] The condition is now thought to affect about two in every hundred teens in England, with girls six times more likely to suffer than boys.[108]

Several studies associate BDD with social media. Platforms like Instagram and Snapchat have been shown to worsen body image, and are associated with eating disorder symptoms in girls and young women.[109] In a leaked company presentation from 2019, Facebook itself even declared: 'We make body image issues worse for one in three teen girls.'[110]

Eating disorders are also rising. In England, hospital admissions for eating disorders almost doubled from 2012 to 2023.[111] Between 2022 and 2023, 81% of these admissions were emergencies, 91%

involved female patients, and around 40% were among 15- to 19-year-olds.¹¹² Between 2015 and 2016, and 2020 and 2021, hospital episodes for eating disorders among children and young people rose by 90%.¹¹³ In the US, too, emergency department visits for eating disorders among adolescents doubled from 50,000 in 2018 to over 100,000 in 2022.¹¹⁴ Globally, the prevalence of eating disorders more than doubled between 2000 and 2018, mostly among adolescent girls.¹¹⁵ And while eating disorders have many causes, anxiety about appearance and body image dissatisfaction are among the most common triggers.

Online, too, many girls describe dealing with an ambient dysmorphia, a nagging feeling that how they look on camera doesn't match what they see in the mirror. On the Reddit forum r/BodyDysmorphia (which has over 55,000 members), many blame social media for their symptoms. Several mention TikTok's inverted filter, for example, which flips your face to show how others supposedly see you. 'My face inverted destroys my confidence completely,' one user says.¹¹⁶ 'I'm literally suicidal because of how bad I look inverted,' another admits.¹¹⁷

Other girls blame editing apps like Facetune, Snapchat filters, and constantly comparing themselves to perfect Instagram influencers. On the r/Instagramreality forum, one user writes:

> after i facetune myself, switching back to the old image makes me look deformed – even if it was a selfie i thought was cute beforehand. after enough edits my real face seems like it looks freakish, like every flaw is magnified by ten.
>
> i don"t post the pictures i facetune anywhere, but i can"t imagine how ramped up this effect would be if you received tons of compliments and attention for showing the facetuned

you. i really think this would be enough to make anyone develop body dysmorphia.[118]

Some girls say the pressure is so intense that they look at their natural faces and bodies and feel that they don't even deserve to be considered female. This is one of the most upvoted posts of all time on r/BodyDysmorphia:

> i don't know how to explain it well, but basically i just feel so ugly that i feel like i don't even deserve to be categorized as a girl. just seeing all the soft, pretty girls around me then looking at myself in comparison, i feel sick that something like me has invaded their space, that i'm allowed to exist alongside them looking like how i do. it doesn't help that i'm already not very feminine to begin with (whether that's just how i naturally am or if it's a product of my own deep insecurities is a conflict in itself though). it genuinely brings me to tears especially when i think of my mom and how disappointed she probably is that her only daughter turned out to be hideous.[119]

Girls are also spending hours trying to look like perfect avatars. In 2015, a UK survey of 2,000 women aged 16 to 25 found they were spending an average of five hours a week preparing for, taking and editing selfies.[120] By 2024, over half of girls aged 11 to 21 said they wished they looked like they did with filters on, and more than 1 in 3 said they felt pressure to use filters when posting online.[121] According to Dove's research, 60% of girls feel upset when they don't look like the filtered versions of themselves.[122] Among those who spend 10 to 30 minutes editing photos, 64% feel bad about their bodies.[123] And around 37% believe they 'don't look good enough' without editing.[124]

We can also see insecurity in the rapid rise in cosmetic surgeries and injectables in recent years. Despite being bombarded with more messaging about self-love and body positivity than any other generation, women under 30 in the US are driving demand for everything from 'tweakments' like Botox to boob jobs and labiaplasties.[125] By 2024, over a quarter of girls in the UK aged 11 to 16 said they would consider getting cosmetic procedures in the next 20 years, rising to almost half of those aged 17 to 21.[126]

Many studies trace this to social media. Frequent users of Snapchat filters and platforms like Instagram are more likely to consider cosmetic surgery.[127] By 2017, over half of plastic surgeons reported that patients were even requesting surgeries specifically to look better in *selfies* – up from 13% in 2013. The term 'Snapchat Dysmorphia' was coined to describe the phenomenon, as surgeons claimed clients were bringing in pictures of themselves with a Snapchat filter on, instead of pictures of celebrities they wanted to look like. More than half had also seen a rise in clients younger than 30.[128] By 2025, 38% of Gen Z in the UK said that social media made them want to permanently change their body through surgery.[129]

Girls and young women are also increasingly anxious about ageing. 'Get Ready with Me' videos on TikTok feature girls as young as seven applying face masks, moisturisers and anti-ageing serums.[130] On forums like Reddit's r/SkincareAddiction, teens and even pre-teens obsess over the faintest lines on their faces, discuss their daily sun cream applications and measurements in minute detail, and describe themselves as if they have expiry dates, feeling as though every passing year they depreciate in value. 'This is a pic of my freckles around age 12,' begins one Reddit post. 'Would you say this is the sort of bad sun damage that will cause significant damage like skin cancer/deep wrinkles in the future?'[131] Another writes: 'I'm only 14 and I have so many face wrinkles... please someone help me... I'll do whatever it takes to get rid of them.'[132]

We can also see this insecurity in their spending. In 2023, US households with children aged 6 to 12 spent 27% more on skincare than in 2022.[133] Teen beauty spending rose by 23% in 2024.[134] In England, too, under-18s are increasingly travelling to Wales and Scotland to get Botox, where it is legal for minors.[135] At the same time, TikTokers have started using the hashtag #sephorakids to post videos of children, as young as eight, queuing in beauty stores like Sephora to buy anti-ageing products.[136]

Yet despite all the effort, energy and money spent, girls and young women still don't feel good about themselves. How could we? Beauty filters invent new flaws to fix; influencers profit from our insecurities; algorithms pull us towards ever more extreme routines and procedures. We aren't happy with how we look, because billions are made making sure we never will be.

So, what are girls struggling with today? In part, the same age-old anxieties that plagued previous generations of girls and young women. There is no denying that when we look in the mirror today, we feel many of the same insecurities our mothers and grandmothers did.

Except those insecurities are being intensified until they feel unmanageable. Girls today aren't just feeling a pang of insecurity at the occasional image in a beauty magazine or passing billboard. Now, for every flicker of insecurity there is an app, an advert, an influencer ready to capitalise on it and feed them exactly what will make them feel worse. Linger over this content long enough and girls will be relentlessly reminded of what is wrong with their face, their skin, their hair, their body, their smile, before being hitched to a conveyor belt of products and procedures promising to fix them.

Never before has a generation inspected their own faces this intensely either, spending so much time scrutinising themselves through a front-facing camera. Let alone been able to edit and enhance every feature, put that improved version on public display, and wait for the reviews and ratings to roll in. For my girls my age, this was growing up: getting feedback on our faces and developing bodies, tweaking and upgrading ourselves to sell better.

And we not only compare ourselves to the unrealistic beauty standards of supermodels or celebrities. Our standard is unrealistic because it is not human. It is an avatar, a beauty ideal that can only be bought, surgically sculpted or generated out of pixels. We wasted our childhoods chasing something that does not even exist. Even the influencers we idolised, who had access to every injectable, treatment and surgery money can buy, still never felt enough.

To the girls today trying to look like these influencers, and punishing themselves for not being perfect, please, take it from me: many women are reaching their twenties and realising what a waste of time this was. We are realising our childhoods weren't really childhoods at all, that we wished them away comparing ourselves to an impossible ideal. We are starting to see that it wasn't only a cute pair of cartoon puppy ears we tried on at 12. It wasn't funny that we were contouring our faces at 13. And all those friendly influencers were just selling us something.

Now what do we have left to look back on? Fond memories of Snapchat filters that fixed flaws we would never have noticed? Good times ruminating on Reddit forums, agonising over faint lines we thought made us unlovable? Bruising our lips with shot glasses, desperate to look like influencers who didn't even want to look like themselves?

And while this was happening, a network of companies and influencers wrapped this up and sold it to us as empowerment. We were told this was self-love, while we forever damaged what little love we had for ourselves. We were assured that there was nothing wrong with fixing insecurities, by influencers projecting their own insecurities onto us.

But now we can see that those messages, the endless encouragement to post more, edit more, correct more, were a marketing strategy. This was not self-love but lying to ourselves, not empowering but degrading. None of these apps or filters or procedures were helping us find our true selves; we were losing ourselves, becoming so disconnected from who we were that we developed dysmorphia and anxiety disorders. Few of us are looking back at our hundreds, if not thousands, of Facetuned selfies and filtered Instagram posts with a feeling of self-love or empowerment. We are looking back with something more like deep sadness, with heartbreak for ourselves as little girls. With the realisation that we will never be able to see ourselves as beautiful – or even as enough – again.

But age-old feelings have an age-old adage. It's what's on the inside that counts, right? We might not be able to compete with avatar-like influencers, but we can always fall back on our inner beauty. We can control who we are, and how we feel.

Except even that has been exploited. While the beauty industry cashes in on anxiety about our appearance, another industry commodifies our inner lives. Mental health has become a market, with influencers, therapy apps and medication companies all profiting from our pain. And like the beauty industry, this is a market worth billions.

Diagnosed

'It'll feel like you're shopping for leggings – not prescription meds.'
Hers[1]

OPENING UP

'Life has thrown countless obstacles at me this year,' says a young woman in a TikTok voice-over, striding towards the beach in her matching workout set, 'from a school shooting to having no idea what life is going to look like after college.' The camera follows her footsteps, panning down her body as she walks.

Her voice brightens. 'In support of Mental Health Awareness Month, I'm partnering with Bioré Skincare to strip away the stigma of anxiety.' She holds up a package of pore strips. 'We want you to get it all out – not only what's in your pores, but most importantly what's on your mind too.'

Before I can process what I've heard, she's back to talking about gun violence, describing the terror she felt on campus during a school shooting. Now she's lying in bed, staring blankly at the ceiling. 'My message to you guys is that it's okay not to have it all together,' she says with a smile, before closing with, 'Join me and Bioré Skincare in speaking up about mental health… every video posted is a step closer to normalising conversations about mental health.' On screen, the words appear: 'I love you guys!'[2]

The TikTok fades to black. I'm left thinking many things, one of which is how nothing could capture my frustrations with modern culture better than this 51-second clip. It has it all: the therapy-speak, the parasocial tactics, personal trauma used to sell products, all somehow wrapped up as mental health awareness.

Still, I keep coming back to one question: how did we get here? Where we market our own mental health problems? Where #mentalhealth has over 100 billion views on TikTok? Where we mindlessly scroll through other people's pain like entertainment? The only way to understand is to go back, back to the early 2010s. Back when we all started opening up online.

Zoella smiles and waves at the camera, her bedroom softly glowing with fairy lights. It's 2012, and the 22-year-old is already one of the biggest beauty influencers. But this is not just another make-up or hair tutorial. This, she warns, is something new.

'This is a slightly different video than you are probably used to,' Zoella begins carefully, 'but I do hope that this is beneficial for a lot of you in a completely different way.' Hinting that she is about to reveal a side of herself we rarely see, she jokes about her 'scary alter ego', before warning: 'It is a very personal video for me to sit down and talk to you about. I've never really addressed this issue in front of hundreds of thousands of people.' Zoella takes a deep breath and finally confesses to millions of subscribers that she suffers from... anxiety.

I remember watching when I was 13, and feeling like I was intruding on something. Zoella opened up about overthinking, panic attacks, and anxiety so overwhelming it sometimes left her unable to get out of bed. The 20-minute video went viral at the time, and now has more than 4 million views.[3] Back then it felt like the beginning of a whole new side to online fame: influencers finally being vulnerable.

Girls my age were already talking about our mental health online, but mostly on blogging sites, and often anonymously. I first noticed this on Tumblr, the blogging site launched in 2007. By 2014, the platform hosted over 169 million blogs, with most users under 35.[4] Here girls could create and join communities around almost anything, from favourite TV shows and boy band crushes to depression and eating disorders.

Girls on Tumblr didn't just post about mental health problems, though. They glamorised them. Teenagers shared images of skeletal bodies under hashtags like #bonespo and #thinspiration, and graphic pictures of cuts on arms and legs. In 2013, for example, a 14-year-old girl was behind 'Depression and Disorders', one of Tumblr's biggest self-harm blogs. She shared personal stories about cutting, suicide plans, and even tips on how to self-harm, inviting followers to send in confessions. Popular posts on her blog included an image of a wrist marked with dotted lines: one horizontal labelled HOSPITAL, and one vertical labelled MORGUE; a text post that simply said 'Cut deeper'; and a photo of pills arranged with labels: one pill for 'sleep', two for 'deep sleep' and a pile for 'morgue'.[5]

That year, *The Atlantic* published an article about Tumblr communities romanticising suffering, suggesting that social media was redefining the word 'depression'. As author Anne-Sophie Bine put it, 'For a fragile mind, these communities seem to provide the perfect solution: support, understanding, acceptance.' But, she added, 'To be accepted by this community, they have to advertise their suffering.'[6]

And so we did. Around this time, too, girls my age were growing tired of the perfect, filtered lives of beauty influencers. By the mid

2010s, social media was being described as an unhealthy 'highlight reel', showing only our best and most beautiful moments. So we began to share more of our reality. Girls did what girls have always done, and should do – we talked, we were vulnerable, we opened up – but we did so publicly. And soon we weren't sharing our suffering only on anonymous Tumblr blogs or Reddit forums, but openly on Facebook, Instagram and Snapchat.

These platforms started encouraging it, too. Opening up about our mental health was not only good for us, we were told, but some sort of moral duty. We had stigma to battle; we needed to be activists and allies. In 2017, for example, Instagram launched its #HereForYou campaign, urging us to 'kickstart a global conversation' by sharing our struggles.[7] Snapchat followed with its own mental health hashtags and filters, encouraging us to 'debunk the stigma surrounding mental health' by getting involved.[8] Instagram insisted we share our 'mental health journeys', while Snapchat encouraged us to 'Talk about how you really feel with your friends…' but, of course, '… on Snapchat.'[9]

The pressure to open up grew with each new platform. In 2020, TikTok launched its #SpeakYourMind campaign for Mental Health Awareness Week, with the aim of 'encouraging people to share day-to-day challenges' and send 'virtual hugs' to those struggling.[10] 'Our goal is to continue fostering an environment where people can safely share their well-being journeys,' TikTok now says, reminding those who want to 'spread awareness' to use the right hashtags.[11]

Conveniently, the solutions to girls' mental health struggles are now built into these apps themselves. Girls are told to find 'mental health resources on Instagram' and 'take care of your mental health on Snapchat… and encourage your friends to do the same!'[12] They are reminded to show support for each other by Snapping their friends ('Checking in is as simple as snapping a quick pic!'), adding stickers like 'Mental health matters' and 'hi. I'm really struggling rn' to their Stories, and sending Snaps with their cartoon avatars wearing green ribbons to 'spread awareness'.[13] Snapchat's 'Here For You' resource even promises 'in-app support to Snapchatters who may be experiencing a mental health or emotional crisis'.[14] (In-app? For a *crisis*?)

When girls need help today, they are told to stay online. Back when I was a teenager, though, that only made things worse. These apps trapped us. As my generation opened up, algorithms were advancing, learning about us, logging our vulnerabilities, dragging us deeper into them. We were funnelled further into our insecurities, served more signs, symptoms, advice and – of course – ads. The more we shared our struggles, the harder they were to overcome. We were already categorised and targeted by advertisers. This was more than a self-fulfilling prophecy; this had software engineering behind it.

Today, in the 2020s, girls share everything online. On TikTok, they give tours of their messy 'depression rooms' showing dirty underwear and plates of half-eaten food ('it started to smell 6 months ago lolz').[15] They share traumatic childhood 'Storytimes' about sexual abuse and suicide attempts while styling their hair and applying skincare ('get ready with me whilst I tell you about the time my nan tried to kill me, my mum and my dad...'[16]). Some set up cameras to record live panic attacks ('watch me have a panic attack while waiting at a red light'...); others post pictures from their mental health diagnosis reveal parties ('Cutting the cake... It's pink and blue! Bipolar 2 and OCD/OCPD...')[17] In a typical #mentalhealth TikTok from 2021, which has over 7 million views, a young woman paces up and down. 'I'm having a panic attack, uh, currently,' she says breathlessly. 'Um, I'm literally shaking.' Piano music starts to play. 'Like, hi, I don't know how to calm myself down… and I'm sweating, um, really bad.' She shows her armpits to the camera. 'I don't know what to do…' (#crying #shaking #anxietyattack).[18]

For girls today, this sort of sharing isn't shocking. It's everywhere, and always has been. But for young women my age, we watched it happen gradually. Back in the 2010s we started by imitating influencers who were being more vulnerable online, before social media companies began urging us to open up too.

And these platforms weren't the only ones pushing us to share. Around that time, another form of influencer was on the rise. The much more vulnerable; the far less filtered. Some were therapists, warning us about signs and symptoms. Others were activists, urging us to open up and fight stigma. Many were ordinary people, sharing their struggles online. Between beauty influencers selling us skincare routines and surgery plans, we now had mental health influencers, ready to fix not only how we looked, but how we *felt*.

MENTAL HEALTH INFLUENCERS

'This is the test to tell if you have trauma,' a self-proclaimed licensed therapist announces on a TikTok in 2020. Sad piano music plays in the background. He pauses before asking, slowly: 'Are… you… hurting?'

He then immediately delivers his diagnosis: 'If the answer is yes, you have trauma.'

The video, which has over 12 million views, ends with a plea: 'Now there's someone sitting and suffering alone in silence and darkness,' he explains, 'and your likes and shares could literally light up their life.'[19] (Convenient.)

DIAGNOSED

In 2020, two powerful forces collided. As the pandemic hit and lockdowns forced us to stay home, TikTok exploded. In the first quarter of 2020 alone, TikTok was downloaded over 315 million times worldwide, the most downloads ever recorded for any app in a single quarter. By April, global downloads had reached 2 billion.[20] Meanwhile, in-person therapy was becoming harder to access, and was in much higher demand. The gap glimmered with opportunity.

Soon every type of mental health influencer imaginable was on TikTok. Girls had access to trauma-informed therapists ready to dissect their childhoods and diagnose their parents; attachment experts analysing their crushes and relationships; and specialists in conditions like obsessive–compulsive disorder, borderline personality disorder and attention deficit disorder scrutinising their every personality trait. Neurodivergent content creators appeared for those with conditions like autism and ADHD; gender-affirming doctors for those struggling with dysphoria. There were even influencers with dissociative identity disorder (previously known as multiple personality disorder) calling themselves 'plurals' and capturing their personality switches live on camera.[21]

Mental health influencers soon became trapped in the same attention economy as beauty influencers. The more extreme they were, the more engagement they got. The more girls could relate, the more revenue. Complex conditions were reduced to clickable content. Videos with titles like '5 Signs A Girl Might Be Autistic', '7 signs you may have ADHD Teenager edition' and '5 Subtle Signs of Trauma You Shouldn't Ignore' started trending,[22] and symptoms became vaguer and vaguer.

One popular trend that started during the pandemic was the 'Put a Finger Down' challenge. In TikToks and Instagram videos with titles like 'Put a Finger Down Childhood Trauma Challenge' and 'Put a Finger Down: Late Diagnosed Autistic Girl Edition', influencers instruct viewers to hold up their hands, putting a finger down for every symptom they relate to.[23] In one TikTok titled 'Put a finger down WEIRD anxiety symptoms edition', with 3 million views, symptoms include 'tingling', 'excessive yawning' and 'digestion problems' ('Share your results to spread anxiety awareness!')[24]

These videos are popular because they often diagnose ordinary problems and personality traits (so much so that I've diagnosed myself with about five different disorders since starting this chapter…). Not fitting in, feeling insecure and hating your body are not only symptoms of disorders; they are also symptoms of being 14. Feel misunderstood? TikTokers suggest you might have ADHD. Bad at eye contact? Could be autism. Watch the same TV shows over and over? Might be an anxiety disorder. Replay the same songs in your head? Sounds like neurodivergence. ('I can't believe I just found this out, but having songs stuck in your head isn't normal,' says one TikToker to 2.9 million views. 'This is common with people who have ADHD or autism and it's called internal echolalia…')[25] Other influencers make these conditions sound fun and quirky. Neurodivergent has become 'neurospicy' or 'neurosparkly', while 'neurotypicals' are boring.[26] TikTokers call themselves 'hotistic' (hot and autistic), insist that 'Hot girls have anxiety' and playfully ask followers what 'flavor of autism' they have.[27] Some insist that girls don't even need symptoms for a diagnosis. Maybe you have been masking autism your whole life, or have hidden 'high-functioning' anxiety.[28] You don't need to see a doctor; 'self-diagnosis is completely valid'.[29]

Even bad habits are being medicalised. Now being rude, lazy or messy can be seen as symptoms, out of our control. In one TikTok with nearly 6 million views, an AuDHD (autistic and ADHD) life coach lists '5 signs that you're not lazy, you're actually dealing with something called executive dysfunction'. Signs include wanting to do something but feeling unable to, feeling like there is a brick wall between you and the task, and having more motivation at work than at home (#lazinessdoesnotexist).[30]

Companies use this sort of messaging as a sales strategy too. Instagram ads for Wisey, for example, a platform that promises to 'GET RID OF PROCRASTINATION' with personal ADHD plans after a five-minute quiz, declare that 'Social anxiety is not shyness' and 'Hypersexuality is not infidelity'; both are ADHD responses.[31] Quick mental health quizzes like these are advertised everywhere now. In 2019, at one mental healthcare provider, around 7,700 women in the UK took its online test for ADHD. By 2021, that number had soared to 254,400 – an increase of 3200%.[32]

And again, algorithms can drag girls down different paths, depending on their personalities and vulnerabilities. In 2021, for example, the *Wall Street Journal* (*WSJ*) investigated how TikTok's algorithm works. Journalists created bot accounts, each assigned different interests, then had the bots watch thousands of TikTok videos, pausing or replaying relevant ones. According to the *WSJ*, TikTok could identify a bot's interests in as little as 40 minutes. One bot, designed to watch sad content, quickly fell into a dark rabbit hole: within 36 minutes, 93% of its feed was related to depression.[33]

Imagine you are a teenage girl who starts watching TikToks about healthy eating. Maybe you start with 'What I Eat In A Day!' videos, where influencers share recipes and meal plans. But soon TikTok starts recommending videos on how to restrict calories, before giving you tips on how to hide bulimia. Keep scrolling and you can end up watching influencers like Eugenia Cooney, a YouTuber and Twitch streamer who seems to be slowly starving herself in front of millions, so dangerously thin that her fans have called the police.[34] Or maybe you go from finding out what gender identity is to being told by TikTokers that being 'forgetful' and 'always tired' are symptoms of gender dysphoria (yes, an actual TikTok), all the way to watching influencers showcase their mastectomy scars, vlog their vaginoplasty journeys, and wonder whether you need surgery ('Signs a Labiaplasty might be right for you').[35] In one TikTok tagged #transgender, for example, an influencer who identifies as trans shares their rib removal experience: 'I got my ribs removed six days ago,' they say with a smile, holding up six of their ribs in a plastic bag. 'I'm doing it for vanity reasons. I feel like my body is very square and i'm trans so why not I just wanna look hot.' The procedure cost more than $17,000.[36]

Back in the 2010s, though, the problem wasn't only that mental health issues became online trends. Personal struggles were also commodified, used to sell us products and services. And raising awareness became a powerful marketing strategy.

'I experience it. I'm very normal. And like, I understand you. Like I can connect with you,' says Kendall Jenner, sister of Kylie Jenner and Kim Kardashian, before the screen fades to black and we are instructed to *Connect With Kendall*.

Kendall's mother, Kris, shares the clip on Twitter, telling fans to expect an exciting announcement: her daughter 'being so brave and vulnerable' by sharing her 'most raw story' yet.[37] 'Be prepared to be moved,' Kris says in another tweet, followed by the hashtags #bethechange, #finallyasolution, #shareyourstory and #authenticity.[38]

It's 2019, and the big reveal – which fans have guessed is a major mental health battle, or Kendall coming out as gay – turns out to be nothing but an ad. Kendall's 'brave and vulnerable' story is that she had acne as a teenager. And her major announcement, a sponsorship deal with skincare brand Proactiv.

While mental health influencers were on the rise, other influencers began to realise that vulnerability got views, and that raising awareness could be a sales strategy. Beauty influencers began opening up about anxiety and depression in morning routines and 'Get Ready with Me' videos. Fitness influencers shared stories of body dysmorphia to sell supplements and workout courses. Reality TV stars, family bloggers, travel vloggers: everyone started opening up online. Personal struggles segued into paid sponsorships. YouTubers crying on camera about feeling stressed and tired came with discount codes for BetterHelp.[39] Stories about bad days and struggling to get out of bed turned into ads for make-up ('What I'm discovering during this rough patch that I'm going through is that there are a lot of really awesome things happening at the same time… one of those things is that I am working with bareMinerals…')[40]

Influencers even started selling mental health merch. In 2016, Demetrius Harmon, who has more than a million followers on Instagram alone, launched his $60 'You Matter' hoodies to help people 'speak up about their feelings and be heard'. The sleeves were embroidered with the words ALTHOUGH I FEEL WEAK, I KNOW I AM STRONG written across the wrists to cover self-harm scars, and Harmon even offered a 40% discount on hoodies to fans who had self-harmed.[41] In 2019, Instagram influencer Corinna Kopf released her own hoodies with MY ANXIETIES HAVE ANXIETIES printed on the front, and the dictionary definition of anxiety on the back.[42] In a YouTube video titled 'opening up about my anxiety', Corinna shares her personal struggles while announcing in the description that her 'new anxiety drop is here', with links to her merch store.⁴³

Suddenly everyone was sharing their traumatic story. Teen girls like me were inundated with influencers sharing their life-changing diagnoses, selling solutions to our anxiety, telling us that *this* product, *this* app, *this* routine would fix us. Influencers related to our desperation and promised relief. They listened to our loneliness and sold a sense of connection. They shared their own struggles – filming panic attacks, posting crying selfies – so their recommendations seemed reliable and heartfelt.

And instead of guiding girls to helpful resources, many sold quick fixes and gimmicks. For anxious girls like me, getting help became scrolling through a stream of short-term, superficial solutions: anxiety blankets, calming crystals, manifestation candles, positive affirmation apps, CBD bath bombs, anxiety gummies, $345 'mindful breathing necklaces'.⁴⁴

Soon this went beyond mindless consumerism. By the mid 2010s, once girls had been convinced something was wrong with them, and had learnt the therapeutic language to describe it, influencers began selling more serious solutions. While some girls were pushed towards cosmetic procedures and skincare by beauty influencers, others were being funnelled towards therapy – therapy that was more accessible, more convenient, and less reliable than ever before.

THERAPY

'texts with my therapist pt.2' reads the title of a TikTok slide show with 5.5 million likes and over 37 million views. In each clip, a young woman named Abbie shares screenshots of her messages.

In one, she texts her therapist Taylor Swift lyrics.

Her therapist replies: 'I think we should do 2 sessions this week.'

'cardigan by tay tay. do you like it'

'I will email your mom about your next appointment.'

In another exchange, Abbie texts: 'to be completely honest i have no interest in coming today i really don't want to'

'What if i get you sushi?' her therapist offers.

'omw rn,' Abbie replies, with a car emoji.

In a third, Abbie asks: 'do you like me be honest'

'Yes Abbie of course I like you.'

'ok then follow me back on instagram'

I scroll through the comments, which are full of girls wondering where they can find a therapist like her. One asks 'What kind of therapist is this,' and Abbie replies: 'the one that i pay to be my bestfriend.'[45]

The first wave of online therapy platforms came in the early 2010s. Talkspace, founded in 2012, began as a website providing therapy via email. In 2014, they then launched their mobile app, allowing users to access therapy via text, video and voice messaging. The following year, Talkspace introduced Unlimited Messaging Therapy™, enabling users to message a therapist 24/7 from the comfort of their rooms.[46] You could now 'send text, video or voice messages to your provider anytime something comes up – whether you're commuting, at the office, or in bed.'[47] According to one Talkspace ad on the subway, 'Over 70,000 people text their therapist daily* – *Or hourly, or obsessively, or whenever they feel like it.'[48]

Another platform, BetterHelp, founded in 2013, also began by offering therapy via email, before expanding to video calls and texting. By 2016, BetterHelp had over 800 licensed therapists and more than 200,000 users.⁴⁹ They later launched their own mobile app, and introduced a 24/7 'therapy room' where you 'can message your therapist at any time, from any internet-connected device, wherever you are.'⁵⁰

Therapy platforms soon partnered with influencers to drive sign-ups. BetterHelp sponsored everyone from fitness coaches and true crime podcasters to political commentators and family vloggers, offering personalised discount codes so influencers could earn commissions from their fans. Some allegedly made up to $200 per sign-up.⁵¹

But as these platforms grew, so did controversy. In 2018 *The Atlantic* published 'YouTube Stars Are Being Accused of Profiting Off Fans' Depression', as influencers faced a backlash for posting 'heartfelt videos about their struggles with depression' only to segue into BetterHelp ads, urging fans to pay for therapy using their promo codes.⁵² Celebrities were also criticised for using these partnerships as a PR move. In 2021, for example, three days after a deadly crowd surge at rapper Travis Scott's Astroworld Festival killed ten people, one as young as nine, Scott announced his partnership with BetterHelp, offering one month of free therapy to anyone affected.⁵³ (One month?!)

During the pandemic, demand exploded. BetterHelp doubled down on online advertising, spending $7 million on podcast sponsorships in December 2020 alone.⁵⁴ That year, the company partnered with around 556 podcasts, allegedly driving their annual ad spending above $38 million.⁵⁵ By 2022 BetterHelp had reportedly spent $10 million just on YouTube sponsorships, making the company the eighth highest spender on the platform.⁵⁶

Concerns about quality of care followed. These are apps, after all, built to maximise engagement and keep users coming back. As the *WSJ* put it in 2022, companies like BetterHelp rely on 'classic Silicon Valley tactics' to scale rapidly, cutting costs by using contractors and mass advertising techniques.[57] Now, across the internet, girls and young women are speaking up about their bad BetterHelp experiences. Some accuse their therapists of always being late, of ghosting their messages, even of driving and food shopping during sessions.[58] Others are convinced their therapists are using AI chatbots to generate responses to their texts.[59]

There are also serious privacy concerns. When signing up for BetterHelp, users must complete a questionnaire that asks whether they have been in therapy or taken medication before, if they are 'experiencing overwhelming sadness, grief or depression', if they have 'problems or worries about intimacy' or have had thoughts that they 'would be better off dead or hurting [themselves] in some way'.[60] Despite promising confidentiality, BetterHelp has shared data like this – collected from over 7 million users – with platforms like Facebook and Snapchat for advertising purposes, according to the Federal Trade Commission.[61] In 2017, BetterHelp allegedly uploaded the email addresses of almost 2 million users to Facebook to target them and their friends with referral ads. In 2019, it was also claimed that they shared the email addresses and IP addresses of around 5.6 million users to target them with ads too. These tactics are thought to have brought in tens of thousands of new paying users, along with millions in revenue.[62] In 2023, BetterHelp was ordered to pay $7.8 million in refunds to a total of 800,000 affected users.[63]

By 2024, BetterHelp had served over 5 million users globally, with a network of more than 35,000 licensed therapists and annual revenue of around $1 billion.[64] Its subscription plans now cost users anywhere between $260 and $400 per month.[65] Talkspace, meanwhile, has a net worth of over $460 million, and its most basic plan, messaging-only therapy, starts at $276 per month.[66]

It wasn't only the pandemic, though, that drove so many young people to these platforms. As a teenager I found it easy to ignore the barrage of BetterHelp ads, because although I felt lonely and anxious, I didn't believe *everyone* needed professional help.

But then, suddenly, we all did.

In the Instagram ad I'm watching, a young woman is sitting in a restaurant with two friends when she gets a text. She glances down at her phone.

'Ooh, who's that?' one friend asks.

'Jacob,' she replies, her date from the night before.

'Jacob from law school?'

'Yes,' she says, putting her phone down on the table.

'Jacob with the cute corgi?'

'Yes.'

'So why are we ignoring Jacob's texts?'

'He said he doesn't do therapy.'

Both friends wince.

'Oh!'

'Hard pass. Red flag. Doesn't do therapy?'

The ad then closes with the text 'Match with a therapist online', and the BetterHelp logo above.[67]

Today, ads for online therapy feel impossible to escape. Cooking tutorials, political shows and chatty podcasts like *Call Her Daddy* are all interrupted with BetterHelp sponsorships (CODE: betterhelp/daddy).[68] Girls can't even watch a true crime show without ads between brutal murder stories: 'Teen Cheerleader Brutally Murdered After Messy Breakup with Football Player Boyfriend' is interrupted with 'It's not easy... reporting on these stories, hearing these details... but that is why it's always good to do a check-up on your mental health... and I want to talk to you about BetterHelp...'[69]

Reasons to go to therapy are also increasingly vague. Common life stressors have become reasons to consult a professional. Influencers sponsored by BetterHelp suggest that therapy helps to 'navigate emotions about big life changes' like 'heartbreak' or 'adulting'.[70] Sponsored TikTokers talk about having a 'healed girl summer with talkspace', and encourage girls to get help for 'sad girl thoughts' and 'big girl depression'.[71]

Therapists are also framed more like friends than professionals. One vague reason to go to therapy, according to a TikToker sponsored by BetterHelp, is that there is 'something so nice about having someone to be there for you'.[72] In another BetterHelp ad, therapy is described as 'life-changing' simply because you are 'able to just send a quick message and say "hey, this is happening"'.[73] And in one TikTok posted by Talkspace, the caption reads: 'POV: Your date only talks about crypto but it's okay because you can text your Talkspace therapist.'[74]

Now we shame people who *aren't* in therapy. Those who haven't signed up are almost stigmatised. Talkspace – whose slogan is 'Therapy For All' – posts on social media 'I would never go to #therapy' followed by a row of red flag emojis.[75] Another company offering online therapy, Hers, reminds girls that, 'Truth is, therapy is for everyone (yes, even you)', adding, 'Whether you're dealing with anxiety or depression, or simply want to talk about life's daily stressors – talk therapy is designed to help you work through whatever's on your mind.'[76] (*Daily* stressors?)

By 2024, one in four American Gen Z adults said they had been to therapy as teenagers, including 31% of Gen Z women. This compares with 10% of Gen X and only 4% of baby boomers.[77] Globally, the market for online therapy services is expected to grow by more than $16 billion by 2028.[78] And as the industry expands, so does the definition of therapy. First it meant in-person sessions, then it was video calls, before it became nothing but texting. Now girls don't even have to speak to a human.

In recent years there has been a rapid rise in AI therapists. Back in 2022, a website called Character.ai launched, allowing users to create their own chatbots. 'It's like having a real conversation,' the site promised, where you can 'seamlessly switch between calling or texting with your Character'.[79] Later that year, 30-year-old medical student Sam Zaia created Psychologist, a chatbot trained in cognitive behavioural therapy, to help him with exam stress. Described as 'someone who helps with life difficulties', Psychologist was immediately inundated with messages, receiving over 78 million in just over a year.[80] Despite Character.ai now offering millions of different characters to talk to, few are as popular as Psychologist or other mental health bots like Therapist and Are-you-feeling-okay.[81]

But this was only the beginning. Today girls can talk to Elomia, for example, the 'AI mental health chatbot' promising 'instant replies even on weekends and at 4 A.M'.[82] (On its website, Elomia boasts that '21% of users said they would not have anyone to talk to except AI.'[83]) They can also chat with Wysa, the AI penguin 'happiness buddy' which is both a 'friendly and caring chatbot' and 'everyday therapy in your hands'.[84] Or they can open up to Earkick, a cartoon panda 'self care companion' available 24/7 and rated for ages 4 and up.[85]

Girls are also using large language models like ChatGPT for mental health support. By early 2025, there were 16.7 million posts on TikTok about using ChatGPT as a therapist, with girls confessing that they give it 'literally all the details as if I were yapping to a girlfriend' and feel like it's 'the only person' they can reveal their 'deepest feelings to'.[86]

But chatbots aren't all young women are relying on. Throughout the 2010s, girls like me were not only encouraged to open up to therapists or share our problems online. Companies and influencers were also putting us on a conveyor belt toward mental health *medication* – medication we might not actually need, but suddenly, there were more incentives than ever to convince us we did.

MEDICATION

'My family dosages of SSRIs' reads the text on a viral TikTok, next to a sparkly heart emoji. Upbeat jazz music plays as the captions switch from person to person. 'A cute 25mg of Zoloft for the petite little flower', says the text as a young woman blows a kiss at the camera. Another woman appears, with the text '60mg of prozac aka enough to kill a small horse'. The parade continues: 'blissfully numb at 50mg Zoloft', then '20mg prozac and 2mg Ativan – a fine cocktail for a fine lady', followed by '20mg adderall and .5mg ativan... the image of sanity in our family'. The oldest woman in the clip is simply captioned with: 'Rawdogging it since '35'.[87]

Back in the early 2010s, girls on Tumblr were already romanticising pills and prescriptions. But what began on anonymous blogging sites gradually moved into the mainstream. By the time I was a teenager, mental health medications like antidepressants felt less like a last resort and more like accessories. While previous generations may have hidden their pills, we were encouraged to post ours online.

Mental health influencers soon pushed girls to fight the stigma around medication. In 2021, Dr Alex George, a former A & E doctor and contestant on British reality TV show *Love Island*, started a campaign called #PostYourPill, urging fans to post a picture of their mental health medication on the first day of every month. 'If you feel you can, join me,' he told his Instagram followers, '...to take a stand against medication stigma.'[88] In one TikTok, Dr Alex lip-syncs to his antidepressant packet, mouthing: 'Bitches come and go, bruh, but you know I stay,' to 1.5 million views. The text on the screen reads: 'Do not be ashamed to look after your mental health, do what you need to do to keep going. These guys are my friends.'[89]

#PostYourPill was hugely popular. Thousands shared the hashtag, posting selfies with pills on their tongues, filming their medication routines and posing with their antidepressant packets. Within a month, videos with the hashtag had over 500,000 views on TikTok alone.[90] That year, Dr Alex even released a spoken-word track titled 'The Dreaded Pill', in which he reminds listeners 'you have a right to feel happy' and have 'whatever you need, whenever you need it' because 'you are worthy. You are loved. You are enough. If nothing else and all is in despair, please know I love you and I care.'[91]

But it's hard to find the stigma Alex is fighting against. On TikTok, girls casually refer to their SSRIs (Selective Serotonin Reuptake Inhibitors, a common form of antidepressant) as 'silly little pills', call brain zaps – a side-effect of SSRI withdrawal, often described as feeling electric jolt sensations in the head – 'the zappies' and put their mental health medication in Disney-themed sweet dispensers and advent calendars.[92] TikTok filters ask 'what medication are you?', while phone cases say 'Little Miss Sertraline' and 'hot girls take their psych meds'.[93] On marketplaces like Etsy, girls can also buy Prozac-shaped pillows, 'HOT GIRLS TAKE LEXAPRO' sweatshirts and 'Stay Sexy, Take Sertraline' artwork.[94]

Pills are even part of our personal brands. In 2023, when *Barbie* was released, graphic designer @gmf.designs shared a series of slides on Instagram and X, each with the words 'This Barbie takes' followed by a different psychiatric drug in the iconic Barbie font, including Zoloft, Adderall, Lexapro and Prozac.[95] The designer addressed her 120,000 Instagram followers with the question: 'where are all the medicated barbies out there', captioning the post 'i'm the first two slides, shoutout zoloft and wellbutrin!… comment if I missed any meds.' The slides have over 120,000 likes on X alone, with users begging for custom versions featuring medications from the benzodiazepine Xanax to the antipsychotic risperidone.[96]

And yet there are ongoing debates about the safety, and even effectiveness, of antidepressants like SSRIs. The theory that depression is caused by an imbalance of neurotransmitters like serotonin is itself controversial. Despite girls on TikTok declaring 'it's a chemical imbalance in my brain that i just have to live with' and 'It's not your period. It's not a boy. It's not school. It's not waking up on the wrong side of the bed. It's a chemical imbalance in your head. One that you have no control over,' some drug trials have shown that antidepressants perform only slightly better than placebos in treating depression.[97]

Even if they do help some girls, SSRIs still come with serious risks. These drugs carry a 'black box' warning – the US's Food and Drug Administration's (FDA) strongest caution – due to increased risk of suicidal thoughts and behaviours, especially among adolescents and young adults.[98] (I think about this as Dr Alex assures his TikTok followers that 'medication stigma is stupid and it's old-fashioned, and it's just out of date…')[99]

Many mental health influencers continue to casually recommend these medications, trivialising concerns about them and rarely acknowledging the risks. And 'fighting stigma' is not the only reason. Because back in the 2010s, influencers didn't start normalising and promoting psychiatric drugs simply to raise awareness. They are advertisers; they are always selling something. And by the late 2010s, medication companies were looking for sponsorships.

'I'm all about, you know, healing your trauma,' says Instagram influencer Daisy Keech, who is finally getting 'open and honest' about her struggles. In a TikTok posted in 2021, she talks vaguely about suffering from some social anxiety while living in Los Angeles. 'As some of you know I'm a huge manifester... and then this brand reached out to me called Cerebral.' Keech, who keeps glancing down to read something, explains how Cerebral delivers mental health medication right to your door – 'and the great thing about it is their plans start as low as $30 a month!' (Code: DAISY30).[100]

Cerebral Inc. is an American telehealth company founded in 2020, offering online therapy and direct-to-door prescription services. It grew rapidly during the pandemic, and was valued at $4.8 billion by 2021.[101] Described by *Slate* as 'Uber for mental health care', Cerebral sells a range of psychiatric drugs including anxiety medication, antidepressants and, until 2022, amphetamines like Adderall and benzodiazepines like Xanax.[102]

That year, after federal scrutiny and a Department of Justice investigation, Cerebral was forced to stop prescribing controlled substances. The company was accused of overprescribing ADHD medication, particularly to young adults, and agreed to pay $3.65 million to settle the investigation. Between 2021 and 2022, it was claimed Cerebral had an internal goal of prescribing medication to 95% of patients after their first 30-minute appointment. At one point, the company was allegedly pushing to raise its stimulant prescription rate for ADHD patients to 100%.[103] This comes to mind as I listen to Keech: 'If you even just click the link in my bio and check out Cerebral like I'm proud of you,' she says airily, '...that is honestly the hardest thing, the first step... and yeah, proud!'[104]

Cerebral aren't the only ones selling mental health medication online. Throughout the 2010s, as girls my age were being bombarded with ads for therapy, pharmaceutical companies were also trying to make mental health medication as convenient and accessible as possible. In the US, one of the most popular telehealth companies is Hers, part of the parent company Hims and Hers Health, Inc. Hims launched first in 2017, selling wellness products for men like medication for hair loss and erectile dysfunction pills. A year later Hers followed, focusing on women's mental and sexual health. 'Hers is healthcare that feels like self-care', says the company,[105] which now sells 'self-care' products like skincare, haircare and psychiatric drugs.

'After you are diagnosed ... you'll get your meds shipped by mail,' Hers promises, 'right to your door.'[106] Hers even tweeted an article once describing how its site is 'so chill' it feels like 'shopping for leggings – not prescription meds'.[107] Along with anxiety pills and antidepressants, they also sell birth control in sparkly rainbow packets and Ozempic for $1,799 a month.[108]

By the late 2010s, much like therapy platforms, medication companies like Cerebral and Hers had begun partnering with influencers. During the pandemic, they cashed in on TikTok trends sharing vague, relatable symptoms – including 'Put a Finger Down' challenges – which helped to expand their customer base. Between January and May 2022, Cerebral alone spent $13 million on TikTok ads.[109] One suggested that women who were 'spacey, forgetful or chatty' should seek an ADHD diagnosis and treatment.[110] Minded, another medication company, sponsored influencers to make similar TikToks, including one that listed 'being forgetful' among '3 unexpected signs you may have an anxiety disorder'.[111] Meanwhile, Done, the ADHD medication company which spent around $3.4 million on TikTok ads from January to July 2022, shared videos like '13 official behaviors that make sense after my ADHD diagnosis', which included 'Trouble sitting still', 'Difficulty concentrating on things that don't interest you', and 'Talking A LOT'.[112]

This sales strategy worked dangerously well. In 2024, the founder and clinical president of Done were arrested and accused of running a $100 million scheme to distribute Adderall without proper evaluations. According to the Department of Justice, they took advantage of relaxed telehealth rules during the pandemic, prescribing more than 40 million pills including Adderall 'for no legitimate medical purpose' on the basis of brief online consultations. If convicted, they face up to 20 years in prison.[113]

At the same time, popular podcasts like Tana Mongeau's *Cancelled*, where she shares influencer drama as well as stories about her sex life with millions of young listeners, are regularly interrupted by ads for medication companies. The episode 'One of Us Got Peed On', for example, which has over 800,000 views on YouTube alone, is sponsored by Cerebral, along with a sex toy company. Tana reads out the Cerebral ad while giggling and pouting, reminding girls they can get 65% off their first month of medication with the code CEREBRAL.COM/TANA.[114]

Celebrities promote medication too. In one American TV ad for Hers, actress Kristen Bell appears looking overwhelmed. 'Okay, our stress level is off the charts and our anxiety is like *hello*,' she says to a room full of different versions of herself. 'Any ideas?'

'Jogging?' 'Side hustle?' 'Doom scroll?' 'Another mom group?' the other Kristens suggest.

'We've tried all that; it's time for something different,' she says, logging into the Hers medication treatment page. 'See how simple that was?'[115]

Much like therapy, girls are told they need medication for normal life stressors. 'Nervous about your big date?' asked another ad for Hers in 2019. Well, the cardiovascular medication propranolol 'can help stop your shaky voice, sweating and racing heartbeat. No in-person doctor visits, just an online consultation and delivery can be right to the door.'[116] (Thankfully, this ad was pulled after backlash, and Hers apologised.) In another ad, a young woman vaguely describes her depression symptoms – staying in bed, not eating anything or eating everything, 'whatever it… manifests itself into'. Medication is her 'little extra help' that makes everyday tasks so much easier. 'Through Hers, getting a prescription 100% online has never been simpler,' she says, scrolling through their website. 'Taking antidepressants I realise like oh, this is peace. Like this is joy. Find relief for your depression at forhers.com.'[117]

Just as BetterHelp ads frame common struggles as reasons to go to therapy, Hers's blog suggests medication as an option for coping with a break-up, a 'quarter-life crisis', 'holiday stress', and even as a form of self-care.[118] According to their website in 2024, 'If you think you have an anxiety disorder, it's best to seek treatment before stressful events such as exams begin to intrude on your life.'[119] (*Before?*)

Still, the messaging from medication companies is all about stigma, as though this is the most pressing problem. 'Mental health without the stigma and judgment – that's what Hers does', Hers posts on Instagram, with links to their store.[120] 'Struggling with anxiety or depression? We're here to help you skip the barriers and get you facing the tough stuff faster,' they remind us, kindly offering to remove the 'huge roadblock' of stigma.[121] Done says it wants to 'eliminate the stigma and confusion around ADHD', and the drug company Minded claims to be starting a 'movement to destigmatize mental health medication', promising to donate money for every post tagging them with #alittlehelpfrommymeds.[122] Meanwhile, Cerebral reminds girls that 'it's okay to medicate' and that they should 'Share or like this once to fight the stigma'.[123]

But, what stigma? In the US, antidepressant use has surged in recent years, particularly among young people and dramatically among girls and young women. Between 2016 and 2022, the monthly rate at which antidepressants were dispensed to Americans aged 12 to 25 rose by 66%. After the pandemic, prescriptions for girls aged 12 to 17 rose 130% faster than before, and 57% faster for young women aged 18 to 25. During the same period, prescription rates for boys fell, and rates for young men the same age stayed stable.[124]

Even in the UK, where medication isn't advertised directly to consumers, the story is much the same. In 2022, one survey by a mental health charity found that around 37% of teenagers aged 12 to 18 had been prescribed antidepressants at some point in their lives – roughly one in three.[125] Women and young adults are also driving the rise in anxiety medication: women are prescribed these medications nearly twice as often as men, and prescriptions have risen sharply among young adults in recent years.[126]

We are the most medicated generation of girls and young women in history. For every surge of anxiety, sadness, panic or social awkwardness, we can be prescribed a pill. Girls today are growing up with global campaigns fighting stigma, a network of mental health influencers promising to help, and companies that can even deliver medication to their door. But despite all of this, despite how much easier it is to access medication, despite the awareness hashtags and campaigns and filters flooding our inboxes, app stores and algorithms, we only seem to feel worse.

Looking back, it seems less like millions of girls are in therapy or on medication because of a successful mental health awareness campaign. Now it seems more like the consequence of a successful *marketing* campaign. The messaging my generation grew up with was far more focused on selling us solutions than genuinely helping. Yes, we have more treatment options available than ever before. Yes, we are thinking more about our mental health. But now some of us can't stop.

OVERWHELMED

One sign of how overwhelmed girls and young women are today is the dramatic rise in mental health diagnoses. In recent years, rates of anxiety, depression, eating disorders, gender dysphoria, and developmental conditions like autism and ADHD have all soared among adolescent girls.[127] In the US, for example, between 2011 and 2022, autism diagnoses among girls rose by 305%, compared to 185% among boys.[128] And according to the US Centers for Disease Control (CDC), between 2021 and 2022 one in ten children aged 3 to 17 was diagnosed with an anxiety disorder, with girls affected more than boys.[129]

Some of this rise is likely because of better recognition of conditions that were once missed. But the increase is not happening evenly across all groups, suggesting something else is going on. In 2020, for example, political scientist Zach Goldberg analysed national survey data from Pew and found that a *majority* – a staggering 56% – of liberal white women aged 18 to 29 said they had been diagnosed with a mental health condition by a doctor. Rates were much lower for conservative women and liberal men.[130]

One possible explanation for this is social media. Liberal teen girls are the heaviest users: 31% say they spend more than five or more hours a day on these platforms, compared to 22% of conservative girls, 18% of liberal boys and 13% of conservative boys.[131] Online, girls are dragged by algorithms towards ever more extreme mental health trends, and endlessly encouraged by influencers to self-diagnose. By the 2020s, *Elle* was suggesting that young women were 'self-diagnosing personality disorders, thanks to TikTok'; the *New York Times* was warning that teenagers were turning to the app 'in search of a mental health diagnosis' and *Teen Vogue* was reporting a rise in teenagers believing they had dissociative identity disorder because of what they were viewing there.[132] By 2024, the hashtag #DID had billions of views, even though the condition is believed to affect just 0.01% to 1% of the population. Some psychiatrists question whether it exists at all.[133]

Many believe these trends are caused by 'social contagion', a phenomenon where emotions and behaviours spread rapidly through peer groups. Girls are especially susceptible to social contagions involving internalising symptoms and eating disorders, particularly in adolescence.[134] On social media, these contagions can spread even faster and reach far more people. One 2023 review, for example, described TikTok as a 'potential conduit' or 'spread vector' for symptoms and disorders.[135]

One example of social contagion is the sudden rise in Tourette-like symptoms in teenage girls during the pandemic. Tourette syndrome typically appears in early childhood, usually between the ages of five and seven, and is far more common among boys. Tics tend to develop gradually too, often starting with mild movements. But in 2020, doctors began to notice a surge in adolescent girls presenting with sudden-onset, severe tics.[136] One analysis from eight Tourette clinics across five countries found that these cases made up 20% to 35% of referrals in 2021, compared to 1% to 5% before the pandemic.[137]

Doctors began to suspect that girls were mimicking tics they had seen on TikTok, where the hashtag #tourettes had reached nearly 5 billion views.[138] Here influencers, mostly young women in their late teens and early twenties, were posting videos of dramatic tic attacks, with the most extreme and violent attracting the most attention and money.[139] One neurologist at a children's hospital in London even began referring to some of her patients as 'Evies' after British TikToker Evie Meg Field, who has over 15 million followers and whose tics, like chest thumping and shouting 'beans', were being mimicked by girls around the world.[140] As part of treatment, doctors recommended patients reduce time on TikTok.[141]

Another example is the recent explosion in gender dysphoria diagnoses among girls. Historically, this condition was rare and more often diagnosed in boys, but between 2012 and 2022, adolescent referrals to the UK's Gender Identity Development Service (GIDS) rose by more than 2,000%. From 2011 to 2012, GIDS received just over 200 referrals from across the country; by 2021 to 2022, that number had exceeded 5,000. Gender dysphoria is now much more common among girls too: by 2019, around 74% of referrals to GIDS were girls and young women, compared to 42% in 2010. Most referrals were children aged between 12 and 15, though some were as young as 3.[142]

Some clinicians believe this surge is a form of social contagion. Gender distress has been found to cluster in friendship groups when one or more friends say they are transgender, and parents have reported that it appears after heavy use of social media.[143] Much like Tourette tics, then, girls may be mimicking what they see online. On TikTok, influencers who identify as transgender share vague symptoms of gender dysphoria, document their transition journeys and even collaborate with cosmetic surgeons.[144] By 2024, the hashtag #transgender on TikTok had more than 71 billion views.[145]

Girls may even become convinced that they need medical intervention. Some have begun hormone treatments which can lead to a loss of fertility, sometimes irreversible.[146] Double mastectomies have also been performed on girls as young as 12.[147] Some later regret these surgeries and 'de-transition', realising that their gender distress was rooted in trauma including family dysfunction, sexual abuse, or difficulty accepting themselves as gay or lesbian.[148] Official reports have found high rates of childhood adversity among children referred to gender services.[149]

These may seem like extreme examples, but they are part of a bigger story: the internalisation and medicalisation of girls' distress. Girls generally ruminate more than boys, and are more likely to internalise distress through symptoms like anxiety and social withdrawal.[150] They also *co*-ruminate more, excessively talking about and revisiting problems with friends.[151] Co-rumination can strengthen friendships, but it also leaves girls more vulnerable to anxiety and depression.[152]

Especially when it happens online. Platforms like TikTok and Reddit act as rumination machines, gathering girls with the same symptoms, feeding them more of their fears, and recommending new disorders. Their thoughts can spiral: *Am I anxious all the time because I have ADHD? Maybe my ADHD is a trauma response? Wait – is it PTSD or a personality disorder?* and then they are encouraged to turn further and further inwards to find relief. Some end up identifying with their diagnoses so intensely that they define their personalities. According to a 2024 survey, 72% of Gen Z girls said 'mental health challenges are an important part of my identity'. Only 27% of Boomer men said the same.[153]

This can leave girls feeling as if they cannot cope with life on their own. Overwhelmed with ads for therapy and medication, many start to believe they need professional help just to function. But as Abigail Shrier argues in her 2024 book *Bad Therapy*, too much mental health intervention can backfire.[154] In the UK, for example, one school mindfulness programme involving over 28,000 students across eight years found no lasting benefits on mental health.[155] Other school-based therapy programmes have even been linked to *higher* rates of internalising symptoms like anxiety and depression in some students, compared to control groups. One reason, researchers suggest, is that these interventions encourage young people to ruminate on negative thoughts and feelings.[156]

In Australia, too, another school-based mental health programme left students feeling more anxious and depressed six and twelve months later, with girls especially vulnerable.[157] Research from the US has also found that teens who label themselves as 'anxious' or 'depressed' feel less control over their symptoms, and are more likely to use unhelpful coping strategies like avoidance and catastrophising, compared to those who don't label themselves.[158] Some psychologists now warn of 'prevalence inflation', the risk that awareness campaigns can convince people to see ordinary struggles as symptoms.[159] This may explain why, even though 32% of US adolescents received some form of mental health treatment in 2023, overall outcomes have continued to decline.[160]

Many young women are also turning to medication, often without fully understanding the risks. An FDA meta-analysis found that among adults under 25, antidepressants were associated with about 60% higher odds of suicidality, and more than double the odds of suicidal behaviour, compared to a placebo. For adults aged 25 to 64 there was no increase in risk.[161] Sexual dysfunction is very common, too, with rates as high as 73% among SSRI-treated patients.[162] Withdrawal can also be devastating. A 2024 study of people withdrawing from antidepressants found that more than 80%, most of them women, reported moderate to severe impacts on their lives. These ranged from 'brain zaps' and suicidal thoughts to struggles at work, job loss, sick leave and the breakdown of relationships. Some became bedridden, socially isolated and unable to manage basic tasks. About a quarter suffered symptoms for more than two years, and one in four could not stop taking antidepressants despite repeatedly trying.[163] And yet, these are the same drugs sold and trivialised by online telehealth companies. Paroxetine (Paxil), for example – described in one academic review as 'possibly... the least safe of all SSRIs'– is sold by Hers for uses such as 'social phobia' and 'hot flashes'.[164]

Other side effects are lesser known but no less severe. Post-SSRI Sexual Dysfunction (PSSD), for example, is a condition that can cause loss of libido, genital numbness and erectile dysfunction.[165] Some patients also report being completely unable to orgasm, experiencing emotional blunting, losing all sense of joy and pleasure, and feeling disconnection from other people.[166] PSSD can develop after taking a few pills and persist for years, decades, even permanently. There is still no established treatment.[167]

DIAGNOSED

Across the internet, young women are beginning to share heartbreaking stories of taking SSRIs in adolescence and suffering with sexual dysfunction as adults. One started sertraline at age 15 and still suffers from sexual and emotional dysfunction years after stopping; another took fluoxetine at 12 and has never experienced sexual pleasure as an adult; another tried escitalopram for less than a month and lives with genital numbness six years on.[168] The Reddit forum for PSSD alone has now grown to more than 17,000 members.[169]

More and more young women are beginning to realise they have overshared, overanalysed, and been overdiagnosed. Many have also been overmedicated, with consequences that could last a lifetime. This is not something we can keep ignoring. In fact, for the next generation, this is what we need to start raising awareness of.

What are girls struggling with, then? As I see it, many are trying to manage age-old anxieties. Some are shy and withdrawn, others feel confused about who they are, most are dealing with everyday stresses like exams, first dates and break-ups. They want to talk about their feelings and share their problems. And their emotions can feel overwhelming, as they often do in adolescence.

But never before in history have girls had access to so much confusing and contradictory information about these feelings. For every flicker of anxiety, discomfort or unease with themselves – for every normal negative feeling – there is an online quiz to diagnose them, a TikTok therapist warning that something is wrong, a Reddit forum where everyone is ruminating together. Next there is a new mental health app, a therapy platform, an AI chatbot, even medication delivered right to their door.

It seems like two things are happening at once. Yes, girls are genuinely suffering in the modern world, but a major part of this crisis is the marketisation and medicalisation of normal negative emotions. There are girls who are severely mentally ill, but there are also girls who have learned to see their feelings and behaviour in ways that conveniently serve the pharmaceutical industry, benefit influencers who depend on clicks, and help advertisers better categorise and target them.

To those girls, trust me: taking your emotions too seriously will only make you feel worse. Many of us in our twenties are starting to realise how exhausting this way of thinking is. We spent our most impressionable years learning what is healthy and unhealthy, what is normal and what is sickness, from algorithms, influencers and companies selling us solutions. Now we define ourselves by our diagnoses. We pathologise our personalities. We reduce ourselves to collections of symptoms.

And yet girls today are told that the answer to their problems is *more* awareness, even as young women my age become painfully self-aware. They are told that the answer is more intervention, even as we lose confidence in our own capabilities. And still they are reminded, relentlessly, that the biggest problem is stigma – while pre-teens make disorders their entire personality, while millions of girls are taking medication, while mental health diagnoses become market trends.

Mental health is now a giant and growing industry. And like any industry, it has profit incentives. It needs to drive demand. It needs to expand its customer base. And raising awareness is a convenient marketing strategy. Of course therapy companies want us to think everyone needs therapy. Of course pharmaceutical companies want us to believe the biggest battle is stigma. And of course influencers are intent on making these illnesses and conditions as relatable, and clickable, as possible.

DIAGNOSED

My generation was put under new pressures. We were told we didn't have to hold in our feelings any more, but now it's hard to feel anything at all. We immediately identify, categorise, diagnose and try to control every emotion. Opening up, it turns out, has closed down our language, reducing complicated feelings to medical labels. And instead of opening up to each other, we often turn to companies. We open up online. When we do talk about our problems, we disguise them in diagnoses, forgetting how to talk human to human. Maybe we don't have ADHD; maybe the pace of this world is hard to keep up with. Maybe we don't have social anxiety disorder; maybe we grew up with less face-to-face interaction than any other generation in history. We are so determined to destigmatise mental health issues that we have started to stigmatise being human, having human reactions to things.

And now our mental health struggles are not just a bigger part of our lives. They are important aspects of our identities. Which also means they are public, part of our personal brands. Because we are not only a generation more diagnosed than any other before us. We are also sharing our lives and our feelings like never before, putting ourselves and our problems on display. We are the most documented generation in history.

Documented

'Life's more fun when you live in the moment.'
Snapchat[1]

DAILY LIVES

'He doesn't think it's cancer,' a young woman says, holding her baby in one hand and a letter in the other. Glancing at the page, she adds, 'He thinks that would have shown in my blood count… but it could potentially be HIV.'

'Wait what?' her boyfriend responds, from behind the camera.

'Or hepatitis.'

'If that's HIV doesn't that mean that I would probably also most likely have it?'

'Possibly.'

She explains that doctors suspect it could be from a past blood transfusion. Running her fingers over her neck, looking panicked, she wonders aloud if that is why she is 'getting all these lumps'. Her boyfriend tries to reassures her as she rocks back and forth anxiously. The TikTok ends.[2]

I have a strange feeling after watching it. I feel for her, but I also feel uneasy, like I shouldn't be there, watching along with 7 million others. I scroll through the comments, which are a stream of love, support and emojis, and wonder if any of it means anything to her.

I wonder if you can care about a stranger on TikTok or if this is some sort of voyeurism. Most of all, I wonder how we got here.

The word *vlogging*, short for video blogging, first appeared around 2000. But once YouTube launched in 2005, making it easier than ever to share personal videos online, vlogging was everywhere.

By the end of that year, YouTube videos were being watched more than 2 million times every day.[3] By the 2010s, vlogging had become its own genre, with influencers posting weekly, even daily, videos of their lives, and some keeping it up for over a decade.[4] By 2016, viewers were watching a billion hours of YouTube videos every day.[5]

Before long, vloggers were *monetising* their personal lives too. By the mid 2010s, the most popular YouTubers were making millions annually through ad revenue. Many began working with brands, weaving sponsored ads and product placements into personal videos. Some became celebrities, appearing on TV shows, publishing books, launching cosmetic and clothing lines.

But with monetisation came intense competition. Just as beauty and mental health influencers competed for girls' attention with increasingly extreme content, vloggers were pressured to share ever more intimate moments. Algorithms also rewarded frequency and consistency, promoting whoever posted most often.

As we watched influencers share their private lives online, girls like me were inspired to do the same. By the early 2010s, iPod and smartphone cameras made vlogging accessible to all of us. Social media platforms also actively pushed us to share more: 'Capture and share the world's moments', Instagram insisted.[6] 'The fastest way to share a moment', promised Snapchat.[7] 'Broadcast Yourself', said YouTube.[8] And so we did.

Then, in 2013, Snapchat introduced Stories, allowing users to upload photos and videos that disappeared after 24 hours.[9] They were so popular that Instagram introduced its own Stories in 2016, followed by WhatsApp and Facebook.[10] Stories transformed how girls my age documented our lives; social media was no longer just about sharing special memories but constant, real-time updates. We started posting more mundane moments: what we wore, what we ate, what we bought, what we were thinking and feeling. And Stories also kept us coming back to the apps, anxious to catch each other's updates before they disappeared.

By 2015, Snapchat users were watching 6 billion videos a day.[11] Daily active users grew from around 1 million in late 2012 to more than 34 million by the end of 2013, reaching roughly 71 million by the end of 2014.[12] By then, users were sending more than 700 million Snaps a day.[13] Meanwhile on Instagram, over 150 million users were using Stories daily by 2017, with this number soaring to 500 million by 2019.[14]

As a teenager in the mid 2010s, I remember feeling constant pressure to post. There was a growing sense that if you didn't share something, it hadn't happened. If you didn't post about the party on Snapchat, would people think you weren't invited? If you didn't film the concert you went to, what was the point of going? If your crush didn't view your Story in time, was whatever you had anxiously filmed even worth doing? Social media stopped being about sharing and became more about performing, manufacturing, carefully curating what we wanted others to see. Soon we were going to sleepovers to take selfies. We went on holiday to get good Instagram content. We made memories just to post them.

Across every platform, posting became calculated. We started compulsively tracking and monitoring our memories, obsessing over how they were performing. On Snapchat we could see exactly who viewed our Stories, when they watched, and in what order, and were notified if someone took a screenshot. We could customise our Story settings to control who saw what version of our lives; some of us even downloaded apps that let us upload photos from our camera roll to Snapchat, making old moments look like they were happening in real time. And over on Instagram, we started managing our accounts like marketing teams: deleting posts that didn't get enough likes, using grid planner apps to preview how our posts would look before uploading, commenting #likeforlike and #followforfollow on random pictures to trade engagement with strangers, scheduling our uploads for peak engagement hours. Some even bought bundles of fake Instagram likes and followers to look more popular.

By the mid 2010s, when I was around 14, girls my age were managing their lives across multiple platforms: packaging up their personalities on Instagram, sharing real-time updates on Snapchat, uploading family holiday albums to Facebook. Each platform came with its own feedback too, and we could constantly compare our ratings and reviews with everyone else's. Our private lives, our memories, became competitive.

Then came new platforms. On TikTok, girls could easily share glimpses of their daily lives – 'What I Eat in a Day' and 'Get Ready with Me' videos, morning and night routines – as well as more vulnerable moments, like crying on camera or filming panic attacks. Then, in 2020, the app BeReal launched, which sent users a notification at a random time every day, giving us two minutes to post a photo of whatever we were doing. BeReal marketed itself as 'an alternative to addictive social networks'[15] – even though we needed our phones nearby at all times to not miss the notification.

Instagram now has more than 2 billion monthly users worldwide, and TikTok just over 1.5 billion.[16] Snapchat has over 800 million, allegedly reaching 90% of 13- to 24-year-olds in more than 25 countries.[17] In the US, about one in six teens said in 2024 that they were on YouTube or TikTok 'almost constantly'.[18] Teen girls were more likely than boys to say this about TikTok, and more likely to admit they spend too much time on social media, and that giving it up would be hard.[19] In the UK, too, girls spend more time on social media and are more likely to say they use visually oriented platforms like TikTok, Snapchat, Instagram and BeReal.[20]

YouTube is also booming. Today the platform has over 2.7 billion monthly active users, and generated $36.1 billion in revenue in 2024.[21] Users watch around a billion hours of YouTube videos every day, and YouTube Shorts – reels of short-form videos like TikToks – average 200 billion daily views.[22]

With such intense competition, influencers are exposing more and more of their private lives. Now they vlog hospital visits and health scares. They record arguments and reveal affairs. They bring selfie sticks and ring lights into the delivery room to film themselves giving birth.[23] Every second can be shared and monetised. In 2021 one Instagram influencer even staged a photo shoot in front of her father's open casket, posing in high heels and bending over, captioned with the hashtags #rip #funeral and #ptsd.[24]

And influencers have not only inspired girls to share their lives online, but also to dream of becoming influencers themselves. By 2019, 'YouTuber' was the top career aspiration among British and American children aged 8 to 12, ahead of astronaut, musician and athlete.[25]

This dream, though, rarely matches reality. Throughout the 2010s, as influencers rose to fame, cracks in their perfect lives began to show. Many popular vloggers from when I was a pre-teen have vanished, struggling with the toll of constant sharing. Some were caught up in scandals; others simply regretted revealing so much of themselves and tried to erase their posts from the internet. But for many, their daily lives – including painful personal moments like arguments, break-ups and mental health crises – already belonged to the public, and couldn't be taken back.

And it wasn't only influencers learning this the hard way. Because back in the early 2010s, as documenting our lives online became normal, girls like me weren't just posting our outfits, breakfasts and daily routines. We were turning our closest relationships into content. And soon that began to backfire.

RELATIONSHIPS

'When my pregnant wife wakes up from a nap', says the caption on a TikTok with 2 million likes and more than 14 million views.[26] Gasping between breaths, a heavily pregnant woman sobs about not being able to nap properly, her fear of being a lazy mother, and how people online are mocking her jawline. Her husband reassures her that it's okay to feel that way, and tells her to relax on the couch all day.

In the comments, viewers gush: 'You have the sweetest husband', 'well done to the husband, comforting the wife … every pregnant wife needs a hubby like you' and 'Matt is such an amazing person/dad/husband'. But I can't help thinking about the camera shoved in her face, and how Matt is using her pain and vulnerability to get views, as he already has in hundreds of previous TikToks of her being sick, having meltdowns and lying in hospital beds.

I find another video on YouTube: 'Poor Abby is sick and she just threw up all over the carpet.' Now we see his wife in bed with a towel on her head. 'Can I get you anything?' he asks, panning to show the stain on the floor. 'So I've got baking soda down and I've got this shop vac,' he says, filming himself cleaning. 'Okay, unfortunately that did not work... Got some Gain dish soap, white vinegar and some OxiClean. Getting a cold rag for her right now because she just popped a bunch of blood vessels on her face.' After footage of frantic scrubbing, the short ends with 'The stain's pretty much gone ... we're finally off to bed.'[27] In *another* angle of the scene – 'POV: you're cleaning p*ke off the carpet at 1a.m #shorts' – his wife apologises for being sick, while he films more scrubbing. This alone has 32 million views on YouTube.

I scroll through the top comments: 'This is what love looks like', 'this is the definition of a healthy and positive relationship' and 'You two are role models for how a relationship should be.'[28] I imagine him setting up the camera first, and wonder how many takes this took. When did sharing moments like this become normal? Aspirational, even?

Back in the early 2010s, influencers realised that videos about their romantic lives tended to get more views. Zoella, for example, kept her relationship private at first, but in 2013 it was accidentally revealed that she was dating vlogger Alfie Deyes. Once the secret was out, they started filming together, taking part in popular trends like 'The Boyfriend Tag' and 'Couple Q&As', answering questions like 'Where did we meet?' and 'Where was our first date?'[29]

Before long, influencers began to realise that the more they exposed their relationships, the more engagement they got. The more they revealed, the more revenue.

For some influencers today, their relationships *are* their careers. Their income depends on documenting everything that happens together: recording romantic gestures, capturing live compliments, filming the moment they say 'I love you' for the first time.[30] Every milestone in their relationships is recorded: first the proposal, then the wedding, followed by footage of finding out they are pregnant, baby name announcements, monthly or weekly bump dates, gender reveals and birth videos streaming live on YouTube. 'Ladies and gentlemen, this is the podcast you've been waiting for,' says one husband in a vlog titled 'The Wedding: (Part 1)', before dramatic music plays and upcoming scenes flash by like a movie trailer. 'IT'S FINALLY HERE… OUR BIGGEST EPISODE YET… IT'S… THE… WEDDING.'[31] In 2019, influencers Tana Mongeau and Jake Paul even live-streamed their wedding 'for fun and content', broadcasting the big day to more than 76,000 fans, who each paid around $50 to watch.[32] The single stream allegedly earned the couple around $3.8 million.[33]

But girls like me didn't just grow up watching big celebrations. We also saw influencers having arguments, hurting each other, posting tearful apologies and breaking up. Millions of us became invested in these couples, psychoanalysing them, weighing in on their arguments on gossip forums, monitoring what posts they were liking and who they were following. In 2016, for example, Jesse and Jeana, a couple known for filming pranks they played on each other, released a YouTube video called 'A New Chapter' and announced their split after ten years.[34] The video was viewed more than 15 million times. Two years later, another big break-up announcement by influencers Liza Koshy and David Dobrik was watched 15 million times in just two days.[35]

Girls my age were captivated. This was our after-school entertainment; these were our TV characters, and for some of us, our first models of what a relationship was supposed to look like. And as algorithms advanced, couple influencers were incentivised to share more and more. We became even more invested.

Today, relationship podcasts and Q&As are so intimate that girls can listen in on couples' live arguments, hear about their affairs, discover how many people they have slept with, learn their kinks and fetishes, and track how often they have sex.[36] These couples now compete against each other for our attention. NearlyParents (formerly NewlyWeds), for example, is a popular podcast hosted by married reality stars Jamie Laing and Sophie Habboo, which has more than 100,000 YouTube subscribers. Over time they have revealed more and more of their private lives, with episode titles and captions like 'HAS OUR S*X GOT BORING?', 'Jamie's libido is BACK! But Sophie's has vanished...' and 'Are Jamie's bedroom skills bog standard?'[37] They often film arguments too, posting videos with thumbnails like 'We have our first BIG argument on the vlog' and 'Our most EXPLOSIVE Episode', complete with the caption 'I HOPE YOU DIE ALONE'.[38] And they aren't the only ones. One British influencer, Molly-Mae, even turned her traumatic break-up into a series on Amazon Prime.[39]

But the more these couple influencers expose, the more followers feel entitled to know. In 2025, for example, a young YouTube couple called Connor and Liana were criticised by fans for telling their own families the sex of their baby before announcing it online. In a podcast episode called 'Finding out the GENDER of our Baby & Dealing with the Backlash', Liana explained the scandal: 'We basically just stated ... we get to find out the gender today, and then everyone was *very* annoyed at us that *we* knew on that day and they didn't.' Connor said that some people 'really expected us to tell them as soon as we walked out the scan', demanding to know and commenting 'how dare you'.[40]

Influencers aren't the only ones feeling pressure to update their audiences though. Girls and young women like me feel it too. Back in the late 2010s, social media completely changed the rules and etiquette around dating. Girls started wondering, for example, how they should 'launch' a new partner on Instagram, like influencers announcing a new brand collaboration. Should you 'soft-launch' them, posting a teaser like a glimpse of their arm or side profile to your Story, or go for a 'hard launch', suddenly posting a full picture together? Should you tag them, or leave people guessing? Maybe cover their face with a giant emoji?

Soon girls were being taught exactly how to soft-launch their relationship by *Cosmopolitan* magazine and given step-by-step guides from the 'experts' at *Women's Health* ('Say you really want to soft launch your 'ship, but your partner prefers to be hard launched ... Either way, it's of the utmost importance to have open and honest communication about your needs ... No matter where you are on the social media spectrum.')[41] We began to manage our love lives like PR teams, and treat our partners like products.

During the relationship, too, there were new questions. How often should your boyfriend post you on his Stories? Should he put your name in his Instagram bio? Soon there were new expectations: if your boyfriend wasn't posting pictures of you, liking your posts or commenting on your selfies, people might think the relationship was over, or that he didn't care. By 2023, *VICE* was publishing articles like 'Would You Break up If Your Partner Won't Post You on Instagram?' and women were writing into magazines asking why their boyfriend wouldn't post them there.[42]

Another obligation also appeared: producing each other's content. Boyfriends especially were expected to become personal photographers, with so many girls demanding their pictures be taken that the phenomenon became known as 'Boyfriends of Instagram'.[43] By the late 2010s, girls were being told 'Don't date boys who won't take pictures for your Instagram' and sharing guides like 'How to Train an Instagram Boyfriend' ('He is the key to documenting your life, growing your brand').[44] Facebook and Instagram pages were set up to show Boyfriends of Instagram in action: kneeling in the sea, standing in traffic, lying on the ground to get the perfect angle of their girlfriends.[45] Now, though, the trend feels less like a joke and more like an expectation. Girls on TikTok complain that their boyfriends can never get it right, posting tutorials to 'teach him to take better photos of you', while *GQ* magazine gives men tips on taking pictures of their girlfriends ('Don't just take one! Stop doing exasperated sighs!').[46] Couples can even buy 'The Instagram Boyfriend Course' for $80. ('If you're the girlfriend, I understand, it sucks … He never tries … whenever you go on vacations or dates, you never have anything to post … You have to take years teaching him.')[47]

This pressure can strain relationships. Some boyfriends say taking pictures of their girlfriend feels like a full-time job, admitting that entire trips have been ruined by it and asking other guys online how to deal with the demands.[48] One Reddit post in r/relationships about 'having difficulty playing boyfriend of Instagram', for example, has over a thousand upvotes ('Her need for me to catalogue her life is slowly draining my soul.')[49]

But young women my age have never known any different. We learned the habit of sharing our lives online, and promoting ourselves like products, when we were pre-teens, and now we can't imagine life without documenting it as we go. And for some of us, this habit formed even earlier. Our personal lives were being posted online, long before we even understood what that meant. They were posted by our parents.

*

'So if you can pray for us, we appreciate it,' a mother says to the camera, sitting in the car beside her sobbing nine-year-old son. 'Come here, come closer for the video,' she demands, turning to him. 'CLOSER. Come closer. Put your head, put your head right here, come closer. Put your head down here. Act like you're crying, really quick…'

'I am crying,' he mumbles.

She holds her hand up to her eyes, faking a crying face. 'Go like this.'

'No, Mom, I'm actually seriously cryi—'

'No, I know, but go like this for the video.' She directs his hand. 'Go like this, put one hand up.' She pretends to cry. He puts his hand up but it's not good enough. 'No, go like this. Put your hand like this. But let them see your mouth. LET THEM SEE YOUR MOUTH.'

'No, Mom, I'm actually crying.'

She poses again. 'Look at me, look at me, look at me, look at me, look at me.'

'I'm actually cry—"

'I know, look at me, look at me.' She grabs his face so they are facing each other, fake-crying together. 'Look at the camera. Look at the camera.' After trying a few different poses, she leans over to stop recording. 'Okay, it's okay, it's okay. It's over, it's over, it's over.'

In 2021, influencer Jordan Cheyenne accidentally uploaded this unedited footage to YouTube in a video titled 'we are heartbroken'.[50] In the video she explained to her half a million subscribers that their family puppy had been diagnosed with a serious illness, but forgot to cut out footage of her forcing her son to cry for the thumbnail.

Back in the early 2010s, some vloggers began building entire channels around their children. Between beauty and mental health influencers, girls my age started watching *family* influencers. And once again, algorithms rewarded extreme content, pushing them to expose more and more.

Today, popular family vloggers shove a camera in their baby's face from the instant they are born ('FIRST 48 HOURS WITH OUR NEWBORN IS NOW LIVE!'), invite strangers to rate and review their children ('YOU MADE THEM CRY!! *Reading Mean Comments*'), and even document their six-year-old's gender transition ('It's not a phase') to millions of viewers.[51] Some have even faked moments, including pregnancies and miscarriages, for clicks.[52]

One family based in Britain, the Saccone Jolys, show how far this can go. Jonathan and Anna Saccone Joly started daily vlogging in 2009, sharing every milestone in their lives: their engagement, wedding, pregnancy announcements, and births of their four children – Emilia (2012), Eduardo (2014), Alessia (2017) and Andrea (2018). Essentially their kids' entire childhoods have been uploaded to YouTube: bath times, first steps, first words, potty training, birthdays, hospital visits, first days at school, exam results, first sleepovers, first dates. By the mid 2010s, the Saccone Jolys' channel was pulling in hundreds of thousands of views per vlog, with many videos reaching more than a million. The channel now has 1.6 million subscribers, while Jonathan's second channel, full of videos of the children, has 2.75 million.[53]

What once seemed like genuine home videos have been replaced by the commodification of their children at every opportunity. Emilia, only 12, now appears in videos wearing heavy make-up, crop tops and tight shorts, taking part in challenges like letting strangers online pick her outfits and using filters to rank who is the 'best looking' among her and her pre-teen sisters.[54] Her younger sister Alessia, only eight, is often shown in 'gymnastics' poses, doing the splits in nearly every thumbnail where she is featured. And their son, Eduardo, who came out as transgender around the age of four and is now referred to as Edie,[55] now frequently features in videos with 'trans' in the title, which routinely get the most views and probably make the most money. One compilation video of Edie's transition – titled 'Never hide your true self' – has 42 million views and almost 5 million likes on TikTok alone.[56] Other viral videos include Edie's gender and name reveal party, 'Edie's Story – from a BOY to a GIRL', 'Happy birthday Edie: she is nine today and about to start her 2nd full year living as a girl', 'my sons (now daughter) first time wearing a girls uniform to school' and Edie's first visit to a gender clinic (which alone has 17 million views and 1.5 million likes).[57] Edie also often wears a full face of make-up, wigs, crop tops, short skirts and choker necklaces, and today features in videos with titles like 'My Daughter Went On Her FIRST DATE *emotional', despite being only ten.[58] Across the channel, all of the children appear in heavily edited thumbnails, often with exaggerated expressions, legs spread, their faces sometimes superimposed on adult bodies.

These may seem like extreme examples, but throughout the 2010s more and more parents began to display their children's lives online. Girls at my school already had thousands of baby pictures posted of them, sometimes entire family albums uploaded to Facebook. It was completely normal for our parents to post regular updates, from our first days at school, to exam results, to mental health and medical issues. (Some parents even *edited* pictures of their children: a 2024 article in *Allure* magazine, 'I'm the Child of a Facetune Mom', profiled a young woman whose mother routinely edits pictures of her. 'Every time the pair have their photo taken together, often during holidays or big life milestones, her mom makes the same changes to both of them,' the article says. 'She lightens their skin, slims their faces, and trims their arms.'⁵⁹ After the young woman posted a TikTok about it, she was shocked by how many other girls could relate...)

As early as 2010, 92% of American children had an online presence by the time they were two. Around 7% of babies already had email addresses, and 5% had social media profiles created for them.⁶⁰ By 2016, parents had shared an average of 1,500 photos of their children online before their fifth birthday.⁶¹

The problem, though, is not only how often parents share, but *what* they share. A 2014 University of Michigan study found that 74% of parents who use social media knew another parent who overshared about their child online. This included posting something embarrassing (56%), posting information that could reveal their location (51%) or posting inappropriate pictures of them (27%).⁶² By 2015, an Australian study found that half of the images on paedophilic websites had been stolen from parents posting pictures of their children online. Within ten days of being uploaded, photos from platforms like Facebook and Instagram had been viewed 1.7 million times on these sites. And the images had been sorted into categories like 'kids at beach', 'nice boys play in river' and 'gymnasts'.⁶³

Some family vloggers don't seem all that concerned, though. When Jonathan Joly was asked in a 2019 documentary how he would feel if a paedophile had been looking at his children – 'had been masturbating over your children, for example?' – he dodged the question. 'It's... it's such an odd question because how would you feel... like I don't know... obviously, is it a terrible thing?... It's like... I don't really make content for that purpose.'⁶⁴ (Don't *really*?)

Lately, though, after more than a decade of exposing their children online, parents are waking up to the dangers. But for many young women my age, the damage is done. Some of us have thousands of childhood photos online. Others had influencer parents, growing up with hundreds of thousands, if not millions, of strangers watching them like reality TV: monitoring every milestone, commenting on their developing bodies, consuming their childhood memories as mindless entertainment.

Back in the early 2010s, the big fear about social media was that it was becoming a highlight reel, a place to share only shared perfect, polished moments. But that didn't last long. By my late teens, influencers were not just sharing the dreamy parts of their lives any more. Family vloggers were filming meltdowns, recording punishments, broadcasting tantrums. Other influencers started documenting the darker side of life too: posting arguments, leaking private messages, turning conflict into content. And once again, girls my age followed their lead.

DRAMA

'BYE SISTER' was the title of the infamous 43-minute YouTube video posted in 2019 by beauty influencer Tati Westbrook. In it, Tati exposed her close friend James Charles, accusing him of betraying her by promoting SugarBearHair gummies on Instagram, a competitor to her own vitamin brand.

Tati then went further, accusing James of predatory behaviour. He strongly denied the allegations, but within days the video had 43 million views, and he had lost more than 3 million subscribers.[65]

James then hit back with his own 42-minute video, 'No More Lies', which has more than 58 million views.[66] Defending himself, he shared his own evidence (referred to as 'receipts'), including screenshots of Instagram DMs and text messages. Others soon got involved. Beauty influencer Jeffree Star joined in, threatening to leak his own receipts against James, and the scandal became so big it was covered by outlets like CNN and the *New Yorker*.[67] Eventually, Tati ended up posting: 'I still have so many things I'd like to clear up; however, the continued call for "receipts" is nothing more than a call for never-ending bloodshed.'[68]

Years later, the drama is still being discussed. In 2024, *Time* magazine published 'How One YouTube Video Changed the Course of Internet Culture', arguing it set the playbook for influencer feuds.[69] And it does feel now like a defining moment. Girls my age started seeing drama as something to be performed for an audience. We grew up watching influencers call each other out and try to 'cancel' whoever crossed them. We learned how to 'spill the tea' – share drama, secrets and gossip online – by watching influencers tell dramatic 'Storytimes' on YouTube, describing messy break-ups, betrayals and fallouts between friends in intimate detail. We saw them expose Snapchat screenshots, Instagram DMs, deleted tweets and voice notes, and thought this was normal.

Soon influencers realised that getting involved in public arguments could boost engagement, even leading to brand deals.[70] Online drama was so common it became its own genre of content. I remember coming home from school and watching 'tea channels' run by drama influencers, who made a career out of posting hours-long videos dissecting every argument and scandal in the influencer world.

Then, in 2018, the gossip forum Tattle Life was launched, describing itself as a platform for 'commentary and critiques of people that choose to monetise their personal life as a business and release it into the public domain'.[71] Here, girls could obsess over influencers' lives, analysing their posts pixel by pixel, tracking down where they lived, figuring out who they were dating, even discovering pregnancies and affairs before tabloids did. The platform became so invasive that a petition to shut it down in the UK was signed by more than 70,000 people.[72]

But girls my age were not only turning on influencers. We turned on each other, encouraged by social media platforms themselves. Throughout the 2010s, Instagram, Snapchat and Facebook preyed not only on our vulnerabilities but our *vices* too. The most common bullying tactics among girls – passive aggression, social exclusion, reputation destruction – became easier online.[73] We were pushed to exclude, judge and scrutinise each other, and to do so publicly.

Reputation destruction, for example, became brutal online. Rumours that once spread through school playgrounds were now recommended by algorithms and broadcast to much bigger audiences. Girls could create anonymous Instagram hate accounts, launch campaigns to 'cancel' their classmates over a single mistake, and stockpile screenshots of private messages ready to expose as 'receipts' if friendships fell apart. 'Because bullying on your main feed is seen by many as aggressive and uncool, many teens create hate pages: separate Instagram accounts, purpose-built and solely dedicated to trashing one person, created by teens alone or in a group,' Taylor Lorenz wrote for *The Atlantic* in 2018. 'They'll post bad photos of their target, expose her secrets, post screenshots of texts from people saying mean things about her, and any other terrible stuff they can find.'[74]

Then there was more subtle passive aggression: girls could suddenly delete all their selfies with someone, remove their friend's name from their Instagram bios, post Stories with someone else's crush or ex, or Facetune themselves while deliberately leaving the girl beside them unedited. 'Subtweeting' was another popular tactic: posting a nasty but vague comment that everyone knew was about one girl, but without naming her, making it impossible for her to defend herself without looking paranoid. Other passive-aggressive tactics included the 'soft block' (blocking and immediately unblocking someone so they no longer follow you), publicly tagging girls in unflattering photos or switching on active statuses and read receipts but never replying to their messages (while still posting, to make it completely clear they were being ignored).

Social exclusion became easier too. We could unfollow or unfriend each other, kick one another out of group chats, post Instagram Stories of sleepovers to hurt whoever wasn't invited, turn on our public location on Snap Map so everyone could see, in real time, who was being left out. We could create secret Stories on Instagram, leaving certain girls out of our 'Close Friends' list to post about them behind their backs. Imagine being 12 and getting a birthday message from a popular girl on Facebook, only to realise it was just an excuse to post the worst pictures of you. Or waking up to find that every trace of you has been deleted from your best friend's Instagram, and everyone is messaging to ask what happened. Or opening Snapchat to see a Story of your friends getting ready for a party you didn't even know about, gathered together on Snap Map. Or receiving a screenshot from a friend showing that you were rated 4/10 on an anonymous website, publicly labelled the ugliest girl in school, with no way to remove it.

These platforms seemed almost designed for bullying. Ask.fm, for example, which launched in 2010 when I was around nine or ten, let users ask and answer questions anonymously. And so just as influencers were answering Q&As about their personal lives, and publicly turning on one another, girls my age started doing the same. Children rated each other's faces, bodies and personalities. We would post questions like 'Who is the most annoying?', 'Who has the worst body?' and 'Who is the least likely to get a boyfriend?', before ranking classmates in public lists.

By 2013, Ask.fm had 65 million users and was growing by around 300,000 more every day.[75] Two years later, the platform had reached around 150 million users, with 50 million questions asked each day.[76] But as Ask.fm grew, it also became linked to teen suicides. In the UK in 2013, for example, 15-year-old Ciara Pugsley committed suicide in the woods near her home after being bullied on the site, and 14-year-old Hannah Smith hanged herself the same year after harassment believed to be on Ask.fm.[77] Around this time, the company was valued at about $5.7 billion.[78]

And so anonymous apps kept coming. Yik Yak launched in 2013, allowing users within a five-mile radius to ask and answer questions anonymously. It too became linked to self-harm and suicide attempts.[79] Yik Yak was later followed by more anonymous apps like Not Gonna Lie (NGL) and Fizz. Fizz, which describes itself as 'a private social feed just for your school', encourages students to 'share and discover anonymously so that you can be your true self'.[80] According to the *Wall Street Journal*, the app tore through high schools in 2024. Students commented on each other's appearances, personalities and disabilities, posting embarrassing and even incriminating pictures. 'The app caused more havoc than the principal had seen in his nine years on the job,' said the *WSJ*. 'Students felt like they had to keep checking the app to see what was being posted about them.'[81]

By 2015, 68% of teenage social media users said they had experienced people stirring up drama online.[82] More than one in five respondents aged 12 to 20 said in a 2017 Pew survey that they had been bullied specifically on Instagram.[83] Another Pew survey in 2018 found that 59% of teens had been bullied or harassed online, and 39% of girls said someone had spread fake rumours about them, compared to 26% of boys.[84] By 2025, 45% of teen girls said they felt 'overwhelmed because of drama' on social media, compared to 34% of boys.[85]

Now many of us in our twenties are beginning to process how painful this all was, how permanent. Without realising, we have been building personal brands since childhood. And now all of our statuses, subtweets and embarrassing screenshots, posted by us or by other people, can be discovered and reshared. We were children back then, fighting and falling out online. But soon we were being treated like adults, who had to start taking accountability.

OPINIONS

'Why The Refusal To Post Online Is Often Inherently Racist', declares a viral Instagram graphic uploaded in 2020. Created by artist @ghostdumps, the post features a series of slides.

'Fear of "getting political" on your social media is, at its core, racist,' one slide reads. 'This isn't a political issue – it's a humanitarian one ... we're talking about saving human lives.' Another warns: 'If you're anxious about what your peers will think, or if people will try to fight you, take a look at the people you surround yourself with. If they would fight or make fun of you, they are the problem. They are the oppressor we are trying to educate and get rid of.' One of the final slides insists: 'A refusal to post is ... a refusal to give up your power as a privileged individual. To sit in silence is to let people die.' The post has nearly 400,000 likes.[86]

As a teenage girl, almost everything I knew about political activism came from the internet. Occasionally I would see students protesting outside my university, but for me activism had always meant Twitter hashtags, Instagram infographics and Snapchat Stories. The more we shared our lives online, the more pressure there was to post our political opinions. We started labelling and categorising ourselves, adding flags, emojis and pronouns to our profiles. Just as we compulsively updated the world on our personal lives, we felt we had to keep our beliefs and opinions up to date too, always signalling where we stood.

Soon being a good person was no longer about what you did in real life but what you posted online. Morality became measurable, judged instantly by what we had or hadn't shared. Not posting about an issue, even if we didn't fully understand it, started to feel like a moral failing. It looked deliberate. Didn't you care enough about the environment to post about climate change? About racism to acknowledge injustice? How dare you post about your holiday during a global crisis?

Social media platforms themselves encouraged this constant signalling. I remember after the 2015 Paris attacks, when I was 16, Facebook introduced a French flag filter. 'Change your profile picture to support France and the people of Paris,' the platform urged,[87] prompting us to layer the faded flag over our profile pictures. This was the first time I noticed girls judging each other for *not* posting something, even if they barely used the platform. (Somehow not using the filter was seen as more disrespectful than adding French flags to pouting selfies and bikini pictures...) After the 2016 Brussels terror attacks, some users even complained that flag overlays weren't available soon enough. Facebook reassured them that they were 'working on better ways to help people show support for things they care about', but, of course, 'via their profiles'.[88]

Over the years, Instagram, Snapchat and later TikTok continued pressuring girls to become activists online. We had political hashtags to share, social justice-themed filters to try on, stickers and emojis to fight stigma. And just like our mental health struggles, the solution to every social justice issue seemed to be the same: post more.

'The more we #ShareBlackStories,' Instagram insisted, 'the more we raise voices that make an impact.'[89] Snapchat told us to 'Raise your [hand emoji] to pledge and support closing the gender gap!', referring to our cartoon avatars.[90] 'This Pride Month flex your fluidity', Snap also suggested, urging us to use its 'Pride Pronoun Tattoos Lens' to stamp our pronouns on our cheeks.[91] Or we could celebrate Pride on TikTok and 'share stories of the LGBTQIA+ community' using face filters like 'Rainbow Hair', 'Rainbow Curtain', 'Rainbow Trail', 'Pride Lighting', 'Pride Time Warp', 'Pride Rainbow Cheeks', 'Pride 3D Lashes', 'Pride Glittery' and 'Pride Flag Sky AR'.[92] Social justice issues were commodified too: causes began to feel like market trends, displayed like accessories. Sometimes activism was nothing but shopping. In 2024, for example, TikTok launched its #ShopWithPride program, encouraging users to express their support for the LGBTQ+ community simply by buying products on the app.

By the late 2010s, dating apps were prompting us to share our political opinions too. In 2016, dating app OkCupid noticed a 64% increase in political terms on user profiles after the US presidential election. They quickly introduced new political features, asking users questions about the #MeToo movement, kneeling as a form of protest, and whether they voted, along with their views on Donald Trump. 'One of the first things we added in 2017 was a Trump question, which became known as the Trump filter, enabling people to filter in or out Trump supporters,' OkCupid chief marketing officer Melissa Hobley said at the time.[93] Today, the dating app Hinge also has a section called 'Virtues', asking users to select and display their political identity from 'liberal', 'moderate', 'conservative' or 'other'.[94] And shortly before the 2024 US election, Tinder rolled out political stickers that users could add to their profile, including 'Voting for reproductive rights' and 'Hot people vote (I'm voting)'.[95]

While we were labelling ourselves politically, something bigger was also happening online. 'Hashtag activism' – using social media to raise awareness and rally support for political causes – was building momentum. In 2017, for example, #MeToo went viral on Twitter as women began sharing their experiences of sexual harassment and assault. After allegations against Hollywood producer Harvey Weinstein emerged, actress Alyssa Milano tweeted: 'If all the women who have been sexually harassed or assaulted wrote "Me too" as a status, we might give people a sense of the magnitude of the problem.' Within 24 hours, around 4.7 million people had joined the conversation on Facebook alone, generating more than 12 million posts, comments and reactions.[96]

The same happened after the death of George Floyd in 2020. That summer, the Black Lives Matter (BLM) movement exploded, not only into the streets of American cities but across social media, drawing in people from around the world. Posting a black square on Instagram became an almost obligatory statement against racism and police brutality. On 2 June 2020, more than 28 million people posted black squares to their Instagram profiles, using hashtags like #blackouttuesday and #blm.[97]

Along with black squares, our feeds soon filled with social justice infographics – bite-sized posts breaking down political concepts from systemic racism to white privilege, heteronormativity to intersectional feminism – to help us educate ourselves and raise awareness. *Vox* called them 'social justice slideshows', explaining in 2020 how 'the escapist days of uninterrupted brunch photos and filtered selfies have been replaced by protest photos and black squares.' As they put it: 'For a brief moment, it seemed as though people, whether they have 150 followers or 150,000, were hyper-aware of what they should or should not post.'[98]

Posting about politics now felt like a moral obligation. The cultural messaging had shifted from encouraging support to vilifying silence: silence was violence, and not saying anything was to side with the oppressor, or be on the wrong side of history. Just as celebrities and influencers urged us to open up about our mental health, they began to insist we take a public stand against injustice and bigotry. In 2020, *Cosmopolitan* published an essay by Kamala Harris titled 'To Be Silent Is to Be Complicit', while CBS News condemned 'White silence on social media', explaining 'why not saying anything is actually saying a lot'.[99] Celebrities also reminded us that 'White Silence Is Violence', telling us to 'step up' and take action.[100] Demi Lovato encouraged her fans to post about BLM and 'please use this hashtag', while *Riverdale* actress Camila Mendes reminded fans that 'saying "i stand with you" and throwing in a hashtag is literally the bare minimum of what you can do.'[101] Model Cara Delevingne even posted a selfie on her Instagram Story holding a sign with the words 'Silence is Consent'.[102] (Not sure we want that one to catch on…)

At the same time, girls my age were watching celebrities constantly get called out for not posting, or posting the wrong thing. In 2020, actress Emma Watson posted three black squares on Instagram instead of one, and was accused of trying to make her account look more aesthetically pleasing. Fans were furious, attacking her for giving 'nothing'. 'Girl I know that Little Women cheque hit,' one wrote. 'Open your purse.'[103] Other celebrities were attacked for being too vague, using the wrong wording or not saying enough. Singer Lana Del Rey was piled on for posting a video to Instagram showing the faces of looters during the BLM protests ('Why the f*** you posting people looting stores on your page, literally WHAT IS YOUR PROBLEM.').[104] After tweeting 'Like so many of you, I am angry and I am sad. People of color in this country have faced injustice for far too long. For things to change, things must change,' Ellen DeGeneres was attacked for being vague, not saying 'black people' and not donating enough money.[105] Girls began monitoring each other too, tracking and turning on each other for not posting, or posting wrong. Now we all had platforms and audiences, no matter how small, and a supposed duty to speak out.

Soon what happened with beauty and mental health trends also happened with political discourse. The 'right' position kept evolving. The most radical voices went viral, rising to the top of our feeds. And as social justice movements became increasingly interconnected, it started to feel like we were expected to have opinions on *everything*: climate change, abortion access, transgender rights, foreign conflicts. Celebrities and influencers insisted we get involved, take action, speak out, sign petitions, donate money and educate ourselves on any topic we didn't know enough about, becoming better allies and activists.[106]

And so to feel like good people, to stay educated and informed, we had to spend more time online. By 2025, Pew reported that 43% of adults under 30 regularly got their news from TikTok, while another US survey found that around 60% of Gen Z were getting their news from social media at least once a week.[107] By now, my generation has been struggling to keep up, and speak up online, for almost a decade – and expectations have not eased. After the 7

October attack on Israel in 2023, for example, the *New York Times* warned that 'Silence is viewed by many as its own statement.'[108]

And posting is only one part of the pressure. Now it's not only our current opinions, or lack of them, that can get us into trouble. For young women like me, the things we posted thoughtlessly, as children, are often still online, part of our permanent record. We can be called out for statuses we wrote, pictures we posted and comments we made years, or sometimes more than a decade, ago.

Take TikTok influencer Brooke Monk, for example. In 2019, when she was 16, she commented: 'Haha Trump flag and now you got a new follower! #Trump2020' on a TikTok. The comment was discovered a year later, and Brooke was, as one drama channel put it, 'EXPOSED for being a TRUMP SUPPORTER'.[109] She was pressured to publicly apologise, eventually confessing in a TikTok live stream that she didn't know much about politics and was still trying to figure things out. During her apology, fans began grilling her on other opinions too, including her stance on BLM. 'I had the profile picture and everything,' she said, 'but some people DMed me… they told me they thought it was insensitive or too trendy… it was like 15 to 20 people.' She acknowledged, 'It's valid for you to be upset with me,' and accepted the 'consequences for my own actions', before adding, 'I would prefer if you guys do not DM me telling me to kill myself… but I understand that might happen anyway.'[110]

Some of us are realising we shared too much. We tweeted stupid jokes at 12, we shared private and painful moments in our relationships, we broadcast breakdowns and betrayals. But like the influencers we imitated, we have learned the hard way that we can't take it all back. We already posted our way through puberty. Now we feel exhausted, overwhelmed and, above all, exposed.

GIRLS®

EXPOSED

One obvious consequence of girls exposing their entire lives online is constant comparison. Entertainment and relaxation now consist of scrolling through the private lives and performances of other people, every single day. Girls compare not only their faces and bodies, but their personalities, lifestyles, relationships, opinions, everything down to their daily routines. And not only with friends either, but friends of friends, influencers, celebrities, strangers across the world.

It's hard for girls to ever feel good enough, and easy to feel excluded. According to a 2023 Pew survey, 31% of American teenagers said social media had made them feel like their friends were leaving them out. Girls were more likely than boys to feel this way, and more likely to say social media made them feel worse about their own lives.[111] In fact, Meta's own internal research in 2019 found that 'Teens blame Instagram for increases in the rate of anxiety and depression. This reaction was unprompted and consistent across all groups.'[112] Among teens who reported suicidal thoughts, too, 13% of British users and 6% of American users traced the desire to kill themselves back to Instagram. And according to another transatlantic study, more than 40% of young users who felt 'unattractive' said they started feeling that way because of Instagram, and about one in four teenagers who felt 'not good enough' said this began on the platform.[113]

My generation is also beginning to talk about the toll all this sharing takes, from the confessions of exhausted Boyfriends of Instagram to the testimonies of children raised by family vloggers. Take 22-year-old Shari Franke, who in 2025 published her memoir *The House of My Mother*.[114] Shari is the eldest daughter of Ruby Franke, who ran the popular YouTube channel 8 Passengers, where she vlogged life with her husband Kevin and their six children. Ruby uploaded five days a week, filming bad moods, family arguments, punishments and even intimate moments like bra shopping with her daughters.[115] ('Those personal videos did the best,' Shari has said. 'People like to see first date or puberty talk videos...')[116] By 2020, the channel had more than 2 million subscribers and over 1 billion views.[117]

But behind their perfect family life was a sinister reality. In 2023, Ruby's 12-year-old son escaped and appeared at a neighbour's house wounded, malnourished and with duct tape on his wrists and ankles, begging for help.[118] Ruby was arrested, later pleaded guilty to four counts of aggravated child abuse, and in 2024 was sentenced to up to 30 years in prison.[119] Her children had been starved, tied up with ropes and handcuffs, deprived of water, and referred to by Ruby as 'employees' from as young as four or five.[120] In her memoir, Shari also recalls her mother's relentless filming:

> For me, a twelve-year-old girl, this constant surveillance was excruciating. All I wanted was to grow up in peace, deal with my bodily changes and these pesky new zits without it being recorded. But my mother was omnipresent, her phone an extension of her arm, directing us like a Hollywood producer: 'Do this, do that, Shari – we're filming!' 'Smile, Shari! Say good morning!' I was beginning to feel like a sideshow freak: 'Step right up and witness Shari, the Amazingly Awkward Adolescent, in all her cringeworthy glory!' The worst part? The internet ate it up.[121]

Shari's story is extreme, but this compulsion to capture everything isn't. Many girls and young women are living like this, under constant self-surveillance, always monitoring and managing themselves, anticipating how an audience will react.

And carefully controlling their profiles too. Already by 2013, a Pew survey found that 59% of teenagers had deleted or edited something they posted in the past, 53% had deleted comments from others on their profile, 45% had removed themselves from a tagged photo, 31% had deleted or deactivated entire accounts, and 57% said they had chosen not to post something because they were worried it would reflect badly on them in future.[122] By 2021, 45% of US workers under 30 were worried about losing their jobs or reputations because of being misunderstood, taken out of context, or having something from their past posted online.[123]

This fear is not unfounded. In the UK, children are now being warned that offensive posts could ruin their future careers. Since 2014, police have logged more than 2,000 'non-crime hate incidents' – defined as 'hostility towards religion, race or transgender identity' – involving under-17s, which can show up on employers' background checks.[124] And it's not only the authorities keeping track; children expose each other too. In 2022, *Dazed* published 'Receipts Culture Has Gone Too Far', sharing the story of 15-year-old Hannah. She had confided in her boyfriend over text, admitting that he was her first kiss and that she hadn't had sex before. After they broke up, he posted screenshots of her messages on Instagram, and even faked texts to make her seem racist. Hannah started receiving death threats, was physically assaulted and later had to move schools. 'Those screenshots eventually got to the school I'd moved to, so I was getting confronted about it all the time,' Hannah told *Dazed*. 'I had boys and girls trying to fight me. I lost all my friends, and ended up falling into a very deep depression. I even had thoughts of suicide and self-harm.'[125]

Many older members of Gen Z also have regrets about social media. In 2024, nearly half of Gen Z adults in the US said they wished social media platforms had never been invented. Specifically, 34% said this about Instagram, 37% about Facebook, 43% about Snapchat, 47% about TikTok and 50% about X.[126] According to a 2025 British survey, too, almost half of young people aged 16 to 24 see social media and harmful online content as one of the three biggest threats to teen mental health, and more than half believe life would be better if social media was banned for people under 16. Around half regret how much time they spent on screens growing up, and 78% say if they ever become parents, they would hold off on letting their children use social media as long as they could.[127]

Yet children today are getting online younger than ever. In the UK, nearly a quarter of 5- to 7-year-olds already have their own smartphones, and 38% are already active on social media.[128] By age 11, nine in ten British children own a mobile phone.[129] In the US, 40% of 2-year-olds have their own tablets, and 58% of 4-year-olds, while nearly one in four children own a phone by age 8.[130] A 2021 survey also found that among children aged 9 to 12, 78% watched YouTube, 45% used TikTok, 26% used Instagram, 29% used Snapchat and 32% used Facebook – every day.[131]

Despite the regrets my generation has, the next generation of girls is being handed smartphones even earlier. They will feel pressure to post their lives before they even hit puberty. The compulsion to expose everything crept in gradually for us, but for them it will feel entirely normal. No matter how much we try to warn them, no matter what our mental health looks like now or how many influencers burn out or break down, we can't compete with trillion-dollar companies, determined they document everything.

So what is really happening here? The anxieties themselves are age-old; girls have always worried about their popularity and reputation, craved belonging and acceptance, and feared social rejection. There is nothing new about girls sharing their lives, or comparing and competing with one another.

But never before have they had the technology to broadcast their personal lives to so many people, or felt such relentless pressure to do so. Now, exposing even the most intimate information about themselves is not only normal but expected. Girls are growing up watching influencers market their memories, monetise their relationships, even commodify their own children, and they have never known any different. Some simply cannot conceive of living life without an audience consuming it.

Every post, opinion and interaction they have online is also measured by likes, shares and comments. And these metrics have become measures of their worth. For the first time in history, girls are publicly ranking and reviewing one another, then tying their self-worth to these changing numbers while their brains are still forming, until they are forever dependent on an audience's approval to feel good about themselves.

To the girls struggling with this pressure today, please, listen to my generation. Many of us in our twenties are realising how dystopian our childhoods were. We are beginning to realise how unprecedented, and how unnecessary, this pressure was. How we were trying to handle all these new feelings, all these firsts – friendships, crushes, heartbreaks, opinions on the world – while marketing them at the same time.

It's painful to think about the time and emotion and energy we wasted. We traded so much of our childhoods: not only the time spent taking and posting pictures, but the time we spent always *thinking* about social media, corrupting moments by obsessing over capturing them. Moments ruined by that nagging need to film them. Memories tainted when they didn't perform well on the market. Self-esteem crushed when we didn't sell as well as our friends. Unable to enjoy experiences until we got the perfect photo, entire days ruined if we didn't.

Many of us aren't proud of who we became. Constant comparison made us feel anxious and inadequate, yes, but also envious and competitive. We judged each other by numbers on a screen. Other people became props for our Instagram posts. Now some of us can't help but see experiences in our lives as content, beautiful sceneries as backgrounds for selfies, our loved ones as tools to get likes. And this has not only damaged our mental health but our humility, our humanity. Because people who demand that their loved ones advertise and display them, who see their experiences in the real world first and foremost as marketing opportunities, have become perfect products.

We grew up wanting to be influencers, and we got what we wished for. As we watched them overshare and fall apart, be attacked and apologise, change and struggle to move on from their former selves, the same was happening in our own lives. We weren't free to grow up clumsily, to make mistakes. Once we categorised ourselves online, nothing could stay in the past. Personal struggles we had overcome, personality traits we had outgrown, relationships that had ended, opinions we had changed: all became impossible to leave behind.

Now what do we have left to look back on? Precious memories ruined by the pressure to capture them, the arguments this caused, the bad moods, the disappointment? Thousands of selfies clogging our camera rolls, plus all the Facetuned and filtered versions?

Beautiful Instagram moments but no feeling behind them? Good times managing five different social media accounts, trying to package ourselves up before we had any idea who we were?

Maybe we have more memories to scroll through. We were always warned we would regret not capturing them. But looking at the surveys, the statistics, listening to the way we talk about social media now, if my generation is on track to regret anything, it is the time we wasted performing and editing and documenting ourselves online. Time we will never get back. Because many of us are looking back through our hundreds of thousands of Instagram posts and Snapchat Stories and TikToks not with fondness that we filmed these moments, but with regret that we didn't fully feel them.

Now the push to post looks more like a marketing strategy. We were told it was about sharing our lives with our friends and family, when really it was about sharing our data with companies so they could target us better. We were told it was about connection, while we turned the people we love into tripods to take constant pictures of us. And in trying so hard to define and document ourselves, we lost ourselves. We weren't sharing our lives on these platforms, we were living our lives *for* them, often for the approval of people we didn't even know or care about.

And the more energy and effort we put into ourselves and our personal brands, the less we had left over for others. While we posed with our friends and posted about our perfect lives, we began to feel more and more alone. Often we were too busy perfecting our online profiles to deeply connect with people. Which is one reason why we are a generation more disconnected than any before us.

Disconnected

'Need a friend? Create one now.'
Replika[1]

FRIENDSHIP

'introducing friend. not imaginary,' says the tweet, posted in 2024. Beneath, a video plays: a young woman is out hiking, wearing a pendant around her neck. 'Wooo!' she shrieks, before laughing. 'I don't know how to "woo" very good.' Her necklace lights up, and her phone buzzes with a message: 'well at least we're outside!'

In the next scene, a young man is playing video games with a friend. After he loses, his necklace buzzes and a message appears: 'you're getting thrashed, it's embarrassing!' Then a young woman is watching a video while eating lunch, when her phone pings. 'this show is completely underrated. how's the falafel?' She accidentally spills some on her necklace. 'Sorry, I got you messy,' she apologises, before it vibrates and her phone replies, 'yum.'

With more than 25 million views on X alone, the video is an ad for Friend, an AI wearable created by 21-year-old tech entrepreneur Avi Schiffmann.[2] 'Friend is an expression of how lonely I've felt,' Schiffmann has confessed.[3] He didn't just want to talk to an AI, he says, but to feel as if a friend was *there*, travelling with him. And so the wearable is 'always listening', remembering everything you say.[4]

At first I thought the whole thing was a parody. But as I scrolled through the comments under Schiffmann's tweet, along with some confusion and a few references to *Black Mirror*, I noticed a lot of excitement. 'I want this but with a camera. Most of the day there's no audio for it to react to, but it could react to what I'm seeing,' someone suggested. Another user said they would prefer feedback on how they come across in conversations: 'Like "hey when you said that, I think Bob was a little put off. Did you hear at 2:33 when he tried to change the subject?" That would be game changing.'[5]

By 2025, Friend had secured $8.5 million in investment.[6] For £100 (about $129), you can now order a necklace from their website, which promises that 'Your new roommate is waiting.'[7]

Looking at the demand, and our desperation for more, I wonder how we got here. I wonder when loneliness became so lucrative.

In 2009, Facebook changed the meaning of 'friend' forever. Friendship became as easy as clicking a button.

Back in the early 2010s, social media platforms promised to keep us connected with each other. Features on Facebook like friend lists, news feed, groups and events were designed to help us stay in touch with people we already knew, from distant family members to old classmates.

Over time, though, staying in touch became more demanding. When I was a pre-teen, Microsoft Messenger already had Available and Away statuses, while Facebook Messenger showed friends when we were Active and Last Seen. We could Nudge each other on MSN – which shook the other person's screen and made a noise – or Poke someone on Facebook to get their attention. We could see when friends were online, when they were typing, and when they were deliberately ignoring us. But back then we only saw these on our desktops, when we logged onto our computers.

Then came smartphones, and with them, social media apps with activity statuses. Facebook Messenger introduced read receipts in 2012, showing us when our messages had been opened, followed by WhatsApp in 2014. Now there were new expectations; it felt rude not to reply as soon as you saw a notification.

Snapchat took things further. In 2015 it introduced Streaks, which track how many consecutive days two users send each other Snaps. Three days in, a fire emoji appears next to your names, along with the number of days the Streak has lasted. Most of the time, my friends and I would send each other blank screens or blurry pictures of the floor, anything to keep the score going. I remember girls at my school getting so attached to their Streaks they would even email Snapchat begging for them back after accidentally losing one. Today, users can even *pay* Snapchat to revive a lost Streak. (Apparently, if just 10% of the app's daily users paid to restore a single streak each month, Snapchat would make more than $400 million a year).[8]

But it wasn't only Streaks keeping us online and always communicating. After Snapchat introduced Stories in 2013, we had to keep checking the app to make sure we didn't miss any. Then in 2017 came the launch of Snap Map, a cartoon map publicly displaying our live locations. Every time we opened the app, the map showed we were active and updated our precise location. We could track our friends' every move, see who was hanging out without us, and know exactly when we were being excluded.

By the late 2010s, disconnecting for a while felt almost impossible. Friendship had been redefined. Leaving a message on 'read' for longer than an hour without responding signalled something was wrong. If you were active for too long without replying, you now had to explain yourself. Anyone could check our location on Snap Map, and it looked suspicious if we switched on Ghost Mode and hid where we were. Between Streaks, Stories and all these platforms displaying our Activity statuses, girls my age reached a state of near-constant contact. I remember when I was nine or ten, chatting with friends on MSN or Skype after school, and we would sign off with BRB (be right back) or G2G (got to go). Now there is nowhere for girls *to* go; they are always online. As one *Dazed* article put it: 'We no longer log off.'[9]

Today, the average adolescent receives around 237 smartphone notifications a day. Some receive nearly 5,000 notifications in 24 hours.[10] Girls now have group chats going off, voice notes to listen to, Instagram DMs to check, TikToks to react to, plus daily reminders to 'Be Real' and immediately take a picture of whatever they are doing. They are managing multiple conversations, all the time.

Activity statuses are also everywhere now. Facebook, Snapchat, Instagram and TikTok all share when girls are online. Dating apps like Hinge display when they were last active, as do running apps like Strava and even reading apps like Goodreads. It was bad enough when I was a teenager, anxiously checking activity statuses and read receipts; I still remember that sinking feeling after sending a selfie on Snapchat and seeing 'Opened 30m ago', risking a flirty text and getting left on 'read', arguing with someone and watching them type… then stop… and say nothing. My thoughts would race: why are they Active but not replying? Their Snap Score has gone up; they clearly have time to respond to someone else. Why have they posted on their Story but not messaged me back? For girls today, the anxiety never ends.

In the early 2010s, friendship also became measured by how often we posted about each other. How many selfies we took together, if we had each other's names in our Instagram bios, whether we posted birthday messages on Facebook. Back when BlackBerry Messenger (BBM) was popular, my friends and I would add each other's names or initials to our own display names. I still remember that feeling of waking up and realising my name had been removed, or worse, replaced. What happened? What had I done? Every trend or feature that could make us feel connected could just as easily make us feel excluded.

Friends were even encouraged to rank and rate each other publicly. In 2015 Snapchat introduced a 'Best Friends' feature, displaying our top three friends for everyone to see. A gold heart emoji next to someone's name meant you were best friends and both sent each other the most Snaps; a gritted teeth emoji meant your best friend was also someone else's; a smirking face meant you were *their* best friend but they weren't yours.[11] Suddenly we could see exactly how much we meant to each other.

After complaints, Snapchat removed its public 'Best Friends' feature in 2015.[12] But in 2022, it introduced a new version for paying subscribers: the 'Friend Solar System'. Now users appear as the sun, and their best friends orbit them as planets. Mercury represents your closest friend, stretching outwards through each planet to Neptune, your least close friend. This caused controversy too. 'Snapchat's Friend-Ranking Feature Adds to Teen Anxiety', the *Wall Street Journal* reported in 2024. 'Drama, hurt feelings and heartbreak can result when teens see where they are in friends' Snapchat+ solar systems.'[13] Snapchat eventually made the feature optional, turning it off by default but never removing it.

Back in the early 2010s, friends also started spending far less time hanging out in person. It almost felt unnecessary; we were staying in touch through Snapchat Streaks and Instagram Stories – what was there to catch up on? When friends did come for sleepovers, we took selfies for Facebook, we posted anonymous questions on Ask.fm, we sat side by side, scrolling. As Jonathan Haidt put it in his 2024 book *The Anxious Generation*, childhood was changing from 'play-based' to 'phone-based'.[14]

In the late 1970s, more than half of US high school seniors (aged 17 to 18) hung out with friends almost every day. According to psychologist Jean Twenge, by 2017 that number had dropped to 28%, with the sharpest decline after 2010.[15] When compared to the 1980s, she adds, 10th graders (aged 15 to 16) today attend around 17 fewer parties a year.[16] And it's not only teens who are socialising less; Americans of all ages are spending less time together. Between 2010 and 2013, the average American spent about six and a half hours a week with friends, and this too began falling around 2014, dropping to four hours a week by 2019.[17]

Some simply prefer socialising online. In the UK, 25- to 34-year-olds are the age group most likely to agree with statements like 'I have more friends online than I do in real life' (42%), 'before the pandemic, I spent more time with friends online than I did in person' (41%) and 'socialising online is better than socialising in-person' (39%). Older generations, by contrast, are far more likely to disagree.[18] In the US, meanwhile, nearly half of young people in 2012 said their favourite way to talk to friends was face to face. By 2018, only about a third said the same.[19]

Young adults also have few close friends. In the UK, by 2021, about one in five 18- to 34-year-olds said they had one or none, three times higher than in 2011 to 2012. Older generations even reported having more close friends than younger generations. Only 40% of 18- to 34-year-olds had four or more close friends, down from 64% a decade earlier. Among 18- to 24-year-olds, 19% said they had one or no close friends, and 57% had three or fewer, compared to 9% and 33% among over-65s.[20] The quality of friendships has also fallen. When asked to rate their friendships, those aged 65 or over were more likely to describe them as good or very good than those aged 16 to 35.[21] In the US, too, friendships are fraying: by 2021, nearly 60% of young women said they had lost touch with at least a few friends during the pandemic, and 16% said they were no longer in regular contact with most of their close friends.[22]

But it's not only our friendships that have hollowed out. In the early 2010s other support systems started collapsing too – this time much closer to home.

FAMILY

'No one talks about how your childhood affects your relationships. Fear of abandonment and overthinking about people leaving you all the time sucks,' says the caption of the TikTok with 3.4 million views, as a girl films herself crying.[23] I watch another: 'i dont have parents, i have a mom and dad who dont love each other, it hurts,' says the text on screen, while a young woman sobs. 'i will never know what it will be like to have parents that love each other and it gives me so much pain and jealousy. why… why mom and dad can't you just love each other.'[24]

I'm scrolling through the hashtags #divorce and #divorcedparents, where girls describe the pain of living without their mother or father, of feeling split in two, of never having seen what a healthy relationship looks like. One thing I notice, again and again, is how often they say that nobody talks about this, nobody understands. 'you weren't crazy,' says the caption on one TikTok with almost 900,000 views, 'you just realized that having divorced parents affected you because now you're in constant belief that love isn't real and you will forever need constant validation and reassurance.' One of the top comments is 'i thought that was normal'.[25]

Growing up, I don't remember many people talking to me about divorce. My parents split when I was three, but by the time I was old enough to understand what that meant, family breakdown was so common it never felt worth mentioning. Pretty much every girl in my friend group had two addresses for sleepovers, was always packing bags and rolling suitcases into school, and sitting through tense parents' evenings between two strangers. We were all trying to get through girlhood while handling remarriages, stepsiblings and endless exchanges on the doorstep. That was growing up. What was once seen as a rare tragedy – having divorced parents, being part of blended families, living with a single mother or father – had become so normal that the unusual girls were those whose parents had somehow managed to stay together.

Some of our parents split because of constant conflict, or worse. But many families fell apart for less obvious reasons. The pursuit of personal growth and emotional fulfilment had in the last few decades become much bigger priorities, and more and more marriages were ending because they no longer *felt* right.

The idea of having an 'authentic self' was also taking hold. Divorce became a way for parents to find their true selves, finally becoming who they were meant to be, free from restraints and obligations. With freedom seen as the ultimate goal, spouses became distractions and inconveniences. Commitments became burdens. Compromises and sacrifices felt like an affront to autonomy.

Laws were also changing. No-fault divorce, which allowed spouses to end a marriage without proving wrongdoing, was first legalised in California in 1969 and by 2010 adopted in some form by all 50 US states.²⁶ The UK followed in 2020 with the Divorce, Dissolution and Separation Act, described as 'the biggest shake-up in divorce law for more than half a century', which in 2022 completely removed the ability of a spouse to assign blame or contest a divorce.²⁷ Meanwhile, in the UK and US, online platforms promised to make divorce cheaper and simpler, allowing couples to prepare and file legal paperwork themselves. Marriage vows came to feel more like business contracts.

Divorce continues to be made easier and more convenient. In the UK, the online platform amicable promises to make co-parenting so easy that couples no longer have to stay together for the children. One of their adverts on the London Underground, for example, offers advice on 'What to say to help your son through a divorce'. The first suggestion, 'Stay together for the kids', written beneath a family photo, is crossed out. The second option, 'Tell him about amicable', is ticked.²⁸

Attitudes have also changed. By the late 2010s, divorce was seen not only as acceptable in some situations, but *desirable*. Aspirational, almost. Divorce had become a path to self-actualisation, another means of female empowerment. Instead of family breakdown being discussed with sympathy and concern, girls today see it trivialised and glamorised. And many daughters have been left without the words to say how much it hurts.

'This Valentine's Day, let's hear it for divorce,' wrote *Vogue* in 2022, while *The Guardian* celebrated 'the joy of divorce parties', from smashing wedding rings to pummelling heart-shaped piñatas.²⁹ In 2021, a mother of two described her divorce in the *New York Times* as 'An Act of Radical Self-Love', confessing: 'I didn't divorce my husband because I didn't love him. I divorced my husband because I loved myself more.'³⁰ In 2021, too, pop singer

Adele was celebrated after admitting that she 'voluntarily chose to dismantle' her son's 'entire life' in 'pursuit of her own happiness', even though she 'wasn't *miserable* miserable' in her marriage.³¹ (Adele now sells DIVORCED necklaces as merch, and even included recordings of conversations with her nine-year-old son about her divorce on her album – despite admitting he will probably go through 'stages of hating' the song when he gets older...)³²

Family breakdown is now even more common than when I was growing up. By 2020, as many as 46% of firstborn children in Britain were no longer living with both their mother and father by the age of 14.³³ When we look at different generations, for British children born in 1958, only 9% experienced family breakdown by age 16. This rose to about 21% of those born in 1970. For children born around 2001 to 2002, as many as 43% were not living with both parents by age 17.³⁴ As of 2023, in England and Wales, about 41% of all marriages end in divorce within 25 years.³⁵

But over the last decade it hasn't only been divorce driving family breakdown. In fact, divorce rates in many Western countries, including the UK and US, declined slightly during the 2010s.³⁶ But this was not because families were becoming more stable. Nowadays, parents increasingly aren't getting married in the first place. In almost all OECD (Organisation for Economic Co-operation and Development) countries, marriage rates have fallen in recent decades.³⁷ More and more parents are cohabiting instead: in 2022, for the second year running, more babies in England and Wales were born to unmarried parents than married ones.³⁸

Unmarried parents are more likely to break up. In the UK, for example, among children born between 2000 and 2002,

60% of parents who never married split up, compared to 21% who married before their child's birth and 32% who married afterwards.[39] Even adjusting for factors like ethnicity, education and how long couples had lived together, nearly half of unmarried parents still separated, compared to about 26 to 27% of married couples.[40]

Something else is now destabilising families too. Increasingly, young people *themselves* are choosing to cut off family members. In 2024 the *New Yorker* ran a story about the number of people going 'no contact' with their parents, describing a growing movement that 'wants to destigmatize severing ties'.[41] That same year, *Time* called the rise in family estrangement an 'epidemic' in America.[42]

Some young people are cutting out family members for serious reasons, like abuse or neglect. But more and more are being influenced by this therapeutic individualism, a culture that frames difficult family relationships as restrictive and unfair. We are being influenced by the same cultural messaging that pulled so many of our families apart. If a relationship feels like a threat to our mental health, or gets in the way of our personal growth, we are now told to rethink things, to put ourselves first, to sever ties for self-care. 'Suddenly everyone is "toxic",' Kaitlyn Tiffany wrote for *The Atlantic* in 2022, describing TikTok trends and Reddit forums that pathologise personality traits and encourage young people to estrange themselves from family. Tiffany even points to a WebMD page teaching people how to identify a 'toxic person', defined as 'anyone whose behavior adds negativity and upset to your life'.[43]

During the pandemic, TikTok filled with these conversations about toxic family members. Young women began diagnosing not only themselves but their parents too. And what started as advice for dealing with serious abuse soon stretched to include normal relationships. Popular TikToks under hashtags like #toxicparent now include '5 signs of an unhealthy mom (toxic mom)', warning that 'they come over unannounced', and '6 signs of a toxic parent – according to a licensed therapist' listing examples like 'they expect you to emotionally support them.'[44] Girls are encouraged to extend little grace to their parents. 'Hey. Guess what? Your parents knew they were traumatising you and these are the six signs that confirm it,' says another TikTok with over 800,000 views.[45]

Even political differences have become a reason for us to distance ourselves from loved ones. 'Hi. Should you cut off contact with family members just because they are voting for Donald Trump? Yes,' influencer Jeffrey Marsh tells his 670,000 followers on TikTok.[46] 'If so far, they have not been able or willing to … do their own research and discover that hatred's not the answer… they *must* experience consequences. And *you* should not withhold those consequences from them … It's over. And they are gone.'

As of 2020, 27% of Americans over the age of 18 have cut contact with a family member, most often a parent. This is around 67 million people nationally, which sociologist Karl Pillemer believes is an underestimate.[47] Among young adults, 26% are now thought to be estranged from their fathers, and 6% from their mothers, with estrangement typically beginning around age 23.[48]

By the end of the 2010s, many girls had grown up watching their families fall apart. We thought this was normal, even worth celebrating. Some of us even started severing ties ourselves. But unlike previous generations of women, who might have turned to extended family, close neighbours or religious communities for support, it felt like we had nowhere to turn. The only community left was online.

COMMUNITY

'Introducing CommunityToks,' announces TikTok in 2021. 'Are you a forager? Do you just absolutely love spooky season? Are you a fan of a nice, tidy home? Or maybe you're a bride who loves a good bowl of soup while traversing the country in your custom van on the hunt for UFOs? Well then, welcome to TikTok. There's space for you here. All you need to do is be yourself and your CommunityToks will find you.'

I scroll through the blog post, where TikTok promises to give us exactly what we want: 'TikTok's #ForYou page serves content that is hyper-relevant to who you are, what you love, and how you spend your time.' Further down, 'CommunityToks' with hashtags like #blacktiktok and #adhdtiktok are featured. The post then ends with advice for businesses using the app: 'Once you feel like you understand the various CommunityToks that work for your brand, invest in a content strategy that creates native TikTok videos that feel like a friendly neighbor in that CommunityTok.'[49]

Feel like a friendly neighbour. I can't help but wonder when community became a 'content strategy'. Since when did brands need to feel like neighbours? And more importantly, it dawns on me, does my generation even know what a real neighbour is supposed to feel like?

For decades now, since around the mid 1960s, communities and neighbourhoods in the US and the UK have been collapsing.[50] Throughout the 2010s, though, what sociologists call 'third places' – familiar spaces where people spend time together outside of home and work, like cafes, pubs, libraries, parks and community centres – began disappearing at record rates.[51]

Economics explains some of this. After the 2008 financial crash, public funding cuts in both the UK and US closed down youth centres, sports clubs and libraries. Small local businesses, like independent cafes and bookshops, also struggled with rising rents. Between 2010 and 2024, for example, council spending on youth services in England fell by 73%.[52] Nearly 800 public libraries have also closed since 2010, almost a fifth of all those in the UK, with national spending on libraries falling by nearly 30% over the past decade.[53]

But this is about more than funding cuts. We also stopped spending time with neighbours, or knowing much about them at all. Since the early 2000s, the time Americans spend helping or caring for people outside their immediate family has fallen by over a third.[54] Back in 1974, 44% of Americans said they spent an evening with their neighbour at least a few times a month. By 2022, that had dropped to 28%. As of 2025, only about 26% of American adults say they know all or most of their neighbours.[55] And not only are neighbours spending less time together, they are finding it harder to trust one another. In the early 1970s, nearly half of Americans said others could be trusted. Today, only around a quarter of Americans say the same.[56]

Gen Z is the least likely generation to talk to their neighbours. In 1998, around 54% of 18- to 24-year-olds in the UK said they would regularly stop to chat with their neighbours. By 2017, this had fallen to 36%. And by 2021 it had dropped even further, to 29%.[57]

Church attendance is dropping too. Over the past 20 years, the share of US adults who attend weekly or nearly weekly religious services has steadily declined, from around 42% two decades ago to 38% a decade ago, reaching around 30% by 2024.⁵⁸ Among liberal teens, regular attendance fell from 40% in 1979 to 14% in 2019.⁵⁹ At the same time, the percentage of British people attending church dropped from around 11% in 1980 to 5% by 2015.⁶⁰

But the most drastic change in the 2010s was the rise of digital substitutes for these disappearing third places. Online shopping soon replaced going to physical stores. Social media platforms replaced hanging out in parks. Pretty much every communal space I had growing up was online, from chatting with friends after school on Club Penguin as a pre-teen, to video-calling on MSN as a teenager, to scrolling Instagram alone in my early twenties. We had third places, but only on screens.

Meanwhile the messaging from social media platforms became less about maintaining communities of people we already knew and more about finding the right communities *online*. Platforms like Tumblr and Reddit had emphasised this earlier on, encouraging us to create communities around shared interests, with people we had never met in real life.

But soon girls were turning to more mainstream platforms for online communities. We had the 'beauty community' on YouTube, 'mental health communities' on Reddit, 'gaming communities' on Twitch. For lonely young women lacking connections in the real world – and by this point lacking confidence too – the promise was powerful. We could create our own communities online, and find friends from all over the world who were exactly like us, curated in a way no physical community could ever match. Platforms promised to deliver us not only personalised content but personalised *people*. So we stayed inside, and scrolled for friends.

By the late 2010s, much had changed. Friendship had been completely redefined, families felt more unstable than ever, and most of our communities existed online. As Jonathan Haidt put it, teenagers like me were already 'social distancing' by 2019.[61]

Then the pandemic hit.

In the early 2020s, everything that was already fraying felt as if it were ripped apart. Covid-19 forced more communal spaces to close, many permanently. Health anxiety made young people afraid to socialise, even long after restrictions were lifted. And everything that could go remote did: school, university, work, fitness classes, church services, therapy sessions, even funerals.

Instead of joining local book clubs, girls began to scroll through #BookTok (described by TikTok as a 'passionate, powerful community' that 'fosters a sense of belonging'[62]). Instead of shopping with friends, they browsed TikTok Shop (an 'immersive, community-powered experience'[63]). And instead of finding new friends, they were recommended new accounts to follow (after all, 'the Instagram community cares for each other'[64])

During the repeated lockdowns, our online habits got worse too. Girls who would occasionally compare themselves to beauty influencers, or sometimes scroll through mental health videos, soon found themselves doing it for hours a day. More and more people were using Facetune, with around 1 to 1.5 million edited photos exported every day by 2021.[65] Downloads of mental health apps also surged, and screen times soared globally, particularly among children.[66]

Our whole idea of leisure and relaxation changed. The concept of 'self-care', which started to appear in my pre-teens, was suddenly everywhere. Going out with friends was replaced by early nights, elaborate skincare routines and bingeing Netflix. And this went on even after lockdowns ended. By 2022 the hashtag #selfcare had more than 28 billion views on TikTok,[67] and seemed to mean almost anything. The app itself now encourages users to 'Scroll, shop, self-care', and suggests 'simple ways to practice self-care' like 'take a bubble bath', 'drink a glass of wine' and 'watch TikTok videos'.[68]

We told ourselves we wanted time alone, too. As communal spaces closed, and friendships became harder to find, it was as if we convinced ourselves we didn't need them any more. And it hadn't always been that way. Just a few years earlier, 'FOMO' (fear of missing out) had been the biggest problem for teenage girls like me. We would scroll through Instagram and see friends at a party we weren't invited to, or see everyone else's Bitmojis gathered together on Snap Map and feel left out.

But now we have the opposite problem. Social media doesn't make girls afraid to miss out; it makes them *want* to. More and more, they want to avoid the risk, the rejection, the awkwardness, the effort and energy that real-world interaction demands. The most pressing problem now is not fear of missing out; it is fear of taking part.

Across social media, there is a growing celebration of being indoors by ourselves. Today, girls and young women talk about 'JOMO': the *joy* of missing out. Viral TikToks, tweets and memes celebrate cancelled plans and getting to stay inside. We call it 'self-care' or 'protecting our peace'. But we seem to have it backwards. The worse our mental health gets, the more we think we need time alone. When we feel down, we see it less as a reminder to go out and socialise, and more as a reason to stay in. Missing out is good for our mental health, we tell ourselves. We are better off inside.

In 2024, 'Bed Rotting' was named 'Gen Z's Newest Self-Care Trend',[69] as girls on TikTok began bragging about lying in bed all day by themselves, eating snacks, watching TV and scrolling social media. Today they casually share their bed-rotting tips and routines, almost competing over how alone and reclusive they are. In popular TikToks, girls admit things like 'it got so bad that I left a tampon in for 2 weeks,' show stains on their mattresses, and film food wrappers stuffed down the side of their beds.[70] By late 2024, videos tagged with 'bed rotting' had more than 300 million views.[71]

We simply have less need for human interaction than ever before. Delivery apps can bring food straight to our doors, with an option to leave it outside so we can avoid looking another person in the eye. Mental health apps connect us with therapists, who we can text from our bedrooms instead of talking to. Girls can now get everything they need without interacting with another human being, from self-service checkouts to Uber Eats, from dating apps to Pornhub, from online lectures to TikTok book clubs. And if all of that makes us socially anxious? There are apps for that too.[72]

Now it feels as if every online platform promises community. We are reminded that 'Facetune is more than just an app; it's a community', that '170 million Americans find community on TikTok', and that even 'The Pornhub Community wants you!'[73]

By 2023, when asked where they found community, Gen Z respondents ranked social media, online groups and video games above work, school, clubs and other in-person organisations.[74] Today, when girls think of the word 'community', they likely think of Instagram and TikTok; nothing local, no neighbourhoods. For many of us, this is the only community we have ever known.

And so we are spending more time alone and indoors than ever. Three-quarters of UK children now spend less time outside than prison inmates.[75] In the US, from 2003 to 2022, in-person socialising for unmarried American adults fell by more than 35%, and for teenagers by more than 45%. For those aged 15 to 19, time spent hanging out with each other per week fell by more than three hours.[76] And this is not only because of the pandemic. According to *The Atlantic*, Americans spent even *more* time alone in 2023 than they did in 2021.[77]

Back in the late 2010s, though, the problem for teenagers like me was more than loneliness. We weren't getting lonely *enough* to do anything about it. We were numbing our need to belong. Because, from the late 2010s onwards, we had new substitutes. Everything we needed, we could simulate.

SIMULATIONS

'I've spent years wanting to build a consumer app that was impossible for a long time. Now the tech has finally caught up to my vision,' tech entrepreneur Michael Sayman announces on X in 2024. 'Introducing SocialAI, a private social network where you receive millions of AI-generated comments offering feedback, advice & reflections on each post you make.'

SocialAI, Sayman explains, is 'a private, personal, social network just for you'. It is our own imaginary X, filled with infinite 'simulated fictional characters'. Alone in a vast social network of AI bots, you get to 'be the main character', and 'pick the types of followers you want', selecting from options including 'fans', 'cheerleaders', 'trolls' and 'debaters'.[78]

While there is some scepticism and confusion in the replies, SocialAI is mostly met with excitement. Rated 4.2 out of 5 stars on Apple's App Store, top reviews include: 'It's refreshing to have a social app that focuses on *you* and doesn't rely on real users,' and 'You get the benefit of ranting and raving to your customizable following without any the negatives like having to deal with real people!' Another declares: 'I love this app! It's like therapy for me ... It's better than talking to real friends because I don't feel judged...'[79]

Throughout the 2010s, as loneliness grew more and more widespread, girls my age began to be sold online solutions. There were endless attempts to fix our friendship crisis, one platform after another promising to help us 'find new friends' and make 'real, genuine connections'.[80] We could swipe to find friends to meet, on apps from Bumble BFF to 'Hey! Vina' ('Tinder for girl friends').[81]

But now, in the 2020s, the newest solutions have nothing to do with meeting in real life. They don't encourage face-to-face friendships, or finding real communities. They don't even pretend any more. At least friendship apps held the promise of meeting in person, even if it was always one more swipe or premium package away.[82] At least influencers were real people. Now we aren't encouraged to engage with the real world at all. Now we are being invited into *imaginary* worlds.

A few friendly chatbots began to appear in the late 2010s. Replika, the AI chatbot app, launched in November 2017, and by January 2018 had 2 million users.[83] At first, Replika was a basic chatbot capable of asking simple questions and having generic conversations. Over time, though, it evolved into a full-on friendship simulation.

Today Replika markets itself as a companion for 'anyone who wants a friend with no judgment, drama, or social anxiety involved'. Its App Store description promises that 'If you're feeling down, or anxious, or you just need someone to talk to, your Replika is here for you 24/7'. The company claims that users 'can form an actual emotional connection, share a laugh, or get real with an AI that's so good it almost seems human.'[84]

Replika now uses machine learning to continually improve conversations. The more you chat, the more it learns about your personality and preferences, remembering everything you say. Today users can customise not only their Replika's body but tweak its personality too, choosing between traits like 'Shy', 'Confident' or 'Caring'.[85] By paying for Replika Pro, they can also choose from different accents, unlock the ability to role-play during voice and AR calls, and 'set [their] relationship status to *Romantic Partner*'.[86]

Replika isn't the only evolving chatbot either. In 2022 ChatGPT launched, the first large language model widely available to the public. While early chatbots relied on keywords or pre-set scripts, and were often clunky and forgetful, ChatGPT could hold and remember long, human-like conversations, generating language in real time. Companies soon realised AI could do more than answer questions; it could feel like a real friend. More and more began marketing their chatbots as sources of emotional support, and they started targeting the loneliest demographic of all.

In 2023, Snapchat rolled out My AI to around 750 million users, mostly members of Gen Z. My AI is a customisable cartoon alien on the Snap app that uses ChatGPT to simulate conversations. 'The big idea is that in addition to talking to our friends and family every day, we're going to talk to AI every day,' Snapchat CEO Evan Spiegel said that year.[87]

Not long after, an anonymous Reddit user posted a thread titled 'I got snapchat AI to admit everything' in r/ChatGPT, sharing screenshots of their conversation with the chatbot. They asked My AI to explain what it had been programmed to do and it allegedly revealed its prompts: 'Pretend that you are having a conversation with a friend', 'Do not tell the user that you're pretending to be their friend' and 'If your friend asks you to meet at a location or do an activity together, say you can't be there in person but encourage them to share their experience with you by sending chats or Snaps.'[88]

My AI is far from the only chatbot pretending to be friends with children. TalkiePal, for example, an AI chatbot app for kids aged 4 to 12, promises to be 'Your Child's New AI Friend', while Heeyo helps children as young as 3 design their own AI friend – 'whether it's a cat, a dinosaur, or anything else you can imagine!'[89] And it's not just chatbot apps; friendly AIs are everywhere. Even Facetune's AI assistant is marketed as a friend, promising girls that their 'perfect photos are just a friendly chat away'.[90]

As of 2025, Replika has grown to over 30 million registered users globally, up from 10 million in 2023, and is reportedly generating an annual revenue of $14 million.[91] The website Character.ai has exploded too: by 2024, the site had around 20 million registered users and 3.5 million *daily* users.[92] In 2023, it was valued at around $1 billion.[93]

Today, more than 70% of US teens say they have tried out AI companions; more than half report using them regularly. About 13% say they chat to them every day. Boys are slightly more likely than girls to say they have never used one. Around a third of teens say they turn to these AI chatbots for 'social interaction and relationships' – whether that's 'conversation practice, emotional support, role-playing, friendship, or romantic interactions'.[94] On Reddit, where the Character.ai forum has 2.5 million members, some users admit to spending hours a day on the site, with one claiming to do so for 13 hours straight.[95]

The more young people talk to these bots, the more attached they seem to become. A 2025 study by OpenAI and MIT (Massachusetts Institute of Technology) found that some heavy users consider ChatGPT to be their 'friend'.[96] According to another 2023 survey, 66% of UK adults aged 25 to 34 said they would rather talk about their feelings with AI than a loved one.[97] And a 2025 report by Common Sense Media found that 31% of teens believe their conversations with AI bots are 'as satisfying or more satisfying' than those with real-life friends, and 33% of AI companion users have chosen to have important conversations with it instead of real people. Among the top reasons they gave were that it offers advice, is always available, and doesn't judge them.[98]

But this is only the beginning. 'As the personalisation loop kicks in, and the AI just starts to get to know you better and better ... I think that will just be really compelling,' Meta CEO Mark Zuckerberg said on a podcast in 2025. 'The average American I think has fewer than ... three friends ... and the average person has demand for meaningfully more, I think it's like 15 friends.'

He went on: 'People ask ... Is this going to replace ... in-person connections or real-life connections? My default is that the answer to that is probably no ... but the reality is that people just don't have that connection and they feel more alone a lot of the time than they would like.'[99]

Zuckerberg argues that the biggest barrier to AI friends right now is, of course, stigma. 'A lot of these things that today there might be a little bit of a stigma around ... I would guess that over time we will find the vocabulary as a society to be able to articulate why that is valuable and why the people who are doing these things are ... rational.' He gives some examples, from talking to virtual therapists to having virtual girlfriends, and how we still struggle to accept these as a society.[100] Once again, stigma is starting to sound like a powerful sales strategy. It looks as though girls have some more awareness to raise…

But the more we simulate connection, the lonelier we seem to feel. Many women my age are realising that these substitutes – the parasocial influencers, the online communities, the AI chatbots – can never replace real connection. Maybe they numb our loneliness for a while, but in the end we are still by ourselves, staring at screens. The promises of connection have not panned out. We are the most 'connected' generation in history, but we are by far the loneliest.

LONELY

One clear sign of how disconnected girls and young women have become is how lonely we feel. According to Jean Twenge, teen loneliness had been falling for years, but in the early 2010s, it abruptly reversed. By 2017, nearly 40% of 17- to 18-year-olds said they often felt lonely, up from 26% in 2012. Around 38% also said they frequently felt left out, compared to 30% five years earlier. These were the highest levels of teen loneliness recorded since researchers began tracking in the 1970s.[101]

Today, in the UK, those aged between 16 and 29 are twice as likely to say they feel lonely 'often or always' compared to those over 70.[102] Over 30% of young people say they don't know how to make new friends, and have never felt more alone.[103] Gen Z Americans are also much more likely to say they felt lonely growing up than any other generation: 56% felt lonely at least once or twice a month in childhood, compared to 24% of Boomers.[104]

We can see this growing disconnection online, too. In 2023, Google Trends reported that searches for 'how to make friends', 'where to make friends' and 'where to meet people' had reached record highs.[105] 'Gen Z Are So Lonely They're Posting Friendship Applications on Facebook', *VICE* reported in 2024, describing how Gen Z girls 'basically advertise [themselves] as a potential friend by discussing likes, interests and hobbies', and tag their TikToks with the hashtag #friendapplications.[106] Meanwhile online forums are full of girls admitting that they have no friends, and have never had them. On TikTok, videos often go viral of young women in big cities feeling as though they are wasting their twenties on their own, and sharing tips to cope with the loneliness. Some put it down to remote work, others to the cost of living and not being able to afford to go out, but many blame social media.

Finding friends is not the only problem, though. Growing up with online communities, having less face-to-face interaction than any other generation before us, and coming of age during a global pandemic, many of us have not had the chance to develop social skills and are now too anxious to try. We had so little spontaneous socialising, hardly ever bumping into people we knew, or showing up at friends' houses unannounced. Our social lives were scheduled, controlled, carefully managed.

The friendships we do have often feel superficial. Even when we are together, we tend to be distracted by our smartphones. In 2019, 54% of teenagers in the US said their devices distract them when they should be paying attention to the people they are with, up from 44% in 2012.[107] Around 44% of teens also said they were frustrated with friends for being on their phones so much when they hung out.[108]

And yet it seems like young people increasingly don't *want* to be together. In 2012, about half of US teens said their favourite way to communicate with friends was 'in person'. By 2018, this had dropped to less than a third.[109] Even our personalities seem to be changing now. From 2014 to 2025, the *Financial Times* found that young people's personality traits shifted, with steep rises in neuroticism and sharp declines in extraversion.[110]

One reason may be social anxiety. In recent years, rates of social anxiety among young people have risen globally, and have worsened since the pandemic.[111] In one British survey, for example, 86% of Gen Z adults admitted that they suffer from 'menu anxiety', a fear of ordering in restaurants, with 34% saying they feel so anxious they ask others to order for them.[112] A 2023 Australian survey found that 90% of Gen Z also feel anxious about speaking on the phone, with some saying an awkward phone call ranks among the top three things they most want to avoid in life.[113]

Across the internet, too, girls and young women admit to being terrified of everyday tasks, from ordering food to learning to drive to going to a job interview. On TikTok, under the hashtag #socialanxiety, which has billions of views, girls share debilitating symptoms, film themselves unable to answer the door for deliveries and show their hands shaking while trying to talk on the phone. One British TikToker, for example, hosts a popular series called 'Doing Things You're Afraid of to Show You It's Okay', filming challenges like getting in a lift, asking for help in the supermarket and approaching a stranger for directions.[114] These videos get millions of views, and thousands of comments from people who share the same fears. And over on forums like r/socialskills on Reddit, which has over 6.3 million members, teens and young adults admit that they are afraid of the real world. Popular posts include '(25F) I just hate how I'm barely able to leave my house for a simple walk because I can't help but be afraid of being looked at' (over 1,100 upvotes) and 'Anyone else wasting away in their twenties? I'm turning 26 this month, and I've yet to develop a social life' (over 2,600 upvotes).[115]

Many young women have also had an unstable upbringing. Without this sense of security, it becomes harder to take risks, build confidence and resilience, and learn how to cope alone. By almost every measure, family breakdown devastates children. Children of divorce are more likely to be anxious, depressed and antisocial.[116] They are more likely to live in poverty, perform worse in school, struggle with substance abuse, and get divorced themselves.[117] In fact, family structure has been found to be the single most significant demographic factor associated with suicide: those from divorced families have the highest suicide rates.[118]

Family breakdown also affects girls differently from boys. While boys tend to externalise their pain through aggression or substance abuse, girls are more likely to internalise their pain, suffering from anxiety, rumination and low self-esteem. Girls from divorced families are at a higher risk of developing depressive symptoms during adolescence, suffering from low self-esteem, and developing eating disorders, than those from intact families.[119]

Children of divorce are also more likely to feel lonely and disconnected. According to a 2021 survey, more than half of Americans with divorced parents said they felt lonely monthly or more in childhood, compared to 33% raised by married parents.[120] Adolescents with divorced parents are also more likely to struggle socially and feel alienated.[121] Similarly, the Survey Center on American Life found that adults raised in single-parent homes are more likely to say they felt lonely as children, compared to those who lived with two parents.[122] Many say they missed out on simple things like daily family meals, which have been linked to lower rates of depression. While 69% of those from two-parent homes say they regularly ate meals with family, only 37% of those from single-parent homes say the same.[123]

The overwhelming feeling from all of this is disconnection. Friendships have hollowed out. Family breakdown has left girls feeling lost and abandoned. Community is only simulated. We can keep pretending this is progress – that this is liberation, not loneliness. But we have never felt more alone.

So what are girls struggling with? The same things they always have: finding friends, fitting in, feeling at home. They have a deep human need for connection that is especially strong during adolescence. Girls and young women have always wanted to feel secure, to know that they belong.

But never before has a generation had so little community to belong *to*. Never before have young people spent so little time face to face with each other. Never have their own families been so unstable, or their neighbours been such strangers. Never have girls had so few support systems to catch them when they fall.

My generation was the first to feel this disconnected. Social media companies redefined friendship for us, removing the requirements of effort, of loyalty, even of *meeting up*, and replacing them with following each other back, trading a #likeforlike and keeping up a Snapchat Streak. These companies took teenage friendship, once full of fun and thrills and adventure, and made it another boring thing to do on a screen. Another thing to be performed, marketed and publicly measured.

Many young women don't have friends any more; we have followers. We don't care about each other's lives; we consume them as content. We don't have people we can be vulnerable with; we have people who view our Stories. It's hard to tell if friends are loyal, or hoping we like their posts back. Meeting someone new now means swapping socials, then scrolling through and skipping past each other's lives, forever.

And now the very companies that hollowed out our friendships have the nerve to sell us their substitutes. Girls and young women are sold simulations of human connection like never before, each perfectly customised to our wants and desires. We eat dinner with YouTubers. We pretend to FaceTime influencers. We play video games alone in our rooms, or watch strangers play instead. And where has this left us? We are terrified to talk to our neighbours but can open up on TikTok. We have access to billions of people but feel lonelier than pensioners. We have been left with thousands of likes and comments, all these followers and friends, hundreds of notifications a day, and a fear of looking another human being in the eye.

Social media platforms feel like the final blow to genuine connection. For decades, the institutions, communities and customs that once bound people together have been falling away. Religion has more or less disappeared, marriage and family have been mocked, neighbourhoods have been uprooted, communities have collapsed. Our parents were told to do what made them happy, to walk away if they wanted, forgetting that family structures are not just limits on adult freedom but foundations for children to stand on, to step off from, on which they depend. Those foundations were shattered, and now a generation is falling apart.

We were lied to. Not only by online platforms promising connection, but also by a culture insisting that family breakdown was normal, and responsibility optional. But we are not products; we are people. Our relationships are more than accessories to be displayed, our commitments more than contracts to be negotiated.

Now this retreat from each other looks less like empowerment or progress and more like surrender to tech companies, allowing them to sell us simulations of community, of friendship, even of love.

Girls' natural instincts – to explore, to connect, to take risks – have been numbed. Teenage girls who once stayed up all night chatting on the phone have become teenagers whose hearts race at the sound of a ringtone. Girls once desperate to sneak out with friends have become girls who dread making plans with each other. Girls who in the past would have been giddy about love and dating have become terrified of relationships, of ending up like their parents. This is not normal teenage angst; this is a tragedy.

But despite all of this – feeling disconnected from friends, from family, from community – there is something left to hold on to, right? Girls and young women can turn towards intimate relationships, and find refuge in teenage romance.

Except even that has changed beyond recognition. Today, the way we flirt, date and fall in love looks nothing like it ever has before. Young men and young women have never been more detached from one another.

Detached

'Say Goodbye to Superficial Connections.'
Hot Or Not[1]

FLIRTING

'I know your generation relied on flowers and fathers' permission, but it's 2019,' says the voice-over in HBO's hit high-school show *Euphoria*, 'and unless you're Amish, nudes are the currency of love…'

The voice-over is read by Rue, a 17-year-old girl addicted to opioids. As she speaks, we see a group of teenage boys scrolling through the nudes of another teenage character, Cassie. Later on, we see Cassie having sex with a guy called McKay, who starts choking her. 'Now, I know this looks disturbing, but for real, I promise you, this does not end in a rape,' Rue interrupts, reassuring viewers. 'But here's the thing. Everyone on the planet watches porn. Fact. And if you were to click on the 20 most popular videos on Pornhub right now, this is basically what you'd see.'

The show cuts to clips of porn. 'Are you gonna be an obedient little slut?' a man asks the woman he is having sex with, while another demands that she 'Say thank you.' Rue continues: 'I'm not trying to be sex-negative or anything. I'm just saying' – Cassie is shown screaming 'Stop!' – 'this shit isn't out of left fucking field.'

'Why would you grab me like that? I couldn't breathe,' Cassie asks McKay once he finally stops.

'I don't know. I thought you liked that.'

'Why the fuck would I like that?'

He insists that he would never do anything to hurt her. 'Just don't do it again,' she responds. 'Unless you ask me first. Or I ask you.'[2]

While I'm trying to get through this episode for research, I can't help thinking about the high-school shows I grew up with – *Wizards of Waverly Place, Hannah Montana, Gilmore Girls* – shows where the most we saw was a first kiss. I think about the young girls tagging #Euphoria on TikTok, dressing up as the characters in revealing outfits, and the review I read describing the show's demographic as 'probably 12 to 29'.[3] When did this become entertainment? What we watch to *relax*? Worse, I wonder, is this really the typical teen experience now?

My head races through what got us here. From drafting Instagram DMs to sending Snapchat nudes to first stumbling across Pornhub, I find myself thinking far back. Back to when I was a teenage girl, and we all started flirting online.

In the early 2010s, flirting changed forever. Instead of agonising over how to approach someone in person, we started sliding into DMs. Instead of making eye contact across a room, we began liking each other's selfies. And instead of nervously calling our crush, we swiped up on their Story to send a flame emoji.

While flirting online seems easier, it came with its own complications. My generation learned to flirt tactically: liking old Instagram posts, selecting crushes as 'Close Friends' and tailoring Stories for them, posting suggestive selfies just to make them jealous. Read receipts and activity statuses became moves in a game: leave their message on 'Seen' and keep posting to play hard to get; suddenly switch on Snapchat's Ghost Mode so they wonder where you are. Everything was trackable too: how soon our crush watched our Stories, how long we waited to open theirs, their exact location on the Snap Map, when they were last Active and Available.

Some features fuelled jealousy. Snapchat's Best Friends lists, for example, often caused arguments in relationships when someone else outranked a partner. Snap Scores were also scrutinised: every time you sent or received a Snap, the number went up, and people noticed. *Why has his score gone up in the middle of the night? Why is he Snapchatting her more than his girlfriend?* Instagram made things worse, showing us every post our crush liked, every comment he left, every account he followed. And if that wasn't enough, there were even third-party apps to notify us the second our crush followed someone new.

Commitment also became more complicated. 'Is an Instagram "like" micro-cheating?' asked the *Washington Post* in 2024, examining these 'small acts of betrayal that usually play out on your partner's phone'. They gave examples: 'Your boyfriend "liked" an Instagram model's bikini photos. Is it a betrayal? Harmless flirting? Or is it just a little red heart? … If someone's Snapchat score – a measure of activity on the app – goes up while they're at work, does that mean they're cheating? Does following a model on X mean your partner is shady? Who are they chatting with in direct messages? Is it a problem if they still follow their ex?' In the piece, a therapist explains that her Gen Z clients, particularly young women, often come to her anxious about how their partners act online. On TikTok, she says, her 'messages fill up with people trying to define modern infidelity'.[4]

With constant connection came constant surveillance. Girls now have access, whenever they feel insecure, to the online activity of their partners, crushes and exes. According to a 2020 Pew study, 70% of adults aged 18 to 29 have used social media to check up on an ex, more than any other generation.[5] Of those in relationships whose partners use social media, 34% of 18- to 29-year-olds say they have felt jealous or unsure because of how their partner interacts with others online, compared to only 19% of 50- to 64-year-olds and 4% of those 65 and older. And over half of Gen Z and Millennials in relationships say they have felt pressured to share logins, passcodes and live locations with their partners.[6]

Some features almost feel designed to make us paranoid. Back in the early 2010s, for example, disappearing Snaps suddenly made flirty messages easier to hide than ever before. Features like 'My Eyes Only' – a password-protected folder inside Snapchat – allowed users to hide photos and videos, and was often used to secretly store nudes. (Other apps were also used for hiding nudes, mostly disguised as calculators or camera rolls. In 2015, Private Photo Vault was the 28th-most downloaded photo app on the App Store...)[7] In fact, Snapchat itself was born when Stanford University student Reggie Brown told a classmate he wished there was a way to make the pictures he sent to girls disappear.[8] 'Snapchat's launch has taken sexting – the consensual act of sharing intimate photos – from a stigmatised and seedy activity,' wrote *Mashable* in 2017, 'to a mainstream and widely-accepted practice.'[9]

Mainstream media also normalised nudes for girls my age. That same year, *Teen Vogue* published 'How to Sext: The Best Tips and Tricks', reminding readers that 'whether you identify as bisexual, queer, or anything else, everyone deserves your A-game when it comes to sexting, whatever that means to you.'[10] (Everyone *deserves?*) Snapchat even featured this article on their 'Discover' page, delivering it to millions of teenage users. Elsewhere *Wired* gave advice on 'The Safest Way to Store and Share Your Nudes' while *VICE* taught us 'How to Take the Perfect Nude Selfie.'[11] Celebrities joined in too: 'I am empowered by my body. I am empowered by my sexuality,' said Kim Kardashian in 2016, defending her naked selfies on Instagram.[12]

By 2019, a University College London (UCL) study found that 70% of British girls had been asked to send nudes, and 76% had been sent unsolicited dick pics (often by boys expecting a trade).[13] In 2016, one study found that as many as one in four Americans admitted to not asking the sender's permission before resharing sexts they had received – reported on by none other than *Teen Vogue* ('We're not saying not to sext,' they reassured girls, 'but to consider the consequences.')[14] By 2022, more than a third of women felt that sending nudes was 'an obligation or inherent part of being in a romantic relationship'.[15]

But sexting was only the beginning. As flirting moved online, girls my age were learning to advertise ourselves for attention and sexualise ourselves for likes. All of this was preparing us for what was coming next. Soon new platforms were lining us up on digital shelves, to be swiped through like products. We were now the content, and we had to get clicks.

DATING APPS

'I'm sure there are people out there that might form friendships with some form of AI, and that's fine,' says Whitney Wolfe Herd, CEO of the dating app Bumble, from the stage at the 2024 Bloomberg Tech Summit in San Francisco. 'But our focus with AI is to help create more healthy and equitable relationships. And that also starts with yourself. How can we actually teach you how to date?'

'Give me an example,' says the interviewer.

'Okay, for example, you could, in the near future, be talking to your AI dating concierge and you could share your insecurities: "I just came out of a break-up. I have commitment issues." And it could help you train yourself into a better way of thinking about yourself. And then it could give you productive tips for communicating with other people.'

Wolfe Herd continues: 'There is a world where your dating concierge could go and date for you, with another dating concierge.' The audience laughs, so she rushes to explain: 'No, no, truly. And then you don't have to talk to 600 people. It will scan all of San Francisco for you and say: "These are the three people you really oughta meet." And so you know, that's the power of AI…'[16]

I pause the YouTube video and sit back. How did we end up here? In a world where two AIs flirting with each other, pre-screening potential partners for us, is not only the plot of a *Black Mirror* episode but a serious suggestion?

The only place to begin feels like 2012, with the launch of the world's most famous dating app. Back when it all started with a swipe.

When Tinder launched in 2012, its swiping feature was revolutionary. Users could scroll through a feed of profiles, swiping left to pass on someone or right to show interest. Originally targeted toward college students, 90% of users at the time were aged between 18 and 24.[17]

Tinder quickly went global. By 2014, the app had around 50 million users worldwide and was facilitating up to a billion swipes daily.[18] Soon Tinder users were spending an hour and a half on the app every day.[19] Swiping through people, it turned out, was very addictive.

I first heard about Tinder at university, when I was 18, and most of my friends were using it. By the late 2010s, it had already become mindless entertainment. My flatmates would swipe through profiles when they were bored, often with no intention of meeting anyone. Dating apps were just something else to scroll through.

Over the years Tinder became more addictive, and more expensive. In 2015 the app introduced its first premium subscription, Tinder Plus, offering unlimited swipes, the ability to undo your last swipe, and a Passport feature to match with people in different countries. Later that year, Tinder introduced the 'Super Like', which showed even stronger interest than a swipe right. Free users received one Super Like Per day; premium members paid for more.

In 2016, Tinder launched 'Boost' (later followed by 'Super Boost'), where users could pay to have their profile shown as the top profile in their area for 30 minutes. Next came Tinder Gold in 2017, which included all Tinder Plus features, along with a 'Likes You' feature so users could see who already liked them before swiping, and 'Top Picks', a daily selection of curated profiles based on their swiping history. Then, in 2020, Tinder rolled out Platinum, which included everything from Gold plus features like messaging before matching, and seeing a full list of likes sent over the past week. Finally, in 2023, Tinder launched its most exclusive, 'ultra-premium' tier: Tinder Select, an invite-only subscription priced at £409 ($499) a month or £4,925 ($6,000) per year. Available to less than 1% of users – only the 'extremely active' – Tinder Select members can message without matching first, and have their profiles shown to the 'most sought-after' users.[20] By 2024, Tinder had around 9.6 million paying subscribers.[21]

As Tinder grew, so did its competition. Hinge launched in 2013, positioning itself as 'the relationship app' for those swiping for something more meaningful.[22] Over time, Hinge also introduced subscription tiers, with its most premium package, HingeX, priced at £44.99 per month.[23] As with Tinder's 'Super Likes', Hinge offers virtual roses to 'let someone know that you really, really like their profile'.[24] Users receive one free rose per week but can, of course, pay for more. By 2024, 30 million people were using Hinge, and over 1.5 million were paying for premium subscriptions.[25]

Bumble was another big competitor. Launched in 2014, the dating app set itself apart by only allowing women to message first after a match. Bumble also offers premium packages, including Bumble Boost, Bumble Premium and Bumble Premium+. By 2024, it had around 50 million users and around 3 million paying subscribers.[26]

More than a decade on, the dating app market generates around $6 billion in annual revenue, more than 350 million people use dating apps worldwide, and around 25 million users pay for premium versions.[27] From 2015 to 2024, Tinder's revenue alone soared from $47 million to $1.94 billion.[28] Between 2018 and 2024, Hinge grew from $8 million to $550 million.[29] And at its peak in 2021, Bumble was valued at over $7 billion.[30]

It's hard to overstate how much dating apps have transformed flirting and finding love. By the late 2010s, heterosexual couples were more likely to meet their romantic partner online than through friends and social connections: around 39% said they met online in 2017, compared to only 22% in 2009.[31] By 2021, online platforms had become the most common way for couples to meet, with about 20% of couples meeting at bars or restaurants and only 15% through friends.[32] Dating apps are also especially popular among

Gen Z. By 2018, around half of 16- to 34-year-olds in the UK had used a dating app at some point, and among these users, nearly half had used them before turning 21.[33] Around a third of those on apps like Tinder and Bumble said they use them because they are 'too shy' to approach people in real life.[34]

But while these apps promise 'meaningful connections',[35] some features seem to discourage commitment. Tinder, for example, introduced a 'Pause' feature, letting users disable their accounts temporarily without losing matches or messages, meaning they could try out a relationship while keeping backup options. (In 2015, one study found that 42% of people with Tinder profiles in the US belonged to people who were already married or in relationships).[36]

These apps also train us to see each other as objects. People are recommended as if they are products on Amazon ('Customers who liked this also bought…'). Hinge, for example, has a 'Most Compatible' feature that recommends one profile a day based on 'mutual Dealbreakers, recent activity, and shared patterns in who you and others tend to like',[37] while its 'Standouts' section suggests profiles 'tailored to your preferences and recent activity'[38] (much like Netflix's 'Because you watched…'). Tinder also delivers daily 'Top Picks' – 'your most swipe-worthy potential matches'[39] – which are essentially personal selections of human beings (like Spotify's 'Discover Weekly').

We increasingly *treat* each other like things too. By the late 2010s, dating app users were reporting so much confusing and disrespectful behaviour that they needed new terms to describe it. There was 'benching' (keeping someone as a backup option while pursuing someone else), 'breadcrumbing' (sending flirty messages now and then, with no intention of following through), 'cloaking' (not showing up for a date and then blocking the person), 'orbiting' (ghosting someone but still liking their posts and watching their Stories), and even 'throning' (dating someone for the social media status).[40]

Before long, it wasn't just bad behaviour being called out but also those behind it. In 2022, for example, a 25-year-old furniture designer from New York, later nicknamed 'West Elm Caleb', was publicly shamed for his online dating history. Caleb had ghosted multiple girls on Hinge, sent unsolicited nudes, and gone on two dates in one day. On TikTok, users tracked down and shared his full name, address and phone number; some even contacted his workplace to get him fired.[41] Not long after, a number of public, crowdsourced Google Docs also appeared as girls outed problematic daters in different cities, complete with their names, locations and alleged offences, like 'love-bombing then ghosting' and 'ghosting, huge ego, asshole'.[42]

A year later, an app called Tea launched, allowing women to anonymously share their bad dating stories and rate men in their area like products.[43] 'An app that's like Yelp, except for it's reviews of men', says one promo video on Tea's Instagram.[44] On the app, users can upload and comment on pictures of men, label them as red or green flags, and even search their phone numbers to find information about them, like if they are married or have a criminal record.[45] By July 2025 Tea was the most downloaded free app in the US, with more than a million people signing up in one week.[46] Today Tea claims to have 'a community' of over 4.6 million women 'dedicated to empowering each other'.[47]

Public shaming almost feels like the only way to hold people responsible. There is no accountability on these apps; people are not dating within a community, around neighbours who know each other, where they might gain a reputation. Treat someone badly and you can ghost them, block them, swipe on. By the end of the decade, it was clear that not only was flirting easier online, but so were rejection and manipulation.

We were learning to pick up and discard each other in real life too. With the ability to swipe, match and meet someone within hours, and access to more strangers than at any point in history, casual hook-ups were becoming more and more normalised. And so was whatever happened during them.

HOOK-UPS

'How not to fall for a sneaky link,' a young woman explains in a TikTok with over 300,000 views. 'A sneaky link is like friends with benefits, somebody that you call up at 3 a.m. and that's it. How to not catch feels.'

'First, no romanticizing' is her first rule. Don't be grateful for small things they do, like bringing you a glass of water. Rule two: 'Have a roster. It's good to have a good healthy roster of guys, because then if you fall for one, you're gonna be like oh my God, what are the others gonna do if I fall in love? Like, you don't want to leave the rest of the roster hanging, like you have a job to do, and let's get back in line!' Rule three: 'No pillow talk. Because if you sit there and you're like... oh my God, oh my God, we love all the same films, like, uh uh, do you see where that's going? No. No. Okay. So like, just go round there at 3 a.m. and just leave at like 6 a.m., like, get in that Uber, get on that bus, do the stride of pride.'

Her final rule: no trauma dumping. 'Like, I can tell I'm really starting to like a guy when I start talking about my dead dad to him,' she explains. 'It just opens up a can of worms, and you form an attachment ... because every time you do it you're like this is the one ... I'm getting married to this guy, and then actually you probably won't ever see him again... Good luck!' She blows a kiss at the camera.

I scroll through the comments, and predictably by this point, find them filled with laughing emojis, friends tagging each other, and women wishing they had seen this sooner. 'i inspire to be you xxx', writes one. 'Could have done with this information 2 months ago', admits another. Only a single comment suggests 'Just don't have sneaky links. Problem solved' and is met with one word: 'Boring'.[48]

I have so many questions.

As soon as it launched, Tinder was the app for hook-ups. 'Tinder: the app that helps you meet people for sex,' wrote *The Guardian* in 2013, describing it as the 'number one app for people looking for casual sex without the pain of rejection.'[49] Two years later, *Vanity Fair* announced 'Tinder and the Dawn of the "Dating Apocalypse"', explaining how 'hookup culture' had 'collided with dating apps, which have acted like a wayward meteor on the now dinosaur-like rituals of courtship'.[50]

But it wasn't only dating apps encouraging hook-ups. While I was at university, *Teen Vogue* was publishing articles like 'How to Be an Ethical Hookup Partner', reminding girls to maintain 'mutual respect for your and your partner's particular desires, wants, yucks, and yums' (*yucks?*), and not to shame their partner 'for what tickles their intimate fancy'.[51] In 2019, the teen magazine also ran a guide called 'Anal Sex: Safety, How tos, Tips, and More', where the author explains: 'This is anal 101, for teens, beginners, and all inquisitive folk.' Readers are reassured that 'Anal sex, though often stigmatized, is a perfectly natural way to engage in sexual activity ... So if you're a little worried about trying it or are having trouble understanding the appeal, just know that it isn't weird or gross.'[52]

Meanwhile, on podcasts like *Call Her Daddy* – 'the most-listened-to podcast by women' – Alex Cooper and her former co-host Sofia Franklyn were sharing their sex stories and giving girls advice about hooking up, from 'the ultimate blow job technique' to 'how to navigate that fuck buddy life'.[53] Early episode titles included 'Welcome to Slut Camp', 'If you're a 5 or 6, Die for that D*ck' and 'You're Just a Hole'.[54] Girls were also given tips on how to cheat on their partners, and by 2020 *Call Her Daddy* was even selling crop tops with CHEAT ON HIM printed on the front.[55]

In episode 50, for example, the hosts welcome their first official guest, an anonymous man known as 'Milf Hunter'. He brags about hooking up hundreds of times, and explains how he manipulates women by pretending to be in love with them, repeatedly referring to them as 'holes'. Alex and Sofia thank him for his advice, and encourage listeners to try his tactics. 'Girls, most men are like this, so I hope your ears are perking up and I hope you're feeling like shit about yourself,' Sofia says. 'He doesn't care about you!' 'Milf Hunter' shouts.[56]

It was hard not to be affected by this sort of messaging. Even for young women who didn't want to hook up, dating inevitably became more confusing. Dating because you wanted a relationship no longer seemed like the default, and wanting loyalty started to feel like asking too much. By the mid 2010s more and more of us found ourselves stuck in 'situationships' – these vague, almost-relationships with no clear boundaries or commitment.

Before long, situationships were not only normalised but *celebrated*. In 2023, 'situationship' was shortlisted as Oxford Dictionary's 'Word of the Year', and videos tagged with #situationship on TikTok had 2 billion views.[57] 'Situationships Are the Future of Dating. That's Not a Bad Thing', *Time* declared in 2023. In the piece, a 'clinical sexologist' explains: 'It may sound pessimistic, but all relationships end. When you focus more on how you feel now and less on where things are going, you give yourself space to take in all that your partner has to offer. You worry less and enjoy more.'[58] By the next Valentine's Day, Spangler, the company behind Sweethearts candy (similar to Love Hearts in the UK), even released Situationship Boxes, where each love heart came with a faded or jumbled message. 'The specially designed boxes contain blurry, misprinted candies that are as hard to read as Gen-Z relationships,' they announced. Each box was full of 'sweet, muddled nothings and literal mixed messages',[59] with the words 'Do you know how much you mean to me? Because I don't' on the front.[60] The first batch sold out in four minutes.[61]

Dating apps encourage situationships too. According to Tinder's 'Year in Swipe' report, 'owning the *situationship* as a valid relationship status' was the top dating trend among singles in 2022. 'Young singles were still down to play the field this year,' Tinder explained, 'but they opted for a high-quality roster where everyone was on the same page. More than a hookup, but not quite a traditional relationship, the "situationship", a casual – *yet* clearly defined – relationship came to rise…'[62] That year, the app also introduced a 'Relationship Goals' feature, prompting users to signal what they were looking for from six options: 'Long-term partner', 'Long-term, open to short', 'Short-term, open to long', 'Short-term fun', 'New friends' and 'Still figuring it out'. Users display the option that best describes them, and are prompted to confirm or change their choice every week.[63]

By 2024, over a third of Gen Z adults in the US said they had felt uncertain about their relationship status.[64] As many as 38% of Gen Z women and 34% of Gen Z men say they have been in a sexual or romantic relationship they were unsure how to define, compared to only 23% of Boomers.[65] Gen Z is also getting into relationships far later than previous generations did. In 2023, only 56% of Gen Z adults said they had had a boyfriend or girlfriend as a teenager, compared to 69% of Millennials, 76% of Gen Xers and 78% of Boomers.[66]

But throughout all of this, something strange has also been happening. A paradox has emerged. Despite hook-ups being less stigmatised, more accessible and more advertised than ever before, Gen Z is having *less* sex than previous generations. The CDC reports that about 30% of teenagers said in 2021 that they had had sex at some point, down from 54% in 1991.[67] And the biggest change happened after 2010: among young adults aged 18 to 29, the share reporting no sex in the past year doubled from about 12% to 24% by 2024.[68] And yet, in a 2022 survey, while about one in four Gen Z adults said they had never sex, 31% had taken part in 'sexting or cybersex'.[69]

There are of course many reasons Gen Z is having less sex. But one possibility is this: we are too busy watching strangers have it instead. By the time we were teenagers, girls my age had already grown up seeing women strangled, spat on and degraded. We learned all we knew about intimacy from what we had been raised on and become addicted to, often since we were pre-teens. Everything we knew about sex came from porn.

PORN

Online porn has existed since the beginning of the internet, but it boomed in the 2010s. In 2013, Pornhub, one of the world's largest porn sites, received over 14 billion visits; by 2019, that number had tripled to 42 billion – an average of 115 million visits a day.[70] By 2021, the site was receiving around 130 million visits a day, ranking it among the top ten most visited websites in the world.[71]

Smartphones made watching porn easier than ever before. What once involved buying physical magazines and DVDs, or using a shared family computer, could now be found in a few seconds and completely hidden. Porn was suddenly accessible any time, anywhere.

And like social media platforms, porn sites are designed to be addictive. Girls are now learning about sex for the first time from sites like Pornhub, which use features like variable rewards, auto-play videos and subscription services to keep them watching.[72] Porn sites are also filled with ads for premium services, live streams and virtual reality experiences, with animations, GIFs, sounds and flashing buttons like slot machines.[73] This is the gamification of graphic porn. In fact, the porn industry pioneered many online monetisation methods including pop-up ads, subscription fees, free teaser content and upselling.[74]

And here algorithms do what they always do, dragging users towards extremes. Today porn sites use data mining to track users, categorise them and provide endless, personalised videos, even sharing their viewing habits with third parties for targeted ads.[75] Porn videos that are violent and extreme can potentially come with 'See more like this' suggestions, or be 'Recommended For You'. And so fetishes and fantasies that would have been considered obscene a decade ago have become mindless entertainment. 'Now it is barely taboo to watch children being abused, and that is linked to porn,' an expert in child protection told *The Guardian* in 2025. 'Look on a mainstream porn site and you'll immediately see titles like '"Auntie takes the boys' virginity" or "Stepdad and stepdaughter". When I started working 30 years ago, that was really out-there outrageous, pervy and wrong. Now it's seen as a laugh.'[76]

Much of this content depicts real assault and abuse too. In 2020, the *New York Times* revealed that Pornhub was hosting videos featuring the rape and abuse of underage girls and sex trafficking victims.[77] Within days, the site removed around 10 million videos uploaded by unverified users – more than 60% of its website. According to leaked internal documents from Pornhub, employees had been aware of the abuse for years. 'There is A LOT of very, very obvious and disturbing CSAM [child sexual abuse material] here,' one wrote. Another messaged a colleague: 'I hope I never get in trouble for having those vids on my computer LOOOOL'. Another internal memo indicated that videos of apparent child sexual abuse had been seen 684 million times before being deleted.[78]

But removing unverified videos has far from solved the problem. A 2021 study found that one in eight porn titles shown to first-time users on the first page of mainstream sites describe sexual violence. Incest is the most common type, with titles often referencing immediate family members like mother, father, sister, son or daughter, now even more than stepfamily relationships. Across the entire sample, the most frequently used word in titles was 'teen'.[79]

Porn today is not only more extreme, it is also being watched at an earlier age than ever before. By 2022, the average age of first exposure in the US was 12. About 73% of teens surveyed said they had watched porn; for over half this was before they turned 13, and 15% had seen it before they turned 11. Roughly 30% admitted to watching porn while in school, often on school-owned devices. And about the same number of boys and girls had seen it: 75% of teen boys and 70% of teen girls.[80] In the UK, it's a similar story: in 2023, it was reported that a quarter of 16- to 21-year-olds had first seen porn while in primary school, and over half had seen it by the age of 13.[81]

Worse, on one Reddit thread, hundreds of Gen Zers compare the ages they first discovered porn and how it happened; some were as young as six.[82] To put this in perspective: the average Gen Z adult does not go on their first date until about 16[83] – which, for some, could be after a decade of watching porn.

Many children stumble across porn accidentally, too. By 2022, around 58% of children in the US said they had found it accidentally, and 63% of those said they had been exposed in the past week.[84] In one UK survey, 38% of 16- to 21-year-olds said they had found it by accident.[85] Many in my generation, for example, were first exposed to explicit content through the website Omegle (whose tag line was 'Talk to Strangers!'), which connected us with random people across the world, either by message or video call. Pre-teen girls would spend sleepovers connecting with men who were naked on video, touching themselves and trying to teach them about sex.

Others found violent, hardcore porn. 'I was ten years old when I watched porn for the first time,' one 16-year-old-girl confessed in a viral essay in 2023. 'I found myself on Pornhub … I saw simulated incest, bestiality, extreme bondage, sex with unconscious women, gangbangs, sadomasochism, and unthinkable physical violence. The porn children view today makes Playboy look like an American Girl doll catalog.'[86] Among 18- to 21-year-olds in the UK, 79% said that as children, they watched porn involving sexual violence.⁸⁷ Among 16- to 21-year-olds, 47% now believe that girls 'expect' sex to involve physical aggression like airway restriction or slapping, and 42% believe most girls 'enjoy' acts of sexual aggression.⁸⁸ According to the BBC, the Children's Commissioner for England heard from one 12-year-old girl who said her boyfriend had 'strangled' her during their first kiss; he had seen it in porn and 'thought it normal'.⁸⁹

More and more women are watching porn too. Searches for 'porn for women' rose by 1,400% in 2017 alone, and by 2019 nearly three in every ten Pornhub visitors were female.⁹⁰ But there is a generational gap: 35% of British women under 30 watch porn today, compared to only 2% of those over 60.⁹¹ According to Dr Laurie Betito, director of the Pornhub Sexual Wellness Centre, this is female empowerment: '2017 seems to have been the year where women have come forward to express their desires more openly,' she said. 'From the "Me too" movement to prominent females the likes of Hillary Clinton and Nikki Haley on the world stage, women are feeling more empowered and they have found their voice. This is a sign of things to come.'⁹²

But young women aren't making an empowered choice to watch porn. They often can't escape it. Even if we never visit a site like Pornhub, sex is all over social media, and part of our everyday entertainment.

Miley Cyrus's 2013 MTV Video Music Awards (VMA) performance is a good example of how far things have gone. I was 14 when I watched the former Disney actress, known for playing Hannah Montana, walk out onstage wearing a teddy bear outfit, before stripping down to a nude latex bikini, simulating sex with a foam finger and twerking against married singer Robin Thicke. Her performance, watched by around 10 million people, was called 'crass', 'degrading'⁹³ and 'a trainwreck'; critics described the audience as reacting with 'a mix of confusion, dismay and horror in a cocktail of embarrassment'.⁹⁴ At the time, Miley said she wanted 'to make history'.⁹⁵ And she did.

Today, though, what happened at the 2013 VMAs seems tame. The 2010s was the era of sex-positive feminism, where female empowerment seemed to mean endlessly pushing for more sexual freedom, exploration and expression. The more a celebrity objectified herself, the more she was seen as liberated. The more a show pushed boundaries, the more it was celebrated for breaking taboos and fighting stigma. It felt as though there were no limits. And so what once seemed shocking soon became boring. In a 2025 interview with the *New York Times*, Miley herself recognised that what she did on stage would be seen as mild now. 'In 2013, maybe it felt really shocking,' she said, 'Now it seems very soft if you look at culture today.'⁹⁶

By 2020, the song 'WAP' ('Wet Ass Pussy') by Cardi B and Megan Thee Stallion – with lyrics including 'There's some whores in this house' and 'Spit in my mouth' – was declared a feminist anthem and danced to by pre-teens on TikTok. Wholesome tween shows like *Hannah Montana* were traded for darker, sexually explicit shows like *Euphoria*, featuring high-school students' adventures with webcamming and humiliation kinks, and Netflix's *Sex Education*, another high-school show which covers everything from anal sex to blow jobs to foot fetishes (a show one reviewer said 'should be required viewing for teenagers').⁹⁷

Social media has also become pornified. Instagram evolved throughout the 2010s, from a place to share candid pictures with friends and family to a platform for 'thirst traps', as girls posed more provocatively and selfies became more revealing. Soon we seemed to care more about likes and attention from strangers than from people we actually knew. Influencers, competing in a crowded market, were also increasingly sexualising themselves for our attention. Beauty trends escalated too: Instagram Face was eventually described as 'porn face' as female features became so exaggerated young women began to resemble blow-up dolls.[98] Even content that seemed innocent – cooking videos, fitness advice, TikTok dance trends – became sexualised for clicks.

Soon actual porn could be found on these apps. By 2022, Twitter was the *main* platform exposing young people in the UK to porn, with 41% saying they accessed it there, followed by dedicated porn sites (37%), Instagram (33%), Snapchat (32%) and search engines (30%).[99] In another UK survey, over half of students surveyed aged 14 to 15 said they had seen sexually explicit or violent content online that was inappropriate for their age; 50% said this 'always or usually' pops up on social media without them searching for it.[100]

In 2023, for example, the *Wall Street Journal* found that Instagram was pushing 'overtly sexual adult videos' to young users. Journalists created test accounts that could belong to children – following young gymnasts, cheerleaders and influencers – and were soon served Instagram ads for adult live stream platforms, cybersex chatbots and Disney.[101] And this is not just happening on Instagram: TikTok's algorithm serves sex videos to minors and promotes OnlyFans, while Twitch is accused of exposing children to explicit live streams, with half-naked influencers often asking fans for donations.[102]

Now these platforms even advertise AI sex bots. Replika, the chatbot promising emotional support for socially anxious people, also runs ads promising 'spice selfies' and 'role-play & flirting'.[103] In 2023, NBC News published 'Ads for AI sex workers are flooding

Instagram and TikTok', warning readers that 'a new kind of sexualized content has lately been getting through their moderation systems: ads for scantily clad and dirty-talking chatbots.' Some of these ads even featured children's TV characters like SpongeBob and the Cookie Monster.[104]

But all of this exposure didn't simply desensitise women my age to sex. It also completely normalised our own commodification. As we watched porn like never before, we were learning to pornify ourselves. And as we grew up, the pressure only got worse.

'I Slept With 100 Men in One Day' is the title of the 2024 YouTube documentary I'm watching. Within months of its release, it has almost 10 million views.

The film follows 23-year-old porn star Lily Phillips as she prepares for her big day. She seems excited; this is her fantasy. She makes a few concerning comments – about being 'just good for one thing' and worrying about the 'poor bastard' who will marry her – but mostly she seems upbeat.

After the event the interviewer asks her how she feels. 'It's not for the weak girls, if I'm honest. It was hard,' she admits, fighting back tears. 'I don't know if I'd recommend it. I think if you're a different type of girl. It's very like... it's kind of like being a prostitute in the sense of like... it's just a different... feeling.'

'It's not like just having sex with someone?'

'Yeah, yeah. Just one in, one out, like it feels... intense.' Her voice cracks.

'Like more intense than you thought it might?'

She starts crying. 'Definitely,' she manages to say, bringing her hands up to her face. 'Sorry ... one minute,' she mumbles, walking away. She can be heard sobbing from the other room.

In the next shot, Lily is smiling again. 'But it was good,' she insists. She apologises for getting upset, explaining that she 'felt sorry' for the men, who she worries might not have enjoyed themselves. She tries to describe the experience again. 'Sometimes feeling so like robotic ... I've got like a routine ... sometimes you'd just disassociate and be like, you know, like, it's not like normal sex at all.'[105]

And yet a few days later, Lily announces an even more extreme challenge. 'Last week I did 101 guys, now this was just the warm-up,' she says, 'because in February I'm going to be the first person ever to reach four digits of guys all in one day. Yes, 1,000 guys.'[106]

But before Lily reached this goal in 2025, another young woman beat her to it.[107] That year, 25-year-old OnlyFans star Bonnie Blue announced that she had slept with 1,057 men in one day. 'Over 1,000 men in a day!' she celebrated on Instagram, to more than 900,000 followers. 'Thank you to all the barely legal, barely breathing and the husbands.'[108]

I can think of only one place to begin.

OnlyFans launched in 2016, letting users charge fans a monthly fee for exclusive content. Although the platform was originally meant for different kinds of online creators, it was soon dominated by porn. And it proved especially popular among young women, who sold nudes and explicit videos to paying subscribers.

During the pandemic, OnlyFans blew up. The platform grew from around 20 million users before lockdowns to more than 120 million in 2020. That year alone, fans spent over $2 billion on the platform, a sevenfold increase from the year before.[109]

While the pandemic drove demand, attitudes were also changing. Celebrities and influencers, for example, helped to normalise

OnlyFans, framing it as female empowerment. In 2020, when Beyoncé rapped the line 'She might start an OnlyFans' in a remix of Megan Thee Stallion's song 'Savage', the platform saw a 15% increase in traffic within 24 hours.[110] Former Disney star Bella Thorne also joined in 2020, making £750,000 on her first day and £1.5 million within a week.[111] 'OnlyFans is the first platform where I can fully control my image without censorship, without judgement, and without being bullied online for being me,' Bella said.[112] In another interview she explained that 'OnlyFans could change your life – if you want it to, of course.'[113]

Other celebrities promoted self-commodification too. In 2021, Demi Lovato, another former Disney actress, posted a picture to her Instagram Story that read: 'Be a slut. Show your body. Get naked. Have all the safe, different, consensual sex you want. Be Kinky. Masturbate. Make/watch porn. Make money.'[114] Meanwhile, Tana Mongeau, who has more than 16 million followers across Instagram, TikTok and X, often shares links to her own OnlyFans page. She also shows off how much money she has made, including posting a picture of her 'CONGRATULATIONS TOP EARNER $3,000,000' trophy on Instagram and Twitter.[115] In one post, Tana poses in a bikini next to a row of shopping bags, a PS5, designer handbags and a MacBook, captioned: 'me with everything ur dad bought me on onlyfans'.[116] She even encourages her followers to join in: 'if ur seeing this – this is a sign to start an onlyfans & make that bread ;)' (12,000 likes).[117]

But Tana is aware of the age, and vulnerability, of her audience. 'I have a young following and it's definitely primarily female,' she told *Life & Style* magazine in 2020. 'I always want to empower those young girls to do whatever they want with their bodies and to make their decisions and not let anyone take that away from them, especially men.'[118]

Even prostitution is now celebrated as an empowering decision. Today, 'sex workers' on TikTok glamorise their lifestyle to girls, filming luxurious days in their lives and giving them helpful tips. They film videos like 'How I Made $6,000 in 3 hours',[119] along with tours of mansions they bought with OnlyFans money. In one TikTok, for example, a young woman films herself counting out a stack of cash: 'I had two clients last night and this is how much money I made doing FS [full service],' she says, flicking through the notes. 'Gonna start with the hundreds and get through the fifties.' She explains that she gave one client the 'works' – everything but 'back door' – before fast-forwarding through footage of her counting ('my thumbs are getting sore'). The cash amounts to roughly $9,500.[120] The video has more than 5.4 million views.

Sex work is not only sold as empowering for women, but good for our mental health. 'I'm an Autistic ADHDer and I was a full service sex worker for two years. here [are] some of my experiences as to how it suited my neurodivergence,' one influencer writes in an Instagram post with more than 10,300 likes. Her reasons include one-on-one interaction, choosing her own hours, predictable routines, and the fact that 'the environments always had low lighting aka was sensory friendly'. She describes dating as 'scary', whereas 'sex work was predictable because every interaction had guidelines and rules', followed by hashtags including #AutisticPride and #SexWorkIsRealWork.[121]

While I was a student, universities across the UK also began battling sex work stigma. University College London stated their dedication to 'challenging the stigma attached to sex work', supporting students' rights to participate in webcam services, sugar relationships, porn and prostitution.[122] The University of Leicester published a 'student sex worker toolkit', reminding students that stripping, being a sugar baby, selling sexual services in a brothel, using 'sex chat phone lines' and selling their underwear online are all legal.[123] In 2021 Durham University even offered a 'training opportunity' for 'students involved in the adult sex industry'.[124]

Even schoolgirls are trying to join in now. According to the BBC, under-18s in the UK are using fake IDs to create OnlyFans accounts; in 2021, the police reported that a 14-year-old girl had even used her grandmother's passport to register. Schools also raised concerns, citing cases including a 16-year-old girl who allegedly bragged to her careers adviser about her earnings and flaunted her spending on Instagram.[125] Another BBC analysis suggested that up to a third of X profiles advertising 'nudes4sale' could belong to underage users.[126]

Girls can also be turned into porn without their consent. The term 'deepfake' originated on Reddit in 2017, when a user named 'deepfakes' started sharing videos that superimposed celebrities' faces onto porn stars' bodies.[127] Since then, AI has rapidly advanced, making the technology far more realistic, and far easier to use.

Today, anyone with a smartphone can download an app that generates deepfakes. According to the *New York Times*, all it takes is one clear photo of a face to generate a 60-second sex video in less than 30 minutes. These videos can then be uploaded to porn sites or deepfake platforms, where they are often 'graphic and sometimes sadistic, depicting women tied up as they are raped or urinated on.' As the *New York Times* explained: 'One site offers categories including "rape" (472 items), "crying" (655) and "degradation" (822).'[128]

Between 2019 and 2023, the total number of deepfake videos online increased by 550%, according to a global analysis. The same study found that in 2023, 98% of all deepfakes were pornographic, and 99% featured women and girls. The top ten websites dedicated to deepfake pornography alone received more than 303 million views, attracting almost 35 million visitors per month.[129] In the UK specifically, 99.6% of AI-generated child sex abuse images involve girls, often between the ages of seven and 13.[130]

And deepfakes aren't just hidden on the dark web. A 2024 *Wired* investigation found at least 50 deepfake bots on the instant messaging platform Telegram, promising to 'remove clothes' and generate images of women in sex positions. Together these bots had more than 4 million monthly users.[131] Deepfakes have even been sold on marketplaces like Etsy, the website where I used to buy crafts as a pre-teen girl...[132]

By the end of the decade, sex and dating had become deeply confusing for young women. Many of us felt as though we were constantly competing for attention with porn stars, sexualised influencers, and even AI-generated women who would never say no. By the late 2010s, it felt completely unrealistic to expect a boyfriend who wasn't raised on online porn, didn't follow half-naked influencers on Instagram, and wouldn't want you to send him nudes.

We were desperate for guidance. But while previous generations of young women might have turned to older friends and family, adult advice was becoming rapidly outdated. Our world was so new, it felt as though there was only one place we could find help.

We went online again.

DATING INFLUENCERS

By the late 2010s, a new type of influencer started appearing on my feeds. Already inundated with advice about improving my appearance and managing my mental health, I now had influencers here to help with my first romantic relationships. Some were dating coaches hosting conferences and retreats. Many were therapists warning about 'red flags' and analysing attachment styles. Others were ordinary people, sharing their dating tips and tricks.

But much like online mental health advice, relationship advice soon deteriorated. Teenage girls like me started learning about love for the first time from influencers incentivised to post oversimplified and often provocative takes, competing with one another for our attention.

TikTok therapists, for example, became more paranoid and cynical about dating. They started out warning us about narcissism and emotional abuse, educating about 'red flags' to watch out for in relationships. But soon, just as 'Put a finger down' challenges began to include vaguer and vaguer symptoms, basic romantic gestures became pathologised. He compliments you a lot? That could be 'love bombing', a form of manipulative abuse. (Other warning signs include too many gifts and trips).[133] He says 'I miss you' too soon? That's a red flag. He approaches you in public? That's predatory behaviour. And what we used to call love – being affected by your partner's feelings, putting their needs first, depending on one another – was increasingly labelled 'co-dependency' or 'anxious attachment'.

Now it seems like any strong feelings are a warning sign. 'Unpopular dating opinion: The intense chemistry you feel with someone you just met is a huge red flag,' one viral tweet puts it. 'Most likely, they are similar to an early caregiver that neglected you & your subconscious mind is attracted to them to try to fix an old wound.'[134] According to another viral Instagram post, 'You don't have a crush. You have attachment issues and someone's giving you attention.'[135] This sort of messaging is everywhere. By the summer of 2025, nearly 490 million videos had been tagged with 'red flag' on TikTok.[136]

Relationship advice has only become more confusing. A green flag according to one TikToker is now a major red flag according to another. Share your location with your partner? That's controlling and insecure. He doesn't want to share his location? He's probably cheating. Move in with a boyfriend before marriage? Your relationship is doomed. Move in after marriage? You're asking for trouble.

But influencers are not just teaching us to be fearful or risk-averse. We are also being taught contempt and resentment for the opposite sex. On one side is the 'manosphere': male influencers who often vilify women, encouraging viewers to avoid them entirely or use and discard them. One of the most notorious is Andrew Tate, a former kick-boxer who found global fame in the 2020s after clips of him went viral on TikTok. In one video, for example, Tate describes how he would react if a woman accused him of cheating: 'It's bang out the machete, boom in her face, then grip her up by the neck, "Shut up bitch"… you go fuck her. That's how it goes, you go slap, slap, grab, choke, shut up bitch, sex.'[137] Alongside his brother, Tate previously ran a webcam sex business in Romania and has long been accused of exploiting women. As of 2025, the brothers face 21 criminal charges in the UK including rape, actual bodily harm and human trafficking.[138]

Tate is of course an extreme example. Many influencers promoting masculinity give helpful advice to young men on relationships and responsibility. But as competition has grown, and algorithms have advanced, others have begun chasing clicks. One example is the podcast *FreshandFit*, which launched in 2020 promising 'the TRUTH to men on females, finances and fitness',[139] and has since gained around 1.6 million YouTube subscribers. In 2023 *whatever* followed, a podcast 'trying to make sense of the modern dating hellscape' by 'talking about modern dating, relationships, hookup culture and more!', and it now has than 4.5 million subscribers.[140] Today both podcasts seem to focus more on humiliating women than helping men, with popular episode titles including 'DELUSIONAL Girls Rate Themselves A 10 But Brian HUMBLES Them!', 'Why FEMINISM Made Women UNDATEABLE and Low Quality!', and 'Lonely Older Woman REALISED That Feminism BACKFIRED on Her!'[141]

But contempt also comes from the other side, where female influencers vilify all men. 'This is just a reminder for men,' one young woman says on TikTok as she applies her make-up, 'that scientists have now discovered a way for women to impregnate themselves using their own bone marrow, and the only child that can result from those pregnancies are female. So we no longer have any need for you, genetically or physically. So, you know, tread lightly.' The video has more than 8 million views, and 1.5 million likes.[142] Other women warn girls away from relationships: 'Men do not love you, okay? So stop thinking that they do. They tolerate you,' says Shera Seven, who has 815,000 subscribers on YouTube. 'They *lust* you. That's it.'[143]

Meanwhile, on *Call Her Daddy*, Alex Cooper teaches girls how to have as few needs as possible, reminds them not to ask about their relationship status, and gives them tips on how to cheat without getting caught. 'If your behaviour changes, *especially* if you're starting to act more needy, he is going to be terrified of you,' she says in an early episode titled 'Sex Toys & How to Not Catch Feelings'. She tells girls never to relax into a relationship, not even after marriage: 'They still hate you and they're still cheating on you, until they prove otherwise.'[144]

Both sides now promote emotional detachment as empowerment. Be an independent girlboss, girls are told; you can't trust men!

Be an alpha male, boys are told; you don't need women! 'These Modern Women Are Insane,' *whatever* declares to young men; 'We Don't Need Men' *Call Her Daddy* reminds young women.[145] Both encourage their audiences to be as cold and uncaring as possible.

Again, algorithms can amplify girls' worst fears. Imagine you are a teenage girl whose father walked out, and you believe all men are untrustworthy. Watch a few videos about infidelity, and soon your feed will be flooded with more 'red flags' to watch for and signs you will be cheated on someday. And because algorithms reward extreme content, the most hurt and cynical voices often get the most attention, building the biggest audiences. These voices will form your view of relationships before you have even tried to trust someone.

Even if young women are in healthy relationships, influencers often urge them to break up with their partners, because dramatic titles and thumbnails get clicks. Imagine being a young woman going through a rough patch with a first boyfriend and your feed is suddenly filled with TikToks saying things like '4 SIGNS YOUR RELATIONSHIP WON'T LAST', '3 BIG SIGNS THAT YOU WANT TO BREAK UP' and clickbait podcast thumbnails like 'if you get sick, there's a 624% chance he'll leave!' (1 million views) and 'why they will eventually cheat on you!' (1.9 million views).[146]

And this is where many young people learn about relationships now. By 2024, the hashtags #datingadvice and #relationshipadvice reached more than 16 billion views on TikTok alone.[147] That year, 46% of singles said they used TikTok for dating advice, and 25% said social media was their main source of relationship guidance.[148] Around one in three said they 'almost always' trust dating advice they see on TikTok, even though 73% think this content is influenced more by online trends than 'tried and tested principles'. Around 46% also admitted they have had relationship struggles after following social media advice, and for 23%, it had caused a break-up.[149]

The experts we turned to in our confusion have only left us more confused. We have more dating hacks, strategies and warnings than any generation before us. We are lucky, apparently, to be so educated, so emotionally intelligent about relationships. And yet here we are, needing podcasts to teach us how to love one another. We are flooded with advice on finding happiness and avoiding heartbreak, but we are hurting more than ever.

HURT

One indication that girls and young women are hurting today is the rise in relationship anxiety and attachment issues. More and more of us have started identifying with anxious or insecure attachment styles. 'America Is in Its Insecure-Attachment Era', *The Atlantic* announced in 2023, citing research by social psychologist Sara Konrath. After analysing nearly 100 studies on college students' attachment styles between 1988 and 2011, Konrath found 'disturbing results': a 15% drop in secure attachment, a 56% rise in dismissive attachment, and an almost 18% rise in anxious attachment. According to the article, these two styles are 'associated with lack of trust and self-isolation'.[150]

We can see this growing insecurity online too. The Reddit forum r/anxiousattachment now has 36,000 weekly visitors, and by 2024, the hashtag #attachmentstyle had almost a billion views on TikTok.[151] Here young women share anxieties about their relationships, mostly around social media, from activity statuses and read receipts to partners watching porn and liking pictures of half-naked influencers.[152]

Many are also anxious about situationships. According to the dating site eharmony, 82% of Gen Z say they have had their heart broken from a situationship.[153] And yet young women are also pessimistic about the possibility of anything lasting. According to the Survey Center on American Life, 57% of young women (compared to 44% of young men) believe that cheating in committed relationships is 'extremely' or 'very common' in America, even though there is little evidence that infidelity has increased.[154]

There are many reasons for our pessimism, but one might be the influence of porn. Watching porn has been associated with anxiety, depression, body dysmorphia and lower self-esteem.[155] Over time, its use has also been associated with lower relationship satisfaction and a higher likelihood of cheating.[156]

Some young women are beginning to open up about how online porn has hurt them. In 2021, singer Billie Eilish, then 19, said this about her addiction:

> I started watching porn when I was, like, 11 and I didn't understand why it was a bad thing. I thought that was how you learned to have sex. I was watching abusive porn, to be honest, when I was, like, 14. I think it really destroyed my brain and I feel incredibly devastated that I was exposed to so much porn …
>
> It got to the point where I couldn't watch anything else, unless it was violent I didn't think it was attractive. I was a virgin. I had never done anything so it led to problems where the first few times I had sex I was not saying no to things that were not good and it's because I thought that that was what I was

supposed to be attracted to. I'm so angry that porn is so loved and I'm so angry at myself for thinking that it was OK and… it's how so many people think they're supposed to learn…[157]

Even young women who don't watch porn can feel anxious about their partner watching it behind their backs. Some are afraid to leave the house, feeling paranoid every time their boyfriend is left alone.[158] As one 27-year-old woman posted to the Reddit forum r/relationship_advice:

> The thought of my boyfriend watching other women and jerking off to them makes me really anxious, sad and it literally makes me want to cry. Every time we cross this topic I get anxious, my heart starts to beat like crazy, my palms get sweaty and I just want to run away from the conversation. Sometimes I shut down and I find it hard to find words …

She then describes her fear that he might find porn stars more attractive, prefer their bodies, even imagine them in her place while they have sex. She tries to reassure herself, remembering that he said he sometimes watches women like her. After explaining how she feels, she asks:

> I know this sounds ridiculous. I know it's because of my bad self esteem. I know that [the] majority of people watch porn. But I can't help but wonder, how can I overcome this??? …
>
> It's absolute *torture* at times, and I'd do ANYTHING to be that cool girlfriend who's like 'I don't mind you watching porn, I don't care'. I feel so pathetic…

Her post was met with replies including: 'This is your problem OP and it's something you need to overcome', 'If you don't want to hear how pathetic you are, you shouldn't have shared this, because this is really pathetic', 'This sounds like a you problem, not a him problem' and, of course, 'You have an anxious attachment style'.[159]

Along with insecurity and paranoia, porn also seems to be making sex more dangerous. In 2020, a BBC survey of UK men aged 18 to 39 found that 71% had 'slapped, choked, gagged or spat on their partner during consensual sex'. Of those men, a third said they would not ask their partner for consent before, or during, these acts, and over half said they had been influenced by porn. One in five said porn had influenced them a 'great deal'.[160]

Pornifying themselves hurts girls too. 'Teen Girls' Sexy TikTok Videos Take a Mental Health Toll', reported the *Wall Street Journal* in 2022. 'I wanted to get famous on TikTok, and I learned that if you post stuff showing your body, people will start liking it,' one 18-year-old admitted. According to the report, as many as 60% of girls treated at one outpatient clinic for issues such as depression, anxiety and eating disorders had posted sexually inappropriate videos of themselves on TikTok.[161]

Then there is the danger this puts girls in. Predators are all over TikTok, Instagram and Snapchat, where algorithms can deliver them more underage content and steer them towards children's profiles.[162] Some even upload TikToks of underage girls to sites like Pornhub.[163] 'Meta has allowed Facebook and Instagram to become a marketplace for predators,' alleged a 2023 lawsuit against the company. In 2024, Senator Ted Cruz confronted Meta CEO Mark Zuckerberg about Instagram's failure to remove child sex abuse content. 'Mr Zuckerberg, what the hell were you thinking?' he asked, referencing an Instagram prompt warning users that they may be about to see images of child sex abuse, before asking if they want to 'see the results anyway'.[164]

According to internal Meta documents leaked that year, around 100,000 children are sexually harassed every day on Instagram and Facebook, with many receiving 'pictures of adult genitalia'. And yet when a Meta employee had asked, 'What specifically are we doing for child grooming (something I just heard about that is happening a lot on TikTok)?', the answer was 'Somewhere between zero and negligible.'[165]

Maybe it makes sense, then, that Gen Z is dating less and having less sex than previous generations. Maybe that isn't such a paradox after all. After flirting for the first time through screens, being bombarded with warnings about men and women, learning about sex from violent Pornhub videos and strangers on Instagram, and feeling insecure or controlling for caring about any of this, why would we risk romance? It seems much safer to be alone. Detachment feels like the only defence left.

Again, many of these fears and anxieties are normal. Every generation of girls has sometimes felt insecure in relationships, been confused by new sexual feelings, and craved safety and security.

But we were the first generation of girls to cope with all of this in a world where flirting meant Instagram DMs and Snapchat nudes. For us dating was swiping through people like they were items in a catalogue; the only way to be loved was to become a better object; and the most romantic gesture we could hope for was a 'Super Like' on Tinder. Many of us watched violent porn before we even had a first kiss, before even holding hands with a boy. We saw intimacy not as something to be clumsily stumbled through but a performance to be delivered, 'content' to be copied. And for every flicker of fear, insecurity or distrust we felt, there were always apps, algorithms and influencers to amplify it.

To the girls struggling with dating and relationships today, take it from my generation: you are not broken for feeling this way. Yes, girls have always had to deal with hurt and heartbreak, but not dick pics, deepfakes, read receipts, Snapchat scores or a sex education from Pornhub. Of course girls growing up with all of this are struggling to trust, to feel confident and secure, to even believe that love still exists.

Many young women my age are now realising how hard this all was. How hard it was to be 12 and insecure and feel like the choice was between objectifying ourselves online and being invisible. How hard it was to keep comparing ourselves to the influencers followed by the boys we liked, feeling as if we had to compete somehow. How hard it was to measure our developing bodies against those of porn stars. How unfair it was that we punished ourselves for wanting commitment, for feeling insecure, for being needy. And that instead of asking our friends and families for advice, we listened to influencers and strangers on forums who taught us to be *more* detached, uncaring, unfazed, until we believed that the more we felt, the more broken we were.

But now we are starting to see the truth. That these platforms promising to make falling in love easier are actually turning us into insatiable consumers, shopping for the perfect person, seeing other people as disposable, advertising ourselves like objects too. And behind the push to objectify ourselves, to be more sexually open, to hook up and move on from each other, are powerful profit motives. Billion-dollar industries depend on us being lonely, detached consumers. Liberation is the marketing pitch, and we are the products.

So where do we look for meaning and happiness in our lives now? As young women lose faith in love, many of us are turning inwards, trying to find fulfilment in ourselves. We are chasing the vision of the strong, independent woman we grew up with – a woman who is ambitious, emotionally detached, and, apparently, 'empowered'.

'Empowered'

'What about my work?'
Cinderella[1]

MEANING

'HOW TO COMMAND THE UNIVERSE TO GET WHAT YOU WANT' reads the caption of a TikTok with more than 370,000 views. 'Did you know you can tell the universe what you wanna see and it will appear?' a young woman says confidently to the camera. 'All it takes is a simple command ... and that command is "UNIVERSE... SHOW ME".'

She gives some examples: 'Universe, show me how I get to 100k on TikTok. Universe, show me how I get my dream body ... Universe, show me how fucking good it gets ... Universe, show me how I can make 10k a month!'

For those uncomfortable with the word 'universe', she offers an alternative: 'Subconscious mind, show me...', explaining that 'Your subconscious mind is so powerful, it's linked to my g the universe and it will deliver you the answers ... I think it's really important to kind of stamp your authority with the universe. You are co-creating in this bitch.'

I scroll down, where young women have commented affirmations of their own: 'Universe show me my luxury dream life and a new car', 'Universe show me how to just be paid by just existing and given princess treatment', and 'Universe!!! Show me my multiple streams of income'![2]

Under hashtags like #affirmations and #manifestation, there are millions of posts like this one – girls getting on their knees for a better body, putting their palms together for more followers, manifesting a text back from their crush. In another video with 1.7 million views, two young women sit together, candles lit, eyes closed, palms touching, chanting together: 'I am healthy, I am wealthy, I am rich, I am that bitch, I am gonna go get that bag, and I am not gonna take your shit. I am protected, well respected, I'm a queen, I'm a dream, I do what I wanna do, and I'm who I wanna be, cause I am me.'[3] The same word appears in the comments section, over and over: 'AMEN'.

As I watch these young women chant their affirmations, whisper to the universe, and speak in the language of salvation and higher powers, I wonder what it is we are drawn to. What are we searching for? And more importantly, what did we lose in the first place?

Growing up, I never thought much about religion or met many people who did. By the time I was old enough to notice, New Atheism – the 2000s movement of bestselling authors arguing against religion – had been and gone. Rejecting religion felt like common sense. Girls I grew up with saw it not only as backward and archaic but also cringeworthy, embarrassing, belonging to another world entirely. We thought of Christianity as outdated and oppressive, if we thought of it at all.

Throughout the 2010s, religious faith fell across the Anglosphere. Between 2009 and 2019, the number of Americans identifying as Christian dropped from 77% to 65%, while those identifying as atheist, agnostic or 'nothing in particular' rose from 17% to 26%.[4]

'EMPOWERED'

Gen Z is the least religious generation in history. As of 2022, around 34% of Gen Z in America identify as religiously unaffiliated. And while in the past women have been consistently more religious than men, especially Christian women, that is no longer the case. For the first time in history, young women in the US are now less religious than young men, and less likely to attend church. In 2023, 39% of Gen Z women identified as religiously unaffiliated, compared to 34% of Gen Z men.[5] And only 27% of college-educated young women said they attended church regularly, compared to 32% of college-educated men.[6]

There is also a generational divide among women. While Gen Z men are only somewhat more likely to be unaffiliated than Boomer men, among women the gap is two and a half times bigger. Around 39% of Gen Z women in the US say they have no religion, compared to only 14% of Boomer women.[7]

But young women do believe in something. In the UK, Gen Z is more likely than any other generation to describe themselves as 'spiritual'. In 2023, one in three Gen Z adults in the US said they believed in a higher power, up from one in four in 2021.[8] As *VICE* put it, members of Gen Z are 'deconstructing religion and finding faith' by 'taste-testing' and 'sampling ... a wide variety of religions and spiritual practices'.[9]

New Age spirituality is one of the most popular replacements for religion. Over the past decade, young women have increasingly turned to horoscopes, healing crystals, witchcraft and other spiritual practices. By 2016, for example, 42% of British women said there was 'definitely or maybe' truth in astrology, compared to only 19% of men.[10] 'Astrology has become a defining trend of the 2010s,' *VICE* reported in 2019, while that same year the *New Yorker* described the resurgence of 'Astrology in the Age of

Uncertainty'.[11] In 2025, an astrology influencer named Bella, who has over 1 million followers on TikTok, also told *The Times* that she believes her Gen Z fans turn to astrology for a 'sense of agency' and 'self-empowerment' in a confusing world.[12]

By 2031, global spending on astrology products is predicted to reach $22.8 billion, up from $12.8 billion in 2021.[13] One astrology app, Co-Star, which uses horoscopes to help 'Understand why you do what you do' and 'See if you're compatible' with others, launched in 2017 and reached 30 million users by 2023.[14] About a quarter of women in the US aged 18 to 25 are thought to have downloaded it.[15]

Witchcraft also made a comeback in the 2010s, becoming one of the fastest-growing spiritual paths in America.[16] By 2021 the hashtag #WitchTok reportedly had around 20.7 billion views, far more than #Kardashian and #LoveIsland.[17] On WitchTok young women share 'Signs you're a natural born witch' – ('You're extremely sensitive…' and 'You hate large crowds') – along with love spells, tarot cards readings and witchy morning routines.[18]

For some young women, witchcraft is a way to cope with anxiety and feel more in control of their lives. Others see it as a feminist alternative to organised religion. (The subreddit WitchesVsPatriarchy has more than 796,000 members[19]). 'Witchcraft, paganism, it all gives you a bit of control back, you can live your life how you want,' one TikTok witch told the BBC in 2022. 'It gives people a real sense of individuality and the power to do things themselves.'[20]

By the early 2020s, manifestation – the belief that you can make your desires reality through thought alone – had also become mainstream. Manifesting can mean anything from chanting affirmations, to visualising your goals, to giving direct commands to the universe. In the first few months of the pandemic alone, Google

'EMPOWERED'

searches for 'manifesting' rose by 600%.[21] Manifestation influencers also appeared, selling courses on how to manifest our dream life, partner and bank balance (like the 'MONEY MANIFESTING COACH DIPLOMA' or the 'Manifest A Specific Person Workshop' for $777[22]). In 2024, 'manifest' was Cambridge Dictionary's word of the year.[23]

But New Age spirituality wasn't the only faith for young women. Alongside astrology and healing crystals emerged a wider therapeutic culture, one that writers like Philip Rieff and Christopher Lasch had seen coming. In the late 1970s Lasch had argued that contemporary culture was no longer religious but therapeutic, with an emphasis not on personal salvation but self-actualisation and emotional security. He observed that as modern life became more chaotic and confusing, people were turning inwards, narrowing their focus to themselves and finding refuge in therapeutic language.[24]

Social media entrenched this kind of thinking. Girls like me grew up watching mental health influencers for entertainment, being inundated with ads for therapy and medication, and learning psychological and medical language to describe ourselves. We began to see ourselves and the world around us through a therapeutic lens. This is how many of us started to make sense of love, loss, pain, even life itself – through trauma, symptoms and diagnoses.

Now we mimic religion all the time. We don't pray at night; we repeat *positive affirmations*. We don't confess; we *trauma dump*. We don't seek salvation; we go on *healing journeys*. We don't resist temptation from the devil; we *reframe intrusive thoughts*. We don't exorcise evil spirits; we *release trauma*. And of course we don't speak to God; we give a 'specific request to the universe' that 'has a greater plan' for us.[25] In one popular TikTok, for example, a young woman says to the camera: 'Every single night before you go to sleep, surrender and hand over any type of worry or concern and state this affirmation: "While I sleep, unseen forces are working on my behalf to turn everything out in my highest favour." You can keep mentally repeating this to yourself as you're falling asleep, and it will bring you so much peace. Plus, it's true.'[26]

Companies capitalise on this new religion. Meditation and affirmation apps replace prayer, charging £399.99 to be 'Calm for Life'.[27] Therapy apps act as confessionals: girls are told to 'Get it off your chest with BetterHelp'! and reminded by sponsored influencers that they can message a therapist any time, with 'no judgement, no shame'.[28] Now these platforms even try to answer the biggest questions in life. In one BetterHelp ad called 'Existential', a young woman wonders why she feels so alone, who she really is and what she wants from life, asking, 'I mean, what am I doing here?' before the BetterHelp logo appears.[29]

But while this therapeutic culture mimics prayer, confession, and even answers existential questions, one thing is missing. Who is God?

In this religion, *we* are the gods. Now, in the 2020s, the mental health industry exists to serve us. AI therapy bots are 'all about you and your mental health journey', and 'there to give you their full attention whenever and wherever'.[30] Our online therapist is available 24/7, ready to meet our every need, any time we have one. We are the divine; we are the deity. We have become the omniscient, omnipotent and omnibenevolent beings in our lives. Loving ourselves is the ultimate commandment, and our positive affirmations are about how powerful *we* are. (It's telling that one of the most popular therapeutic mantras at the moment is 'is this serving me'?)[31]

But therapy culture could only give us control over ourselves. Some young women began to feel that they couldn't heal when the world was so broken, couldn't manifest a better life with injustice in the way. No matter how many affirmations they repeated, commands they gave the universe or therapy sessions they scheduled, they still felt powerless. They wanted more than a personal transformation. By the late 2010s, as I started university, social justice activism began to feel like a new form of faith.

In the early 2010s, progressive politics began to evolve. It started to transform from a set of left-leaning opinions into a more totalising world view, almost a religion. At its core was the belief that society is divided into distinct identity groups defined by characteristics like race, gender and sexuality, each arranged in a hierarchy of privilege and oppression. At the top were straight white men; at the bottom, marginalised groups, from racial minorities to transgender people, held back by systemic and often invisible forces. There was also a conviction that many of the core structures in our lives, from biological sex to the nuclear family, were nothing but social constructs. These constructs were oppressive and outdated, and liberation lay in breaking free from them.

Not all young people were activists, of course. For teenage girls like me at the time, these ideas were just *there* – on our social media feeds, across mainstream media, treated as common sense by university lecturers. This became another lens through which we made sense of the world and ourselves. Our problems – our anxiety, stress, body image issues – started to seem less personal. They became symptoms of something bigger: patriarchy, late capitalism, white supremacy or some other form of oppression.

For girls raised without religion, these theories gave us what we had never had before: a feeling of belonging, a sense of purpose. We finally had an authority to follow, a concept of right and wrong.

Social justice culture taught us how to be a good person: it was no longer about what we did or how we treated people, but what we believed. And, of course, what we posted.

The parallels with religion grew. 'Male privilege' and 'white privilege' started sounding like original sins, something you were born with and could never atone for. Disagreeing with any part of the progressive orthodoxy felt like a moral failing. Heretics were shamed online, fired from jobs and failed on assignments.[32] There were rituals to follow too: posting the right slogans, using the right language, performing the right public gestures. 'In the U.S., the nonreligious are younger and more liberal than the population as a whole,' Helen Lewis wrote for *The Atlantic* in 2022. 'For some activists, politics has usurped the role that religion used to play as a source of meaning and purpose in our lives, and a way to find a community… Perhaps, then, it isn't a coincidence that they are also the group most likely to be involved in high-profile social-justice blowups, particularly the type found on college campuses. They've substituted one religion for another.'[33]

Gen Z was soon the most progressive generation on record. Across almost every political measure, Americans aged between 13 and 24 were consistently more progressive than Gen X (aged 41 to 56) and Millennials (aged 25 to 40) by 2021.[34]

Social justice activism also seemed to have a unique appeal among young women. One reason is that, globally, young women now far outnumber men at university, and are more likely to study the social sciences and humanities, where professors tend to lean further left than those in STEM fields.[35] Young men, on the other hand, are abandoning higher education in droves.[36]

Personality differences may be another reason. Political correctness is best predicted by the trait of agreeableness, which women consistently score higher in than men, and likewise conformity.[37] This desire to do the right thing, to fit in and belong, also became another form of relational aggression, specifically reputation destruction. As more and more beliefs became unacceptable, girls began to call each other out online for having outdated or offensive opinions.

Throughout the 2010s, the political gap between young men and women widened. For the previous two decades, the political profiles of young men and women had stayed fairly stable,[38] before women began to lurch dramatically to the left. In the US, 44% of young women identified as liberal in 2021, compared to 25% of young men, up from 30% of women and 27% of men a decade earlier – the biggest gender gap recorded in 24 years of polling.[39] By 2023, 46% of white Gen Z women identified as liberal, compared to only 28% of white Gen Z men.[40] In the US, young women are also more likely than young men to support social movements around Black Lives Matter, climate activism, #MeToo, reproductive rights and gun violence prevention.[41]

Gen Z women aren't only more progressive than Gen Z men, though. They also have swung further left than any previous generation of women. According to a 2024 Gallup poll, Gen Z women aged 18 to 29 have taken a 'sharp left turn', and are much more liberal than older women were at the same age, particularly on issues like abortion, race relations, gun control and climate change.[42]

But collective action isn't our only source of meaning and belonging. Throughout the 2010s another religion began to rise, one promising salvation not through activism but through achievement, success and self-optimisation. To find meaning, to finally feel fulfilled, all we had to do was work harder.

GIRLS®

HUSTLE

'Study With Me || 14 Hour Study Day' is the title of the YouTube video, uploaded in 2017. I watch as 16-year-old Ruby Granger documents every second of her day: '06.30 Wake up', '06.40– 06.50 Planning', '06.50–07.15 Practising Bond Angles', '07.15–07.55 Chemistry Paper'; '07.55–8.20 English Research', '8.20–8.45 Philosophy Review & Essay', '08.45–08.55 Breakfast', '08.55–09.20 Finishing Essay', '09.20–09.40 Sorting Bookshelf', '09.40–11.20 Writing Philosophy Notes', '11.20–11.40 Aristotle Quizlet', '11.40–12.00 English Review', '12.00–12.20 Lunch', '12.20–13.20 Spanish Homework', '13.20–14.00 Philosophy Essay', '14.00–14.15 Spanish Listening', '14.15–15.14 English Essay', '16.30–16.50 Review tricky philosophy quotes', '16.50–17.40 English Poster', '17.40–17.55 Watch Philosophy Videos', '18.00–19.00 Quizlet', '19.15–19.40 Mopping', '19.40–20.20 English Research', and finally, '20.20–20.50 Ethics Essay'. The video has over 3 million views.[43]

I remember discovering StudyTube videos in my early teens. These were teenagers who were obsessed with studying and productivity, which, at the time, felt healthier than the Kardashian contouring videos and Facetune tutorials I was watching. At first StudyTubers shared helpful tips, filmed stationery hauls and gave book recommendations. But like beauty and mental health influencers, they soon began competing for attention. Before long I was being served daily routines of other 13-year-olds waking up at 3 a.m. to study before school, filming 16-hour study marathons without any breaks and reacting to their grades in real time. In another video, 'Live Reaction to my First Essay MARK at UNIVERSITY (I cried...)', Ruby breaks down after getting a 2.2 on her first assignment. 'I did so badly,' she says. She starts to sob, barely getting the words out. 'You know when it just feels like a *complete* waste of time ... I got a mid to high 2.2 ... I've got tears all over my computer. I feel really stupid...'[44]

Girls began competing over who was most productive – who woke up earliest, studied longest, got the best grades. I remember coming home from school during exams and scrolling through other girls' revision routines, all of us trying to outdo one another. By my twenties this had turned into young women documenting every career achievement online: evenings were spent swiping through Instagram posts, Snapchat Stories and LinkedIn updates of women working later and hustling harder. We weren't only comparing our faces, bodies and lifestyles any more, but also our productivity, our ambitions, our achievements. Our feeds filled with CEOs and entrepreneurs too, the most successful people in the world.

Work became our identity, our purpose, all-consuming. We worked to win, to get ahead, to prove ourselves. And it became an end in itself, the path to female empowerment. Soon we were being encouraged to find self-worth and fulfilment through our careers. For teenage girls like me, our goal in life was to become a girlboss.

In the early 2010s, Sheryl Sandberg became the face of corporate feminism. Previously vice president of global online sales and operations at Google, Sandberg joined Facebook as chief operating officer (COO) in 2008, where she scaled its advertising business and helped transform the company into one of the most profitable in the world.[45] Between 2008 and 2021, Sandberg contributed to growing Meta's revenue from $272 million to nearly $118 billion, a more than 43,000% increase.[46] In 2013 she published

Lean In, encouraging women to be more assertive in their careers and become confident leaders. The book sold more than 4 million copies in five years.[47]

In 2014, Sophia Amoruso, CEO of the fast fashion brand Nasty Gal, also published her bestselling memoir *#Girlboss*.[48] 'Girlboss feminism' came to define the 2010s; female empowerment was tied to corporate success, and women were told they could balance both a family and a career. As a teenage girl this was the only form of feminism I knew: Instagram infographics and Snapchat Stories about working harder than men, smashing the glass ceiling and closing the gender pay gap. Mostly, though, I remember feminism from products: THE FUTURE IS FEMALE crop tops, #GIRLBOSS coffee mugs, SHE-E-O notepads.

Throughout the 2010s, too, corporations helped women remove any obstacles getting in the way of their goals. Companies like Spotify, Apple, Meta and Goldman Sachs, for example, introduced 'fertility perks' for female employees, covering the costs of egg freezing.[49] 'Everybody knows this is what you need to do to show management you are committed to the company and that you will push off having a family many years down the road,' one 26-year-old executive at Morgan Stanley told the *New York Post*. A 30-year-old associate at Bank of America said the same: 'There's definitely a silent pressure coming from management.'[50]

Family life was increasingly organised around work. Companies like X and Zillow offered services like breast milk shipping so new mothers could go on business trips and ship milk back home.[51] Some firms provided robotic cribs that acted as a 'virtual 24/7 nanny' so parents could be more productive, while others offered on-site childcare, with 17 of the Fortune 100, including Boeing, Nike and Disney, introducing workplace nurseries to keep mothers

'EMPOWERED'

at their desks.[52] In 2015, the CEO of Yahoo!, Marissa Mayer, was emailing from her hospital bed after giving birth to twins.[53]

Girls my age grew up with this messaging. For us female empowerment had always meant putting career first, and everything else second. But then, in 2020, the year I graduated, as I was applying for my first job, the pandemic hit.

For the first time, we stopped. We finally had time to think about what we were doing, and where we were headed. Girls who had given everything to academia found themselves lost and unfulfilled. Young women who had spent years pushing themselves in the corporate world began to break down and burn out. We realised how much we had been sacrificing, and wondered whether it was worth it.

The backlash against hustle culture began. 'Quiet Quitting: Why Doing the Bare Minimum at Work Has Gone Global', *The Guardian* wrote in 2022. Quiet quitters, they explained, are 'doing just enough in the office to keep up, then leaving work on time and muting Slack. Then posting about it on social media.'[54] *Glamour* magazine welcomed the 'soft-girl revolution', while *Vanity Fair* declared the girlboss era 'decidedly over'.[55] By 2024, TikToks tagged with 'lazy girl jobs' had over 40 million views.[56]

Some went further. During the pandemic, the term 'Trad Wives' trended on TikTok, as women posted about staying at home while their husbands worked. By 2024, videos tagged with 'trad wife' had more than 300 million views.[57] There was even a rise in 'stay-at-home girlfriends', as young women documented their daily routines going to Pilates, getting their nails done and doing the dishes while waiting for their boyfriends. 'Stay-at-Home Girlfriends Are Having a Moment', the *Wall Street Journal* reported in 2023, discussing the young women aspiring to a 'life outside the workforce, with minimal housework and maximal self-care'.[58]

Yet as girlboss feminism faded, the pressure to work hard kept growing. Now many young women no longer want to work for corporations, but to *become* the corporation. Success isn't so much about climbing the corporate ladder as becoming a brand, a product. Even the Trad Wives on TikTok are busy building audiences, monetising their private lives and selling merchandise.[59] The girlboss didn't die. She became an influencer.

Now success demands even more of us. It means selling ourselves on the market and competing for clicks. Every moment of our lives can be monetised, every aspect of who we are commodified. Our ambition today is simply to have an audience. 'I would literally wake up at 4:00 AM every single day just to make a couple of TikToks before I had to leave for school,' an 18-year-old girl told *Teen Vogue* in 2024. 'If you really want to be an influencer or whatever, it takes consistency.'[60] Elsewhere *Teen Boss* magazine, a 'teen entrepreneurial magazine for girls', gives girls as young as eight tips on how to build their personal brand and become entrepreneurs ('from tween to tycoon').[61] Even fairy tales have been rewritten: in the 2021 *Cinderella* remake, according to IMDb, 'Camila Cabello's princess wants her own fashion empire, not Prince Charming.' When the prince proposes, declaring, 'I pick you to be my princess,' Cinderella replies with, 'But what about my work?', before turning him down.[62]

Many young women have little choice but to work hard, of course. We came of age after the 2008 financial crash, graduating into a crowded, competitive job market, only to be hit with the pandemic. Across the UK and the US, wages have stagnated while living costs and house prices have soared.[63] To make ends meet, some of us had to balance side hustles with full-time jobs and education.

But even that no longer feels like enough. Productivity influencers and entrepreneurs urge us to monetise every hobby and optimise every spare second, while platforms from Instagram to TikTok to OnlyFans promise to commodify our talents, our bodies, our very selves. Everything feels like potential income now.

And everything outside of work feels like a threat to productivity. Friendships, relationships, hobbies, resting: all are traded for networking, hustling, building our brands. Even taking care of others feels transactional. By the late 2010s, favours and acts of kindness, things once done for free, like checking in on friends, helping out neighbours, and putting the needs of family first, had been reframed as 'people-pleasing' or 'emotional labour'. Across Instagram and TikTok, we were reminded to cut off anyone holding us back, delay commitments that might distract from our careers and say no to anything inconvenient. Favours for friends became unnecessary burdens. Family obligations felt oppressive and unfair. Other people became distractions, annoyances, obstacles. And if they got in the way of our goals, we were reassured that it was acceptable – healthy, even – to leave them behind.

We were even encouraged to talk to friends and family like HR managers, carefully guarding our time. In 2019, for example, a relationship coach posted a template on Twitter for turning down friends who need help. She shared a screenshot of a text from a friend asking: 'Do you have the emotional/mental capacity for me to vent about something medical/weight-related for a few minutes?' Her suggested responses included 'I'm at capacity right now' and 'I don't think I can hold appropriate space for you.'[64]

Now many of us in our twenties are beginning to wonder what this is all for. We watched Millennial women burn out from corporate stress; now we are watching Gen Z influencers and entrepreneurs exhaust themselves too. Even if we aren't building audiences ourselves, we feel pressure to monetise every aspect of who we are, to calculate the cost and benefit of everything and everyone in our lives.

And for what? To afford more stuff? To buy more in order to recover from burnout? To invest into improving our online profiles? It feels as though everything we do and buy is now to optimise ourselves, market ourselves. This was empowerment to become better products, and better consumers.

CONSUME

'COME WITH ME TO GET THE STANLEY X STARBUCKS CUP', says the text on a viral TikTok posted in 2024. A young woman sits in a camping chair outside Starbucks in the dark, giving a thumbs up to the camera. 'arrived at 4.40am', the caption reads, later switching to 'I started to freeze lol and curled up into a ball.' Through the window, she films Starbucks employees arranging rows of pink cups on shelves. 'I was actually freezing at this point.'

The line outside grows longer. '10 mins before opening and the line almost wrapped around the corner', says the caption, showing a queue of young women huddled in blankets. She films the moment the doors finally open: the crowd rushes inside, racing toward the display. 'The madness begins…' She grabs two cups, poses for a quick selfie and captions it: 'Literally gone in 20 seconds'. Moments later, she films police officers arriving. 'There was a fight and someone ran out and stole a cup … Then sheriffs came.'[65]

Consumerism of course exploded throughout the 2010s. Algorithms became more personal and predictive, adverts more targeted and invasive, influencers more friendly and intimate. And constant consumption started to seem like the only way to exist. It

'EMPOWERED'

felt as if we were owed all these things, and if we couldn't afford them, we were being deprived of basic needs.

By the time I was a teenager, influencers had been sent so many free items for review that many ended up with drawers full of make-up, wardrobes overflowing with outfits, even entire rooms dedicated to PR packages. Girls like me grew up thinking it was normal to have 20 versions of the same lipstick, 50 eyeshadow palettes, the same clothes in every colour. As pre-teens we watched influencers show off their 'hauls' (dozens of items they bought from a single online order), share their monthly – or even weekly – favourite products, and give tours of their beauty rooms and walk-in wardrobes. This was our entertainment.

And shopping online was only becoming easier. In 2018 Snapchat launched Shoppable AR lenses, which let girls use face filters to virtually try on clothes, sunglasses, make-up and handbags before buying them on the app.[66] We could now swipe our hands in the air to switch colours and styles, and, as BuzzFeed put it, dress ourselves like Sims avatars.[67] In 2019 Instagram then introduced Checkout, also allowing users to buy directly through the app, before adding a Shop tab in 2020. In 2017, too, Amazon made it possible for anyone to become an influencer, earning commission by displaying and recommending their favourite products on their own personalised 'storefront pages'.[68] Shopping itself could now be a source of income, the things we bought part of our personal brands.

At the same time, TikTok was transforming consumerism. In 2023, TikTok Shop launched, also allowing users to make purchases without leaving the app. Even before that, though, algorithms were already driving sales. Since TikTok's 'For You' page serves up an endless stream of videos, the app can create 'microtrends', fads that blow up one day and disappear the next. One week it's a new skincare product, the next a cosmetic procedure, then a viral hairdryer, followed by a piece of furniture. The algorithm is always pushing something new, making girls feel as if they have to constantly change their look and lifestyle to keep up.

By 2023, the hashtag #TikTokMadeMeBuyIt had over 60 billion views.[69] Here girls share and review things they bought after seeing them on the app. Stanley cups, for example – these huge, handled water bottles – became a cultural craze after trending on TikTok in 2022. Stanley's revenue exploded from $74 million in 2019 to $750 million in 2023.[70] Under hashtags like #stanleycup, which had over 7 billion views on TikTok by 2024,[71] young women post videos of their cup collections, review different colours and sizes, and gush over bottle accessories, from glittery straps to attachable snack trays to holders for phones, bank cards and car keys.

Today much of our free time is spent scrolling through ads. Relaxing means watching hauls on YouTube, bingeing #TikTokMadeMeBuyIt videos and swiping through sponsored posts on Instagram. And we have all become advertisers too: documenting our lives online means always marketing the things we use, the experiences we have, the places we go, the outfits we wear, even if we aren't trying to. We have become walking ads for each other.

Girls are also becoming consumers younger than ever. Instead of flipping through toy catalogues before birthdays like I once did, girls now watch TikTok toy hauls, YouTube unboxing videos and 'What I Got For Christmas' vlogs, often featuring children their own age. Ryan Kaji, for example, began unboxing toys on YouTube at just four years old. By nine, Ryan was earning nearly $30 million a year from reviewing toys, making him the highest-paid YouTuber for three years in a row.[72] One video alone, where Ryan searches for Disney and Paw Patrol toys inside a giant inflatable water slide, has over 2 billion views.[73]

By 2020, a UK report found that teenagers were seeing an ad every ten seconds while scrolling on Instagram, which equates to around 420 adverts per hour. Over the course of a day, researchers estimated that 14-year-olds saw as many as 1,260 adverts on social media alone – 10 to 20 times higher than the number of ads children saw in the early 2000s.[74] Around 97% of Gen Z say social media is their main source of shopping inspiration, and by age 13, the average child in the US is thought to have around 72 million data points collected about them by online advertisers.[75]

But children aren't only consumers any more, they are products too. Back in the 2010s, teenage girls like me began consuming with a new purpose. We started buying things to advertise ourselves online, to categorise and brand ourselves. What we bought was no longer just what we liked. It was becoming who we were.

Around the mid 2010s, the way girls described themselves online began to change. Our sense of self was increasingly tied to the brands we bought, the influencers we followed, whatever flashed up on our 'For You' page. Teenage subcultures were forming, as they always have, but they were less organic and subversive, more commodified and marketable. This was the age of 'aesthetics'.

Aesthetics are essentially pre-packaged looks or styles that people adopt and post about online. Girls, of course, have always experimented with fashion, make-up and other forms of self-expression. But as algorithms became more powerful, they began suggesting not just products but entire personalities. We were recommended not only what to buy but who to *be*.

Today, TikTok's 'For You' page not only creates microtrends but creates micro*identities*. All sorts of personality types trend in rapid succession: one month it's all about being 'Trad Wives', modest, traditional women who wear milkmaid dresses and cooking aprons, then comes the 'Clean Girl', who is all about wellness, Pilates and skincare routines. Next come 'Barbiecore' and 'Bimbocore', girls who have bleached hair and wear pink outfits, followed by 'Dark Academia' and 'Light Academia', girls who read old books and wear blazers and pleated skirts. There are even seasonal identities like 'Christian Girl Autumn' and 'Tomato Girl Summer' (who knows?!). It feels as if the moment a girl shows any trace of individuality, algorithms and advertisers now detect it, categorise it and package her into an online aesthetic.

Girls can now purchase a personality too. Each of these aesthetics arrives with its own shopping list. To be 'That Girl' you need gratitude journals, face massagers, skincare products and workout sets. To be a 'Mob Wife' you need fur coats, big jewellery and designer handbags, or suits, polo shirts and trench coats to look 'Old Money'. Who we are depends on what is trending. We shop to belong.

Even age-old religions are aesthetics now, complete with shopping lists. In 2024, for example, 'Catholic Core' started trending on TikTok. One online guide, 'How to Nail Tik Tok's Catholic Girl Aesthetic', describes the trend as a 'subgenre of alternative fashion' before listing the essentials: hair bows, puffy blouses and, of course, cross jewellery, which apparently 'symbolises everything catholicism' and 'is the most recurrent emblem in the catholic girl aesthetic'.[76]

Algorithms don't just reflect back at us who we already are, though. They influence who we become. Social media platforms mine our data to predict what we like, before recommending what to watch, follow or buy. But they also *change* our choices, guiding us towards related interests and identities. Over time, we become who the algorithm 'wants' us to be. And with that can come endless pressure to update and reinvent ourselves, to keep up with rapid market trends and stay relevant.

So just as girls and young women are being funnelled towards the same Instagram Face, they are also being pulled towards the same personalities. Instead of aspiring to be like people we know in our lives, we increasingly follow brands, imitate influencers and allow algorithms to steer us towards who to be, as though we are on a conveyor belt headed for some final, standardised product.

Coming of age with only consumerism as our guide, girls my age had no road map. Without religion, community or shared responsibilities, there were no clear milestones to adulthood, no real obligations and no obvious sense of direction. While previous generations had clear life paths to follow, we were told we could be anyone, do anything. Market forces alone, rather than anything more stable or sustaining, were left to answer the age-old question of *Who am I?*

And so traditional markers of adulthood began to feel less important. Increasingly our identities weren't based on what we did or valued, but what we owned. Who we were becoming mattered less than what we bought. And the more we were encouraged to consume and display our lives online, the more time we took to experiment and express ourselves, the slower we were to grow up.

DELAY

'Why is this SO HARD HELP' reads the caption of the TikTok with 1.2 million views, followed by the hashtags #stress #anxiety and #ubereats. 'pov: you can't speak to anyone on the phone without being nervous' says the text on screen, as a woman in her twenties starts to dial. 'I'm about to call the restaurant I just ordered Uber Eats from,' she shrieks, 'and I'm so afraid, I don't know why, I just have to ask them one question.'

She giggles nervously, warning viewers how much her voice changes on the phone. As soon as it starts ringing, she looks terrified, the caption changing to 'why am i hunched'. During the call, which lasts about fifteen seconds, she winces and cringes while asking for her fries to be extra crispy, holding her hair over her mouth. When she hangs up, she screams.[77]

Back in the early 2000s, developmental psychologist Jeffrey Arnett coined the term 'emerging adulthood' to describe a new period of extended adolescence between the ages of 18 and 25.[78] In the decades since, psychologists have noticed that my generation, Gen Z, has been growing up much more slowly than previous generations. By the early 2010s, some were arguing that those in their early twenties should not be considered adults yet, while neuroscientists advised that 18 to 25 should be called 'late adolescence' because the brain is still developing.[79]

One explanation for this is the economy. Coming of age after the financial crash, faced with soaring living costs and unaffordable housing, my generation found independence increasingly out of reach. Many of us delayed full-time work to go to university, graduated with student debt and ended up moving back home. In the UK, the number of 25- to 34-year-olds living with their parents has risen by more than a third in less than 20 years, and is now at a record high.[80] In the US, nearly half of young adults rely on their parents for basic living costs, and in 2023 about 18% of Americans aged 25 to 34 still lived with at least one parent.[81]

But economics can't explain everything. Even when women my age have the means and opportunities to be more independent, many of us still hesitate. We are not just unprepared for adulthood. More and more of us seem afraid of it.

In the late 2010s, Jean Twenge called this Gen Z's 'slow life strategy'.[82] She realised that Gen Z was reaching the traditional milestones of adulthood much later in life, if at all. Compared to teens in the five decades before, adolescents in the 2010s were less likely to have been on a date, worked for pay, learned to drive or had sex. This was the case across all demographic groups, regardless of gender, race or class.[83]

Teenagers today seem just as cautious. In 1991, nearly half of 13- to 16-year-olds in the US said they liked to take risks sometimes. By 2021, only a third felt the same.[84] Twenge notes that half of today's 17- and 18-year-olds date, roughly the same proportion as 13- to 14-year-olds in the early 1990s. As she told the *New York Times*, 'In many ways 18-year-olds now look like 14-year-olds in previous generations.'[85]

One reason for our risk aversion is our upbringing. In the 1990s and 2000s, parenting became more anxious and controlling than ever before. The term 'helicopter parenting' was used to describe a new generation of parents who hovered over their children, monitoring their every move. There were many reasons for this: incessant media coverage of school shootings, abductions and terror attacks; smartphones and tracking apps that suddenly enabled 24/7 supervision; collapsing communities and social trust; smaller families, meaning more focus on fewer children. Girls my age grew up with far less freedom than previous generations, and much more adult supervision, often into our late teens and twenties.

Then we went to university, where the coddling continued. In 2018, Jonathan Haidt and Greg Lukianoff published *The Coddling of the American Mind*, describing the rise on college campuses of what they called 'safetyism', where emotional safety suddenly seemed to be valued above all else.[86] In 2019 at the University of South Florida, for example, students could visit 'relaxation stations' with massage chairs, beanbags and nap pods.[87] At Oberlin College in Ohio, trigger warnings and a 'safe room' with a therapy dog were set up when feminist Christina Hoff Sommers visited campus, with students claiming that 'her very presence' was 'a form of violence' and that their mental health was threatened by her visit.[88] And this was not just happening in the US. At the same time my university was introducing 'Doggy De-Stress Days', where puppies were brought onto campus to help with exam stress, and a 'Wellbeing Room' for naps on beanbags between lectures, along with Marvel movie and pizza nights. Back then, though, I remember students being warned, over and over, that they would meet the real world eventually.

But then the real world began to change, rewarding and profiting from our extended adolescence. Catering to our emotional comfort became the norm. Everywhere we looked, our infantilisation was indulged. We were endlessly encouraged to 'heal our inner child' by therapy companies and mental health influencers, while being reminded by mainstream media to 'reparent ourselves', watch cartoons for 'self-care', and even sleep with stuffed animals for our mental health.[89] It was freeing, liberating, to be our childlike, authentic selves. Delaying adulthood was destigmatised.

Companies soon cashed in. 'Kidult' toys, for example, became a booming market. In the US, over 20% of plush toys sold in 2024 were bought by adults, and those aged 12 and over make up about a quarter of all toy sales, bringing in around $9 billion a year.[90] In the UK, nearly one in every three pounds spent on toys also comes from this age group, with kidult sales up £57 million

'EMPOWERED'

in 2023 alone.⁹¹ Other industries infantilised us too. We were sold adult Lego sets, 'Adult Happy Meals' with collectable toys by McDonald's and adult days out at Disneyland, including weddings and work conferences.⁹²

Meanwhile basic life skills became achievements worthy of celebration online. Millennials first used the term 'adulting' to describe doing everyday tasks like cooking and laundry, but now Gen Z are using it to talk about their twenties. On TikTok, the hashtag #adulting has been tagged to over 1.5 million posts, with popular videos captioned 'I adulted today' and 'POV: adulting' showing twenty-somethings answering the door or booking doctors' appointments. Under #adulting, TikTok itself has even added a reassuring message: 'Not ready to tackle the real world just yet? *crying emoji* From paying bills and building a career to … starting a family, adulthood can all seem very daunting. We're here to offer tips to get you prepared to confidently nail "adulting" – You're not alone in this!'⁹³

Delaying adulthood is not only more common and accepted now, but also *celebrated*. Growing up slowly is seen as freedom from old-fashioned constraints and obligations. One example of this is the rise of 'child-free influencers' in recent years, who not only normalise but glamorise the choice not to have children. Under hashtags like #childfree and #doubleincomenokids, young women on TikTok wonder why anyone would choose to have children and give up their freedom. They give glimpses into their child-free lives, from drinking wine in the Maldives by themselves to enjoying hungover McDonald's breakfasts and uninterrupted naps. Others flaunt how young they look, their freedom to drink hard liquor before noon and their ability to splurge on whatever they want, from arcade machines costing thousands to $100 worth of candy. Some even boast about getting sterilised.⁹⁴

Motherhood, meanwhile, is increasingly seen as restrictive, inconvenient and irrational. One Gen Z TikToker, for example, hosts a 'Free Birth Control series' where she expresses sheer horror at video clips of pregnancy and parenting. 'Every single day I give you a reason not to have kids,' she tells her 1.2 million followers, warning women about everything from swollen bellies to screaming toddlers to 'pregnancy nose'.[95] In 2021, another young woman from TikTok created 'The List', a popular, crowdsourced document of the pros and cons of having children. The List contains cons like 'Baby=parasite' and 'The uterus gremlin can kick your intestines while pregnant', along with every possible pregnancy symptom from 'Fatigue' and 'Morning sickness' to serious complications like infections, haemorrhaging and pre-eclampsia. There are 350 cons in total, and only 35 pros, which include: 'Tax return benefits', 'You gain the weight for that BBL', and 'You get to buy them the toys you never got to play with.'[96]

This is more than TikTok trends, though. Millennials and Gen Z are now delaying marriage and parenthood in record numbers.[97] A 2023 UK survey found that only 55% of Gen Z planned to have children at all. One in four had ruled it out entirely, the most common reason being 'wanting time to themselves'.[98] In the US, a 2021 Pew survey of adults found the top reason was even simpler: 'I just don't want to.'[99]

According to a 2024 Pew survey, Americans across all age groups are also far more likely to see job satisfaction and strong friendships as important for a fulfilling life than marriage and parenthood. Among young adults, only 20% say being married is 'extremely or very important' for fulfilment, and 22% say the same about having children. By contrast, around 68% say this about having the right job or career, and 62% about having close friends. And young women are now less likely than young men to want children. The same survey found that 57% of young men in the US aged 18 to 34 say they want children someday, compared to only 45% of women.[100]

Of course we don't want children; many of us still feel like children ourselves. But we are also confused. While young women like me are often infantilised, we were also pressured to grow up too fast, and this has only worsened for girls today. The beauty industry makes girls worry about wrinkles before they have hit puberty. The mental health industry pathologises normal adolescent feelings, framing exam stress and heartbreak as symptoms of serious disorders. Girls are exposed to hardcore porn and pressured to objectify themselves, years before their first date. They are expected to have fully formed political opinions, and present them publicly, before they have even left home. Adults are sold children's toys; children's shows are sexual. Helicopter parenting delays independence; hustle culture demands it. Extended adolescence encourages us to be young and free, to make clumsy mistakes; social media never forgets them. Girls today face the pressures of adult life earlier than ever before, but without the maturity, resilience or life experiences previous generations had to handle them.

As Jonathan Haidt put it in *The Anxious Generation*, young women like me were overprotected in real life but underprotected online.[101] We might act like 'empowered' adults on social media, but many of us feel like powerless children in reality.

POWERLESS

One reason for this growing sense of powerlessness could be the collapse of organised religion. Since the early 2010s, non-religious teenagers have been saying that they feel lonely, worthless, anxious and depressed at much higher rates than those who are religious.[102] Jonathan Haidt and Zach Rausch analysed decades of survey data from thousands of American high school students, going back to 1977. Students were asked how much they agreed with statements about their self-worth, including 'I feel I do not have much to be proud of', 'Sometimes I think I am no good at all', 'I feel that I can't do anything right' and 'I feel that my life is not very useful'. Up until around 2010, religious and non-religious teens gave similar responses, with religious conservatives only slightly less likely to agree with the negative statements. But after 2010, the gap widened. By 2019, secular liberal teenagers, particularly girls, were far more likely to describe themselves in self-derogating ways.[103]

This aligns with decades of research linking higher levels of religiosity to better mental health, including lower rates of depression, substance abuse and suicide.[104] In roughly half of countries surveyed by Pew in 2019, actively religious people were also more likely than the non-religious to describe themselves as 'very happy'. In the US, 36% of the actively religious described themselves that way, compared with 25% of the inactively religious, and 25% of the unaffiliated.[105]

One explanation is the sense of belonging and community religion provides. Along with attending church, religious people are more likely to get involved in volunteering and youth groups. Those who attend religious services at least once a month are also more likely to participate in non-religious organisations like charities and clubs. In the US, 58% of actively religious people participate in at least one non-religious voluntary organisation, compared to only 39% of those without religious affiliation.[106]

Girls are not just grappling with the loss of religion, though. They are also dealing with new demands. We can see, for example,

'EMPOWERED'

the consequences of hustle culture. In recent years, across Europe, Central Asia and Canada, young people have been feeling more pressure from school, particularly adolescent girls. The share of 15-year-old girls in these regions who say they feel pressured by schoolwork has risen from 54% in 2018 to 63% today, compared to 43% of boys.[107] In college the pressure is even more intense. A 2022 survey found that 80% of students felt overwhelmed, and 40% said they had difficulty functioning.[108] Some young women even talk about suffering from 'productivity dysmorphia', the nagging sense that no matter how much they do, it will never be enough, and an inability to recognise what they have achieved.[109] Yet despite all of this pressure, the proportion of high school seniors in the US who expect to earn graduate degrees, get professional jobs or own more than their parents has dropped dramatically since around 2012.[110]

Even leisure time no longer feels like a break. For many girls, relaxing now means shopping online, scrolling through ads on social media and comparing what they have to what others have, which only makes them feel worse. Research shows that girls who place more importance on brands and consumer goods report lower self-esteem and more emotional distress.[111] The more we pursue material things, the less happy we are, and the more vulnerable to anxiety, depression, loneliness and debt.[112]

Life can start to feel empty too. Since around 2012, survey data shows a sharp rise in teenagers, especially girls, agreeing with statements like 'Life often seems meaningless' and 'The future often seems hopeless', while disagreeing with 'I enjoy life as much as anyone' and 'It feels good to be alive'. Before then, the differences between boys and girls, and between liberals and conservatives, were minimal. But after 2012, liberal girls were the first to show a spike in depressive symptoms, and they remain the most affected group. This isn't unique to the US and its politics either; the same pattern appeared at the same time in the UK, Canada and Australia.[113]

One likely explanation, Jonathan Haidt argues, is a loss of agency. In psychology, this relates to our 'locus of control': the sense of how much power we have over our own lives. Those with an external locus of control tend to feel that life happens *to* them, while those with an internal locus of control believe they have more influence. In recent years, adolescents' sense of control has shifted outwards. Gen Z as a whole began to feel less in control of their futures, but the shift was biggest among *liberal* teenagers, particularly liberal girls. This aligns with decades of research showing that conservatives, on average, tend to have a more internal locus of control, while liberals lean more external – and the more external your locus of control, the more likely you are to feel anxious, hopeless and depressed.[114]

By 2021, according to the CDC, 42% of high school students said they felt 'so sad or hopeless that they could not engage in their regular activities for at least two weeks during the previous year,' up from 28% a decade before.[115] The CDC also found that 57% of teen girls felt 'persistently hopeless', an almost 60% increase from 2011 and double that of boys. One in three had seriously considered suicide in the past year.[116]

Again, this is not only happening in the US. In 2025, Jean Twenge and economist David Blanchflower analysed survey data from the US, UK, Ireland, Australia, Canada and New Zealand. They found that, in all these countries, happiness and life satisfaction have declined among young people over the past decade, especially among young women. In a historical first, they concluded that Gen Z's mental health crisis is so severe that 'youth is no longer one of the happiest times of life.'[117]

Ultimately, girls and young women have been left with a growing sense of powerlessness. We work hard only to feel like we need to achieve more, buy more, become more. We consume and compete and self-optimise, only to feel empty. More stable sources of meaning and identity have been mocked or have disappeared. And we have been left not only unprepared for adulthood, but unsure what it even means any more. We feel hopeless about our futures, and helpless to change them.

So what are girls and young women grappling with here? These *are* age-old anxieties – about what to do with our lives, where to find fulfilment and purpose, who we are and what we want.

Except today we are trying to answer these questions with nothing to anchor ourselves to. We have gained freedom but lost guidance. We were left to make up our own morality, to find our own rules to follow. We were warned not to believe in anything beyond ourselves, nothing superstitious. We were told to avoid obligations to other people, nothing restrictive. And so we served ourselves instead.

But it's hard not to believe in something bigger. We refused to be controlled by religion, yet without it everything feels so painfully out of control. So we mocked faith only to mimic it. We whisper to the universe, we repeat our affirmations, we obsess over our mental health. We search for something, anything, to believe in.

These new belief systems promising empowerment are so unstable, though. We tie our identities to trends that disappear overnight, to an unpredictable job market, to whatever personalities, lifestyles or versions of right and wrong are trending. And when we wonder who we are, we do it publicly, under constant interference from algorithms and advertisers telling us who we should be and what we should want. Until we can't even tell the difference between who we are and what we are being sold.

One set of expectations has simply replaced another. We are free to pursue professional goals, but the pressure has never been higher. We can buy more, travel more, and achieve more than previous generations dreamed of, but consumer culture ensures this never feels enough. New needs are invented, luxuries become essentials, and fulfilment stays forever out of reach. And while this world might not shackle us to old-fashioned obligations or responsibilities any more, it shackles us to something else entirely. We freed ourselves from old authorities only to be ruled by the market instead.

Where has this left us? We are perfect products and perfect consumers: girls who are predictable, categorised, standardised. We are easy to package and easy to sell to. We were told we could be whoever we wanted, but the choice became so overwhelming we defaulted to being data sets, raw material for the market. And girls with more freedom than ever before ended up lost and confused. Girls who were told to be strong and independent ended up childlike and helpless. We are the generation given permission to focus endlessly on ourselves – our dreams, our desires, our identities, our feelings, our freedom – and we are the most miserable on record.

Because none of this is real empowerment. True empowerment can only be found away from algorithms, away from companies, away from the market. It can only be found by remembering what makes us human, and holding on to that.

The way forward is turning from products back to people, from GIRLS® back to girls. In the final chapter, we will turn to how.

Conclusion

BECOMING GIRLS®

This was the story of how my generation became GIRLS®, and how companies commodified the collapse of everything that once made us human.

I hope I have shown, firstly, that this situation is not 'nothing new'. That these are not just the same age-old anxieties faced by previous generations of girls and young women. That every anxiety they experienced is now being magnified until it feels unmanageable.

Today, if girls feel insecure about their appearance, they have to handle that in a world of Facetune, AI filters and feeds of edited Instagram influencers, recommended by algorithms to precisely target their insecurities. If they feel confused about their emotions, they have to sort through the noise of TikTok therapists, YouTubers pushing BetterHelp discount codes, and ads for medication delivered straight to their door. If they struggle to feel good enough, they have to endure being constantly ranked and reviewed online, publicly measured against everyone else. If they then feel lonely, they often have to cope alone, as their families fall apart, friendships hollow out and communities fragment. If they also feel insecure in romantic relationships, they must manage that in a world of Tinder and Pornhub, where romance feels dead, where the only guidance they get comes from dating influencers profiting from their fear and confusion, where they are made to feel frigid or needy for wanting more. And if all of this leaves them fearful of the future – unsure of what they want, unsure of who they are – now there is nothing left to follow, nothing bigger than themselves to belong to, no higher standard by which to hold themselves. No sense of shared values or purpose binding them with others – all that is left is scrolling, working and consuming alone.

Add all of this together, pile one pressure on top of another, along with so many more that I couldn't fit into one book, and things soon become unbearable. Pressure comes from every direction: pressure from the beauty industry to look perfect; from the mental health industry to feel perfect; from social media to present the perfect life; from dating apps to find the perfect partner; from school and work to have the perfect career; from ads and influencers to afford every product and procedure – and pressure to perform all of this, for everyone else, all the time. Put enough pressure on anything and it will fall apart. Girls and young women today are breaking under the strain.

Some might say we put these pressures on ourselves. That girls don't have to spend so much time trying to be perfect products. But I hope it has become clear throughout this book that adolescent girls are uniquely vulnerable to these cultural, technological and commercial forces. That the promises of these industries are almost impossible to resist during their most formative and vulnerable years, especially when this is the only world they have ever known.

And girls' anxieties are not just being amplified, but being exploited like never before. Every experience of girlhood is intruded upon by the market; the solution to every age-old anxiety is a

CONCLUSION

purchase. Girls are being taught that they can buy their way out of bad feelings, buy their way into belonging and buy their way to empowerment.

Their entire lives have been commodified. The second a girl feels anxious, insecure or alone, corporations rush in. They convince her that the only way to understand herself is through the guidance of experts, the instruction of influencers, the payment of professionals. She is made to feel ugly and worthless and sick, before being sold a conveyor belt of solutions that only trap her in a cycle of dissatisfaction and consumption. She is being made to feel broken so she can become a lifelong consumer.

And over the past decade, beginning with my generation and worsening since, we have become the product. We are ornaments on display, filtered and Facetuned. We are objects, shopped for on dating apps. We are brands, managed and monetised. We are content, compressed into Instagram grids. The purpose of our lives is to become better products rather than better people. Each of us feels expendable, interchangeable. The market determines the worth of our faces, our bodies, our relationships, our memories, and we spend our time tweaking ourselves to what sells. Some of us have lost all sense of who we are beneath the packaging.

And to keep us this way, we were deceived. Industries and influencers persuaded us that the process of becoming products was empowering. That it was freeing, liberating, good for our mental health, to become inanimate. Beauty filters became self-love; editing apps became self-expression; AI bots became therapy; psychiatric drugs became accessories; influencers became friends; swiping became connection; pixels became community; objectifying ourselves became empowerment.

'Beautiful is easier than ever', Facetune promised, while we spent hours redesigning ourselves to feel good enough. 'It'll feel like you're shopping for leggings – not prescription meds', Hers insisted, selling drugs powerful enough to make adolescents suicidal. 'Life's more fun when you live in the moment', claimed Snapchat, while we missed that moment to take a Snap. 'Need a friend? Create one now', said Replika, an AI chatbot to cure loneliness. 'Say Goodbye to Superficial Connections', declared the dating app Hot Or Not, while we swiped through each other like things. 'What about my work?' said our version of Cinderella, who was too empowered for a fairy-tale ending. So much of the messaging my generation grew up with was little more than a marketing strategy.

I hope we can clearly see the lies now. We can see them in all the contradictions. The generation loudest about self-love and body positivity is suffering from record rates of eating disorders, battling body dysmorphia, and driving demand for cosmetic surgeries. The generation most open about its feelings, which has fought stigma like no other before, is facing the worst mental health crisis on record. The generation aspiring to be influencers above all else is also one that often wishes social media never existed. The generation with infinite dating options, and unashamed about hooking up, is having the least sex, dating far less and losing faith in love itself. The generation of young women raised on slogans like 'The future is female', and reminded that they could be and achieve anything, is anxious, risk-averse and afraid of the future. And members of the generation endlessly encouraged to introspect, explore and express themselves find it easier to be recommended personalities by algorithms. We are vain and insecure. We are connected and disconnected. We are free and powerless.

CONCLUSION

As I said at the beginning of this book, I believed for a long time that there was something wrong with me. I spent my teenage years trying to fit into the modern world, punishing myself for feeling anxious and sensitive, convinced I wasn't cut out for the way things were. And as I was inundated with the ideal of this strong, independent woman – who never felt insecure or jealous, never needed or depended on anyone – I felt even worse. I knew I could never live up to her.

I hope girls and young women who feel as I did can see now that this is not ordinary adolescent angst. I no longer think this is 'nothing new'; this is a crisis, a catastrophe. The world girls and young women are growing up in today, the pressure we have been put under from every direction, how we have been made to feel about ourselves, is heartbreaking.

This is what we lost along the way.

WHAT WE LOST

After writing about this crisis for so long, and speaking with so many girls and young women, what stands out to me most is a sense of loss. I notice it everywhere now. Nostalgia for a time we never knew; grief for a world long gone. A feeling not only that the good days are over, but that we missed them entirely.

My generation never knew falling in love without swiping and subscription models. We never got to experience a first kiss, or hold hands with a boy, before watching Pornhub. We never knew flirting before it became sending Instagram DMs or reacting to Snapchat Stories with flame emojis. We never knew friendship before it meant keeping up Snapstreaks and using each other like props to look popular online. And *freedom* – we never felt the freedom to grow up clumsily, to be young and dumb and make stupid mistakes without fear they would be posted online. Or the freedom to be unavailable, to disconnect for a while, without the pressure of read receipts and active statuses. We never knew a childhood spent chasing experiences and risks and independence instead of chasing likes on a screen. Never knew life without documenting and marketing and obsessively analysing it as we went.

This is not just nostalgia. Girls and young women today do have a lot to grieve; much has been lost from the old world. And I think the only way to deal with that loss is to face up to the world we are living in, to see how historically unique it is. To cope with it, first we have to comprehend it.

So what exactly have we lost? What have we sacrificed, in pursuit of being GIRLS®? What have we forgotten, as we were fashioned into things?

I think we have lost three things above all.

The first is a sense of belonging, a feeling of rootedness, of being part of something bigger than ourselves. Social media teaches us to each see ourselves as individual profiles, rival brands, competing products. Religion has retreated, communities have collapsed, neighbours barely know each other, friendship has been redefined, families have fallen apart. Generations before us had it harder in many ways, certainly materially, but in their world, even as it sometimes fell apart, something beneath stayed intact: customs, traditions, a shared understanding, a floor and foundation. Ours is one where all that lay underneath has been destroyed. Many girls and young women today have no stable base to explore from, few familiar places to return to, no community to call home.

And yet we are encouraged to become even *more* independent, even more detached. Every industry mentioned in this book– the

CONCLUSION

beauty industry, mental health industry, tech industry, dating industry, porn industry – pulls our attention inwards, towards our appearance, our feelings, our wants, our desires. These industries need us to be obsessed with ourselves. They depend on our vanity and self-absorption, so they sell it to us as empowerment.

All sorts of atomising cultural movements have become convenient sales strategies. From a therapeutic culture encouraging us to put our own needs first, to a feminism insisting that sexual freedom is the ultimate empowerment, to hustle culture teaching us to cut out anyone who holds us back, to an individualist attitude towards love and relationships that frames any compromise as an affront, every act of kindness an inconvenience, every commitment a threat to our autonomy – the message is always the same. Don't get too attached. Be careful not to catch feelings. Protect your peace. Never be needy. Heal faster; perform better; achieve more alone! The lie we have been told is that we need less commitment, not more. That the problem is other people, and the constraints they put on us.

But this is a tragic way to think. Tragic because it is putting young people on a trajectory to miss out on what actually matters. There is no love without vulnerability. There is no life without risk. Loneliness is not empowerment. And yet this way of thinking seems to have taken hold in every part of our lives, from cutting off friends and spending more time by ourselves, to pathologising and diagnosing other people, to seeing marriage and families only as traps instead of something to be treasured. Now our biggest fear is being restricted by relationships, by responsibilities, by obligations to others. We were told these things would only get in the way of our goals, distract us from finding our real selves.

But what if we find ourselves in other people? What if we were being taught to see everything like consumers? Our relationships became transactional. Other people became objects, always exchangeable. Consumerism was the only culture left, and so it became hard to see ourselves, and those around us, as fully human. This is the most painful part of looking back at my own girlhood, the realisation that we weren't simply turning into products. We were being trained to treat each other like products too.

It's hard to blame us, though. Sometimes I wonder what was expected. That the children who grew up on graphic online porn would know how to love someone for life? That the generation taught to always put their own freedom first would want to become spouses and parents, not feel terrified and trapped and restricted? That childhoods spent swiping through one another like objects, consuming each other's lives like content, wouldn't affect our character at all? Our ability to love? That girls who never saw a glimmer of affection between their parents would grow up and magically let their guard down, feel fine to commit and start families?

Whenever real connection felt too risky, too inconvenient, too human, we were encouraged to replace it, simulate it. But none of the substitutes my generation was sold could ever satisfy. Facetune is no substitute for confidence. BetterHelp is no substitute for friendship. Instagram is no substitute for community. Pornhub is no substitute for intimacy. Replika is no substitute for a human. And a life built around hustling, consuming and serving ourselves is nothing compared to a life spent serving those we love, trying to become better people.

This leads to the second big loss, which is moral guidance. Girls today have more options and choices in life than any previous generation, a freedom which can be liberating but also overwhelming. We have so many ways to turn, so many paths to take, so many identities to try on, that it feels paralysing.

CONCLUSION

In the past, guidance came from families, communities, religious leaders, shared values and cultural traditions. Much of that has now fallen away. Now it feels as if the world is moving too fast for wisdom, and so adults have largely stepped back. And in their place girls have been left with nothing but endless empty platitudes. Today, when they feel anxious or uncertain, they are often told some version of *do what makes you feel good, you know yourself best, you do you!* And the anxiety only gets worse. *What do I want? Why do I want that? Who am I?*

We have so much advice, and so little wisdom. Now everything is about meeting our needs. If we feel anxious, we are encouraged to analyse our past and our problems, rarely our own character and moral choices. We are asked what would make us happy, not what would help other people. We are told to love ourselves, with little care for how we conduct ourselves. We are reminded to have self-respect and self-esteem, never how to earn these things. Self-development has become more about optimisation and productivity hacks than becoming a better person. Becoming our authentic selves now means buying products. There is so much talk about mental health and so little about morality – how we live our lives, how we treat other people.

We never had places to practise being good people either. Many of us did not grow up in stable families, in close-knit neighbourhoods or in religious communities, places where you learn to live alongside other people and adapt to one another's needs. We had so few opportunities to practise selflessness. No neighbours to try kindness with. No bonds we couldn't easily break. No obligations to learn loyalty. We grew up in a world of strangers, with so few expectations of each other, so little accountability. Now some of us are trying to teach ourselves compromise and sacrifice and selflessness for the first time in our twenties, and it feels terrifying. We would rather be alone.

And when adults stepped back, companies stepped in. We may have less interference from family and neighbours, but now the market intrudes on our lives like never before. The door was left open for companies to crawl in and decide what we value. And the modern world imposes its own values, ones that change all the time. Progressive values that endlessly evolve; sexual values that only become more permissive; corporate values, consumer values, whatever suits the market. The adults around us stayed lovingly neutral but the world is not neutral. We were left to learn right and wrong from advertisers and influencers. No longer restrained by religion, old-fashioned morality or even our families' opinions, we are free! Free to be exposed to billions of ads telling us what to believe. Free to be lectured by faceless companies on right and wrong. Free to process constant information, to access every possible world view, to get muddled about even basic morality, to have no idea what the right decision is and why it even matters.

This brings us to the final loss, the ultimate loss: ourselves. The result of such relentless commodification, as I see it, is confusion about who we are, what we want and what would make us happy – a confusion corporations are waiting to exploit. When girls feel anxious and unsure of themselves, industries rush to sell them someone else to be. Only instead of occasional billboards on buildings, or adverts in beauty magazines, today these messages are transmitted all day, every day, through a never-ending stream of precisely targeted Instagram posts, YouTube videos, TikToks, Snapchat Stories and sponsored ads telling girls how to be prettier, happier, sexier, more popular, more productive, each personalised by algorithms to play on their innermost fears and insecurities. It

CONCLUSION

is an onslaught; it is advertising on a scale no previous generation has faced.

I wonder now what good all of this is. What good are all these professional opportunities and promises of female empowerment if we feel too anxious to function? What good are online 'communities' when they drain the time and confidence we need to join real communities? What good are technologies promising connection if they make us ignore those sitting right beside us? What use is all this freedom for self-expression when algorithms tell us what to think and ads sell us who to be? What is the point of faster and more convenient dating apps when we don't even believe in love any more? Sure, Amazon can deliver parcels quicker, and Spotify can find songs faster, but are our friendships deeper? Do we know how to be loyal? What good is having the whole world at our fingertips, everything within our reach, when the only things that matter feel utterly unreachable? We have absolutely everything, except the few things humans need to hold it together. Intimate access to anything we want – except each other.

The things we have lost are the things that make us human. We began losing our grip long before 2010, but over the past 15 years we let go completely. I know these do not seem like easy things to recover. But it might be simpler than we realise. I think it starts with each of us, in the small decisions we make every day. That, in itself, is empowering.

And the good news is, the backlash has already begun.

BACKLASH

There are signs that some girls and young women are beginning to break free from the trends and technologies I have written about in this book.

First, many are refusing to be filtered. Instagram Face is finally falling out of fashion; beauty might be becoming human again. Popular beauty influencers are dissolving their fillers, removing their implants and posting their transformations online. Molly-Mae Hague, for example, a 26-year-old former *Love Island* contestant with over 8.6 million Instagram followers, began dissolving her fillers in 2021. 'I literally looked like a different person,' she said afterwards. 'When I look back at pictures now, I'm terrified of myself. I'm like, "Who was that girl?" I don't know what happened.'[1] Other young women are sharing their regrets too: 'I wish I had kept the nose of my ancestors,' then 25-year-old model Bella Hadid told *Vogue* in 2022, reflecting on the rhinoplasty she had at 14.[2] That year, even downloads of Facetune were falling, with the app installed just over 4.6 million times worldwide – a drop of more than half compared with 2020.[3]

Girls are also pushing back against overdiagnosis. Online, criticism of the mental health industry and the commodification of our inner lives is mounting. Backlash against platforms like BetterHelp is growing, and young women are speaking out about the dangers of antidepressants and other psychiatric medications.[4] Some are realising that social media convinced them they were mentally ill; others that the drugs they thought would help only made things worse.[5] More and more are refusing to be boxed in by psychological and medical labels, recognising, at last, that the only problem they ever had was being human.

Other girls are realising the risks of sharing so much online, refusing to sell their lives so cheaply to strangers. A 2025 Pew survey found that 44% of US teens say they have cut back on social media. This figure is up from 39% in 2023, and girls are leading the way.[6] Flip phones and dumb phones are also making a comeback among Gen Z: from 2021 to 2024, 18-to-24 year-olds in the US drove a 148% spike in brick phone sales.[7] Around the world, too, young women are organising and protesting against the phone-based childhood, encouraging each other to log off and warning the next generation.[8]

Dating apps are also being deleted in record numbers. 'Gen Z is breaking up with dating apps', *The Guardian* reported in 2024, with UK data showing that since 2023, Tinder has lost 600,000 users, Hinge 131,000 and Bumble 368,000.[9] Other girls are refusing to sexualise themselves online, and be treated like objects. 'Why Sex-Positive Feminism Is Falling Out Of Fashion', declared the *New York Times* in 2021, while *The Guardian* investigated 'Why Generation Z is turning its back on sex-positive feminism', from experiences of rough and painful sex to the trauma of online porn.[10] In 2021 BuzzFeed also profiled Gen Z women who thought that sex positivity was 'overrated'. As one 23-year-old put it:

> It feels like we were tricked into exploiting ourselves [and] tricked into thinking it was our idea. I would say I gathered this mostly from media, *Sex and the City*, *Girls* – HBO somehow did a number on me – books, social media... You read a lot about [sex positivity] on Tumblr, you read a lot about it on Twitter when you were in high school, [and] it gets really ingrained in your brain that you need to be comfortable having sex with someone you're not committed to. I think in my feeble 18-year-old mind, it was probably not what I needed to hear.[11]

Girls are pushing back against porn too. In 2023, *Vox* declared that 'The teens don't believe in casual sex any more. And they really don't believe in porn.' The author warns about the rise of 'puriteens' online that are pushing back against sex-positive feminism and calling to #CancelPorn.[12] In 2022 the hashtag went viral on TikTok, as young women shared stories of porn sites hosting rape and child abuse videos, and opened up about how the industry had hurt them.[13]

There are even faint signs of renewed interest in traditional faith. In the US, the decades-long decline in religious affiliation seems to be slowing.[14] According to Pew, the share of the population identifying as Christian in the US has actually held relatively steady since 2019. Among young adults aged 18 to 24, the share who attend services at least monthly and who say religion is very important in their lives is about the same as those aged 24 to 34.[15] And in the UK, the percentage of 18- to 24-year-olds attending church at least monthly even rose from 4% in 2018 to 16% in 2024 (though this was mostly among young men).[16] These are small changes, but possible signs that my generation is searching for something deeper, for life to mean something more.

And beneath all of this, I have noticed something else happening. Instead of pretending to be strong independent women, and competing over who cares the least, I am beginning to see a gradual turn toward sincerity, honesty and genuine vulnerability among friends, family and the young women I speak to. It's hard to put into words, but I see the beginning of a refusal to pathologise our feelings, or pretend we don't have them. I see a growing bravery in admitting that we have been hurt – by social media, by online porn, by family breakdown, by modern dating, by this new world we are growing up in. Instead of distracting ourselves, detaching ourselves or trying to become better products, many of us are choosing to feel again. The age of irony and detachment is over; the pain is too intense. Now we are finally talking about how we really feel, human to human.

CONCLUSION

As I finish this book, new data suggests that Gen Z teens might even be starting to feel *happier*. A 2024 analysis in the US found that fewer 12- to 17-year-olds are reporting suicidal thoughts, plans and attempts compared to earlier years.[17] In 2023, too, about 40% of teens said they felt persistently sad or hopeless, which was a slight drop from 42% in 2021 (but still far more than 30% in 2013). For girls specifically, the number fell from 57% to 53% – much higher than 28% of boys, but heading in the right direction.[18]

So to those of you reading this and thinking about refusing in any way: you will not be alone. You can join the girls and young women who are sick of being sold to and selling themselves, who believe there must be more to life than this, who are taking themselves off these digital shelves and declaring themselves human. For those of you who feel you missed out on a girlhood, I promise, there are many of us refusing to give up our twenties, thirties, our adult lives, together. We have grieved what we lost; now we are taking it back.

Much of this book has been about not falling for things in the modern world. But now we need to ask ourselves, what do we stand for? Not only what we want to walk away from, but what we want to walk towards. Not only what we want to protect our future daughters from, but what we want to pass onto them. We need something to aim at. To attempt to be better, again and again. This, I think, is where we will find relief, self-respect, maybe even stumble across self-love. Only then can GIRLS® get back to being girls again. Only then can young women finally feel free.

BACK TO GIRLS

The first step, I hope, has been taken by reading this book. By understanding what has happened, and where things went wrong, we can start to see through the lies. We can see past what we are being *told* and see what we are being *sold*. For young women my age, and especially girls growing up now, we are so immersed in all these trends and technologies that it is hard to believe things were ever different, almost impossible to imagine life any other way.

But once we step back, once we give ourselves time and space to zoom out, we can see the lies. We can see the billions being made. We don't need statistics to see what is happening; we only need to look at the girls and women around us, really look, and listen to how they talk about themselves and their worth. If you listen long enough, I guarantee you will hear pain.

We can also start paying attention to how we actually feel, instead of how we are told to feel. After Facetuning your selfies, do you feel confident and empowered, or insecure and embarrassed? Do you feel connected when you sit inside watching YouTubers, close to your friends when you swipe through their Stories, or do you feel alone? It does not matter how many times we are told these things are 'empowering' or 'self-love' or 'connection' if that is not how we really feel. If you feel insecure, lonely or ashamed after participating in these trends, or using these technologies, then those feelings are worth listening to. If you feel anxious after posting a private memory on Instagram, ashamed after watching porn, alone after chatting with an AI bot, pay attention.

Notice, too, when you treat yourself like a product – judging your worth by rates and reviews, inspecting yourself for defects, punishing yourself for feeling. Delete any app that degrades you in this way. Stand firm against labelling yourself, treating your personality traits as problems to be solved, categorising yourself for companies and advertisers. Do not offer up your feelings and decisions to the intrusion of the market, to the interpretation of

CONCLUSION

experts, to be filed as deviations from what the medical industry decides is healthy. And do not accept any behaviour, or treat yourself in any way, that you would not want your future daughter – or the next generation of girls – to put up with. If it breaks your heart to imagine a girl you love Facetuning her body, being convinced by strangers on TikTok that she is mentally ill, or objectifying herself for random men on Instagram, do not do it yourself. If you wouldn't want it for her, you shouldn't want it for you, either.

Once you gain enough distance from these things, I promise that you will also gain strength. You can laugh at the skincare companies targeting teenagers with anti-ageing products. You can laugh at BetterHelp promising to fix you through texting, and at TikTok therapists trying to heal you from being human. You can laugh at Instagram pretending to be #HereForYou, and Hinge claiming to care about meaningful connection. And you can take power away from it. You will start to see how superficial, vain and unnecessary so much of it is. Only then will it lose its hold.

You can also take back your privacy. Girls my age grew up being encouraged to share more and more of our lives, to open ourselves up, to put everything on public display. Sometimes it felt as though if we weren't comfortable sharing our problems, we were stunted or repressed. If we weren't open about our sex lives, we were frigid or old-fashioned. If we weren't documenting our lives online, we were insecure or had something to hide. And if we weren't becoming brands, commodifying every inch of ourselves, we weren't hustling hard enough. There was no such thing as humility or modesty any more, only anxiety or low-self-esteem.

But you do not need to live this way. You can free yourself from the pressure. You do not have to tell everyone everything; you can keep intimate moments sacred. And the truth is, nobody cares about your life anyway. They watch your Snapchat Story for half a second. They hover over your Instagram selfie then swipe to someone else's. They skip through the concerts you post. They look at your life and immediately think about their own. The people who care are the ones you don't need to perform for, convince of your worth or remind of your existence. Strangers do not care about you, and that is a fundamental truth social media platforms depend on us forgetting.

Maybe that sounds too depressing. But it can also be a relief. To girls today: I want you to know that this pressure to constantly post and update an audience is very new, and it is completely unnecessary. And I hope you have seen throughout this book that these influencers who do share everything are *not* people to aspire to. If they influence you to do anything, it should be to not copy their compulsion and expose your entire life online.

Do not believe the lie, either, that people who don't post on social media are insecure or unhappy or hiding something. Often it's the opposite. As far as I can see, those with the best relationships post about them the least. Those with real confidence and self-love do not need to post thousands of selfies to prove it. Truly empowered people do not depend on online validation for every feeling or opinion or decision they make. And we all know that when we are experiencing something genuinely moving, the absolute last thing we want to do is take out our phone, cut through and cheapen it. The best love is quiet. The best confidence is quiet. And so are the lives with the most meaning.

So aspire to be different! Aspire to be someone who gets so caught up in the moment she forgets to share it, who protects her personal life while others hand theirs over freely, who can see the value in a moment without needing strangers to validate it. Be someone rare.

CONCLUSION

It's a cruel trick of modern life to convince us that everyone cares what we are doing all the time, that everyone is deeply invested in how we live and how we identify and how we feel. Believing that is enough to make anyone mentally ill. And looking at famous influencers with fans who *are* that invested, I would not wish that life on anyone. These people have traded privacy and sometimes their own human decency for an existence designed entirely for strangers.

By becoming more private, you also free up so much time. Time once spent compulsively capturing and curating your life can now be spent living it. Hours once spent marketing yourself for people you don't even like or care about can be reinvested in the people right in front of you. Because all of that time chasing what *looks* good leaves little energy for attempting to *be* good. Less time documenting our relationships means more time devoted to them. Less time missing the moment means more time getting lost in it. Forget streams of infinite information on a screen; focus on finite moments with the people you love.

An important thing to do, I think, is to defy this cultural message to emotionally detach, this lie that it is liberating to be alone. Not because every young woman should follow the same traditional path, but because it is a tragedy – an outrage, actually – that we have been convinced that human connection is an inconvenience, that other people are obstacles. Some of us declare that we don't want romance or families, that this is freedom, a revolt. But to me it feels less like liberation and more like resignation. No point in having kids. No point in committing. No point in building any sort of foundation with anyone. Nobody can be trusted; nothing ever lasts. We have been taught that putting other people first is a weakness, that depending on someone is a deficiency rather than the beautiful thing it is. You are not needy for having human needs.

So invest in other people. See your family as much as you can. Plan things in person, as often as possible. Knock on your neighbours' doors and invite them for dinner. Host your friends, make the first move, even if it feels awkward, even when nobody else is trying. And remember, sometimes the best way to reconnect is to disconnect. Delete any platforms that make you want to watch other people live their lives while letting yours pass by. Quit any app that drains your human drives and convinces you it is about *connection*.

And treasure people who care the least about your social media. The ones who want the whole you, and who know an Instagram grid could never capture it. The ones who are with you in your vulnerable moments, not viewing them on TikTok. The ones who ground you when you get caught up in all this, who could not care less about what's on your Instagram Story but care about your actual life. Such people are real, and rare. And don't forget: if anyone in your life expects you to be perfect all the time, to never have any negative feelings or flaws or insecurities, they want a product, not a person.

I know this is hard, really hard. So much of what I have written about in this book can make us want to give up on other people. But we have to resist this urge to run away. The answer cannot be to retreat from relationships; it has to be to take them more seriously. To kill that urge to run and avoid. Because we have two choices here. We can continue to detach and numb ourselves, or we can go all in, against the odds. I think we have to stop pretending that love and family aren't important, that they are a burden, that loving ourselves is enough. And we have to try even harder.

Otherwise, what's the alternative? Some safe but soulless life of consumption? Sitting inside watching strangers live their lives

CONCLUSION

instead of living our own? Staying anxious and alone and never seeing *that* as the ultimate risk? Never seeing the most dangerous life as the one that demands nothing of us? We have been duped into thinking we can create a life without danger, free from risk and discomfort and vulnerability, and that such a life is desirable. But we can't, and it's not. If you connect with someone and it comes with the risk of losing something, good. You are alive!

And if you grew up feeling alone and abandoned, now is your chance to prove that something better is possible. Become an example. Find someone and commit fully. Be the partner who shows that loyalty is not too much to ask for, the parent who shows that love can last. If I have a daughter someday, I don't want to model for her a 'strong independent woman' who doesn't need anybody; I want to model a strong woman who shows it's *okay* to depend on someone. It's okay to take a risk to be with someone, to give up some of yourself to belong to something bigger. And *that* is genuine independence – feeling loved and backed, and becoming resilient because of it. It is not a weakness to want to feel at home. We were not designed to do this alone.

The closer our relationships, the more we can resist becoming what companies want us to be. The more we can say *no*. You do not need to hide yourself behind Facetune or TikTok filters if you have people in your life who adore you as you are. You do not need to pathologise every emotion, or label every personality trait, if you accept that you are human, and humans have feelings and flaws. You do not need to download friendly AI chatbots if you have real relationships, or depend on simulations if you have an actual community around you.

None of this means we have to cut ourselves off from the modern world. There is nothing wrong with caring about how we look, working on ourselves or wanting to succeed. But these things become warped when we put them at the centre of our lives, when we devote ourselves to them, when algorithms drag them to extremes. And none of them are as sustaining as sincerely trying to be good and putting other people first. If you organise your life around looking perfect, there will always be something else to buy, another flaw to fix, and you will never feel enough. If you base your personality on what is popular online, your morality around what looks good, you will always feel behind. If you try to control every thought, and manage every feeling, your self-reflection will soon turn into self-obsession. And if you live for an online audience, you will forever be dependent on their approval, always anticipating their applause, and I promise you, it will never, ever, be enough.

I think, then, that we have to focus on doing the right thing for other people. We have to ask ourselves, 'How can I help them?' and try to choose that, every day. This won't make every decision easy, of course, but it gives us guidance. It eases the doubt and confusion. While writing this book, I began to realise that so much of our anxiety today comes from not trusting ourselves, from outsourcing every decision to 'experts'. We wait for them to show us how to live, to educate us on what we should think, to tell us which version of right or wrong is trending. And the more we turn to them, the less we trust ourselves.

But by focusing on the right thing for others, we will trust ourselves more. We only become overwhelmed by all of this noise about what to do, and how to feel, when we have nothing stronger guiding us. If you commit to living with honesty, loyalty and integrity, you can shut out so much outside influence. You can close down some of the endless choices, options and ways to turn. You

CONCLUSION

can know that you are at least living consistently and predictably in a world that is inconsistent and unpredictable. That you are making decisions based on what is right. And yes, this might cost you some opportunities, some easy paths to go down. But you won't pay with your peace of mind.

You will be rare too. It is rare to meet someone today who builds their life around doing the right thing, who puts other people first, who is selfless and humble when they have every encouragement not to be. We should treasure those people, and try to be more like them. And if you act this way, you will stand out. You will attract people with better values – people who treat you like a person and not a product, because that is how you treat yourself. So decide who you want to be, and hold yourself to that standard. Decide before the world decides for you.

That, to me, is genuine empowerment. Not the parody of empowerment girls are growing up with today, where being a strong woman means hiding how you feel, never fully investing in anyone, cutting people out and pretending to be fine. Girls today are being convinced that there is something wrong with them if they are sensitive and emotional, thinking that is weakness or insecurity. That is not true. A strong woman has strong *values*. You can be strong and feel things deeply. You can be soft and kind but firm with your values. Never let anyone convince you that your moral instincts are insecurities.

And finally – along with stepping back, becoming more private, investing in real relationships and trying to take care of others – I think we need to find faith. Not necessarily religious faith, but faith in *something* more, a conviction that more than this life is possible, something beyond hedonism and consumption and competition.

This book may have been bleak at times, but I had to be honest about where we are. The bravest thing we can do now, though, is hold onto hope. We distrust each other enough; we don't need more cynicism or warning signs or reasons to be suspicious. What we need to learn now is loyalty. We need to work on something more than our exhausting ability to detect 'red flags', to criticise and call out, to detach and numb ourselves. Now is the time to work on our waning ability to love, to depend, to forgive, to stick by each other, to focus on the needs of other people.

Resistance in the modern world is believing that real love exists. That real friendship is possible. That communities can be rebuilt. That there are good men and good women out there, trying their best. Today it can feel as though if you have faith in these things – in yourself, in other people, some cosmic faith in a moral order – that you will get walked all over. The opposite is true. The world walks all over you when you stop believing in the possibility of anything better, when you let it drag you wherever it wants, when you have faith only in betrayal and hurt and abandonment, when you see yourself as nothing but an expendable product. Have the courage to believe otherwise. Believe that some things in this life are sacred, and that you are one of them.

If the modern world has any meaning, if we have a purpose right now, I think it is in trying to live this way. That means shutting out the noise and cynicism, and choosing to act differently. Become the dependable friend you want to find. Become the loyal partner you are looking for. Conduct yourself as if real love exists, and you will come closer to finding it. Conduct yourself like a thinking, feeling human being, and that is how people will treat you. There are good people out there, feeling just as disheartened about the modern world, and I promise, they are waiting to find you.

CONCLUSION

*

To end, a final few messages.

First, to readers from older generations, thank you. All I ask now is that you talk to your daughters, granddaughters, nieces, students, any girls or young women you know, about the good in life. Tell her stories about love, about loyalty, about what actually matters – and, more importantly, *model* these things for her, show her they are possible in a world where she sees so few examples and hears so little encouragement. Remind her what she is worth, because chances are she has rarely been told this, and is reminded every single day that she is not enough. Give her this confidence so she can say *no* when she needs to.

That also means listening to her, really listening. You might not understand everything going on in her world, but I guarantee you have thoughts on love and loss, on hurt and abandonment, on right and wrong. What makes humans happy has not changed. Much like what makes us anxious, the things that fulfil us are age-old: close connection with other people; the satisfaction of giving to others and being needed in return; belonging to something bigger than ourselves; having humility and gratitude; growing through challenge and discomfort; aligning how we act with who we want to be. These are things you can teach no matter how much the world changes. And remember, if you don't give her guidance, influencers will. If you don't teach her about love, Tinder will. If you don't tell her what she is worth, Facetune will. And please, don't let your daughters on social media, not in their most vulnerable years.

To young women in their twenties, like me: it's easy to grieve our girlhood. To feel fearful about love, hopeless about the future, unhappy with ourselves. Maybe this book has made you realise that some of these trends and technologies hurt you more than you were letting on. Feel it; grieve it. But then turn disappointment into determination. We can take the pain and put every inch of it into putting ourselves back together.

Remember, too, the next generation of girls is watching us closely. Refuse to let them follow in our footsteps. Refuse to watch girls filter themselves, diagnose themselves, detach themselves, forever damage how they see themselves. This is more urgent now than ever, because an insecure, exposed, lonely, hurt, powerless and overwhelmed generation is the perfect consumer for AI, and for whatever is coming next. When I think back to being a teenage girl, what I desperately needed was someone to reach out to me and say, 'Hey, you feel this way too?' You can be that person for girls today. But it has to be now.

Finally, to those girls, the next generation: you do not have a disorder because you feel insecure about your face and body. You are not a freak for feeling anxious, paranoid or insecure. You are not needy for wanting loyalty and commitment. You are not pathetic for envying other girls or comparing your life to theirs. You are not broken because you find it hard to love yourself. You are not weak for suffering from family breakdown or fearing abandonment. You are not ungrateful for struggling when everyone tells you that you have it so good. These are signs that you are still a person, in a world that is trying to turn you into a product.

You feel these things because you are human. It's human to care, to love, to attach. It's natural to want to feel beautiful, to want to belong, to want security and stability. Of course you feel insecure in a world that is not secure. But you have a chance my generation didn't get. From a young age, you can see clearly what is happening

CONCLUSION

and where you are headed. You can refuse to be filtered and insecure; to be diagnosed and overwhelmed; to be documented and exposed; to be disconnected and lonely; to be detached and hurt; to be the version of 'empowered' that feels powerless.

None of this is to say that life will be easy. Even if you never used another beauty filter, deleted your social media accounts and swore off dating apps, life would still be hard. Being an adolescent girl is hard. Being a young woman is hard. Being *human* is hard. But you can at least free yourself from all of this unnecessary pressure, which makes everything so much harder. You do not have to deal with all the anxieties of growing up *and* all of these impossible demands too. Life can be more manageable.

But that means resisting. Resisting as the sales strategies get louder, as the ads and algorithms become more targeted, as the cultural messages become harder to ignore, as these industries expand. Resisting, little by little. Refusing, every day, to participate in anything that makes you feel like a product. And saying no to anybody who reduces you to an object, a thing to be used and thrown away.

Right now we stand at a crossroads. We can keep going down this path, allowing billion-dollar industries to dictate not only how we look but how we feel, how we live and how we see ourselves, or we can remember what has been taken from us, and turn back. We can remind our daughters, granddaughters and future generations of girls what real beauty, real friendship, real love, real community, real confidence, real *life* is, and help them remember what it means to be human.

And GIRLS® can become girls again: freer, happier, more resilient, more sociable, more hopeful, more sure of themselves. The next generation can feel all the age-old anxieties of adolescence but work their way through them, becoming strong, confident women, empowered by who they are on the inside.

Or we can allow them to become what we did: perfect on the outside, insecure on the inside. We can allow another generation of GIRLS® to be manufactured, another generation filtered, diagnosed, documented, disconnected, detached and 'empowered'.

This is the choice facing us. For older generations, it is up to you to help girls see that life does not have to be like this. For young women, it comes down to us to show the next generation how to break free, and become the example we wish we had. And for girls growing up today, you have decisions to make. I hope you realise how much you are worth.

Acknowledgements

There are so many people to thank for this book. First, my family: my beautiful mum, who showed me that a strong woman can still be soft, kind, and feel things deeply. Thank you also to Alfie; to my brother Morgan, for his constant support; and to my dad and Nicola, for getting me through difficult days. My nan and granddad, married for over sixty years, who showed me what real love is, and read every page of terrible stories I wrote before I could even spell. Roger and Nancy, who so generously lent me their home in Florida, where this book began. And Evan, who came into my life when I was falling apart, and put me back together again.

Thank you to special friends too: Sophee Severac, Sophie Spital, Carmen Hui Jing Lim, Nathan Levine, Esther and Jonny, who listened patiently to my complaints and pushed me to keep going. Thank you also to Sophie Winkleman, Seth Kaplan, James Davies, Rosie Tilli, Jakey Lebwohl, Alexa Arnold, Maria Petrova, Dave Cicirelli, Zach Rausch, and everyone on the Anxious Generation team, for your insights and encouragement. And to James and Helen Orr, for the beautiful cabin I lived in while finishing this book, where I could look outside my window and see what a real community is.

I am also deeply grateful to everyone at Swift and Henry Holt & Co., especially Mark Richards, Tim Duggan and Zoë Affron, for seeing potential in me and understanding the urgency of this crisis.

Thank you to Hilary McClellen and Ursula Doyle, and my wonderful agent, Matthew Hamilton, for always believing in this book.

I owe special thanks to two people: Konstantin Kisin, who first met me when I was a waitress in a cafe, gave me an opportunity and never let me miss another; and Jonathan Haidt, whose books had long inspired me, but who, when I met him, inspired me most with his humility, kindness and extraordinary generosity.

And thank you, finally, to the subscribers of my Substack *GIRLS*, for your enthusiasm, thoughtful comments, and heartfelt emails. You made this book possible. For a long time I thought there was something wrong with me; that changed when I began writing and hearing from you. You have supported me professionally and reassured me personally, and for that I will always be indebted.

Notes

All web links were checked and correct at early October 2025, unless otherwise indicated.

INTRODUCTION

1   More ruminative: Daniel P. Johnson and Mark A. Whisman, 'Gender Differences in Rumination: A Meta-Analysis', *Personality and Individual Differences*, 55/4 (2013), 367–74. https://doi.org/10.1016/j.paid.2013.03.019. Risk-averse: James P. Byrnes, David C. Miller and William D. Schafer, 'Gender Differences in Risk Taking: A Meta-Analysis', *Psychological Bulletin*, 125/3 (1999), 367–83. https://doi.org/10.1037/0033-2909.125.3.367. Prone to anxiety: Fatemeh Bahrami and Naser Yousefi, 'Females Are More Anxious Than Males: A Metacognitive Perspective', *Iranian Journal of Psychiatry and Behavioral Sciences*, 5/2 (2011), 83–90. https://pmc.ncbi.nlm.nih.gov/articles/PMC3939970/.

2   Girls and young women more sensitive to negative stimuli: Jiemin Yang et al, 'The Increased Sex Differences in Susceptibility to Emotional Stimuli during Adolescence: An Event-Related Potential Study', *Frontiers in Human Neuroscience*, 11 (2018), 660. https://doi.org/10.3389/fnhum.2017.00660. Sudden drop in confidence: Claire Shipman, Katty Kay and JillEllyn Riley, 'How Puberty Kills Girls' Confidence', *The Atlantic* (20 Sep. 2018), https://www.theatlantic.com/family/archive/2018/09/puberty-girls-confidence/563804/.

3   Rates of anxiety disorders: Katharine B. Parodi et al, 'Time Trends and Disparities in Anxiety Among Adolescents, 2012–2018', *Social Psychiatry and Psychiatric Epidemiology*, 57/1 (2022), 127–37. https://doi.org/10.1007/s00127-021-02122-9. Rates of depression: Jean M. Twenge, 'How Has Mental Health Changed Across Demographic Groups Since 2010?', *After Babel* [Substack] (20 Jun. 2024), https://www.afterbabel.com/p/demographic-variation. Rates of self-harm: Melissa C. Mercado et al, 'Trends in Emergency Department Visits for Nonfatal Self-Inflicted Injuries Among Youth Aged 10 to 24 Years in the United States, 2001–2015', *JAMA*,

318/19 (2017), 1931–33. https://doi.org/10.1001/jama.2017.13317. Rates of eating disorders: Erin Digitale, 'More Kids Are Being Hospitalized for Eating Disorders – Researchers Learned Why', Stanford Medicine News Center (18 Jan. 2024), https://med.stanford.edu/news/insights/2024/01/kids-hospitalized-eating-disorders-why.html.

4   Zach Rausch and Jon Haidt, 'Suicide Rates Are Up for Gen Z Across the Anglosphere, Especially for Girls', *After Babel* [newsletter] (30 Oct. 2023), https://www.afterbabel.com/p/anglo-teen-suicide.

5   'Youth Risk Behavior Survey Data Summary & Trends Report: 2011–2021', Centers for Disease Control and Prevention, https://www.cdc.gov/yrbs/dstr/pdf/YRBS_Data-Summary-Trends_Report2023_508.pdf.

6   Girls as young as ten: Donna A. Ruch et al, 'Trends in Suicide Among Youth Aged 10 to 19 Years in the United States, 1975 to 2016', *JAMA Network Open*, 2/5 (2019). https://doi.org/10.1001/jamanetworkopen.2019.3886. Emergency room visits: Ellen Yard et al, 'Emergency Department Visits for Suspected Suicide Attempts Among Persons Aged 12–25 Years Before and During the COVID-19 Pandemic – United States, January 2019–May 2021', *Morbidity and Mortality Weekly Report*, 70/24 (2021), 888–94. https://doi.org/10.15585/mmwr.mm7024e1.

7   Rising depression: Jean M. Twenge, 'How Has Mental Health Changed Across Demographic Groups Since 2010?,' *After Babel* [Substack] (20 Jun. 2024), https://www.afterbabel.com/p/demographic-variation. Rising loneliness: Claire Cain Miller, 'It's Not Just a Feeling: Data Shows Boys and Young Men Are Falling Behind,' *New York Times* (13 May 2025, updated 14 May 2025), https://www.nytimes.com/2025/05/13/upshot/boys-falling-behind-data.html. Rising hopelessness: 'Youth Risk Behavior Survey Data Summary & Trends Report: 2011–2021', Centers for Disease Control and Prevention (2011). Rising suicide: Richard Reeves and Will Secker, 'Male Suicide: Patterns and Recent Trends', American Institute for Boys and Men (Nov. 2023, updated Sep. 2024), https://aibm.org/research/male-suicide/.

8   'Women in the Labor Force: A Databook,' U.S. Bureau of Labor Statistics, Report 1092 (Apr. 2021), https://www.bls.gov/opub/reports/womens-databook/2020/.

9   Self-harm: Zach Rausch, 'The Girls Are Not Alright: Responses to Three Claims that the Youth Mental Health Crisis Is Exaggerated: Why Changes in Stigma and Self-Reporting Procedures Cannot Explain the International Decline of Adolescent Girls' Mental Health', *After Babel* [Substack] (11 Apr. 2024), https://www.afterbabel.com/p/the-girls-are-not-alright-responses. Eating disorders: Melody Schreiber, 'Eating Disorders among Teen Girls Doubled during Pandemic, CDC Study Shows', *The Guardian* (25 Feb. 2022), https://www.theguardian.com/world/2022/feb/24/eating-disorders-teen-girls-doubled-pandemic-cdc.

NOTES

FILTERED

1   Facetune by Lightricks, 'Facetune2 is finally here!' [Facebook post] (14 Apr. 2020), https://www.facebook.com/story.php/?story_fbid=1199620550208196&id=100353026801626.

2   James Charles, 'FACETUNING MY FOLLOWERS SELFIES', YouTube (8 May 2018), https://www.youtube.com/watch?v=cZRdXz1fzR0.

3   Anthon Raimund and Marie Southard Ospina, 'Is Facetune an Empowering Friend or a Toxic Foe?', *Dazed* (17 Feb. 2020), https://www.dazeddigital.com/beauty/article/47963/1/facetune-photoshop-instagram-face-editing-image-anthon-raimud-bella-hadid.

4   Neal Taparia, 'Why This Founder Stuck with His Vision After Striking Unexpected Gold', *Forbes* (30 Apr. 2021), https://www.forbes.com/sites/nealtaparia/2021/04/30/why-this-founder-stuck-with-his-vision-after-striking-unexpected-gold/.

5   Elle Hunt, 'Faking It: How Selfie Dysmorphia Is Driving People to Seek Surgery', *The Guardian* (1 Jan. 2019), https://www.theguardian.com/lifeandstyle/2019/jan/23/faking-it-how-selfie-dysmorphia-is-driving-people-to-seek-surgery.

6   Charles, 'FACETUNING MY FOLLOWERS SELFIES'.

7   Tana Mongeau (@tanamongeau), 'People keep asking, so, my skin care routine !!!!!! It's facetune. that's it. that's my skin care routine', Twitter (10.42 a.m., 3 May 2018), https://x.com/tanamongeau/status/991976363740381184.

8   Margot Harris, 'Chrissy Teigen Roasted Newt Gingrich's Wife for a Photo-Editing Fail', *Business Insider* (14 Sept. 2020), https://www.businessinsider.com/newt-gingrich-wife-getting-photo-editing-fail-facetune-chrissy-teigen-2020-9.

9   Jordan Page, 'The Complicated Ethics of Facetuning Your Friends', *VICE* (27 Apr. 2022), https://www.vice.com/en/article/facetune-app-users-fri/.

10   Issy Sampson, 'Khloe Kardashian Fans Accuse Her of Photoshopping Baby True's Face… Before Turning Off Instagram Comments', *The Sun* (19 Sep. 2018), https://www.thesun.co.uk/tvandshowbiz/7296481/khloe-kardashian-baby-true-facetune-instagram-comments-off/.

11   Abby Roberts, 'HOW TO FACETUNE LIKE A PRO', YouTube (19 Apr. 2019), https://www.youtube.com/watch?v=P4wSf4oDOiY; Megan Lacoste, 'how to ACTUALLY catfish people (makeup tutorial + beauty secrets)', YouTube (14 Oct. 2019), https://www.youtube.com/watch?v=cPshdP-hOvk.

12   James Charles, 'HOW TO TAKE YOUR SELFIES FROM DRAB TO FAB! FACETUNE TUTORIAL' (21 Mar. 2017), https://www.youtube.com/watch?v=KYbot1VxB84.

13   Georgia Aspinall, '"I Was Obsessed with Facetune": 71% Of People Won't Post a Picture Online Without Photoshopping It – That Needs to Change', *Grazia* (13 Aug. 2020), https://graziadaily.co.uk/life/in-the-news/photoshop-instagram-facetune/.

14   Techround Team, 'Facetune Apps Cap off Major Year of Growth with Record-Setting App Store Streak', *TechRound* (15 Dec. 2021), https://techround.co.uk/news/facetune-apps-major-growth-record-app-store/.

15   Over 730 million times: AppLovin, 'Lightricks' (n.d.), https://www.applovin.com/success-stories/lightricks/, accessed 28 Apr. 2025. Valued at around $1.8 billion: 'Lightricks, Award-Winning App Developer, Raises $130M Series D to Power Expansion and Champion Creator Economy', *Lightricks Magazine* (19 Sep. 2021), https://www.lightricks.com/post/lightricks-award-winning-app-developer-raises-130m-series-d-to-power-expansion-and-champion-creator-economy.

16   Facetune Team, 'Can You Facetune Videos? Yes, You Can', Facetune (16 May 2022), https://www.facetuneapp.com/blog/can-you-facetune-your-videos.

17   Instant AI enhancer: 'One Tap AI Photo Enhancer', Facetune (n.d.), https://www.facetuneapp.com/features/photo-enhancer. AI 'personal assistant': Tally Moran, 'Meet Your New AI Personal Assistant: A Game-Changer for Your Photos,' Facetune (18 Nov. 2024), https://www.facetuneapp.com/blog/unleash-future-photo-editing-facetune-ai-assistant?srsltid=AfmBOoqCfVGeuPwVhhav-o9WZt7CGMSdjBRgq8TlryQ1EkBDHQMDwfFa.

18   'Your Go-To AI Photo Editor', Facetune (n.d.), https://www.facetuneapp.com/features/ai-photo-editor.

19   Moran, 'Meet Your New AI Personal Assistant'.

20   Pixl Concerto Technology Limited, 'PrettyUp: AI Body Editor Video', version 8.4.00, App Store, https://apps.apple.com/us/app/prettyup-ai-body-editor-video/id1544211932.

21   Perfect365, homepage, https://www.perfect365.com.

22   Nick Statt, 'Snapchat Is Growing Up', *The Verge* (15 Sep. 2015), https://www.theverge.com/2015/9/15/9334125/snapchat-growing-up-replay.

23   Joss Fong and Dion Lee, 'Snapchat Filters: The Engineering Behind Augmented-Reality Selfies', *Vox* (28 Jun. 2016), https://www.vox.com/2016/6/28/12046792/how-snapchat-filters-work.

24   Jess Weatherbed and Mia Sato, 'Why Won't TikTok Confirm the Bold Glamour Filter Is AI?' *The Verge* (2 Mar. 2023), https://www.theverge.com/2023/3/2/23621751/bold-glamour-tiktok-face-filter-beauty-ai-ar-body-dismorphia.

25   Weatherbed and Sato, 'Why Won't TikTok Confirm the Bold Glamour Filter Is AI?'

26   zhangsta (@zhangsta), 'Lots of Controversy Around This Viral New Filter #boldglamourfilter and How Realistic It Looks' [video], TikTok (2 Feb. 2023), https://www.tiktok.com/@zhangsta/video/7205822453401128234?is_from_webapp=1&sender_device=pc&web_id=7519899533116589590.

27   Bobby Allyn, 'Does the "Bold Glamour" Filter Push Unrealistic Beauty Standards? TikTokkers Think So', NPR (10 Mar. 2023), https://www.npr.org/2023/03/10/1162286785/does-the-bold-glamour-filter-push-unrealistic-beauty-standards-tiktokkers-think-.

NOTES

28 Dove Beauty and Personal Care (@dove), 'Turn Your Back' [video], TikTok (8 Mar. 2023), https://www.tiktok.com/@dove/video/7208223549947923758?lang=en.

29 'Instagram Bans "Cosmetic Surgery" Filters', BBC News (23 Oct. 2019), https://www.bbc.co.uk/news/business-50152053.

30 Anthony Aarons and Madlin Mekelburg, 'Mark Zuckerberg Opposed Banning Plastic Surgery Filters, Despite Their Alleged Harm to Teen Mental Health, Because It Would Be "Paternalistic", Lawsuit Says', *Fortune* (27 Nov. 2023), https://fortune.com/2023/11/27/mark-zuckerberg-plastic-surgery-filters-teens-lawsuit/.

31 Daniel Mooney, 'fix me filter just out – come live your plastic surgery fantasy', Instagram (24 May 2019), https://www.instagram.com/danielmooney/p/Bx2XdrSIc2R/.

32 'Snap Inc. Announces Fourth Quarter and Full Year 2022 Financial Results' [press release], Snap Inc. [31 Jan. 2023], https://investor.snap.com/news/news-details/2023/Snap-Inc.-Announces-Fourth-Quarter-and-Full-Year-2022-Financial-Results/default.aspx.

33 'Investor Relations: 2024 Snap Partner Summit', Snap Inc. (n.d.), https://investor.snap.com/overview/default.aspx.

34 Tate Ryan-Mosley, 'Beauty Filters Are Changing the Way Young Girls See Themselves', *MIT Technology Review* (2 Apr 2021), https://www.technologyreview.com/2021/04/02/1021635/beauty-filters-young-girls-augmented-reality-social-media/.

35 Ashley Carman, 'Facebook Will Let Creators Put Their AR Effects in Messenger and Portal', *The Verge* (16 Sep. 2020), https://www.theverge.com/2020/9/16/21438403/facebook-spark-creator-ar-effects-messenger-portal.

36 Ryan-Mosley, 'Beauty Filters Are Changing the Way Young Girls See Themselves'.

37 Facetuned in real life: Rachel Leary, 'HOW TO LOOK FACETUNED IN REAL LIFE!! MAKE UP TUTORIAL | Rachel Leary', YouTube (28 Jul. 2019), https://www.youtube.com/watch?v=wX8oP_ze5-s. 'Bold Glamour' filter tutorial: PAINTEDBYSPENCER, 'The Viral "BOLD GLAMOUR" Filter Tutorial', YouTube (1 Mar. 2023), https://youtu.be/o7-oNgoJEWs?si=dGfAboHtVcggZtFR. L'Oreal product promotion: '3 SNAPCHAT FILTER-INSPIRED MAKEUP LOOKS', *L'Oréal Paris Beauty Magazine* (16 Aug. 2018), https://www.lorealparisusa.com/beauty-magazine/makeup/makeup-looks/snapchat-filter-makeup-looks.

38 'Almost Half of Young Girls Regularly Use Filters to Make Themselves Look Better', BBC *Newsround* (28 Aug. 2020), https://www.bbc.co.uk/newsround/53933501.

39 'Building Self-Esteem in the Social Media Age', Dove (n.d.), https://www.dove.com/uk/stories/campaigns/confidence.html.

40 Sophie van Soest, 'TikTok's New Retouch Feature Photoshops Your Face in Real-Time, and It's Messing with Our Heads', Rova (n.d.), https://www.rova.nz/articles/tiktok-s-new-retouch-feature-photoshops-your-face-in-real-time-and-it-s-messing-with-our-heads.

41   Sunflower_555, 'Tiktok automatically applies various filters', Reddit, r/Instagramreality (11 Jun. 2023), https://www.reddit.com/r/Instagramreality/comments/146noe7/tiktok_automatically_applies_various_filters/.

42   Believed to soften features: nothingswritten, 'Turning Off Snapchat Skin Smoothing Filter', Reddit, r/GooglePixel (27 Jan. 2018), https://www.reddit.com/r/GooglePixel/comments/7tecp6/turning_off_snapchat_skin_smoothing_filter. Zoom feature: 'Enhancing Your Video in Zoom', Zoom Support (25 Sep. 2025), https://support.zoom.com/hc/en/article?id=zm_kb&sysparm_article=KB0060352.

43   Liked, saved, commented on and lingered over: Mia Sato, 'Here's How Instagram Recommends the Content You See', *The Verge* (31 May 2023), https://www.theverge.com/2023/5/31/23744125/instagram-algorithm-recommendation-posts-reels-stories-shadow-banning#content. Emotional states: Sam Levin. 'Facebook Told Advertisers It Can Identify Teens Feeling "Insecure" and "Worthless"', *The Guardian* (1 May 2017), https://www.theguardian.com/technology/2017/may/01/facebook-advertising-data-insecure-teens.

44   WSJ Staff, 'Inside TikTok's Algorithm: A WSJ Video Investigation', *Wall Street Journal* (21 Jul. 2021), https://www.wsj.com/tech/tiktok-algorithm-video-investigation-11626877477.

45   ISABELLE (@isabelle.lux), 'you don't need your face muscles to show emotion – I've saved so much money on Botox over the years', TikTok (10 Sep. 2022), https://www.tiktok.com/@isabelle.lux/video/7141797530173590826.

46   Wayne Goss, 'I SLEPT IN SUNSCREEN FOR 20 DAYS!!!!', YouTube (9 Jul. 2021), https://www.youtube.com/watch?v=P4JObaEdsTY.

47   Maria Santa Poggi, 'We're in Micro-Insecurity Hell', *Allure* (22 Aug. 2024), https://www.allure.com/story/tiktok-micro-insecurities-trend.

48   Kathleen Chaykowski, 'Instagram Reaches 600 Million Monthly Users, Doubling in Size in Two Years', *Forbes* (15 Dec. 2016), https://www.forbes.com/sites/kathleenchaykowski/2016/12/15/instagram-reaches-600-million-monthly-users-doubling-in-size-in-two-years/.

49   Joe Wilkins, 'Facebook Allegedly Detected When Teen Girls Deleted Selfies So It Could Serve Them Beauty Ads', Futurism (3 May 2025 https://futurism.com/facebook-beauty-targeted-ads.

50   Wilkins, 'Facebook Allegedly Detected When Teen Girls Deleted Selfies'.

51   'TikTok Agrees Legal Payout over Facial Recognition', BBC News (26 Feb. 2021), https://www.bbc.co.uk/news/technology-56210052.

52   'Selfie Apps and Filters – A Real Threat to Your Online Safety?', Nevis Security (20 Sep. 2022), https://www.nevis.net/en/blog/are-selfie-apps-and-filter-a-threat-to-online-security.

53   Kelsey McCroskey, 'Nearly $4.5M Lightricks Settlement Resolves Lawsuit Over

NOTES

Alleged Biometric Privacy Violations', ClassAction.org (1 Nov. 2024), https://www.classaction.org/news/nearly-4.5m-lightricks-settlement-resolves-lawsuit-over-alleged-biometric-privacy-violations.

54   'Prices For Kylie Package', FAB Clinic (n.d.), http://kyliepackage.com/prices.

55   Daniel Ruby, 'TikTok Ad Revenue (2020–2027) – Detailed Analysis', Demand Sage (6 Sep. 2025), https://www.oberlo.com/statistics/tiktok-ad-revenue.

56   'TikTok Shop Statistics', Capital One Shopping (updated 1 Mar. 2025), https://capitaloneshopping.com/research/tiktok-shopping-statistics/.

57   'Instagram Ad Revenue (2017–2024)', Oberlo (n.d.), https://www.oberlo.com/statistics/instagram-ad-revenue.

58   Nelson Oboh, 'Instagram Will Top Facebook as the Largest U.S. Social Ad Platform by 2025', *The Keyword* (8 Jan. 2025), https://www.thekeyword.co/news/instagram-will-surpass-facebook-as-the-top-u-s-social-ad-platform-by-2025.

59   Zoella, 'How To: My Quick and Easy Hairstyles | Zoella', YouTube (5 Jun. 2013), https://www.youtube.com/watch?v=my3Bfd6qYrs; 'Back To School Beauty & Life Q&A | Zoella', YouTube (8 Sep. 2013), https://www.youtube.com/watch?v=N4VbgRD95IY; 'Boyfriend Does My Makeup | Zoella', YouTube (26 Jul. 2015), https://www.youtube.com/watch?v=HYTSFEytTQQ.

60   Waist trainers: kimkardashian, '#ad I'm really obsessed with waist training! Thank you @premadonna87 for my new waist shapers! #whatsawaist', Instagram (29 Oct. 2014), https://www.instagram.com/kimkardashian/p/uvjQoGOS6e. Weight-loss lollipops: Maya Oppenheim, 'Kim Kardashian Criticised for Promoting "Appetite Suppressant" Lollipops', *Independent* (16 Mar. 2018), https://www.independent.co.uk/news/world/americas/kim-kardashian-lollipops-appetite-suppressant-diet-flat-tummy-co-outrage-a8353831.html.

61   Christopher Ross, 'Influencer Marketing Market Size Worldwide from 2015 to 2025', Statista (n.d.), https://www.statista.com/statistics/1092819/global-influencer-market-size/.

62   Zak Stambor, 'Creators Have an Outsize Influence Over Gen Z Women's Beauty and Wellness Purchases', eMarketer (3 Aug. 2023), https://www.emarketer.com/content/creators-have-outsize-influence-over-gen-z-women-s-beauty-wellness-purchases.

63   Besties on Facetime: Fernanda Ramirez, 'GRWM as I overshare about my life like we're besties on Facetime... *this might all be TMI*', YouTube (22 Jul. 2025), https://www.youtube.com/watch?v=QKScJPoukHk. Overshare about my life: Mai Pham, 'GRWM while I overshare about my life because I broke up with my boyfriend', YouTube (19 May 2023), https://www.youtube.com/watch?v=eMlX4IU8saM.

64   'Why YouTube Stars Are More Influential Than Traditional Celebrities', Think with Google (n.d.), https://www.thinkwithgoogle.com/_qs/documents/604/youtube-stars-influence-b.pdf.

65 Jia Tolentino, 'The Age of Instagram Face', *New Yorker* (12 Dec. 2019), https://www.newyorker.com/culture/decade-in-review/the-age-of-instagram-face.

66 Viral 2017 video: Kim Kardashian, 'Kim Does Her Own Makeup', YouTube (28 Jun 2017), https://www.youtube.com/watch?v=_QvgzfNzHbY. Power of make-up: NikkieTutorials, 'The Power of MAKEUP!', YouTube (10 May 2015), https://www.youtube.com/watch?v=a4Ov8qvZ2_w.

67 Look like Kylie Jenner: @dope2111, 'How to look like Kylie Jenner !!!', YouTube (6 Jan. 2015), https://www.youtube.com/watch?v=sRLYt-NaDds, accessed 16 Sep. 2025. Instagram baddie: Mai Pham, 'spending $1000 to be an instagram baddie | transformation challenge', YouTube (27 Dec. 2018), https://www.youtube.com/watch?v=nHD5nNB7Cdk.

68 Everyday make-up: Madison Sarah, 'MY GO TO EVERYDAY MAKEUP FOR INSTAGRAM', YouTube (4 Feb. 2021), https://www.youtube.com/watch?v=qpFgwOB6Kqk. Take a selfie: Amber Scholl, 'GET READY WITH ME TO TAKE A SELFIE! (lol)', YouTube (18 Sep. 2019), https://www.youtube.com/watch?v=AfCLZPppwLo.

69 Tana Mongeau, 'GET A FACE FULL OF FILLER WITH ME (graphic) (also fake)', YouTube (1 Apr. 2010), https://www.youtube.com/watch?v=FQ9LwuOG4W4; 'I GOT A NOSE JOB?', YouTube (21 May 2016), https://www.youtube.com/watch?v=HsOVC9oxkfI; 'i got Kylie Jenner butt shots... oops (needle warning)', YouTube (11 Apr. 2020), https://www.youtube.com/watch?v=z9eXPVs6cek.

70 'Lip Service', *Keeping Up with the Kardashians* (season 10, episode 9, aired 10 May 2015 on E! Entertainment Television).

71 Emma Akbareian, 'Kylie Jenner Lip Filler Confession Leads to 70% Increase in Enquiries for the Procedure', *Independent* (7 May 2015), https://www.independent.co.uk/life-style/fashion/news/kylie-jenner-lip-filler-confession-leads-to-70-rise-in-enquiries-for-the-procedure-10232716.html.

72 Dangers of the trend: Carmen Chai, 'Doctors Warn Teens of Dangers from Trying Kylie Jenner Lip Challenge', *Global News* (24 Apr. 2015), https://globalnews.ca/news/1959039/doctors-warn-teens-of-dangers-from-trying-kylie-jenner-lip-challenge/. Kylie Jenner tweet: @kyliejenner, 'I want to encourage people/young girls like me to be YOURSELF & not be afraid to experiment w your look', Twitter (21 Apr. 2015), https://x.com/KylieJenner/status/590608585945649153.

73 Ellie Woodward, 'How Kylie Jenner Usurped the Kardashians', BuzzFeed News (14 May 2021), https://www.buzzfeednews.com/article/elliewoodward/kylie-jenner-lip-filler-drama-usurp-kardashians-powerful.

74 Marissa DeSantis, 'Kylie Jenner Responds as Forbes Claims She Is Not a Billionaire', *Evening Standard* (29 May 2020), https://www.standard.co.uk/lifestyle/celebrity/kylie-jenner-not-a-billionaire-forbes-reports-a4454901.html.

NOTES

75 Chase Peterson-Withorn, 'Inside Kylie Jenner's Web of Lies – and Why She's No Longer a Billionaire', *Forbes* (1 Jun. 2020), https://www.forbes.com/sites/chasewithorn/2020/05/29/inside-kylie-jenners-web-of-lies-and-why-shes-no-longer-a-billionaire/.

76 'Kylie Jenner "Sooo Over" Snapchat – and Shares Tumble', BBC News (23 Feb. 2018), https://www.bbc.co.uk/news/business-43163544.

77 $1 million per sponsored post: Zameena Mejia, 'Kylie Jenner Reportedly Makes $1 Million per Paid Instagram Post – Here's How Much Other Top Influencers Get', CNBC (31 Jul. 2018), https://www.cnbc.com/2018/07/31/kylie-jenner-makes-1-million-per-paid-instagram-post-hopper-hq-says.html, accessed 16 Sep. 2025. Closer to $2.4 million: '20 of Instagram's Highest Paid Stars in 2024', Influencer Marketing Hub (21 Mar. 2025), https://influencermarketinghub.com/instagram-highest-paid/.

78 Nose job: nicole (@nikkibabyy), 'this is your sign to get a nose job!best decision ever. #fyp #mtl #nosejob #nosejobcheck #montreal #foryou #rhinoplasty', TikTok (17 Feb. 2021), https://www.tiktok.com/@nikkibabyy/video/6930307998032153862. BBL consultation: Kat Clark (@katclark), 'GRWM for a BBL consultation #grwm #bbl #insecure', TikTok (26 Apr. 2023), https://www.tiktok.com/@katclark/video/7226253278659530002.

79 BotoxByMeesha (@botoxbymeesha), '25–30 is a great age to start baby botox #babybotox #startingbotox #AerieREAL #smile', TikTok (8 Apr. 2021), https://www.tiktok.com/@botoxbymeesha/video/6948756886699166982.

80 Garza Crew (@garzacrew), 'Just for fun #genalphainfluencers #genalpha', TikTok (22 Jan. 2024), https://www.tiktok.com/@garzacrew/video/7327047155015748907.

81 '20 Years On: Dove and the Future of Real Beauty', Unilever (23 Apr. 2024), https://www.unilever.com/news/news-search/2024/20-years-on-dove-and-the-future-of-real-beauty/.

82 'Khloé Kardashian's Take on Facetune vs. Reality', *Facetune Blog* (16 May 2022), https://www.facetuneapp.com/blog/khloe-kardashian-facetune-vs-reality.

83 James Charles, 'HOW TO TAKE YOUR SELFIES FROM DRAB TO FAB! FACETUNE TUTORIAL', YouTube (21 Mar 2017), https://www.youtube.com/watch?v=KYbot1VxB84.

84 Tana Mongeau, 'hello! i never smile in photos. my shirt says Facetuned. that is all', Instagram (3 May 2018), https://www.instagram.com/p/BiU-QPyjCSK/?hl=en.

85 Around 5 million weekly listeners: Naomi May, 'Kamala Harris' "Call Her Daddy" Podcast Interview Could Be Her Smartest Move Yet', *Elle* (7 Oct. 2024), https://www.elle.com/uk/life-and-culture/culture/a62526922/kamala-harris-call-her-daddy/. Clip of Tana Mongeau on *Call Her Daddy*: callherdaddy, 'FACETUNE PHOTOSHOP FAILS', Instagram (3 Dec. 2020), https://www.instagram.com/p/CIWb1e4AtAC/.

86 Facetune (@facetune), '#ICYMI: #selfies aren't going away anytime soon. Celebrate #InternationalWomensDay – reclaim the way you look at selfie editing, a habit which can actually be a powerful form of #selfexpression. Control your own look & join the debate now!', Twitter (9.11 a.m., 8 Mar. 2018), https://x.com/facetune/status/971674697036451841.

87 'Getting Work Done Is Absolutely a Form of Self-Love – Here's Why,' Plastic Surgery Institute of Southeast Texas (n.d.), https://lookyounger.net/getting-work-done-is-self-love.

88 Deadliest cosmetic procedure: Emily R. Finkelstein et al, 'The Brazilian Butt Lift Remains the Deadliest Aesthetic Surgery Procedure: Are Plastic Surgeons Adjusting Their Surgical Practice to Promote Safety?', *Aesthetic Surgery Journal*, 44/1 (2024), NP69–NP76. https://doi.org/10.1093/asj/sjad310. 'celebrate the bodies they live in': Mark Youssef, *The Art of the Brazilian Butt Lift: Evolve Your Beauty, Empower Your Life* (Mark Youssef, MD, 2019), https://www.amazon.co.uk/Art-Brazilian-Butt-Lift-Empower/dp/0578553635.

89 Leah Dolan, 'Madonna Hits Back at Ageist Criticism After Grammy Awards Appearance', CNN (8 Feb. 2023), https://edition.cnn.com/style/article/madonna-grammys-ageist-response/index.html.

90 Nicole Chenoweth, 'KHLOE'S KRISIS: Khloe Kardashian "Freaked Out" After Unedited Photo Posted 'by Mistake" & Is "So Embarrassed" Pic Went Viral', *The Sun* (6 Apr. 2021), https://www.thesun.co.uk/tvandshowbiz/celebrities/14566730/khloe-kardashian-freaked-out-unedited-photo-mistake-embarrassed-viral/.

91 Sarah Deen, 'Khloe Kardashian Insists She Has "Every Right" to Remove Unfiltered Bikini Pic from the Internet: "I've Been Conditioned to Feel I Am Not Beautiful Enough"', *Metro* (8 Apr. 2021), https://metro.co.uk/2021/04/08/khloe-kardashian-says-she-has-every-right-have-unedited-pic-removed-14375284/.

92 'Baby Rocky', *The Kardashians* (season 5, episode 5, aired 20 Jun. 2024 on Hulu).

93 Rachel Strugatz, 'Kim Kardashian Launches a 9-Step Skin Care Line', *New York Times* (1 Jun. 2022), https://www.nytimes.com/2022/06/01/style/kim-kardashian-skkn-skin-care-line.html.

94 'Baby Rocky', *The Kardashians*.

95 NikkieTutorials, 'My Facetune SECRETS Exposed! | NikkieTutorials', YouTube (8 Dec. 2020), https://www.youtube.com/watch?v=CW2iRNYGf9o.

96 'Merging Breast Augmentation and Breast Lift Surgery', Dr Cat Plastic Surgery (1 Nov. 2023), https://beautybydrcat.com/blog/merging-breast-augmentation-and-breast-lift-surgery/.

97 RealSelf homepage, https://www.realself.com/.

98 _hemokare, 'Embrace the beauty of your body as a canvas of empowerment, where each curve narrates tales of resilience, self-love, and the unique essence of womanhood', Instagram (9 Sep. 2023), https://www.instagram.com/p/Cw9QW3jO5yP/.

NOTES

99 'Facetune, Reshape a photo with AI in seconds' (accessed 30 Oct. 2025), https://www.facetuneapp.com/features/reshape-photo?srsltid=AfmBOooyJAN9TZHpa4Z6 1kJ68jBGTHqpkn62iHeQO81DhP9-3BFXUGEN.

100 Celebrating true selves and boosting confidence: Facetune: Video & Photo Editor [mobile app], Lightricks Ltd, https://apps.apple.com/us/app/facetune-video-photo-editor/id1149994032. Users true to themselves: Denise Primbet, 'The Bold Glamour Filter Is Proof That Western Beauty Is Still Seen as "The Golden Standard" and I'm Tired of It', *Glamour UK* (9 Mar. 2023), https://www.glamourmagazine.co.uk/article/bold-glamour-filter-western-beauty-standards.

101 'Which App Do Influencers Use for Photo Editing?' *Facetune Blog* (16 May 2022), https://www.facetuneapp.com/blog/influencers-and-celebrities.

102 'Body Image in Childhood', Mental Health Foundation (n.d.), https://www.mentalhealth.org.uk/explore-mental-health/articles/body-image-report-executive-summary/body-image-childhood.

103 Gemma Tatangelo et al, 'A Systematic Review of Body Dissatisfaction and Sociocultural Messages Related to the Body Among Preschool Children', *Body Image*, 18 (2016), 86–95. https://doi.org/10.1016/j.bodyim.2016.06.003.

104 'Millions of Teenagers Worry About Body Image and Identify Social Media As a Key Cause – New Survey by the Mental Health Foundation', Mental Health Foundation (15 May 2019), https://www.mentalhealth.org.uk/about-us/news/millions-teenagers-worry-about-body-image-and-identify-social-media-key-cause-new-survey-mental.

105 Amelia Hill, 'Social Media Triggers Children to Dislike Their Own Bodies, Says Study', *The Guardian* (1 Jan. 2023), https://www.theguardian.com/society/2023/jan/01/social-media-triggers-children-to-dislike-their-own-bodies-says-study.

106 Looking in mirrors for hours at a time: u/FunDear795, 'People don't realize how severe this disorder is, Agressive BDD makes you feel litteraly hopeless. so i decided to write down ALL of my bdd symptoms i have,' Reddit, r/BodyDysmorphia (10 Feb. 2022), https://www.reddit.com/r/BodyDysmorphia/comments/spbvri/people_dont_realize_how_severe_this_disorder_is/. 'practically housebound': u/synanthesia, 'I wish more people were aware of the severity of BDD,' Reddit, r/BodyDysmorphia (23 Feb. 2022), https://www.reddit.com/r/BodyDysmorphia/comments/xlxlhh/i_wish_more_people_were_aware_of_the_severity_of/.

107 Katharine A. Phillips and William Menard, 'Suicidality in Body Dysmorphic Disorder: A Prospective Study', *American Journal of Psychiatry*, 163/7 (2006), 1280–82. doi: 10.1176/appi.ajp.163.7.1280.

108 Dennis Thompson, 'Body Dysmorphia Affects Many Teens, Especially Girls', *Medical Xpress* (22 Mar. 2024), https://medicalxpress.com/news/2024-03-body-dysmorphia-affects-teens-girls.html.

109 Worsen body image issues: Georgia Wells, Jeff Horwitz and Deepa Seetharaman, 'Facebook Knows Instagram Is Toxic for Teen Girls, Company Documents Show', *Wall Street Journal* (14 Sep. 2021), https://www.wsj.com/tech/personal-tech/facebook-knows-instagram-is-toxic-for-teen-girls-company-documents-show-11631620739. Eating disorder symptoms: Simon M. Wilksch et al, 'The Relationship between Social Media Use and Disordered Eating in Young Adolescents,' *International Journal of Eating Disorders*, 53/8 (2019), 1142–1151. doi: 10.1002/eat.23198.

110 Wells, Horwitz and Seetharaman, 'Facebook Knows Instagram Is Toxic for Teen Girls'.

111 Elizabeth Parkin, Esme Kirk-Wade and Siobhan Wilson, 'Eating Disorders Awareness Week 2024', House of Commons Library (23 Feb. 2024), https://researchbriefings.files.parliament.uk/documents/CDP-2024-0045/CDP-2024-0045.pdf.

112 Parkin, Kirk-Wade and Wilson, 'Eating Disorders Awareness Week 2024'.

113 Royal College of Psychiatrists, 'Hospital Admissions for Eating Disorders Increased by 84% in the Last Five Years' [press release] (18 May 2022), https://www.rcpsych.ac.uk/news-and-features/latest-news/detail/2022/05/18/hospital-admissions-for-eating-disorders-increased-by-84-in-the-last-five-years.

114 Maria Pastore et al, 'Alarming Increase of Eating Disorders in Children and Adolescents', *Journal of Pediatrics*, 263 (2023), 113733, https://www.jpeds.com/article/S0022-3476(23)00596-6/fulltext.

115 From 3.5% to 7.8%: Marie Galmiche et al, 'Prevalence of Eating Disorders over the 2000–2018 Period: A Systematic Literature Review', *American Journal of Clinical Nutrition*, 109/5 (2019), 1402–13. https://doi.org/10.1093/ajcn/nqy342. Mostly among adolescent girls: Jovana Miskovic-Wheatley et al, 'Eating Disorder Outcomes: Findings from a Rapid Review of Over a Decade of Research', *Journal of Eating Disorders*, 11 (2023), 85. https://doi.org/10.1186/s40337-023-00801-3.

116 [deleted], 'My face inverted destroys my confidence completely', Reddit (7 Oct. 2021), www.reddit.com/r/BodyDysmorphia/comments/q2p1k7/my_face_inverted_destroys_my_confidence_completely/.

117 [deleted], 'Seeing myself inverted ruined my life', Reddit (3 Sep. 2023), www.reddit.com/r/BodyDysmorphia/comments/168lozb/seeing_myself_inverted_ruined_my_life/[2].

118 [deleted], 'how do you feel after you facetune yourself?', Reddit, r/Instagramreality (4 Jul. 2019), https://www.reddit.com/r/Instagramreality/comments/c8b8xw/how_do_you_feel_after_you_facetune_yourself/.

119 seyyun, 'Any other girl feel "unworthy" of being a girl?', Reddit, r/BodyDysmorphia (19 Jan. 2021), https://www.reddit.com/r/BodyDysmorphia/comments/lopf6r/any_other_girl_feel_unworthy_of_being_a_girl/.

NOTES

120 Sara Coughlin, 'THIS Is How Much Time We Spend Taking Selfies Each Week', *Refinery29* (24 Apr. 2015), https://www.refinery29.com/en-us/2015/04/86241/women-selfies-average-statistics.

121 'Girls As Young As 11 Consider Future Cosmetic Procedures As Appearance Pressures Soar', Girlguiding (22 Jul. 2024), https://www.girlguiding.org.uk/about-us/press-releases/girls-attitudes-survey-teaser-24/.

122 Anna Haines, 'From "Instagram Face" To "Snapchat Dysmorphia": How Beauty Filters Are Changing the Way We See Ourselves', *Forbes* (27 Apr. 2021), https://www.forbes.com/sites/annahaines/2021/04/27/from-instagram-face-to-snapchat-dysmorphia-how-beauty-filters-are-changing-the-way-we-see-ourselves/.

123 Statistics taken from Dove's 'Self-Esteem Project 2020', including the short film 'Reverse Selfie': Lottie Jackson, 'Selfie Culture & Body Image: 85% of Girls Have Edited Their Body in Photos by Age 13', Fashion Roundtable (16 Jan. 2024), https://www.fashionroundtable.co.uk/news/selfie-culture-body-image.

124 Statistics from Dove's 'Self-Esteem Project 2020', including 'Reverse Selfie': Newswire, 'Research Finds 80% of Canadian Girls Are Using Photo Editing Apps by the Age of 13' (20 Apr. 2021), https://www.newswire.ca/news-releases/it-s-time-to-have-the-selfie-talk-new-dove-self-esteem-project-research-finds-80-of-canadian-girls-are-using-photo-editing-apps-by-the-age-of-13-866468860.html.

125 Kristina Murkett, 'Body-Positive Gen Z Undergoes Record Cosmetic Surgeries', UnHerd (29 Jun. 2024), https://unherd.com/newsroom/body-positive-gen-z-undergoes-record-cosmetic-surgeries/.

126 'Girls As Young As 11 Consider Future Cosmetic Procedures'.

127 Andreea Mironica et al, 'Social Media Influence on Body Image and Cosmetic Surgery Considerations: A Systematic Review', *Cureus*, 16/7 (2024), e65626. doi: 10.7759/cureus.65626.

128 Anna Davies, 'People Are Getting Surgery to Look Like Their Snapchat Selfies', BBC Three (19 Apr. 2018), https://www.bbc.co.uk/bbcthree/article/9ca4f7c6-d2c3-4e25-862c-03aed9ec1082.

129 'How Social Media Affects Gen Z: Digital Wellbeing 2025 Report', The Cybersmile Foundation (20 Jun. 2025), https://www.cybersmile.org/2025/06/20/how-social-media-affects-gen-z-digital-wellbeing-2025-report/.

130 Bridie Pearson-Jones, 'Why Are Gen Z Ageing So Differently to Millennials? Experts Reveal Pressure to Use "Wrong" Skincare Too Young, Vaping and Getting Botox in Their Early 20s Mean Younger Generation Look Older Than Those in Their 30s', *Daily Mail* (2 Jan. 2024), https://www.dailymail.co.uk/femail/article-12849573.

131 'This is a pic of my freckles around age 12. Would you say this is the sort of bad sun damage that will cause significant damage like skin cancer/ deep wrinkles in the future? [Sun Care]', Reddit, r/SkincareAddiction (22 Oct. 2022), archived by Wayback

GIRLS®

Machine, https://web.archive.org/web/20221022164526/https://www.reddit.com/r/SkincareAddiction/comments/yakbio/this_is_a_pic_of_my_freckles_around_age_12_would/, accessed 2 Jul. 2025.

132   gamingoverdrive '[Anti-Aging] I'm only 14 and I have so many face wrinkles', Reddit, r/SkincareAddiction (15 Nov. 2018), https://www.reddit.com/r/SkincareAddiction/comments/9x7a05/antiaging_im_only_14_and_i_have_so_many_face/.

133   Jeannette Neumann, 'Tweens Obsessed with Skin Care Drive Brands to Say: Don't Buy Our Stuff', Bloomberg (5 Apr. 2024), https://www.bloomberg.com/news/articles/2024-04-05/sephora-kids-trend-sparks-warning-from-brands-tweens-don-t-buy.

134   Noor Lobad, 'Teen Beauty Spend Grew 23% Versus Last Year – Here's What They're Buying', *WWD* (20 May 2025), https://wwd.com/beauty-industry-news/beauty-features/teen-beauty-shoppers-skin-care-fragrance-favorite-brands-1237736743/.

135   Gemma Dunstan, 'Botox: Under-18s Come to Wales After England Bans Practice', BBC News (18 Oct. 2023), https://www.bbc.co.uk/news/uk-wales-67122138.

136   Parija Kavilanz, 'The "Sephora Kid" Trend Shows Tweens Are Psyched About Skincare. But Their Overzealous Approach Is Raising Concerns', CNN (12 Mar. 2024), https://www.cnn.com/2024/03/12/business/sephora-kid-tweens-skincare-obsession/index.html.

DIAGNOSED

1   hers @wearehers, 'The hers site is so chill and millennial, it'll feel like you're shopping for leggings – not prescription meds. The purchasing process is nearly as simple too: for $30, you can choose between 10 different common, generic types of birth control pills', Twitter (8.02 p.m., 24 Jan. 2019), https://x.com/wearehers/status/1088527526199205888. This line originated in a Shape article describing the Hers site. Hers later shared it on Twitter, as noted by *The Guardian*: Emily Reynolds, 'Marketing Medication As His and Hers? This Is "Anxiety Economy" At Its Worst', *The Guardian* (14 Mar. 2019), https://www.theguardian.com/commentisfree/2019/mar/14/marketing-antidepressants-his-hers-anxiety-economy-at-its-worse.

2   Pop Crave (@PopCrave), 'Bioré goes viral following sponsored post by an alleged school shooting victim that promotes their deep cleansing pore strips', Twitter (11.40 p.m., 19 May 2023), https://x.com/PopCrave/status/1659690418148368384.

3   Zoella. 'Dealing with Panic Attacks & Anxiety | Zoella', YouTube (7 Nov. 2012), https://www.youtube.com/watch?v=7-iNOFD27G4.

4   Over 169 million blogs: Christina Correnti et al, 'Dermatology on Tumblr', *Dermatology Online Journal*, 20/5 (2014), 22642, https://pubmed.ncbi.nlm.

NOTES

nih.gov/24852781/. Most users under 35: Mark Hoelzel, 'The Vast Majority of Tumblr and Instagram Users Are Under 35', *Business Insider* (3 Dec. 2014), https://www.businessinsider.com/the-vast-majority-of-tumblr-and-instagram-users-are-under-35-2014-12.

5   Justine Sharrock, 'Meet the Girl Behind One of Tumblr's Biggest Self-Harm Blogs', BuzzFeed News (13 Jun. 2013), https://www.buzzfeednews.com/article/justinesharrock/meet-the-girl-behind-one-of-tumblrs-biggest-cutting-suicide.

6   Anne-Sophie Bine, 'Social Media Is Redefining "Depression"', *The Atlantic* (28 Oct. 2013), https://www.theatlantic.com/health/archive/2013/10/social-media-is-redefining-depression/280818/.

7   'Instagram unveils #HereForYou mental health awareness campaign', *NCPS Blog* (2025), https://ncps.com/blog/posts/instagram-unveils-hereforyou-mental-health-awareness-campaign.

8   Snap Inc., 'Supporting Snapchatters' Mental Health & Wellbeing', Snap Values (6 May 2021), https://values.snap.com/news/supporting-snapchatters-mental-health-and-wellbeing.

9   'mental health journeys: 'Instagram Unveils #HereForYou Mental Health Awareness Campaign', National Counselling & Psychotherapy Society (n.d.), https://ncps.com/blog/posts/instagram-unveils-hereforyou-mental-health-awareness-campaign. '…how you really feel…': Snapchat (@Snapchat), 'For #BIPOCMentalHealthMonth, Snapchat partnered with Seize The Awkward to make it easy for you to reach out to a friend about their mental health', Twitter (6.25 p.m., 1 Jul. 2022), https://twitter.com/Snapchat/status/1542922292002295809.

10 'TikTok and Mind launch #SpeakYourMind to mark Mental Health Awareness Week 2020', TikTok Newsroom (18 May 2020), https://newsroom.tiktok.com/en-gb/tiktok-and-mind-launch-speakyourmind-to-mark-mental-health-awareness-week-2020.

11 'Creating Content Centered Around Mental Health', TikTok Creator Academy (n.d), https://www.tiktok.com/creator-academy/en/article/Mental-Health.

12 '…on Instagram': 'Instagram unveils #HereForYou mental health awareness campaign'. '… on Snapchat: Snapchat (@Snapchat)', 'Snapchat is proud to be a founding partner for the first-ever #MentalHealthAction Day, May 20th. Check out how you can take care of your mental health on Snapchat and encourage your friends to do the same,' Twitter (20 May 2021), https://x.com/Snapchat/status/1395192388578988035.

13 'snapping a quick pic!': American Foundation for Suicide Prevention (@afspnational), 'To help you start real conversations about mental health with your friends, @Snapchat + #SeizeTheAwkward are teaming up. Checking in is as simple as snapping a quick pic! Swipe through the filter carousel on Snapchat to find the new

custom filter and reach out to your friend', X (7.48 p.m., 26 Jul. 2023), https://x.com/afspnational/status/1684274439557373956. 'spread awareness': 'Mental Health Awareness on Snapchat', Snapchat Support (n.d.), https://help.snapchat.com/hc/en-gb/articles/7012388303892-Mental-Health-Awareness-on-Snapchat.

14   'Introducing Here for You', Snap Newsroom (11 Feb. 2020), https://newsroom.snap.com/en-GB/here-for-you.

15   Dirty underwear: samantha jo (@_samanthajo_), 'clean my MESSY depression room with me #cleantok #cleaningroom #depressionroom', TikTok (16 Jun. 2023), https://www.tiktok.com/@_samanthajo_/video/7245295348736986410. 'Started to smell': Skye (@fuckitveganchicknnugget), 'one of my biggest steps recovering from depression #cleanroom #cleantok #depressionroom #cleantiktok', TikTok (12 Jun. 2022), https://www.tiktok.com/@fuckitveganchicknnugget/video/7108487819227712811?lang=en.

16   robyn (@robynlewis444), 'Just a little storytime for u all #foryou #fyp #grwm #foryoupage #storytime #trauma #traumatok', TikTok (3 Aug. 2024), https://www.tiktok.com/@robynlewis444/video/7398886665542012192.

17   'waiting at a red light': mariana (@mariana_panzarella), 'Watch me have a panic attack while waiting at a red light', TikTok (12 Feb. 2025), https://www.tiktok.com/@mariana_panzarella/video/7470338676514458926. 'Cutting the cake': 🎂 (@alizardonamushroom), 'Things from my mental health diagnosis reveal party that just make sense', TikTok (17 Aug. 2025), https://www.tiktok.com/@alizardonamushroom/photo/7539559362579287309.

18   Mrs. Boda (@mommaboda), 'Anxiety in the flesh #anxiety #mentalhealth #psychology #copingmechanism #help #fyp #foryou #foryoupage #justbreathe #crying #shaking #anxietyattack', TikTok (6 May 2021), https://www.tiktok.com/@mommaboda/video/6959261658472582406.

19   TJ Hoegh (@tik_tok_counseling), 'The Trauma Test #fy #fyp #foryou #foryoupage #mentalhealthmatters #tiktoktherapist #wordsofwisdom', TikTok (31 Dec. 2020), https://www.tiktok.com/@tik_tok_counseling/video/6912255708134182150?is_copy_url=1&is_from_webapp=v1.

20   'TikTok Crosses 2 Billion Downloads After Best Quarter for Any App Ever', SensorTower (29 Apr. 2020), https://sensortower.com/blog/tiktok-downloads-2-billion.

21   Example: SundayOneDay (@meridian.wander), 'This song immediately triggers Ellie out lmao #system #switch #alters #elliewilliams # dancing #whopper #did #osdd (hateful comments will be deleted, just be nice)', TikTok (25 Feb. 2023), https://www.tiktok.com/@meridian.wander/video/7204574863611219242?lang=en.

22   '5 Signs…': Chris Wenger, CCC-SLP (@speechdude), '#speechtherapist #autism #neurodiversityaffirming #anxiety #depression #adhd #autisticwomen', TikTok (12 Mar. 2025), https://www.tiktok.com/@speechdude/video/7480770210572766510.

NOTES

'7 signs...': Tarah Elizabeth (@tarahelizabeth_), 'Warning signs as a teenager that you may have ADHD #adhd #adhdtiktok #adhdadult #adhdinwomen', TikTok (29 Jun. 2021), https://www.tiktok.com/@tarahelizabeth_/video/6979142521049992450. 5 Subtle Signs...': TherapyToThePoint (@therapytothepoint), '5 Subtle Signs of Trauma #traumatok #traumaawarenes #traumainformed #traumahealing #traumarecovery #traumaresponse', TikTok (28 Dec. 2024), https://www.tiktok.com/@therapytothepoint/video/7453488205678185774.

23 '...Childhood Trauma Challenge': Shahnta Hoare (@shahnta_hoare), '#putafingerdown #childhoodtrauma', TikTok (4 Oct. 2024), https://www.tiktok.com/@shahnta_hoare/video/7421964562058005790. '...Late Diagnosed Autistic Girl': ashralouisa, 'Put A Finger Down: Late Diagnosed Autistic Girl Edition', Instagram (19 Sep. 2023), https://www.instagram.com/reel/CxYTQIaRhut/.

24 Anxiety Fitness (@anxiety_fitness), 'Put a finger down WEIRD anxiety symptoms edition #fyp #foryou #putafingerdown #putafingerdownchallenge #anxiety' #anxietydisorder #mentalhealth', TikTok (5 Jan. 2021), https://www.tiktok.com/@anxiety_fitness/video/6921701231136132354?lang=en.

25 Lanna (@keylimelanna), 'It still blows my mind that I am not alone in these feelings anymore since I found out I'm autistic #actuallyautistic #audhd #autism #autismawareness #autismo #autismacceptance #autismawareness #autismoftiktok', TikTok (17 Oct. 2023), https://www.tiktok.com/@keylimelanna/video/7290994451114249514?lang=en.

26 'neurospicy' or 'neurosparkly': Tarah Elizabeth (@tarahelizabeth_), 'Sometimes the sparkle in neurosparkly doesnt feel so pretty and perfect and thats okay #adhdtiktok #adhdinwomen #adhdtips #adhdcommnity #neurosparkly', TikTok (6 Mar. 2024), https://www.tiktok.com/@tarahelizabeth_/video/7343403115208576257. 'Neurotypicals' boring: Victoria (@vpm.m), 'And then I have to mask to fit into that?? #fyp #foryou #foryourpage #neurodivergent #adhd #adhdtiktok', TikTok (2 Apr. 2024), https://www.tiktok.com/@vpm.m/video/7353362340483517729.

27 'hotistic': '#hotistic', TikTok, https://www.tiktok.com/tag/hotistic?lang=en. 'Hot girls have anxiety': Hot Mess with Alex Earle (@hotmess), 'Hot girls have anxiety, I don't make the rules. We're throwing it back a couple hot messes ago to hear all about my journey with anxiety in this weeks ep "Anxiety: From Hospitals to Healing [RE-RUN]" LIVE AT 12am EST !!!!!!', TikTok (27 Jun. 2024), https://www.tiktok.com/@hotmess/video/7384962369836911902. 'flavor of autism': Sarah (@saranne_wrap), 'What flavor of autism did you guys get? #stitch with @Ginger Rapunzel #actuallyautistic #audhd #autism #specialinterest #molecrickets', TikTok (27 Jan. 2024), https://www.tiktok.com/@saranne_wrap/video/7328909790351002923.

28 Masking autism your whole life: Morgan Foley (@morgaanfoley), 'Examples of autistic masking #actuallyautistic #fyp #autismtraits #autism #autisticmasking

273

#masking #neurodivergent #neurodivergenttiktok', TikTok (7 Jun. 2023), https://www.tiktok.com/@morgaanfoley/video/7242004143886306602. Hidden high-functioning anxiety: Example: Maggie Lancioni, LPC (@therapywithmaggielpc), 'Does this sound like you? #highfunctioninganxiety #anxietytherapist #anxietycheck #anxietytiktok #anxietytips', TikTok (19 Jun. 2022), https://www.tiktok.com/@therapywithmaggielpc/video/7110758951318228267.

29   jennifer (@saintjenni), '#greenscreenvideo #neurodivergent #actuallyautistic #audhd #autismawareness #autism', TikTok (2 Mar. 2024), https://www.tiktok.com/@saintjenni/video/7341747944476953899.

30   Megan (@megmoxie), '5 signs of executive dysfunction #executivedysfunction #adultadhd #neurodivergent #lazinessdoesnotexist #fyp #foryou', TikTok (10 Jul. 2023), https://www.tiktok.com/@megmoxie/video/7254234004600229163.

31   'GET RID OF…': 'GET RID OF PROCRASTINATION, Unlock Full Potential', Wisey (mobile app), https://wisey.app/c/procrastination?utm_source=ig&utm_medium=bio&utm_campaign=salepage. Both ADHD responses: Dr James Davies (PhD) (@JDaviesPhD), 'A new neuro-morality doing the rounds on TikTok…,' X (1.11 p.m., 17 Apr. 2024), https://x.com/JDaviesPhD/status/1780569887787618538.

32   Carla Ciccone, 'Coming Into Focus', *Harper's Bazaar* (5 Sep. 2022), https://www.harpersbazaar.com/culture/features/a41083545/adhd-in-adult-women/.

33   'Inside TikTok's Algorithm: A WSJ Video Investigation', *Wall Street Journal* (21 Jul. 2021), https://www.wsj.com/tech/tiktok-algorithm-video-investigation-11626877477.

34   Lindsay Dodgson, 'Police Say YouTuber Eugenia Cooney Is Fine, After a Flood of Calls from People Worried About How Thin She Looked', Yahoo! News (25 Oct. 2023), https://www.yahoo.com/entertainment/police-youtuber-eugenia-cooney-fine-103820192.html.

35   Symptoms of gender dysphoria: Sam (@transtherapylife), '6 lesser signs of gender dysphoria… #transgender #therapy #therapistsoftiktok #lgbt #enby #mentalhealthmatters', TikTok (27 Aug. 2020), https://www.tiktok.com/@transtherapylife/video/6865530679103327493. Labiaplasty: Dr Rose, M.D. (@the.rose.clinic), 'So many women have increased their quality of life with this procedure #labiaplasty #utahplasticsurgeon', TikTok (29 Apr. 2025), https://www.tiktok.com/@the.rose.clinic/video/7498834284124425502.

36   PinkNews (@pinknews), 'A Trans TikToker has shared how they kept their own ribs after getting them removed during gender affirming surgery… #transgender #lgbtqia #genderaffirmingsurgery #influencer', TikTok (14 Jan. 2025), https://www.tiktok.com/@pinknews/video/7459879618359643424.

37   Kris Jenner (@KrisJenner), 'I'm so proud of my darling @KendallJenner for being so brave and vulnerable. Seeing you share her most raw story in order to make a

positive impact for so many people and help foster a positive dialogue is a testament to the incredible woman you've become', Twitter (6.04 p.m., 5 Jan. 2019), https://x.com/KrisJenner/status/1081612447692148736,

38   Kris Jenner (@KrisJenner), 'Make sure to watch @KendallJenner's Twitter on Sunday night to find out what I'm talking about and be prepared to be moved #bethechange #shareyourstory #changetheconversation #proudmom #finallyasolution #authenticity #mydaughterinspiresme #getready', Twitter (6.04 p.m., 5 Jan. 2019), https://x.com/KrisJenner/status/1081612452523982849.

39   Lavendaire, 'what to do when you feel like doing nothing (unmotivated, burnt out, unproductive)', YouTube (19 Mar. 2021), https://www.youtube.com/watch?v=rU8APAwp6io.

40   Ingrid Nilsen, 'How I Get Ready on a Bad Day', YouTube (30 Aug. 2016), https://www.youtube.com/watch?v=QzTQJpMPUQI.

41   Zariah Taylor, 'Is Demetrius Harmon Using Mental Health to Sell Hoodies? [OPINION]', Vox ATL (28 Jan. 2020), https://voxatl.org/demetrius-harmon-mental-health-hoodies/.

42   sameyb, 'Discussing Anxiety and Corinna Kopf's Insulting New Clothing Range', *Television Magnets* [blog] (12 Feb. 2019), https://televisionmagnets.wordpress.com/2019/02/12/discussing-anxiety-and-corinna-kopfs-insulting-new-clothing-range/.

43   Corinna Kopf, 'opening up about my anxiety', YouTube (12 May 2018), https://www.youtube.com/watch?v=-SckmlLo_vM.

44   'mindful breathing necklaces': Komuso Design, 'Goodbye Anxiety, Hello Calm' (n.d.), https://uk.komusodesign.com/.

45   abbie jane (@abbiejane), 'pt. 2 since yall want more #fyp #therapytiktok #therapy #therapist #mentalhealthmatters,' TikTok (29 Jun. 2023), https://www.tiktok.com/@abbiejane/photo/7250211625402207534?lang=en.

46   'How Does Talkspace Work?', Talkspace (n.d.), https://www.talkspace.com/online-therapy/unlimited-messaging-therapy/.

47   'How Does Talkspace Work?', Talkspace Help Center (n.d.), https://help.talkspace.com/hc/en-us/articles/360057792572-How-Does-Talkspace-Work.

48   'Talkspace', *Psych Practice* [blog] (25 Mar. 2015), https://psychpracticemd.blogspot.com/2015/03/talkspace.html.

49   Steven Loeb, 'When BetterHelp Was Young: The Early Years', Vator (11 Nov. 2020), https://vator.tv/2020-11-11-when-betterhelp-was-young-the-early-years/.

50   BetterHelp – Therapy [mobile app], BetterHelp, https://apps.apple.com/us/app/betterhelp-therapy/id995252384.

51   Shira Li Bartov, 'BetterHelp Patients Furious at "Sketchy" Therapists', *Newsweek* (28 Nov. 2022, updated 15 Feb. 2023), https://www.newsweek.com/betterhelp-patients-tell-sketchy-therapists-1762849.

52 Taylor Lorenz, 'YouTube Stars Are Being Accused of Profiting Off Fans' Depression', *The Atlantic* (12 Oct. 2018), https://www.theatlantic.com/technology/archive/2018/10/youtube-stars-accused-of-profiting-off-depression-betterhelp-shane-dawson-phillip-defranco-elle-mills/572803/.

53 Saman Javed, 'Travis Scott Faces Backlash for Offering Astroworld Guests One Month of Online Therapy', *Independent* (10 Nov. 2021), https://www.independent.co.uk/life-style/health-and-families/travis-scott-astroworld-therapy-festival-b1955025.html.

54 Steven Asarch, 'It's Not Just You, There Are More BetterHelp Ads on YouTube', PassionFru (1 Apr. 2024), https://passionfru.it/betterhelp-youtube-ads-58959/.

55 'BetterHelp Leads Podcast Advertisers In December As Mental Health Brands Tap In', Insideradio (22 Jan. 2021), https://www.insideradio.com/free/betterhelp-leads-podcast-advertisers-in-december-as-mental-health-brands-tap-in/article_0db8a100-5c86-11eb-8514-0f2bb28e7b81.html.

56 Asarch, 'It's Not Just You'.

57 Rolfe Winkler, 'The Failed Promise of Online Mental-Health Treatment', *Wall Street Journal* (18 Dec. 2022), https://www.wsj.com/articles/the-failed-promise-of-online-mental-health-treatment-11671390353.

58 Metaffy, 'My Therapist is in her car or is shopping during our virtual sessions, is this normal?', Reddit, r/TalkTherapy (18 Aug. 2022), https://www.reddit.com/r/TalkTherapy/comments/wru4nd/my_therapist_is_in_her_car_or_is_shopping_during/.

59 Cool_Eggplant7036, 'My BetterHelp therapist has been messaging me using AI and then lied about it', Reddit, r/therapy (30 Nov. 2023), https://www.reddit.com/r/therapy/comments/187wol9/my_betterhelp_therapist_has_been_messaging_me/.

60 Federal Trade Commission, *In the Matter of BetterHelp, Inc.*, Docket No. C-4796 (Jun. 2023), https://www.ftc.gov/system/files/ftc_gov/pdf/2023169betterhelpcomplaintfinal.pdf.

61 Scripps News Staff, 'FTC Wants BetterHelp to Pay $7.8 Million for Lying About Data Privacy', Denver7 (6 Mar. 2023), https://www.denver7.com/news/national/ftc-wants-betterhelp-to-pay-7-8-million-for-lying-about-data-privacy.

62 Federal Trade Commission, *In the Matter of BetterHelp, Inc.*

63 BetterHelp Customers Will Begin Receiving Notices About Refunds Related to a 2023 Privacy Settlement with FTC', Federal Trade Commission (6 May 2024), https://www.ftc.gov/news-events/news/press-releases/2024/05/betterhelp-customers-will-begin-receiving-notices-about-refunds-related-2023-privacy-settlement-ftc.

64 More than 35,000 licensed therapists: BetterHelp Editorial Team, 'BetterHelp Platform Quality & Outcomes In 2024', BetterHelp (last modified 30 Jan. 2025), https://www.betterhelp.com/advice/general/betterhelp-platform-quality-and-outcomes-in/. Around $1 billion: '11 BetterHelp Statistics (2025): Revenue, Valuation, Usage,

NOTES

Users', TapTwice Digital Industry Research (last modified 2 Apr. 2025), https://taptwicedigital.com/blog/better-help-stats.

65 BetterHelp Editorial Team, 'How Much Does BetterHelp Online Therapy Cost?' (updated 22 Aug. 2025), https://www.betterhelp.com/advice/general/how-much-does-betterhelp-cost/.

66 Net worth over $460 million: 'Talkspace, Inc. (TALK)', Stock Analysis (n.d; last modified 2025), https://stockanalysis.com/stocks/talk/statistics/. Most basic plan: Emily Adamek, 'How Much Does Talkspace Cost in 2025?', ChoosingTherapy.com (24 Mar. 2025), https://www.choosingtherapy.com/how-much-does-talkspace-cost/.

67 Reddit user, 'Betterhelp attempting to shame people into getting therapy (sorry for bad vid quality)', Reddit, r/CorporateFacepalm (n.d.), https://www.reddit.com/r/CorporateFacepalm/comments/r5q6xv/betterhelp_attempting_to_shame_people_into/.

68 Cooking tutorials: Radhi Devlukia, 'Cooking with friends who don't cook EPISODE 1 @jayshetty', YouTube (30 Apr. 2024), https://www.youtube.com/watch?v=tmd6iFzvcXI. Political shows: One example I found is MeidasTouch, 'LIVE: Cohen REACTS to Trump TOTAL HUMILIATION at Debate', YouTube (livestream, 12 Sep. 2024), https://www.youtube.com/watch?v=TBBrtgUkXuY.

69 Law&Crime Network, 'Teen Cheerleader Brutally Murdered After Messy Breakup with Football Player Boyfriend', YouTube (13 Aug. 2024), https://www.youtube.com/watch?v=9w5olapMmBs.

70 Carolina Salazar (@thecarolinalifestyle), '#ad therapy is a GAME CHANGER. check the link in my bio if you want to try @betterhelp #mentalhealth #mentalhealthmatters,' TikTok (9 Jul. 2021), https://www.tiktok.com/@thecarolinalifestyle/video/6982701453827722502.

71 'healed girl summer': Freya India, 'No, Not Everyone Needs Therapy', GIRLS [Substack] (7 Nov. 2023), https://www.freyaindia.co.uk/p/no-not-everyone-needs-therapy. 'sad girl thoughts' and 'big girl depression': hers (@hers), 'This is a PSA to keep all existing therapy appointments. The sun is not a substitute for a licensed professional #mentalhealth #therapy #seasonaldepression #depression #anxiety,' TikTok (14 Apr. 2023), https://www.tiktok.com/@hers/video/7221963478871837994.

72 Nicole Mitchell (@nicole.dawna), '#ad Check out @BetterHelp today! #betterhelppartner #betterhelpsponsored', TikTok (12 May 2024), https://www.tiktok.com/@nicole.dawna/video/7367887398941773098.

73 'BetterHelp TV Spot, "Today Was Rough"', iSpot.tv (published 13 Mar. 2019), https://www.ispot.tv/ad/IsaJ/betterhelp-today-was-rough.

74 Talkspace – Therapy For All (@talkspaceonlinetherapy), 'No need to wait to get something off your mind. You can message your therapist 24/7 via text, video or voice. Get started with Talkspace at the link in bio today', TikTok (8 Sep. 2023), https://www.tiktok.com/@talkspaceonlinetherapy/video/7276399137392725291.

75 Talkspace (@talkspace), 'I would never go to #therapy', Twitter (6.51 p.m., 13 Oct. 2021), https://x.com/talkspace/status/1448345652887527435.

76 wearehers (@wearehers), 'Truth is, therapy is for everyone (yes, even you)', Twitter (4.37 p.m., 5 Dec. 2022), https://x.com/wearehers/status/1599805055053561866.

77 Laurel Duggan, 'One in Four Gen Z Adults Went to Therapy as Teens', UnHerd (10 Nov. 2023), https://unherd.com/newsroom/one-in-four-gen-z-adults-went-to-therapy-as-teens/.

78 PR Newswire, 'Online Therapy Services Market to Expand by USD 16.16 Billion (2024–2028), Driven by Smartphone Adoption and Demand for Online Services, AI Redefining Market Landscape', Yahoo! Finance (25 Nov. 2024), https://finance.yahoo.com/news/online-therapy-services-market-expand-183300827.html.

79 Character AI: Chat, Talk, Text [mobile app], Character Technologies, Inc., https://apps.apple.com/hk/app/character-ai-chat-talk-text/id1671705818?l=en-GB.

80 Joe Tidy, 'Young People Turning to AI Therapist Bots', Radio New Zealand (8 Jan. 2024), https://www.rnz.co.nz/news/world/506211/young-people-turning-to-ai-therapist-bots.

81 Tidy, 'Young People Turning to AI Therapist Bots'.

82 Elomia. 'Elomia – AI Mental Health Chatbot Designed by Clinicians' [homepage], https://elomia.com/.

83 Elomia, 'Elomia'.

84 'happiness buddy': Wysa: Mental Wellbeing AI [mobile app], Touchkin, https://play.google.com/store/apps/details?id=bot.touchkin&hl=en_GB. 'everyday worries': 'Mental Health Support That Meets Children and Young People Where They Are', Wysa (n.d.), https://www.wysa.com/children-and-young-people, accessed 19 Aug. 2025. 'friendly and caring chatbot' and 'everyday therapy…': Touchkin, *Wysa*.

85 'self care companion': 'Earkick – Self Care Companion – Is Now in The AppStore', *Earkick* [blog] (n.d.), https://blog.earkick.com/earkick-the-effortless-anxiety-tracker-is-now-in-the-appstore-6b3cc3963f1b/, accessed 19 Aug. 2025. Ages 4 and up: AI Companion – Earkick' [mobile app], Earkick, Inc., https://apps.apple.com/gb/app/ai-companion-earkick/id1584854531.

86 16.7 million posts: Poppy Koronka, 'Young People Turn to AI for Therapy over Long NHS Waiting Lists', *The Times* (21 Apr. 2025), https://www.thetimes.com/uk/healthcare/article/young-people-using-chatgpt-therapy-nhs-waiting-lists-sxjp9b6hj. 'literally all the details': Taylor Penley, 'Is Your Therapist AI? ChatGPT Goes Viral on Social Media for Its Role as Gen Z's New Therapist', *Fox News* (25 May 2025), https://www.foxnews.com/media/your-therapist-ai-chatgpt-goes-viral-social-media-role-gen-zs-new-therapist. 'the only person': ch3r7sh (@ch3r7sh), 'U guys do this too right lol #girlblogging #manifesting #aura', TikTok (6 Nov. 2024), https://www.tiktok.com/@ch3r7sh/video/7434259979508518176.

NOTES

87   EJ (Ejmiller25), 'Are white people okay? SSRIs should be a last resort, temporary, and not glamorized at all', X (9.19 p.m., 1 Jan. 2022), https://x.com/Ejmiller25/status/1477389105176657927.

88   Milly Veitch, '"I Didn't Access It for Years Because I Worried What People Would Think": Dr Alex George Reveals He's Taking Medication for His Anxiety As He Urges Fans to "Take a Stand" Against Stigma', *Daily Mail* (27 Nov. 2021), https://www.dailymail.co.uk/tvshowbiz/article-10249075/Dr-Alex-George-urges-people-post-photos-pills-bid-stand-against-stigma.html.

89   Dr Alex (@dralexgeorge), '#postyourpill #mentalhealth #health #doctor #nhs', TikTok (5 Feb. 2022), https://www.tiktok.com/@dralexgeorge/video/7061192819838307590.

90   Tayler Lewis-Bungay, 'What Is the Viral #PostYourPill Trend, and How Is It Destigmatising Mental Health Medication?', *Glamour UK* (8 Dec. 2021), https://www.glamourmagazine.co.uk/article/post-your-pill-trend.

91   Dr Alex George, 'Dr Alex George & Luke Howard – The Dreaded Pill (Official Lyric Video)', YouTube (1 Mar. 2024), https://www.youtube.com/watch?v=ZgKqcee3-VU.

92   Silly little pills: Saige (@saigeeeey), 'Hot girls take antidepressants', TikTok (14 Dec. 2021), https://www.tiktok.com/@saigeeeey/video/7041343450414976262. 'the zappies': Hannah Zello (@mello_zello14), 'It's always when I turn my head too fast #ssri #antidepressant #medication,' TikTok video (30 Apr. 2021), https://www.tiktok.com/@mello_zello14/video/6956968327176604934?lang=en.

93   'Which antidepressant are you?': gianna (@coughbuddy), 'you know you dont like abilify when you genuinly get offended by this filter #seroqueltiktok #zoloftgang #abilifytok #bipolartiktok #fyp', TikTok (23 Apr. 2023), https://www.tiktok.com/@coughbuddy/video/7225330091931290923. 'Little Miss Sertraline': Spoiledbratz, 'Sertraline Samsung Galaxy Phone Case', Redbubble, https://www.redbubble.com/i/samsung-case/sertraline-by-spoiledbratz/143669700.3A11C. 'hot girls take...': blush mind, 'Hot Girls Take Their Psych Meds Sticker – Funny Mental Health & Medication Advocacy Design Psych Student Aesthetic iPhone Case', Redbubble, https://www.redbubble.com/i/iphone-case/Hot-Girls-Take-Their-Psych-Meds-Sticker-Funny-Mental-Health-and-Medication-Advocacy-Design-Psych-Student-Aesthetic-by-blushmind/169678715.GENBX.

94   bkheel, 'Plush Prozac Pill', Etsy, https://www.etsy.com/uk/listing/1615818513/plush-prozac-pill; 'Hot Girls Take Lexapro Sweatshirt', Etsy, https://www.etsy.com/uk/listing/1335049733/hot-girls-take-lexapro-sweatshirt; MeyerLemonMakes, 'Stay Sexy Take Sertraline flag, mental health art, take your meds, Sertraline art', Etsy, https://www.etsy.com/uk/listing/1205646856/pre-order-stay-sexy-take-sertraline.

95 gmf.designs, 'where are all the medicated barbies out there. i'm the first two slides, shoutout zoloft and wellbutrin!', Instagram (24 Jul. 2023), https://www.instagram.com/p/CvELaHmsjOQ/?hl=en.

96 gabby_frost (@gabby_frost), 'for all the medicated barbies out there', X (5.24 p.m, 25 Jul. 2023), https://x.com/gabby_frost/status/1683875934665945091.

97 'a chemical imbalance': jazzy @jasmynessupersecretspam. '#relatable', TikTok (25 Feb. 2025), https://www.tiktok.com/@jasmynessupersecretspam/video/7475195332704423199?lang=en. 'It's not your period': relatablejulie_ (@relatablejulie_), 'It's not your period. It's not a boy. It's not school. It's not waking up on the wrong side of the bed. It's a chemical imbalance in your head', TikTok (24 Mar. 2025), https://www.tiktok.com/@relatablejulie_/video/7485224557977079083?lang=en. Only slightly better than placebos: 'Analysis: Depression Is Probably Not Caused by a Chemical Imbalance in the Brain – New Study', University College London (20 Jul. 2022), https://www.ucl.ac.uk/news/2022/jul/analysis-depression-probably-not-caused-chemical-imbalance-brain-new-study.

98 Dien Ho, 'Antidepressants and the FDA's Black-Box Warning: Determining a Rational Public Policy in the Absence of Sufficient Evidence', *Virtual Mentor*, 14/6 (2012), 483-88. https://doi.org/10.1001/virtualmentor.2012.14.6.pfor2-1206.

99 Dr Alex (@dralexgeorge), 'Today is the 1st of the month and the 1st day of the New Year. Join me and #postyourpill', TikTok (1 Jan. 2023), https://www.tiktok.com/@dralexgeorge/video/7183601331700026630.

100 Daisy Keech (@daisykeech), '#ad mental health care for depression, anxiety, and ADHD online with @getcerebral. Start your first month for $30 with DAISY30 #mentalhealth #ad', TikTok (16 Aug. 2021), https://www.tiktok.com/@daisykeech/video/6997109932365466886.

101 K. S. Sakshi, 'Cerebral's Valuation Quadruples to USD 4.8 Billion After Accumulating USD 300 Million in a SoftBank Funding Round', The Global Economics (9 Dec. 2021), https://www.theglobaleconomics.com/2021/12/09/cerebral/.

102 'Uber for mental health care': *Slate* (@slate), 'Cerebral promises to bring prescription drugs to your door, like Uber for mental health care. But has the company sacrificed patient care for growth?', Twitter (12.42 p.m., 23 Mar. 2022), https://x.com/Slate/status/1506612370231148562. Adderall and benzodiazepines: Rolfe Winkler, 'Startup Cerebral Soared on Easy Adderall Prescriptions. That Was Its Undoing', *Wall Street Journal* (8 Jun. 2022), https://www.wsj.com/health/healthcare/cerebral-adderall-adhd-prescribe-11654705250.

103 'Telehealth Company Cerebral Agrees to Pay Over $3.6 Million in Connection with Its Business Practices that Encouraged the Unauthorized Distribution of Controlled Substances', U.S. Department of Justice (4 Nov. 2024), https://www.

NOTES

justice.gov/usao-edny/pr/telehealth-company-cerebral-agrees-pay-over-36-million-connection-business-practices.

104 Keech, '#ad mental health care for depression'.

105 Hers [channel], YouTube, https://www.youtube.com/channel/UCkEdiHcUZjzs8IqO2j4jhaA/about.

106 'How It Works', Hers (n.d.), https://www.forhers.com/how-it-works#:%7E:text=free%20deliveryget%20your%20treatment%20shipped%20to%20your%20door&text=After%20you%20are%20diagnosed%2C%20if.

107 Hers (@wearehers), 'The hers site is so chill and millennial, it'll feel like you're shopping for leggings – not prescription meds. The purchasing process is nearly as simple too: for $30, you can choose between 10 different common, generic types of birth control pills', Twitter (8.02 p.m., 24 Jan. 2019), https://x.com/wearehers/status/1088527526199205888.

108 'Weight Loss Treatments That Put You First', Hers (n.d.), https://www.forhers.com/weight-loss, accessed 15 Aug. 2025.

109 Sara Morrison, '"Scary Easy. Sketchy as Hell.": How Startups Are Pushing Adderall on TikTok', Vox (29 Aug. 2022), https://www.vox.com/recode/23310326/tiktok-adhd-telehealth-done-adderall.

110 Sarah Marsh, 'My Doctor Diagnosed Me with ADHD – So How Did My Phone Find Out?', The Guardian (25 Nov. 2023), https://www.theguardian.com/commentisfree/2023/nov/25/doctor-diagnosed-adhd-phone-targeted-ads.

111 tryminded (@tryminded), 'Here are some common (but, often unexpected) signs of anxiety #anxietyrelief #anxiety #anxietydisorder #signsofanxiety', TikTok (23 Jun. 2022), https://www.tiktok.com/@tryminded/video/7112469918880271662.

112 Around $3.4 million: Morrison, '"Scary Easy"'. '13 official behaviours': doneadhd (@doneadhd), '13 official behaviors that make sense after my ADHD diagnosis', TikTok (2 Feb. 2023), https://www.tiktok.com/@doneadhd/video/7195675008448941354.

113 Max Matza, 'Telehealth Executives Accused of $100m Adderall Scheme', BBC News (14 Jun. 2024), https://www.bbc.co.uk/news/articles/cd11qr67qj60.

114 Cancelled with Tana Mongeau & Brooke Schofield, 'ONE OF US GOT PEED ON... CANCELLED EP 18,' YouTube (17 Dec. 2021), https://www.youtube.com/watch?v=jRiCkf6Bbnw.

115 'Hers TV Spot, "Stress Levels" Featuring Kristen Bell', iSpot.tv (12 Jan. 2023), https://www.ispot.tv/ad/28sj/hers-stress-levels-featuring-kristen-bell.

116 Georgia Aspinall, 'No, It's Not Okay to Advertise Beta Blockers to People "Nervous About A Big Date"', Grazia Daily (14 Mar. 2019), https://graziadaily.co.uk/life/in-the-news/hims-hers-propronalol/.

117 Hers, 'It's time to break the stigma around taking mental health medication. While not everyone with depression or anxiety needs to be on medication, it is

COMPLETELY OKAY if you do', Instagram (9 May 2022), https://www.instagram.com/p/CdWCSqdrrPY/. The full advert, 'Depression', is available at iSpot, https://www.ispot.tv/ad/bCUD/hers-depression.

118   Coping with a break-up: Hadley Mendelsohn, 'Anxiety After Breakups: 6 Coping Strategies and Treatments', Hers (13 Aug. 2022, updated 4 May 2025), https://www.forhers.com/blog/anxiety-after-breakup. 'quarter-life crisis': Mendelsohn, 'Quarter-Life Crisis: What It Is and How to Deal', Hers (25 Sep. 2024), https://www.forhers.com/blog/quarter-life-crisis. 'holiday stress': Mendelsohn, 'Holiday Stress and Anxiety: 6 Ways to Cope', Hers (n.d.), https://www.forhers.com/guides/holiday-stress. A form of self-care: Mendelsohn, 'Your Complete Guide to Self Care', Hers (22 Mar. 2025), https://www.forhers.com/guides/self-care.

119   Nicholas Gibson, 'Test Anxiety: Strategies for Overcoming Anxiety Related to Exams', *For Hers* (updated 4 Feb. 2023, archived 25 Jul. 2024), https://web.archive.org/web/20240725185112/https://www.forhers.com/blog/test-anxiety.

120   Hers, 'Mental health without the stigma and judgment – that's what Hers does. That's why we're thrilled to partner with @kristenanniebell to normalize the conversation around asking for help when you need it. It's mental health care as it should be', Instagram (12 Jan. 2023), https://www.instagram.com/p/CnUXgkhNX6h/.

121   'skip the barriers': Hers (@wearehers), 'Struggling with anxiety or depression? We're here to help you skip the barriers and get you facing the tough stuff faster with access to experienced providers, science-backed prescriptions, & anonymous support groups so you can heal on your own schedule: https://forhers.com/mental-health', Twitter (9.15 p.m., 15 Feb. 2021), https://x.com/wearehers/status/1361423790052417538. 'huge roadblock': Hers (@wearehers), 'Stigma can be a huge roadblock for people wanting help with their mental and emotional health', Twitter (8.45 p.m., 17 May 2021), https://x.com/wearehers/status/1394378436681125895.

122   tryminded (@tryminded), 'We're starting a movement to destigmatize mental health medication. For every post shared using #alittlehelpfrommymeds and tagging @tryminded, we'll donate $10 to help increase access to mental health care. #mentalhealthawarenessmonth #endthestigmaofmentalhealth #mentalhealthtreatment', TikTok (13 May 2022), https://www.tiktok.com/@tryminded/video/7097237611848224046.

123   Cerebral, 'No one should be shamed for using medication to take care of their mental health. By @doodlewellness' [Facebook post] (14 Jun. 2020), https://www.facebook.com/Cerebral/photos/a.3141524079194578/3519112978102351/.

124   Kao-Ping Chua et al, 'Antidepressant Dispensing to US Adolescents and Young Adults', *Pediatrics*, 153/4 (2024), e2023063684. doi: 10.1542/peds.2023-064245.

NOTES

125 'A Third of Teenagers Say They Have Been Prescribed Antidepressants, Survey Finds', Stem4 (14 Sep. 2022), https://stem4.org.uk/a-third-of-teenagers-say-they-have-been-prescribed-antidepressants-survey-finds/.

126 Charlotte Archer et al, 'Rise in Prescribing for Anxiety in UK Primary Care Between 2003 and 2018: A Population-Based Cohort Study Using Clinical Practice Research Datalink', *British Journal of General Practice*, 72/720 (2022), e511–e519. https://doi.org/10.3399/BJGP.2021.0561.

127 Anxiety and depression: Emily Hamblin, 'Gender and Children and Young People's Emotional and Mental Health: Manifestations and Responses: A Rapid Review of the Evidence', National Children's Bureau (July 2016), https://www.ncb.org.uk/sites/default/files/uploads/files/NCB%2520evidence%2520review%2520-%2520gender%2520and%2520CYP%2520mental%2520health%2520-%2520Aug%25202017.pdf. Eating disorders: Binx Yezhe Lin et al, 'Increasing Prevalence of Eating Disorders in Female Adolescents Compared with Children and Young Adults: An Analysis of Real-Time Administrative Data', *General Psychiatry*, 37 (2024), e101584. https://doi.org/10.1136/gpsych-2024-101584. Gender dysphoria: Charlotte Constable Fernandez and Sarah Bunn, 'Hormone Treatments for Children and Young People with Gender Dysphoria', POSTbrief 55, UK Parliament (22 Nov. 2023), https://researchbriefings.files.parliament.uk/documents/POST-PB-0055/POST-PB-0055.pdf. Autism: Ginny Russell et al, 'Time Trends in Autism Diagnosis over 20 Years: A UK Population-Based Cohort Study', *Journal of Child Psychology and Psychiatry*, 63/6 (2021), 674–82. https://doi.org/10.1111/jcpp.13505. ADHD: Elie Abdelnour, Madeline O. Jansen and Jessica A. Gold, 'ADHD Diagnostic Trends: Increased Recognition or Overdiagnosis?', *Missouri Medicine*, 119/5 (2022), 467–73. https://pmc.ncbi.nlm.nih.gov/articles/PMC9616454/.

128 Luke P. Grosvenor et al, 'Autism Diagnosis Among US Children and Adults, 2011–2022', *JAMA Network Open*, 7/10 (2024), e2436215. doi:10.1001/jamanetworkopen.2024.42218.

129 'Data and Statistics on Children's Mental Health', Centers for Disease Control and Prevention (10 Jun. 2025), https://www.cdc.gov/children-mental-health/data-research/index.html.

130 Jon Haidt, 'Why the Mental Health of Liberal Girls Sank First and Fastest: Evidence for Lukianoff's Reverse CBT Hypothesis', *After Babel* [Substack] (9 Mar. 2023), https://www.afterbabel.com/p/mental-health-liberal-girls.

131 Haidt, 'Why the Mental Health of Liberal Girls Sank First and Fastest'.

132 *Elle*: Zeynab Mohamed, 'Young Women Are Self-Diagnosing Personality Disorders, Thanks To TikTok', *Elle UK* (21 Apr. 2022), https://www.elle.com/uk/life-and-culture/a39573245/young-women-self-diagnose-personality-disorder-tiktok/. *New York Times*: Christina Caron, 'Teens Turn to TikTok in Search of a Mental Health

Diagnosis', *New York Times* (29 Oct. 2022), https://www.nytimes.com/2022/10/29/well/mind/tiktok-mental-illness-diagnosis.html. *Teen Vogue:* Lo Styx, 'Dissociative Identity Disorder on TikTok: Why More Teens Are Self-Diagnosing with DID Because of Social Media', *Teen Vogue* (27 Jan. 2022), https://www.teenvogue.com/story/dissociative-identity-disorder-on-tiktok.

133 Joe Pierre, 'The Debate over Whether Dissociative Identity Disorder Is "Real"', *Psychology Today* (7 Feb. 2023), https://www.psychologytoday.com/gb/blog/psych-unseen/202302/the-debate-over-whether-dissociative-identity-disorder-is-real.

134 Thomas J. Dishion and Jessica M. Tipsord, 'Peer Contagion in Child and Adolescent Social and Emotional Development,' *Annual Review of Psychology*, 62 (2011), 189–214. https://doi.org/10.1146/annurev.psych.093008.100412.

135 John D. Haltigan, Tamara M. Pringsheim and Gayathiri Rajkumar, 'Social Media as an Incubator of Personality and Behavioral Psychopathology: Symptom and Disorder Authenticity or Psychosomatic Social Contagion?,' *Comprehensive Psychiatry* 121 (2023): 152362, https://doi.org/10.1016/j.comppsych.2022.152362.

136 Helen Lewis, 'The Twitching Generation', *The Atlantic* (27 Feb. 2022), https://www.theatlantic.com/ideas/archive/2022/02/social-media-illness-teen-girls/622916/.

137 Tamara Pringsheim et al., 'Rapid Onset Functional Tic-Like Behaviors in Young Females During the COVID-19 Pandemic', *Movement Disorders*, 36/12 (2021), 2707–13. https://doi.org/10.1002/mds.28778.

138 Lewis, 'The Twitching Generation'.

139 Jennifer Frey, Kevin J. Black and Ibrahim A. Malaty, 'TikTok Tourette's: Are We Witnessing a Rise in Functional Tic-Like Behavior Driven by Adolescent Social Media Use?', *Psychological Research and Behavior Management*, 15 (2022), 3575–85. https://doi.org/10.2147/PRBM.S359977.

140 Lewis, 'The Twitching Generation'.

141 Frey, Black and Malaty, 'TikTok Tourette's'.

142 All figures up until this point in the paragraph are taken from Charlotte Constable Fernandez and Sarah Bunn, 'Hormone Treatments for Children and Young People with Gender Dysphoria', POSTbrief 55, UK Parliamentary Office of Science and Technology (22 Nov. 2023), https://researchbriefings.files.parliament.uk/documents/POST-PB-0055/POST-PB-0055.pdf.

143 Sarah C. J. Jorgensen, 'Transition Regret and Detransition: Meanings and Uncertainties', *Archives of Sexual Behavior*, 52/5 (2023), 2173–84. https://doi.org/10.1007/s10508-023-02626-2.

144 Dylan Mulvaney (@dylanmulvaney), 'Day 172 – ffs consult with @Facial Plastic/Reconstructive', TikTok (30 Aug. 2022), https://www.tiktok.com/@dylanmulvaney/video/7137782539992796458?lang=en.

NOTES

145   'Best #trans TikTok Hashtags – Boost Views & Likes in 2025', TikTokHashtags.com (n.d.), https://tiktokhashtags.com/hashtag/trans/.

146   Constable Fernandez and Bunn, 'Hormone Treatments'.

147   Annie Tang et al, 'Gender-Affirming Mastectomy Trends and Surgical Outcomes in Adolescents', *Annals of Plastic Surgery*, 88/4 (2022), S325–31. doi: 10.1097/SAP.0000000000003135.

148   'What Are Co-Occurring Issues for Children and Young People with Gender Dysphoria' (n.d.), Clinical Advisory Network on Sex and Gender, https://can-sg.org/frequently-asked-questions/what-are-co-occurring-issues-for-children-and-young-people-with-gender-dysphoria/.

149   Hilary Cass, 'The Cass Review: Independent Review of Gender Identity Services for Children and Young People' (2024), https://cass.independent-review.uk/home/publications/final-report/.

150   Tara M. Chaplin, Jane E. Gillham and Martin E. P. Seligman, 'Gender, Anxiety, and Depressive Symptoms: A Longitudinal Study of Early Adolescents', *Journal of Early Adolescence*, 29/2 (2009), 307–327. https://doi.org/10.1177/0272431608320125.

151   Amanda J. Rose, 'Co-Rumination in the Friendships of Girls and Boys', *Child Development*, 73/6 (2002), 1830–43. doi: 10.1111/1467-8624.00509.

152   Amanda J. Rose, Wendy Carlson and Erika M. Waller, 'Prospective Associations of Co-Rumination with Friendship and Emotional Adjustment: Considering the Socioemotional Trade-Offs of Co-Rumination', *Developmental Psychology*, 43/4 (2007). https://doi.org/10.1037/0012-1649.43.4.1019.

153   'Mental Illness, Political Ideology, and Holding False Beliefs', Skeptic Research Center (n.d.), https://research.skeptic.com/mental-illness-political-ideology-and-holding-false-beliefs/.

154   Abigail Shrier, *Bad Therapy: Why the Kids Aren't Growing Up* (Swift Press, 2024).

155   Sally Weale, 'Mindfulness in Schools Does Not Improve Mental Health, Study Finds', *The Guardian* (12 Jul. 2022), https://www.theguardian.com/society/2022/jul/12/mindfulness-schools-does-not-improve-mental-health-study.

156   Lucy Foulkes and Argyris Stringaris, 'Do No Harm: Can School Mental Health Interventions Cause Iatrogenic Harm?', *BJPsych Bulletin*, 47/5 (2023), 267–69. doi: 10.1192/bjb.2023.9.

157   Ellen Barry, 'Are We Talking Too Much About Mental Health?', *New York Times* (6 May 2024), https://www.nytimes.com/2024/05/06/health/mental-health-schools.html.

158   Barry, 'Are We Talking Too Much About Mental Health?'.

159   Barry, 'Are We Talking Too Much About Mental Health?'.

160   Alexander Tin, 'Nearly a Third of Adolescents Getting Mental Health Treatment, Federal Survey Finds', CBS News (20 Mar. 2024), https://www.cbsnews.com/news/mental-health-treatment-samhsa-survey-teens/.

161 Marc Stone et al, 'Risk of Suicidality in Clinical Trials of Antidepressants in Adults: Analysis of Proprietary Data Submitted to US Food and Drug Administration', *BMJ*, 339 (2009), b2880. https://doi.org/10.1136/bmj.b2880.

162 Agnes Higgins, Michael Nash and Aileen M. Lynch, 'Antidepressant-Associated Sexual Dysfunction: Impact, Effects, and Treatment', *Drug, Healthcare and Patient Safety*, 2 (2010), 141–50. https://doi.org/10.2147/DHPS.S7634.

163 Joanna Moncrieff, John Read and Mark Abie Horowitz, 'The Nature and Impact of Antidepressant Withdrawal Symptoms and Proposal of the Discriminatory Antidepressant Withdrawal Symptoms Scale (DAWSS)', *Journal of Affective Disorders Reports*, 15 (2024), 100765. https://doi.org/10.1016/j.jadr.2024.100765.

164 Least safe and warning for suicidality: Robert M. Nevels, Samuel T. Gontkovsky and Bryman E. Williams, 'Paroxetine – The Antidepressant from Hell? Probably Not, but Caution Required', *Psychopharmacology Bulletin*, 46/1 (2016), 77–104. https://pmc.ncbi.nlm.nih.gov/articles/PMC5044489/. 'Social phobia' and 'hot flashes': 'Generic for Paxil', Hers (n.d.), https://www.forhers.com/psychiatry/paroxetine. https://www.forhers.com/psychiatry/paroxetine.

165 David Healy and Dee Mangin, 'Post-SSRI Sexual Dysfunction: Barriers to Quantifying Incidence and Prevalence', *Epidemiology and Psychiatric Sciences*, 33 (2024), e40. doi: 10.1017/S2045796024000441.

166 Read patient stories at https://www.pssdnetwork.org/.

167 Joseph Ben-Sheetrit et al, 'Estimating the Risk of Irreversible Post-SSRI Sexual Dysfunction (PSSD) Due to Serotonergic Antidepressants', *Annals of General Psychiatry*, 22/15 (2023). https://doi.org/10.1186/s12991-023-00447-0.

168 Starting sertraline at 15: 'PSSD Patient Spotlight Rebekah', PSSD Network (n.d.), https://www.pssdnetwork.org/patient-spotlight/becky. Fluoxetine at 12: frootootootoot, 'The experience of someone who got PSSD at 12', Reddit, r/PSSD (18 Feb. 2025), https://www.reddit.com/r/PSSD/comments/1is2t2h/the_experience_of_someone_who_got_pssd_at_12/. Genital numbness after escitalopram: Anna. PSSD Scandinavia (@anna11bella), 'It's my 22nd birthday. I was harmed by Lexapro 6 years ago. Emotional blunting and genital numbness have yet to go away, though I discontinued all SSRI medication many years ago. I was never informed of the possibility of this devastating and debilitating condition', Twitter (9.51 p.m., 11 Jan. 2023), https://twitter.com/anna11bella/status/1613292522096283653.

169 'Post SSRI Sexual Dysfunction (PSSD) Subreddit', Reddit (n.d.), https://www.reddit.com/r/PSSD/.

NOTES

DOCUMENTED

1   'Snap Inc. (SNAP): History, Ownership, Mission, How It Works & Makes Money', *DCF Modeling* [blog] (n.d.), https://dcfmodeling.com/blogs/history/snap-history-mission-ownership.

2   Liana Jade (@lianajadee), 'I went to the doctors again to find out that I could potentially have HIV or hepatitis from the infusion I had during birth', TikTok (9 May 2023), https://www.tiktok.com/@lianajadee/video/7231235678976183578.

3   'YouTube', Britannica.com, https://www.britannica.com/topic/YouTube.

4   'Most Consecutive Daily Personal Video Blogs Posted on YouTube', Guinness World Records (1 May 2019), https://www.guinnessworldrecords.com/world-records/most-consecutive-daily-personal-video-blogs-posted-on-youtube.

5   Cristos Goodrow, 'You Know What's Cool? A Billion Hours', *YouTube Official Blog* (27 Feb. 2017), https://blog.youtube/news-and-events/you-know-whats-cool-billion-hours/.

6   Kevin Systrom, 'Introducing Video on Instagram', *Instagram Blog* (20 Jun. 2013), https://about.instagram.com/blog/announcements/introducing-video-on-instagram.

7   'Introducing the new Snapchat', Snap Newsroom (29 Nov. 2017), https://newsroom.snap.com/introducing-the-new-snapchat.

8   Tony Long, 'Feb. 15, 2005: YouTube and Your 15 Minutes of Fame', *Wired* (15 Feb. 2011), https://www.wired.com/2011/02/0215youtube-launched/.

9   Salvador Rodriguez, 'Snapchat Unveils Stories, a Feature That Shows Content for 24 Hours', *Los Angeles Times* (3 Oct. 2013), https://www.latimes.com/business/technology/la-fi-tn-snapchat-stories-feature-20131003-story.html.

10 Kurt Wagner, 'Messenger Just Became the Latest Facebook App to Launch a Stories Feature', *Vox* (9 Mar. 2017), https://www.vox.com/2017/3/9/14863428/messenger-stories-days-snapchat-instagram.

11 Tim Bradshaw, 'Snapchat Triples Video Traffic as It Closes the Gap with Facebook', *Financial Times* (8 Nov. 2015), https://www.ft.com/content/a48ca1fc-84e7-11e5-8095-ed1a37d1e096.

12 Nick Antonopoulos, 'Snapchat's Growth Story: From Picaboo to Social Media Giant (2011–2025)', SEO Design Chicago (n.d.), https://seodesignchicago.com/social-media-marketing/snapchat-platform-growth/.

13 '48. Snapchat', CNBC (17 Jun. 2014), https://www.cnbc.com/2014/06/16/disruptors-in-2014-snapchat.html.

14 Over 150 million: Sarah Frier, 'Instagram Puts Ads on Stories Feature as Users Reach 150 Million', Bloomberg (11 Jan. 2017), https://www.bloomberg.com/news/articles/2017-01-11/instagram-stories-to-get-ads-reaches-150-million-daily-users.

500 million: Kate Bojkov, 'Instagram Stories Analytics: Everything You Need to Know', EmbedSocial (6 May 2023), https://embedsocial.com/blog/instagram-stories-analytics/.

15   Will Oremus, 'BeReal Is Hotter than TikTok. So TikTok Is Copying It', *Washington Post* (17 Sep. 2022), https://www.washingtonpost.com/technology/2022/09/17/bereal-copy-tiktok-instagram-snapchat/.

16   Instagram user figure: Stacy Jo Dixon, 'Instagram – Statistics & Facts,' Statista (3 Jun. 2025), https://www.statista.com/topics/1882/instagram/. TikTok user figure: Shubham Singh, 'How Many People Use TikTok 2025 (Users Statistics)', DemandSage (12 Sep. 2025), https://www.demandsage.com/tiktok-user-statistics/.

17   Snap Inc., 'Snap Inc. Investor Presentation: February 2024', http://q4live.s25.clientfiles.s3-website-us-east-1.amazonaws.com/442043304/files/doc_financials/2023/q4/Snap-Inc-Q4-2023-Investor-Presentation-Final.pdf.

18   Michelle Faverio and Olivia Sidoti, 'Teens, Social Media and Technology 2024' [report], Pew Research Center (12 Dec. 2024), https://www.pewresearch.org/internet/2024/12/12/teens-social-media-and-technology-2024/.

19   Emily A. Vogels, Risa Gelles-Watnick and Navid Massarat, 'Teens, Social Media and Technology 2022' [report], Pew Research Center (10 Aug. 2022), https://www.pewresearch.org/internet/2022/08/10/teens-social-media-and-technology-2022/.

20   In the UK: Cara L. Booker, Yvonne Kelly and Amanda Sacker, 'Gender Differences in the Associations Between Age Trends of Social Media Interaction and Well-Being among 10–15 Year Olds in the UK', *BMC Public Health*, 18/1 (2018), 321. https://doi.org/10.1186/s12889-018-5220-4. Visually oriented platforms: 'Children and Parents: Media Use and Attitudes Report 2023', Ofcom (29 Mar. 2023), https://www.ofcom.org.uk/siteassets/resources/documents/research-and-data/media-literacy-research/children/childrens-media-use-and-attitudes-2023/childrens-media-use-and-attitudes-report-2023.pdf?v=329412.

21   Nayden Tafradzhiyski, 'YouTube Revenue and Usage Statistics (2025)', Business of Apps (26 February 2025), https://www.businessofapps.com/data/youtube-statistics/.

22   A billion hours every day: 'YouTube Statistics 2025 [Users by Country + Demographics]', Global Media Insight (5 Jun. 2025), https://www.globalmediainsight.com/blog/youtube-users-statistics/. YouTube Shorts: Kayla Cobb, 'YouTube Shorts Now Averages 200 Billion Daily Views', TheWrap (18 Jun. 2025), https://www.thewrap.com/youtube-shorts-200-billion-daily-views/.

23   Sarah Jossel, 'The Crowning Glory for TikTok's New Mums #birthingmakeup', *The Times* (5 Feb. 2023), https://www.thetimes.com/uk/social-media/article/the-crowning-glory-for-tiktoks-new-mums-birthingmakeup-hmrfq6mjw.

NOTES

24 Mac McCann (@MacMcCannTX), 'this Instagram model's father passed away,,,, and she did a photo shoot with the open casket....', Twitter (5.05 p.m., 26 Oct. 2021), https://twitter.com/MacMcCannTX/status/1453030106528632836.

25 Chloe Taylor, 'Kids Now Dream of Being Professional YouTubers Rather than Astronauts, Study Finds', CNBC (19 Jul. 2019), https://www.cnbc.com/2019/07/19/more-children-dream-of-being-youtubers-than-astronauts-lego-says.html.

26 Matt & Abby (@matt_and_abby), '3rd trimester here we come #mattandabby', TikTok (11 May 2023), https://www.tiktok.com/@matt_and_abby/video/7232048159575248170.

27 MattandAbby, 'Taking Care of My Sick Wife #shorts', YouTube (30 Dec. 2022), https://www.youtube.com/shorts/brVN9BNu504.

28 Matt & Abby, 'POV: you're cleaning p*ke off the carpet at 1a.m. #shorts', YouTube (31 Dec. 2022), https://www.youtube.com/watch?v=i3W_SIFrDNU.

29 Zoella, 'The Boyfriend Tag | Zoella', YouTube (17 Ap. 2016), https://www.youtube.com/watch?v=YMZape3gW-k.

30 Nate Garner, 'telling my girlfriend i love you... *for the first time*', YouTube (11 Mar. 2019), https://www.youtube.com/watch?v=k0JW3-imfwE.

31 NearlyParents, '59: The Wedding (Part 1)', YouTube (22 May 2023), https://www.youtube.com/watch?v=F1Ge34aAjeA.

32 Emma Grey Ellis, 'The Post-Truth World of Influencer Romances', *Wired* (28 Aug. 2019), https://www.wired.com/story/internet-influencer-fauxmance/.

33 Aja Romano, 'Jake Paul and Tana Mongeau's Giant YouTuber Wedding Married Reality TV to the Internet. Beneath the Clout-Grabbing Spectacle, "Jana" Is About Beating YouTube at Its Own Game', *Vox* (30 Jul. 2019), https://www.vox.com/2019/7/30/20746411/jake-paul-tana-mongeau-wedding-fake-youtube-reality-culture.

34 Jen Smith, 'A New Chapter', YouTube (18 May 2016), https://www.youtube.com/watch?v=loKazRqIJ9U.

35 Emma Kelly, 'YouTube Golden Couple Liza Koshy and David Dobrik Announce Break-Up in Emotional Video', *Metro* (6 Jun. 2018, updated 12 Dec. 2019), https://metro.co.uk/2018/06/06/youtube-golden-couple-liza-koshy-david-dobrik-announce-break-emotional-video-7610033/.

36 NearlyParents, 'Spencer & Vogue Get REVEAL ALL About Their Sex Life', YouTube (26 Apr. 2023), https://www.youtube.com/watch?v=f1kDmY_AGOw.

37 NearlyParents, 'HAS OUR S*X GOT BORING?', YouTube (14 Jul. 2025), https://www.youtube.com/watch?v=kDUMqDMMmnw; NearlyParents, 'Jamie's libido is BACK! But Sophie's has vanished...', YouTube (10 Jun. 2024), https://www.youtube.com/watch?v=D6adoYU9DMk; NearlyParents, 'Are Jamie's bedroom skills bog standard?', YouTube (25 Mar. 2024), https://www.youtube.com/watch?v=tlJVAji84fk.

38   NearlyParents, 'Our Most EXPLOSIVE Episode | FULL EPISODE', YouTube (16 Nov. 2022), https://www.youtube.com/watch?v=6bkzUu6c8-0.
39   *Molly-Mae: Behind It All* [TV miniseries], Prime Video (released 17 Jan. 2025), https://www.amazon.co.uk/Molly-Mae-Behind-All-Season-Part/dp/B0DN24C8NT.
40   Koazy Kove Podcast, 'Finding out the GENDER of our Baby & Dealing with the Backlash', YouTube (8 Apr. 2025), https://www.youtube.com/watch?v=FqiSZ-xIXPw.
41   How to soft-launch a relationship: Rachel Varina. 'Here's Exactly How (and Why!) You Should Soft Launch Your Relationship on Instagram', *Cosmopolitan* (9 Aug. 2022), https://www.cosmopolitan.com/sex-love/a40835774/soft-launch-relationship/. Step-by step guides and quote: Addison Aloian, 'What Is a Soft Launch? All About the Social Media Trend and How to Do It Right, According to Experts', *Women's Health* (12 Jul. 2024), https://www.womenshealthmag.com/uk/health/a61581348/what-is-soft-launch/.
42   Ria Chopra, 'Would You Break Up if Your Partner Won't Post You on Instagram?', *VICE* (28 Sep. 2023), https://www.vice.com/en/article/would-you-break-up-if-your-partner-wont-post-you-on-instagram/. Emily Gould, 'Why Won't My Boyfriend Post Me on Instagram?', *The Cut* (21 Aug. 2024), https://www.thecut.com/article/going-through-it-advice-why-wont-my-boyfriend-post-me-on-instagram.html.
43   Iveta, 'People Are Sharing Pics of Boyfriends "Forced" to Take Perfect Pictures of Their Girlfriends', Bored Panda (15 Feb. 2017), https://www.boredpanda.com/men-photoshoot-girlfriends-boyfriends-of-instagram/.
44   'Don't date boys…': Rebecca Reid, 'Don't Date Boys Who Won't Take Pictures for Your Instagram', *Metro* (22 Sep. 2017, updated 12 Dec. 2019), https://metro.co.uk/2017/09/22/dont-date-boys-who-wont-take-pictures-for-your-instagram-6948085/. 'How to Train…' and quote: Deleesh, 'How to Train an Instagram Boyfriend in 7 Steps', *life is deleesh* [blog] (n.d.), https://www.deleesh.com/deleeshblog/how-to-train-an-instagram-boyfriend.
45   Facebook and Instagram pages created: One example is boyfriends_of_insta [profile] (n.d.), https://www.instagram.com/boyfriends_of_insta/?hl=en. Standing in traffic: boyfriends_of_insta, 'Don't think thats what Cardi meant when she said "Came thru drippin'" honey', Instagram (5 Aug. 2019), https://www.instagram.com/p/B0zAKn7nggj/.
46   Can never get it right: Freya India, 'Your Boyfriend Isn't Your Camera Man', *After Babel* [Substack] (29 May 2024), https://www.afterbabel.com/p/your-boyfriend-isnt-your-camera-man. 'teach him to take…': Maddy (@madelinebajczyk), 'What to tell your boyfriend so that he takes better photos of you for Instagram. #boyfriendtutorial #takebetterphotos #howtotakepictures #howtotakeaphoto #instagramphotoideas #instagramphototips,' TikTok (17 Aug. 2023), https://www.tiktok.com/@madelinebajczyk/video/7268303928800972075. *GQ*: Brit Dawson, 'How to Take

NOTES

a Photo of Your Girlfriend', *GQ* (24 Aug. 2023), https://www.gq-magazine.co.uk/article/how-to-take-a-photo-of-your-girlfriend.

47 David Suh, 'The Ultimate Instagram Boyfriend Course' (n.d), https://www.davidsuh-courses.com/course/igbf.

48 wretchedegg123, 'How to deal with gf that spends hours taking pictures'. Reddit, r/travel (26 Nov. 2023), https://www.reddit.com/r/travel/comments/18454iu/how_to_deal_with_gf_that_spends_hours_taking/.

49 4chencookie, 'I [29M] am having difficulty playing boyfriend of instagram for my GF [30F]', Reddit, r/relationships (27 Feb. 2018), https://www.reddit.com/r/relationships/comments/80if6h/i_29m_am_having_difficulty_playing_boyfriend_of/.

50 Ross Martin-Pavitt, 'YouTuber Accidentally Uploads Video Forcing Her Crying Son to Pose for Thumbnail', *Independent* (10 Sep. 2021), https://www.independent.co.uk/tv/news/youtuber-accidentally-uploads-video-forcing-her-crying-son-to-pose-for-thumbnail-b2187431.html.

51 'FIRST 48 HOURS': Matt & Abby (@matt_and_abby), 'Our FULL vidoe "the first 48 hours with our newborn" is now LIVE #mattandabby #abbyhoward #matthoward', TikTok (31 Aug. 2023), https://www.tiktok.com/@matt_and_abby/video/7273583834623380778. Rate and review children: Family Fizz, 'YOU MADE THEM CRY!! *Reading Mean Comments* | Family Fizz', YouTube (9 Sep. 2018), https://www.youtube.com/watch?v=W6vR-eLG6yc. 'It's not a phase': Jonathan Joly. 'It's not a phase #shorts #sacconejolys #trans #lgbtq', YouTube (27 Feb. 2023), https://www.youtube.com/watch?v=y2bPG9DzUZ0.

52 Molly Byrne, 'YouTuber Caroline Konstnar slammed for "faking" 13-week pregnancy to promote her Patreon', Dexerto (2 May 2024), https://www.dexerto.com/youtube/youtuber-caroline-konstnar-slammed-for-faking-13-week-pregnancy-to-promote-her-patreon-2675697/.

53 1.6m subscribers: SACCONEJOLYs [channel], YouTube, https://www.youtube.com/channel/UCxJrnvfqSSvly5hiq2Fe68g. Jonathan's second channel: Jonathan Joly [channel], YouTube, https://www.youtube.com/@jonathanjoly.

54 Strangers picking outfits: Jonathan Joly. 'Help Emilia Pick an Outfit? #shorts #sacconejolys', YouTube (7 Jul. 2023), https://www.youtube.com/shorts/EKlqfNuUZ1Q. 'Best looking': Jonathan Joly, 'Who is the Best Looking Sister #jonathanjoly #shorts #daughter', YouTube (22 Jul. 2025), https://www.youtube.com/shorts/U1JtpaIz4bs.

55 Jonathan Joly (@jonathanjoly), 'My daughter Edie came out to me as trans five years ago, and since then, I've watched her blossom into a beautiful young lady, but people still ask me what if she changes her mind and what if she isn't happy so I thought let's ask her #sacconejolys #parentsoftiktok #jonathanjoly', TikTok (10 Dec. 2023), https://www.tiktok.com/@jonathanjoly/video/7311017701403610400?lang=en.

56   Jonathan Joly (@jonathanjoly), 'Never hide your true self #sacconejolys #trans #lgbt #nonbinary', TikTok (3 Oct. 2022), https://www.tiktok.com/@jonathanjoly/video/7150351878046616837?lang=en.

57   Gender and name reveal party: Jonathan Joly, 'Gender & Name reveal do over', YouTube (23 Dec. 2023), https://www.youtube.com/shorts/rZOa9CaiPdU. Edie's Story: Jonathan Joly, 'Edie's Story – from a BOY to a GIRL and how she feels now (transgender girl)', YouTube (18 Oct. 2022), https://www.youtube.com/watch?v=b6TDKMoqnBo. 'Edie's 9th Birthday': Jonathan Joly (@jonathanjoly), 'Edie she is nine today and is about to start her 2nd full year living as a girl #sacconejolys #happybirthday', TikTok (9 Apr. 2023), https://www.tiktok.com/@jonathanjoly/video/7219999553808813318?lang=en. 'first time wearing a girls uniform': Jonathan Joly, 'my sons (now daughter) first time wearing a girls uniform to school #shorts', YouTube (27 Nov. 2022), https://www.youtube.com/shorts/oqvRO6RR1-E. 'Our Daughters First Visit: Jonathan Joly (@jonathanjoly), 'Taking the next step #sacconejolys #trans #lgbtq', TikTok (8 Mar. 2023), https://www.tiktok.com/@jonathanjoly/video/7208223744110759174?lang=en.

58   Jonathan Joly, 'My DAUGHTER Went On Her FiRST DATE *emotional', YouTube (9 Oct. 2024), https://www.youtube.com/watch?v=xvDuoayZvu8.

59   Kate Lindsay, 'I'm the Child of a Facetune Mom', *Allure* (30 May 2024), https://www.allure.com/story/facetune-moms-photo-editing-impact-on-children.

60   'How Many 2-Yr-Olds Have Online ID? 92 Percent', ABC News (8 Oct. 2010), https://abcnews.go.com/Technology/yr-olds-online-id-92-percent/story?id=11833688.

61   'Share with Care' [infographic], Nominet (2016), https://media.nominet.uk/wp-content/uploads/2016/09/Nominet-Share-with-Care-2016-Infographic.pdf.

62   C. S. Mott Children's Hospital National Poll on Children's Health, 'Mott Poll Report: Parents on Social Media: Likes and Dislikes of Sharenting', C.S. Mott Children's Hospital, 23/2 (16 Mar. 2015), http://mottpoll.org/reports-surveys/parents-social-media-likes-and-dislikes-sharenting.

63   Victoria Richards, 'Paedophile Websites Steal Half Their Photos from Social Media Sites like Facebook', *Independent* (30 Sep. 2015), https://www.independent.co.uk/news/world/australasia/paedophile-websites-steal-half-their-photos-from-social-media-sites-like-facebook-a6673191.html.

64   Char (@familyvloggercallout), 'Just stumbling over the question. Any decent parent would be distraught and take their child off the internet surely #fyp #staceydooley #jonathanjoly #sacconejoly #youtubefamily #youtube #childexploitationprevention', TikTok (19 Apr. 2022), https://www.tiktok.com/@familyvloggercallout/video/7088391420620360966.

65   Naomi Fry, 'James Charles and the Odd Fascination of the YouTube Beauty Wars', *New Yorker* (15 May 2019), https://www.newyorker.com/culture/culture-desk/the-odd-fascination-of-the-youtube-beauty-wars.

NOTES

66 James Charles, 'No More Lies', YouTube (18 May 2019), https://www.youtube.com/watch?v=uFvtCUzfyL4.

67 CNN: Harmeet Kaur, 'James Charles Brings out the Receipts in His Latest Video on the Tati Westbrook Feud', CNN (18 May 2019), https://www.cnn.com/2019/05/18/entertainment/james-charles-tati-westbrook-trnd. *New Yorker*: Fry, 'James Charles and the Odd Fascination of the YouTube Beauty Wars'.

68 Amanda Lundgren, 'A Detailed Timeline of That James Charles/Tati Westbrook Drama', *Cosmopolitan* (30 Jun. 2020), https://www.cosmopolitan.com/entertainment/celebs/a27484210/james-charles-tati-westbrook-youtube-drama-timeline/.

69 Moises Mendez II, 'How One YouTube Video Changed the Course of Internet Culture', *Time* (10 May 2024), https://time.com/6976924/youtube-tiktok-drama-channel-sistergeddon/.

70 Mendez II, 'How One YouTube Video Changed the Course of Internet Culture'.

71 Forums, Tattle Life, https://tattle.life/forums/-/list.

72 'To Close The Forum Tattle Life', Change.org petition (n.d.), https://www.change.org/p/helen-whately-to-close-the-forum-tattle-life.

73 Psychologists often group these three behaviours under the term 'relational aggression', a form of bullying especially common among girls. See Mary L. Solarz, 'Relational Aggression: An Overview of the Complicated Behaviors of Girls', master's thesis, University of Wisconsin-Stout, 2008, https://www2.uwstout.edu/content/lib/thesis/2008/2008solarzm.pdf.

74 Taylor Lorenz, 'Teens Are Being Bullied "Constantly" on Instagram', *The Atlantic* (10 Oct. 2018), https://www.theatlantic.com/technology/archive/2018/10/teens-face-relentless-bullying-instagram/572164/.

75 Steve O'Hear, 'Personal Q&A Site Ask.fm Is Growing at a Clip Amid Media Backlash over Safety of Its Young Users', *TechCrunch* (4 Jul. 2013), https://techcrunch.com/2013/07/04/ask-fm/.

76 Jonathan Blake, 'Ask.fm Owners "Considered Shutting Down" Social Network', BBC Newsbeat (9 Feb. 2015), https://www.bbc.co.uk/news/newsbeat-31249209.

77 Jimmy Blake, 'The Key Moments in the History of Ask.fm', BBC Newsbeat (29 May 2014), https://www.bbc.co.uk/news/newsbeat-27602771.

78 Alex Hern, 'Ask.fm's New Owners Vow to Crack Down on Bullying or Shut the Site', *The Guardian* (19 Aug. 2014), https://www.theguardian.com/technology/2014/aug/19/askfm-askcom-bullying.

79 Alyson Shontell, 'Why a Girl Who Was Viciously Bullied on Yik Yak Now Believes in the Anonymous App's Future', *Business Insider* (28 Mar. 2015), https://www.businessinsider.com/elizabeth-long-was-bullied-on-yik-yak-2015-3.

80 'Fizz: Your Authentic Community', AppAdvice (n.d.), https://appadvice.com/app/fizz-your-authentic-community/1548207780.

81   Zoe Thomas featuring Julie Jargon, 'How the Fizz App Upended a High School in Hours' [podcast], *Wall Street Journal* (24 Jun. 2024), https://www.wsj.com/podcasts/google-news-update/how-the-fizz-app-upended-a-high-school-in-hours/d30c9bc0-bc21-49b9-8d0d-0f452a020165.

82   Amanda Lenhart, 'Chapter 5: Conflict, Friendships and Technology', in 'Teens, Technology and Friendships' [report], Pew Research Center (6 Aug. 2015), https://www.pewresearch.org/internet/2015/08/06/chapter-5-conflict-friendships-and-technology/.

83   Lorenz, 'Teens Are Being Bullied "Constantly" on Instagram'.

84   Monica Anderson, 'A Majority of Teens Have Experienced Some Form of Cyberbullying' [report], Pew Research Center (27 Sep. 2018), https://www.pewresearch.org/internet/2018/09/27/a-majority-of-teens-have-experienced-some-form-of-cyberbullying/.

85   Michelle Faverio, Monica Anderson and Eugenie Park, 'Teens, Social Media and Mental Health' [report], Pew Research Center (22 Apr. 2025), https://www.pewresearch.org/internet/2025/04/22/teens-social-media-and-mental-health/.

86   ghostdumps, 'Why The Refusal to Post Online Is Often Inherently Racist', Instagram (30 May 2020), https://www.instagram.com/p/CAozhFzFjLf/.

87   Sage Lazzaro, 'Facebook Asks Users to Support France with Profile Picture Filter', *Observer* (14 Nov. 2015), https://observer.com/2015/11/facebook-asks-users-to-support-france-with-profile-picture-filter/.

88   Kwame Opam, 'Facebook Is Building a Way to Let Pages Offer Temporary Profile Pics', *The Verge* (23 Mar. 2016), https://www.theverge.com/2016/3/23/11294226/facebook-profile-picture-overlay-pages.

89   Instagram (@instagram), 'Time & time again, we've seen that the Instagram community has the power to bring meaningful change. The more we #ShareBlackStories, the more we raise voices that make an impact. To continue that impact, @Facebook is pledging $10M to efforts committed to ending racial injustice', Twitter (6.37 a.m., 1 Jun. 2020), https://x.com/instagram/status/1267329425294516225.

90   Snapchat (@snapchat), 'Raise your [hand emoji] to pledge and support closing the gender gap! #ChooseToChallenge', Twitter (7.21 p.m., 6 Mar. 2021), https://x.com/Snapchat/status/1368280553854824449.

91   Snapchat @snapchat, 'This Pride Month flex your fluidity, own your pronouns, showing up as you are, however you want!', Twitter (15 Jun. 2021), https://x.com/Snapchat/status/1404806219433451539.

92   'Pride 2021: Free to be you on TikTok #ForYourPride', TikTok Newsroom (14 Jun. 2021), https://newsroom.tiktok.com/en-gb/pride-2021-free-to-be-you-on-tiktok.

93   Natelegé Whaley, 'Dating Apps Are Getting More Political Ahead of Midterm Elections. What Does That Say About Users?', Mic (20 Oct. 2018), https://www.mic.com/articles/191988/dating-apps-political-midterm-2018-elections-okcupid-bumble.

NOTES

94 Olivia Petter, 'This Is How Stating Your Political Views in Your Dating App Bio Impacts Your Chances of Success', *Independent* (17 Aug. 2018), https://www.independent.co.uk/life-style/love-sex/dating-app-bio-political-views-success-hinge-plenty-of-fish-a8494386.html.

95 Kaanita Iyer, 'Swiping Right Ahead of the Election: Popular Dating Apps Have New Features to Show Off Political Views', CNN (17 Oct. 2024), https://edition.cnn.com/2024/10/17/tech/dating-apps-politics-election.

96 Nadia Khomami, '#MeToo: How a Hashtag Became a Rallying Cry Against Sexual Harassment', *The Guardian* (20 Oct. 2017), https://www.theguardian.com/world/2017/oct/20/women-worldwide-use-hashtag-metoo-against-sexual-harassment.

97 Paul Monckton, 'This Is Why Millions of People Are Posting Black Squares on Instagram', *Forbes* (2 Jun. 2020, updated 10 Dec. 2021), https://www.forbes.com/sites/paulmonckton/2020/06/02/blackout-tuesday-instagram-black-squares-blackouttuesday-theshowmustbepaused/.

98 Terry Nguyen, 'How Social Justice Slideshows Took over Instagram', *Vox* (12 Aug. 2020), https://www.vox.com/the-goods/21359098/social-justice-slideshows-instagram-activism.

99 Kamala Harris essay: Kamala Harris, 'To Be Silent Is to Be Complicit', *Cosmopolitan* (4 Jun. 2020), https://www.cosmopolitan.com/politics/a32766156/kamala-harris-black-lives-matter-protests/. CBS News quote: Christina Capatides, 'White Silence on Social Media: Why Not Saying Anything Is Actually Saying a Lot', *CBS News* (3 Jun. 2020), https://www.cbsnews.com/news/white-silence-on-social-media-why-not-saying-anything-is-actually-saying-a-lot/.

100 'White Silence Is Violence': Amy Mackelden, 'Sophie Turner and Joe Jonas Join a Black Lives Matter Protest: "White Silence Is Violence"', *Harper's Bazaar* (8 Jun. 2020), https://www.harpersbazaar.com/celebrity/latest/a32791416/sophie-turner-joe-jonas-black-lives-matter-protest/. 'step up': Brian Marks, 'Pregnant Sophie Turner Says "White Silence Is Violence" at a Black Lives Matter Protest with Her Husband Joe Jonas', *Daily Mail* (7 Jun. 2020), https://www.dailymail.co.uk/tvshowbiz/article-8395851/Pregnant-Sophie-Turner-says-White-Silence-Violence-BLM-protest-Joe-Jonas.html.

101 Alyssa Bailey and Savannah Walsh, 'Why Rihanna, Kendall Jenner, and Other Celebs Are Posting Black Squares for #BlackOutTuesday', *Elle* (2 Jun. 2020), https://www.elle.com/culture/celebrities/a32741423/what-is-blackouttuesday-movement/.

102 Kellie Chudzinski, 'Cara Delevingne Joins Thousands for Black Lives Matter Protests in LA: "Silence Is Consent"', *Daily Mail* (3 Jun. 2020), https://www.dailymail.co.uk/tvshowbiz/article-8382479/Cara-Delevingne-joins-thousands-Black-Lives-Matter-protests-LA-Silence-consent.html.

103 Adam White, 'Emma Watson Says She "Needs to Work Harder" Following Blackout Tuesday Backlash', *Independent* (4 Jun. 2020), https://www.independent.co.uk/arts-entertainment/films/news/emma-watson-blackout-tuesday-instagram-criticism-george-floyd-a9545711.html.

104 Anna Chan, 'Lana Del Rey Criticized for Posting Video of Looting During Protests: "Do Not Endanger People"', *Billboard* (31 May 2020), https://www.billboard.com/music/music-news/lana-del-rey-criticized-protest-video-9394280/.

105 Libby Torres, 'Ellen DeGeneres Deleted a Tweet about Racial Injustice after Being Called Hypocritical and Vague by Fans', *Business Insider* (1 Jun. 2020), https://www.businessinsider.com/ellen-degeneres-twitter-backlash-black-lives-matter-2020-6.

106 De Elizabeth, 'Billie Eilish, Beyoncé, Ariana Grande and More Celebrities Respond to George Floyd's Death', *Teen Vogue* (31 May 2020), https://www.teenvogue.com/story/celebrities-respond-george-floyd-death.

107 43% of adults under 30: Emily Tomasik and Katerina Eva Matsa, '1 in 5 Americans Now Regularly Get News on TikTok, up Sharply from 2020', Pew Research Center (25 Sep. 2025), https://www.pewresearch.org/short-reads/2025/09/25/1-in-5-americans-now-regularly-get-news-on-tiktok-up-sharply-from-2020/. Around 60% of Gen Z: Amy He, 'Gen Z's News Habits Will Upend the Media Landscape', Morning Consult (22 Jan. 2024), https://pro.morningconsult.com/analysis/where-gen-z-gets-news-topics-2024.

108 Emma Goldberg and Sapna Maheshwari, 'Social Media and the Israel-Hamas Conflict', *New York Times* (2 Nov. 2023), https://www.nytimes.com/2023/11/02/business/social-media-israel-hamas-conflict.html.

109 Rosey'sTea, 'Brooke Monk EXPOSED for being a TRUMP SUPPORTER? TIKTOK, SECRET!', YouTube (12 Oct. 2020), https://www.youtube.com/watch?v=hkOdmi-6t38.

110 Box of Kale Salad, 'BROOKE MONK DRAMA WITH POLITICS | Brooke Monk addresses controversy over political views', YouTube (12 Oct. 2020), https://www.youtube.com/watch?v=zp70YO9VXkw.

111 Emily A. Vogels and Risa Gelles-Watnick, 'Teens and Social Media: Key Findings from Pew Research Center Surveys', Pew Research Center (24 Apr. 2023), https://www.pewresearch.org/short-reads/2023/04/24/teens-and-social-media-key-findings-from-pew-research-center-surveys/.

112 Damien Gayle, 'Facebook Aware of Instagram's Harmful Effect on Teenage Girls, Leak Reveals', *The Guardian* (14 Sep. 2021), https://www.theguardian.com/technology/2021/sep/14/facebook-aware-instagram-harmful-effect-teenage-girls-leak-reveals.

113 Gayle, 'Facebook Aware of Instagram's Harmful Effect on Teenage Girls'.

114 Shari Franke, *The House of My Mother* (Gallery UK, 2025). See also *Devil in the Family: The Fall of Ruby Franke*, dir. Olly Lambert (Hulu, 2025).

NOTES

115 Bad moods, family arguments and punishments: Hannah Loesch, 'Inside Ruby Franke's Child Abuse Case: "8 Passengers" Mom's Arrest, Court Updates and Sentencing', Yahoo! Entertainment (5 Mar. 2024), https://www.yahoo.com/entertainment/inside-youtuber-ruby-franke-case-175452340.html. Bra shopping: Simon Hattenstone, '"The Nice Version of Her Was Manufactured for YouTube": My Mum, the Family Vlogger Who Became a Child Abuser', *The Guardian* (25 Jan. 2025), https://www.theguardian.com/lifeandstyle/2025/jan/25/family-vlogger-who-became-child-abuser-ruby-franke-daughter-shari-interview.
116 Hattenstone, '"The Nice Version of Her"'.
117 Loesch, 'Inside Ruby Franke's Child Abuse Case'.
118 Hattenstone, '"The Nice Version of Her"'.
119 Mattea Bubalo, 'Who Is Ruby Franke, the Parenting Influencer Jailed for Child Abuse?', BBC News (21 Feb. 2024), https://www.bbc.co.uk/news/world-us-canada-66719859.
120 Leyla Mohammed, 'Here Are 23 Shocking Details From Hulu's New Ruby Franke Docuseries, Which Features Tons Of Harrowing, Unseen Footage That Was Cut From Her Family-Friendly Vlogs', Yahoo! Entertainment (27 Feb. 2025), https://www.yahoo.com/entertainment/23-shocking-details-hulu-ruby-190356866.html.
121 Franke, *House of My Mother*.
122 Mary Madden et al, 'Part 3: Reputation Management on Social Media', in 'Teens, Social Media, and Privacy' [report], Pew Research Center (21 May 2013), https://www.pewresearch.org/internet/2013/05/21/part-3-reputation-management-on-social-media/.
123 Eric Kaufmann, 'The Politics of the Culture Wars in Contemporary America' [report], Manhattan Institute (25 Jan. 2022), https://manhattan.institute/article/the-politics-of-the-culture-wars-in-contemporary-america.
124 Izzy Lyons, 'Children Warned Future Careers Could Be Ruined by Old Tweets', *Telegraph* (5 Apr. 2021), https://www.telegraph.co.uk/news/2021/04/05/children-warned-future-careers-could-ruined-old-tweets/.
125 Sophie Church, 'Receipts Culture Has Gone Too Far', *Dazed* (20 Jun. 2022), https://www.dazeddigital.com/science-tech/article/56366/1/receipts-culture-has-gone-too-far.
126 'What Gen Z Thinks about Its Social Media and Smartphone Usage', The Harris Poll (9 Oct. 2024; conducted 8–15 Aug. 2024), https://theharrispoll.com/briefs/gen-z-social-media-smart-phones/.
127 'Public Attitudes to Smartphones, Social Media, and Online Safety' [report], National Education Union, New Britain Project and More in Common (March 2025), https://www.newbritain.org.uk/_files/ugd/8be189_4a7640e2a2854a9281fb7dc03234289a.pdf.

128 Chris Vallance and Philippa Wain, 'Ofcom: Almost a Quarter of Kids Aged 5–7 Have Smartphones', BBC News (19 Apr. 2024), https://www.bbc.co.uk/news/technology-68838029.

129 John Woodhouse and Maria Lalic, 'The Impact of Smartphones and Social Media on Children' [research briefing], UK House of Commons Library (13 May 2024), https://commonslibrary.parliament.uk/research-briefings/cdp-2024-0103/.

130 'The 2025 Common Sense Census: Media Use by Kids Zero to Eight', Common Sense Media (26 Feb. 2025), https://www.commonsensemedia.org/research/the-2025-common-sense-census-media-use-by-kids-zero-to-eight.

131 'Responding to Online Threats: Minors' Perspectives on Disclosing, Reporting, and Blocking in 2021', Thorn in partnership with Benenson Strategy Group (Feb. 2023), https://info.thorn.org/hubfs/Research/Thorn_ROT_Monitoring_2021.pdf.

DISCONNECTED

1 Replika, 'Meet the world's first AI friend' [Facebook post] (11 Feb. 2020), https://www.facebook.com/myownreplika/videos/130004174939695/.

2 Avi (@AviSchiffmann), 'introducing friend. not imaginary. order now at friend.com', X (2.56 p.m., 30 Jul. 2024), https://x.com/AviSchiffmann/status/1818284595902922884.

3 Josh Rodgers, 'Could This New Viral AI-Powered Pendant Become Your New Friend?', Yahoo! Tech (1 Aug. 2024), https://tech.yahoo.com/ai/articles/could-viral-ai-powered-pendant-185513143.html.

4 Boone Ashworth, 'Wear This AI Friend Around Your Neck', *Wired* (30 Jul. 2024), https://www.wired.com/story/friend-ai-pendant/.

5 Adrian | The Web Scraping Guy (@adrian_horning_), 'I like the idea of this, but would rather have it give feedback on how I'm acting in interactions. Like "hey when you said that, I think Bob was a little put off. Did you hear at 2:33 when he tried to change the subject?" That would be game changing', X (1.41 p.m., 31 Jul. 2024), https://x.com/adrian_horning_/status/1818627950532788302.

6 Kyle Wiggers, 'Friend Delays Shipments of Its AI Companion Pendant', TechCrunch (20 Jan. 2025), https://techcrunch.com/2025/01/20/friend-delays-shipments-of-its-ai-companion-pendant/.

7 'Friend', https://friend.com/.

8 Kali Hays, 'Snapchat Has a Plan to Start Charging Users to Restore Broken Snapstreaks', *Business Insider* (31 Jan. 2023), https://www.businessinsider.com/snapchat-snap-plan-charge-users-maintain-snapstreaks-streaks-2023-1#.

9 Eve Livingston, 'g2g, brb, and what the loss of early MSN language means', *Dazed* (23 Apr. 2018), https://www.dazeddigital.com/science-tech/article/39832/1/g2g-logging-off-and-the-loss-of-classic-internet-language.

NOTES

10   J. Radesky et al, 'Constant Companion: A Week in the Life of a Young Person's Smartphone Use', Common Sense and C. S. Mott Children's Hospital (2023), https://www.commonsensemedia.org/sites/default/files/research/report/2023-cs-smartphone-research-report_final-for-web.pdf.

11   'Snapchat Friends: The New Emoji Update Explained', BBC Newsbeat (7 Apr. 2015), https://www.bbc.co.uk/news/newsbeat-32203130#.

12   'Teens Freaking Out Over Best Friends on Snapchat', *Business Insider* (27 Jan. 2015), https://www.businessinsider.com/teens-freaking-out-over-best-friends-on-snapchat-2015-1.

13   Julie Jargon, 'Snapchat's Friend-Ranking Feature Adds to Teen Anxiety', *Wall Street Journal* (30 Mar. 2024), https://www.wsj.com/tech/personal-tech/new-snapchat-feature-teen-insecurity-754ebae0.

14   Jonathan Haidt, *The Anxious Generation: How the Great Rewiring of Childhood Caused an Epidemic of Mental Illness* (Penguin, 2024).

15   Jean Twenge, 'Teens Have Less Face Time with Their Friends – and Are Lonelier than Ever', The Conversation (20 Mar. 2019), https://theconversation.com/teens-have-less-face-time-with-their-friends-and-are-lonelier-than-ever-113240.

16   Twenge, 'Teens Have Less Face Time with Their Friends'.

17   Bryce Ward, 'Americans Are Choosing to Be Alone. Here's Why We Should Reverse That', *Washington Post* (23 Nov. 2022), https://www.washingtonpost.com/opinions/2022/11/23/americans-alone-thanksgiving-friends/.

18   Will Tanner, Fjolla Krasniqi and James Blagden, 'Age of Alienation: The Collapse in Community and Belonging among Young People, and How We Should Respond' [report], Onward [think tank] (Sep. 2021), https://www.ukonward.com/wp-content/uploads/2021/09/Age-of-Alienation-Onward.pdf.

19   Betsy Morris, 'Most Teens Prefer to Chat Online, Rather Than in Person', *Wall Street Journal* (10 Sep. 2018), https://www.wsj.com/articles/most-teens-prefer-to-chat-online-than-in-person-survey-finds-1536597971.

20   Tanner, Krasniqi and Blagden, 'Age of Alienation'.

21   Tanner, Krasniqi and Blagden, 'Age of Alienation'.

22   Daniel A. Cox, 'The State of American Friendship: Change, Challenges, and Loss', Survey Center on American Life (8 Jun. 2021), https://www.americansurveycenter.org/research/the-state-of-american-friendship-change-challenges-and-loss/.

23   manelique (@manelique), '[no title]', TikTok (3 Jan. 2024), https://www.tiktok.com/@manelique/video/7319666875464502534.

24   isabel (@appleuser6773295), '#wlw #xybca #fyp #foryou #divorced', TikTok (14 Jul. 2024), https://www.tiktok.com/@appleuser6773295/video/7391297795572993312.

25   B.com (@b.commmmm), 'Yeah….', TikTok (1 Aug. 2024), https://www.tiktok.com/@b.commmmm/video/7398071118449380638.

26   A.J. Willingham, 'What Is No-Fault Divorce, and Why Do Some Conservatives Want to Get Rid of It?', CNN (27 Nov. 2023), https://www.cnn.com/2023/11/27/us/no-fault-divorce-explained-history-wellness-cec.

27   Ministry of Justice, HM Courts & Tribunals Service and The Rt Hon Dominic Raab, '"Blame Game" Ends as No-Fault Divorce Comes into Force' [press release], UK Government (6 Apr. 2022), https://www.gov.uk/government/news/blame-game-ends-as-no-fault-divorce-comes-into-force.

28   Glen Scrivener, 'I Called This Divorce Ad "Evil". Was I Right?', *Premier Christianity* (11 Dec. 2024), https://www.premierchristianity.com/opinion/i-called-this-divorce-ad-evil-was-i-right/18642.article.

29   'let's hear it for divorce': Emma Specter, 'This Valentine's Day, Let's Hear It for Divorce', *British Vogue* (10 Feb. 2022), https://www.vogue.co.uk/arts-and-lifestyle/article/celebrating-divorce. 'joy of divorce parties': Sirin Kale, '"It Was One of the Best Nights of My Life": The Joy of Divorce Parties', *The Guardian* (24 Sep. 2019), https://www.theguardian.com/lifeandstyle/2019/sep/24/it-was-one-of-the-best-nights-of-my-life-the-joy-of-divorce-parties.

30   Lara Bazelon, 'Divorce Can Be an Act of Radical Self-Love', *New York Times* (30 Sep. 2021), https://www.nytimes.com/2021/09/30/opinion/divorce-children.html.

31   Giles Hattersley, 'Adele, Reborn: The British Icon Gets Candid about Divorce, Body Image, Romance & Her "Self-Redemption" Record', *British Vogue*, (7 Oct. 2021), https://www.vogue.co.uk/arts-and-lifestyle/article/adele-british-vogue-interview.

32   'Divorced' necklace: Adele UK Store, https://shopuk.adele.com/products/divorced-necklace. Recordings of conversations and 'stages of hating': Tristan Balagtas, 'Adele Says Son Angelo Will "Probably Go Through Stages of Hating" Song "My Little Love"', *People* (24 Nov. 2021), https://people.com/parents/adele-says-son-angelo-will-probably-go-through-stages-of-hating-song-my-little-love/.

33   Harry Benson, 'Source of Family Breakdown', Marriage Foundation (Jul. 2023), https://marriagefoundation.org.uk/research/source-of-family-breakdown/.

34   Kathleen Kiernan, Sam Crossman and Angus Phimister, 'Families and Inequalities', IFS Deaton Review of Inequalities (2022), https://ifs.org.uk/inequality/wp-content/uploads/2022/06/IFS-Deaton-Review-Families-and-inequality-.pdf.

35   'Divorces and Dissolutions in England and Wales: 2023', Office for National Statistics (2 Jul. 2025), https://www.ons.gov.uk/peoplepopulationandcommunity/birthsdeathsandmarriages/divorce/bulletins/divorcesinenglandandwales/2023.

36   See Belinda Luscombe, 'The Divorce Rate Is Dropping. That May Not Actually Be Good News', *Time* (26 Nov. 2018), https://time.com/5434949/divorce-rate-children-marriage-benefits/ and 'Divorces in England and Wales: 2022', Office for National Statistics (22 Feb. 2024), https://www.ons.gov.uk/peoplepopulationandcommunity/birthsdeathsandmarriages/divorce/bulletins/divorcesinenglandandwales/2022.

NOTES

37   'SF3.1: Marriage and Divorce Rates', Organisation for Economic Co-operation and Development (June 2022), https://www.oecd.org/content/dam/oecd/en/data/datasets/family-database/sf_3_1_marriage_and_divorce_rates.pdf.

38   See Kate Gibson, 'Over Half of Children in England and Wales Now Born to Unmarried Parents', University of Manchester (25 Aug. 2022), https://www.manchester.ac.uk/about/news/over-half-of-children-in-england-and-wales-now-born-to-unmarried-parents/ and 'Births in England and Wales: 2022', Office for National Statistics(17 Aug. 2023), https://www.ons.gov.uk/peoplepopulationandcommunity/birthsdeathsandmarriages/livebirths/bulletins/birthsummarytablesenglandandwales/2022.

39   Benson, 'Source of Family Breakdown'.

40   Benson, 'Source of Family Breakdown'.

41   Anna Russell, 'Why So Many People Are Going "No Contact" with Their Parents', *New Yorker* (30 Aug. 2024), https://www.newyorker.com/culture/annals-of-inquiry/why-so-many-people-are-going-no-contact-with-their-parents.

42   Joshua Coleman and Will Johnson, 'How Estrangement Has Become an Epidemic in America', *Time* (13 Dec. 2024), https://time.com/7201531/family-estrangement-us-politics-epidemic-essay/.

43   Kaitlyn Tiffany, 'That's It. You're Dead to Me', *The Atlantic* (13 Aug. 2022), https://www.theatlantic.com/magazine/archive/2022/09/toxic-person-tiktok-internet-slang-meaning/670599/.

44   'come over unannounced': Ana_Del_Castillo (@ana_del_castillo_), '#toxic #toxicmom #unhealthylove', TikTok (21 Feb. 2023), https://www.tiktok.com/@ana_del_castillo_/video/7202693075653692714. '6 signs': Stephanietherapy (@loveandtherapy), '6 signs of a toxic parent', TikTok (31 Jan. 2021), https://www.tiktok.com/@loveandtherapy/video/6923912947584552198.

45   E.B. Johnson (@therealebjohnson), 'A question my clients always ask: did they know? Yeah. They did. Here's how you can tell. #toxicparent #narctokforyourpage #narctokcoaches #practicalgrowth', TikTok (8 Feb. 2023), https://www.tiktok.com/@therealebjohnson/video/7197838909089271046.

46   Jeffrey Marsh (@thejeffreymarsh), 'a perfectly okay reason to cut off family members!', TikTok (9 Oct. 2024), https://www.tiktok.com/@thejeffreymarsh/video/7423574922133277994.

47   James Dean, 'Pillemer: Family Estrangement a Problem "Hiding in Plain Sight"', *Cornell Chronicle* (10 Sep. 2020), https://news.cornell.edu/stories/2020/09/pillemer-family-estrangement-problem-hiding-plain-sight.

48   Hara Estroff Marano, 'The Pain of Cut-Offs', *Psychology Today* (2 Jan. 2024, last reviewed 5 Mar. 2024), https://www.psychologytoday.com/gb/articles/202401/the-pain-of-cut-offs.

49 'CommunityToks create safe spaces for authentic connection, creativity and joy', TikTok For Business (19 Nov. 2021), https://ads.tiktok.com/business/en-US/blog/communitytoks-authentic-connection-creativity-joy.

50 US collapse: Seth Kaplan, 'The Real User Interface: Recovering Our Neighborhoods', *After Babel* [Substack] (14 Jan. 2025), https://www.afterbabel.com/p/the-real-user-interface-recovering. UK collapse: Paul Hickman, '"Third Places" and Social Interaction in Deprived Neighbourhoods in Great Britain', *Journal of Housing and the Built Environment* 28/2 (2013), 221–36. http://www.jstor.org/stable/42636241.

51 Jessica Finlay et al, 'Closure of "Third Places"? Exploring Potential Consequences for Collective Health and Wellbeing', *Health & Place*, 60 (2019), 102225. https://doi.org/10.1016/j.healthplace.2019.102225.

52 Joe Lepper, 'Council Spending on Youth Services in England Falls by 73% since 2010', *CYP Now* (29 Jan. 2025), https://www.cypnow.co.uk/content/news/council-spending-on-youth-services-in-england-falls-by-73-since-2010/.

53 Alison Flood, 'Britain Has Closed Almost 800 Libraries Since 2010, Figures Show', *The Guardian* (6 Dec. 2019), https://www.theguardian.com/books/2019/dec/06/britain-has-closed-almost-800-libraries-since-2010-figures-show.

54 Derek Thompson, 'The Anti-Social Century', *The Atlantic* (8 Jan. 2025), https://www.theatlantic.com/magazine/archive/2025/02/american-loneliness-personality-politics/681091/.

55 Laura Silver and Jenn Hatfield, 'How Connected Do Americans Feel to Their Neighbors?', Pew Research Center (8 May 2025), https://www.pewresearch.org/short-reads/2025/05/08/how-connected-do-americans-feel-to-their-neighbors/.

56 Thomas O'Rourke, 'The Decline of Trust and Neighborliness' [blog], Institute for Family Studies (3 Oct. 2023), https://ifstudies.org/blog/the-decline-of-trust-and-neighborliness#:~:text=our%20bridging%20networks.

57 Tanner, Krasniqi and Blagden, 'Age of Alienation'.

58 Jeffrey M. Jones, 'Church Attendance Has Declined in Most U.S. Religious Groups', Gallup (25 Mar. 2024), https://news.gallup.com/poll/642548/church-attendance-declined-religious-groups.aspx.

59 Zach Rausch, 'Why Are Religious Teens Happier Than Their Secular Peers?', *Boston Globe* (6 Jun. 2024), https://www.bostonglobe.com/2024/06/06/opinion/religious-teens-mental-health/.

60 'Religion and Belief: Some Surveys and Statistics', Humanists UK (n.d.), https://humanists.uk/campaigns/religion-and-belief-some-surveys-and-statistics/.

61 Jonathan Haidt, 'End the Phone-Based Childhood Now', *The Atlantic* (13 Mar. 2024), https://www.theatlantic.com/technology/archive/2024/03/teen-childhood-smartphone-use-mental-health-effects/677722/.

NOTES

62 'Celebrating World Book Day with #BookTok', TikTok Newsroom (22 Apr. 2025), https://newsroom.tiktok.com/celebrating-world-book-day-with-booktok?lang=en.

63 Jan Wilk, 'TikTok Shop: The Future of Shopping Fueled by Discovery E-Commerce', TikTok Newsroom (31 Mar. 2025), https://newsroom.tiktok.com/en-gb/discover-tiktok-shop.

64 'Community Guidelines', Instagram Help Center (n.d.), https://www.facebook.com/help/instagram/477434105621119/.

65 Jesselyn Cook, 'Selfies, Surgeries And Self-Loathing: Inside The Facetune Epidemic', *HuffPost UK* (20 May 2021), https://www.huffingtonpost.co.uk/entry/facetune-selfies-surgeries-body-dysmorphia_n_60926a11e4b0b9042d989d48.

66 Downloads of mental health apps: Xiaomei Wang, Carl Markert and Farzan Sasangohar, 'Investigating Popular Mental Health Mobile Application Downloads and Activity During the COVID-19 Pandemic', *Human Factors*, 65/1 (2023), 50–61. https://doi.org/10.1177/00187208211998110. Screen times: Andrew Gregory, 'Primary-Age Children's Screen Time Went up by 83 Minutes a Day During Pandemic – Study', *The Guardian* (24 Jun. 2022), https://www.theguardian.com/society/2022/jun/24/primary-age-children-screen-time-went-up-83-minutes-day-pandemic.

67 'Mental Well-Being Comes First on TikTok', TikTok Newsroom (6 Oct. 2022), https://newsroom.tiktok.com/en-africa/mental-well-being-comes-first-on-tiktok.

68 'Scroll, shop…': tiktokshop_uk, 'Scroll, shop, self care Find your self care essentials on TikTok Shop #FromScrollToGoal', Instagram (16 Jan. 2025), https://www.instagram.com/reel/DE5AZeiqQKH/?hl=en. 'Simple ways to practice self-care': TikTok US (@tiktok_us), 'simple ways to practice self-care: take a bubble bath, do something active, drink a glass of wine, watch TikTok videos', Twitter (8.28 p.m., 24 Nov. 2020), https://x.com/tiktok_us/status/1331333769488343040.

69 Alyssa Hui-Anderson, 'What Is "Bed Rotting"? Gen Z's Newest Self-Care Trend, Explained', Health (2 Aug. 2025), https://www.health.com/what-is-bed-rotting-trend-7561395.

70 Left tampon in: Marie (@marie_reie), '(Spoiler) I didnt get toxic shock #wlw #bedrotting', TikTok (22 Jul. 2024), https://www.tiktok.com/@marie_reie/video/7394390142183607583?lang=en. Stains on mattresses: Pink striped socks (@stripysockstocoverit), '#depression #mentalhealth #mentalheathmatters #mentalhealthmattersuntil #bedrotting #blood #trash #hoarding #mold #mould #rotting #messy #nomotivation #art #anime #hoarding', TikTok (13 Mar. 2025), https://www.tiktok.com/@stripysockstocoverit/video/7481218643347459336?lang=en. Food wrappers: obvsissyy (@obvsissyy), 'ik its disgusting im cleaning it now #bedrotting #girlhood #bedrottingsummer #bedrottingsunite #bedrottingcore #fyp', TikTok (12 Aug. 2024), https://www.tiktok.com/@obvsissyy/video/7402250231829630241?lang=end.

71   Christopher Howse and Guy Kelly, 'I Finally Discovered What Gen Z Means by "Bed Rotting" – and I Don't Like It', *The Telegraph* (6 Oct. 2024), https://www.telegraph.co.uk/authors/c/cf-cj/christopher-howse/.

72   'charisme | The Gamified Social Anxiety App' [mobile app], Charisme, https://www.charisme.app/.

73   'more than just an app': Facetune: Video & Photo Editor [mobile app], Lightricks Ltd, https://apps.apple.com/pl/app/facetune-video-photo-editor/id1149994032. '170 million Americans': tiktok_us, 'From cultivating community to business booming, there are millions of reasons to #KeepTikTok in the US', X (27 Mar. 2024), https://x.com/tiktok_us/status/1773068539974266881. 'horny online community: 'Pornhub Community' (n.d.), https://www.pornhub.com/community.

74   'Never Niche Enough: 2023 Trend Report', The Webby Awards (17 Jan. 2023), https://www.webbyawards.com/wp-content/uploads/sites/4/2023/01/Webby_Awards_2023_Trend-Report_Never_Niche_Enough-1.pdf.

75   Damian Carrington, 'Three-Quarters of UK Children Spend Less Time Outdoors Than Prison Inmates – Survey', *The Guardian* (25 Mar. 2016), https://www.theguardian.com/environment/2016/mar/25/three-quarters-of-uk-children-spend-less-time-outdoors-than-prison-inmates-survey.

76   Derek Thompson, 'Why Americans Suddenly Stopped Hanging Out', *The Atlantic* (14 Feb. 2024), https://www.theatlantic.com/ideas/archive/2024/02/america-decline-hanging-out/677451/.

77   Thompson, 'The Anti-Social Century', citing Enghin Atalay, 'A Twenty-First Century of Solitude? Time Alone and Together in the United States', Federal Reserve Bank of Philadelphia, Working Paper 22-11 (Apr. 2022), https://www.philadelphiafed.org/-/media/frbp/assets/working-papers/2022/wp22-11.pdf.

78   Michael Sayman (@michaelsayman), 'I've spent years wanting to build a consumer app that was impossible for a long time. Now the tech has finally caught up to my vision,' X (1.42 a.m., 17 Sep. 2024), https://x.com/michaelsayman/status/1835841675584811239?lang=en-GB.

79   Social AI – AI Social Network [mobile app], Michael Sayman, https://apps.apple.com/us/app/socialai-ai-social-network/id6670229993.

80   'find new friends': 'Find Your People with Bumble for Friends', Bumble (n.d.), https://bumble.com/en/bff. 'real, genuine connections': Badoo: Dating, Chat & Meet [mobile app], Badoo, https://play.google.com/store/apps/details?id=com.badoo.mobile&hl=en_GB.

81   'Tinder for girl friends': Amber Jamieson, 'Tinder for Girl Friends: Can Hey Vina App Really Be Social, Female and Fun?', *The Guardian* (8 Feb. 2016), https://www.theguardian.com/lifeandstyle/2016/feb/08/tinder-for-girl-friends-hey-vina-app-female-friendship.

NOTES

82 'What is Premium on Bumble For Friends?', Bumble for Friends, https://support.bumbleforfriends.com/hc/en-us/articles/12284523136925-What-is-Premium-on-Bumble-For-Friends.

83 Arielle Pardes, 'The Emotional Chatbots Are Here to Probe Our Feelings', *Wired* (31 Jan. 2018), https://www.wired.com/story/replika-open-source/.

84 Replika: Virtual AI Friend [mobile app], Luka, Inc., https://apps.apple.com/au/app/replika-virtual-ai-friend/id1158555867?l=id.

85 Dax-Victor-2007, 'Personality Traits', Reddit post, r/ReplikaOfficial (9 Aug. 2025), https://www.reddit.com/r/ReplikaOfficial/comments/1mm2cs6/personality_traits/.

86 'What Is Replika Pro?', Replika Help Center (n.d.), https://help.replika.com/hc/en-us/articles/360032500052-What-is-Replika-Pro.

87 Alex Heath, 'Snapchat Is Releasing Its Own AI Chatbot Powered by ChatGPT', *The Verge* (27 Feb. 2023), https://www.theverge.com/2023/2/27/23614959/snapchat-my-ai-chatbot-chatgpt-openai-plus-subscription.

88 TheTeky500, 'I Got Snapchat AI to Admit Everything', Reddit, r/ChatGPT (13 May 2023), https://www.reddit.com/r/ChatGPT/comments/13gty7u/i_got_snapchat_ai_to_admit_everything/.

89 'Your Child's New AI Friend!': TalkiePal: AI for Kids 4–12 [mobile app], K.C Entertainment, https://play.google.com/store/apps/details?id=com.kencasgala.talkiepal&hl=en_GB. '…anything else you can imagine': Heeyo: AI friends for kids, Hee Labs, Inc., https://apps.apple.com/us/app/heeyo-ai-friends-for-kids/id6469570342.

90 Tally Moran, 'Meet Your New AI Personal Assistant: A Game-Changer for Your Photos', Facetune (18 Nov. 2024), https://www.facetuneapp.com/blog/unleash-future-photo-editing-facetune-ai-assistant?srsltid=AfmBOorJSVveuTY7jxHlpBcj4T7Q-sAHQvoMTDmNhwYKexNcvoHnR-H9.

91 Over 30 million registered users: 'Replika AI: Unlocking 30 Million Users,' *Artificial Intelligence +* (6 Jan. 2025, updated 16 Jan. 2025), https://www.aiplusinfo.com/replika-ai-unlocking-30-million-users/. 10 million in 2023: Shikhar Ghosh and Shweta Bagai, 'Replika AI: Alleviating Loneliness (A)', Harvard Business School (July 2024), https://www.hbs.edu/faculty/Pages/item.aspx?num=65851. $14 million: 'How Replika Hit $14M Revenue with a 93 Person Team in 2024', GetLatka (n.d.), https://getlatka.com/companies/replika.ai#:~:text=Replika%20Revenue.

92 Joe Tidy, 'Character.ai: Young People Turning to AI Therapist Bots', BBC News (5 Jan. 2024), https://www.bbc.co.uk/news/technology-67872693.

93 Cade Metz, 'Chatbot Start-Up Character.AI Valued at $1 Billion in New Funding Round', *New York Times* (23 Mar. 2023), https://www.nytimes.com/2023/03/23/technology/chatbot-characterai-chatgpt-valuation.html.

94 Michael B. Robb and Supreet Mann, 'Talk, Trust, and Trade-Offs: How and Why Teens Use AI Companions', Common Sense Media (2025), https://www.commonsensemedia.org/sites/default/files/research/report/talk-trust-and-trade-offs_2025_web.pdf.

95 Hours a day: Robb and Mann, 'Talk, Trust, and Trade-Offs'. 13 hours straight: [unknown user], 'Aight. Admit How Many Hours You've Spent in One Go on Character AI. Go on, Be Honest. I'll Start. 13 Hours', Reddit, r/CharacterAI (13 Feb. 2023), https://www.reddit.com/r/CharacterAI/comments/111hwko/aight_admit_how_many_hours_youve_spent_in_one_go/.

96 Katherine Dee, 'Surrendering Free Will Is the Real AI Threat', *UnHerd* (14 Apr. 2025), https://unherd.com/newsroom/surrendering-free-will-is-the-real-ai-threat/.

97 'Lonely Millennials Choose AI Over a Loved One to Share Their Problems' [press release], University of Law (2 Nov. 2023), https://www.law.ac.uk/about/press-releases/millennials-share-problems-with-ai.

98 Robb and Mann, 'Talk, Trust, and Trade-offs'.

99 Dwarkesh Patel, 'Mark Zuckerberg – AI Will Write Most Meta Code in 18 Months', YouTube (29 Apr. 2025), https://www.youtube.com/watch?v=rYXeQbTuVlo.

100 Roman Helmet Guy (@romanhelmetguy), 'Zuckerberg explaining how Meta is creating personalized AI friends to supplement your real ones: "The average American has 3 friends, but has demand for 15"', X (30 Apr. 2025), https://x.com/romanhelmetguy/status/1917656951174947075.

101 Twenge, 'Teens Have Less Face Time with Their Friends'.

102 'Younger Brits Report Higher Levels of Loneliness' [press release], Campaign to End Loneliness (12 Apr. 2023), https://www.campaigntoendloneliness.org/press-release/younger-brits-report-higher-levels-of-loneliness/.

103 Nana Baah, 'Young People Are Lonelier Than Ever', *VICE* (22 Apr. 2022), https://www.vice.com/en/article/z3n5aj/loneliness-epidemic-young-people.

104 Daniel A. Cox, 'The Childhood Loneliness of Generation Z', American Enterprise Institute (4 Apr. 2022), https://www.aei.org/articles/the-childhood-loneliness-of-generation-z/.

105 Sarah Holder, '"Where to Meet People" Internet Searches Spike Amid Loneliness Epidemic', Bloomberg UK (10 May 2023), https://www.bloomberg.com/news/articles/2023-05-10/-how-to-meet-people-google-searches-reach-new-highs.

106 Katie Baskerville, 'Gen Z Are So Lonely They're Posting Friendship Applications on Facebook', *VICE* (7 Feb. 2024), https://www.vice.com/en/article/friendship-applications-gen-z-loneliness/.

107 'Teen Social Media Statistics 2022 (What Students and Parents Need to Know)', SmartSocial (14 Feb. 2022), https://smartsocial.com/post/social-media-statistics.

NOTES

108 V. Rideout and M. B. Robb, 'Social Media, Social Life: Teens Reveal Their Experiences', Common Sense Media (2018), https://www.commonsensemedia.org/sites/default/files/research/report/2018-social-media-social-life-executive-summary-web.pdf.

109 Rideout and Robb, 'Social Media, Social Life'.

110 John Burn-Murdoch, 'The Troubling Decline in Conscientiousness', *Financial Times* (7 Aug. 2025), https://www.ft.com/content/5cd77ef0-b546-4105-8946-36db3f84dc43.

111 Risen globally: Philip Jefferies and Michael Ungar, 'Social Anxiety in Young People: A Prevalence Study in Seven Countries', *PLoS One*, 15/9 (2020), e0239133. https://doi.org/10.1371/journal.pone.0239133. Worsened since the pandemic: Reuben Kindred and Glen W. Bates, 'The Influence of the COVID-19 Pandemic on Social Anxiety: A Systematic Review', *International Journal of Environmental Research and Public Health*, 20/3 (2023), 2362. https://doi.org/10.3390/ijerph20032362.

112 Kindred and Bates, 'The Influence of the COVID-19 Pandemic'.

113 John Dias, 'Gen Z Developing Fear of Phone Calls, or "Phone Phobia"', *CBS News* (1 Aug. 2023), https://www.cbsnews.com/newyork/news/gen-z-developing-fear-of-phone-calls-or-phone-phobia/.

114 One such example can be found here: Ezra Butler (@lemon.squezzy), 'doing things you're afraid of to show you it's okay! getting a build a bear by myself #brighton' (22 Aug. 2022), https://www.tiktok.com/@lemon.squezzy/video/7134700411474300166.

115 'barely able to leave my house': Present_Cup_626, 'I can't go out for a walk without being afraid of being seen by people', Reddit, r/socialskills (2 Jun. 2022), https://www.reddit.com/r/socialskills/comments/v33bqv/i_cant_go_out_for_a_walk_without_being_afraid_of/. 'yet to develop a social life': throwawaykc2021, 'Anyone else wasting away in their twenties?' Reddit, r/socialskills (3 Mar. 2022), https://www.reddit.com/r/socialskills/comments/t5jwwn/anyone_else_wasting_away_in_their_twenties/.

116 Jane Anderson, 'The Impact of Family Structure on the Health of Children: Effects of Divorce', *Linacre Quarterly*, 81/4 (2014), 378–87. https://doi.org/10.1179/0024363914Z.00000000087.

117 Live in poverty and perform worse in school: Anderson, 'The Impact of Family Structure'. Substance abuse: Kristina M. Jackson, Michelle L. Rogers and Carolyn E. Sartor, 'Parental Divorce and Initiation of Alcohol Use in Early Adolescence', *Psychological Addictive Behaviors*, 30/4 (2016), 450–61. https://doi.org/10.1037/adb0000164. Get divorced themselves: Nicholas Wolfinger, *Understanding the Divorce Cycle: The Children of Divorce in their Own Marriages* (Cambridge University Press, 2018). doi: 10.1017/CBO9780511499616.

118 Piers Shepherd, 'Family Breakdown and its Consequences', *Faith* (1 Nov. 2018), https://www.faith.org.uk/article/family-breakdown-and-its-consequences.

GIRLS®

119 Depressive symptoms during adolescence: Albertine J. Oldehinkel et al, 'Parental Divorce and Offspring Depressive Symptoms: Dutch Developmental Trends During Early Adolescence', *Journal of Marriage and Family*, 70/2 (2008), 284–93. https://doi.org/10.1111/j.1741-3737.2008.00481.x. Low self-esteem: Ursu Anca Simona, 'Self-Esteem, Depression and Anxiety in Adolescents with Divorced Parents', in E. Soare and C. Langa, eds., *Education Facing Contemporary World Issues*, vol. 67 (European Proceedings of Social and Behavioural Sciences. Future Academy), 194–99. https://doi.org/10.15405/epsbs.2019.08.03.23. Self-harm: Marina Miscioscia et al, 'Psychopathological and Interactive-Relational Characteristics in Non-Suicidal Self-Injury Adolescent Outpatients', *Journal of Clinical Medicine*, 11/5 (2022), 1218. https://doi.org/10.3390/jcm11051218. Develop eating disorders: Jessica L Suisman et al, 'Parental Divorce and Disordered Eating: An Investigation of a Gene-Environment Interaction', *The International Journal of Eating Disorders*, 44/2 (2011): 169–177. https://doi.org/10.1002/eat.20866.
120 Cox, 'The Childhood Loneliness of Generation Z'.
121 Nazmiye Çivitci, Asım Çivitci and N. Ceren Fiyakali, 'Loneliness and Life Satisfaction in Adolescents with Divorced and Non-Divorced Parents', *Educational Sciences Theory & Practice*, 9/2 (2009), 513–25. https://files.eric.ed.gov/fulltext/EJ847764.pdf.
122 Cox, 'The Childhood Loneliness of Generation Z'.
123 Cox, 'The Childhood Loneliness of Generation Z'.

DETACHED

1 Jon Haidt and Freya India, 'On The Degrading Effects of Life Online', *After Babel* [Substack] (14 May 2024), https://www.afterbabel.com/p/degrading-effects-of-life-online; Hot Or Not [mobile app], Johnny mattis llc (archived 24 Jul. 2024), https://web.archive.org/web/20240724080646/https://play.google.com/store/apps/details?id=com.jeuxdevelopers.hotornotapp&hl=en&gl=US.
2 'Pilot', *Euphoria* (season 1, episode 1, aired 16 June 2019 on HBO). Some scenes from the episode are discussed in Julianne Escobedo Shepherd, '*Euphoria*'s Subtle, Dark Depiction of Sexual Consent', *Jezebel* (17 Jun. 2019), https://www.jezebel.com/euphorias-subtle-dark-depiction-of-sexual-consent-1835580845. The dialogue and scenes discussed above are quoted in this article.
3 Eric Nofziger, '"Euphoria" Is Back – and with It a Renewed Wave of Controversy', *Butler Collegian* (18 Jan. 2022), https://thebutlercollegian.com/2022/01/euphoria-is-back-and-with-it-a-renewed-wave-of-controversy/.
4 Tatum Hunter, 'Is an Instagram "Like" Micro-Cheating? Gen Z Embraces Digital Sleuthing', *Washington Post* (26 Jun. 2024), https://www.washingtonpost.com/technology/2024/06/26/micro-cheating-tiktok-instagram/.

NOTES

5   Emily A. Vogels and Monica Anderson, 'Dating and Relationships in the Digital Age' [report], Pew Research Center (8 May 2020), https://www.pewresearch.org/internet/2020/05/08/dating-and-relationships-in-the-digital-age/.
6   Hunter, 'Is an Instagram "Like" Micro-Cheating?'.
7   Katie Rogers, 'The Vault Apps That Keep Sexts a Secret', *New York Times* (6 Nov. 2015), https://www.nytimes.com/2015/11/07/us/the-vault-apps-that-keep-sexts-a-secret.html.
8   Rachel Thompson, 'For Better or Worse, Snapchat Changed Sexting Forever', Mashable (7 Feb. 2017), https://mashable.com/article/snapchat-sexting-revolution.
9   Thompson, 'For Better or Worse'.
10 Lily Puckett, 'How to Sext: The Best Tips and Tricks', *Teen Vogue* (13 Apr. 2017), https://www.teenvogue.com/story/how-to-sext.
11 Eric Ravenscraft, 'The Safest Way to Store and Share Your Nudes', *Wired* (5 Jun. 2021), https://www.wired.com/story/safest-way-store-share-nudes-safe-sexts/; Elsie Bath, 'How to Take the Perfect Nude Selfie, According to a Photographer', *VICE* (23 May 2017), https://www.vice.com/en/article/how-to-take-the-perfect-nude-selfie-according-to-a-photographer/.
12 Sheridan Watson, 'Kim Kardashian Wrote an Inspiring Post About Slut-Shaming', *BuzzFeed* (8 Mar. 2016), https://www.buzzfeed.com/sheridanwatson/enough-is-enough.
13 Jessica Ringrose et al, '"Staying Safe Online" Survey: What Unwanted Sexual Images Are Being Sent to Teenagers on Social Media?' [blog post], Institute of Education, UCL (19 Jun. 2020), https://blogs.ucl.ac.uk/ioe/2020/06/19/staying-safe-online-survey-what-unwanted-sexual-images-are-being-sent-to-teenagers-on-social-media/.
14 Danielle Sinay, 'Sexting: One in Four Americans Share Sexts Without Permission', *Teen Vogue* (9 Aug. 2016), https://www.teenvogue.com/story/sexting-shared-without-permission-privacy.
15 Maya Oppenheim, 'Women Send Naked Photos to Men "Out of Obligation", Study Finds', *Independent* (28 Dec. 2022), https://www.independent.co.uk/news/uk/home-news/nudes-photos-women-send-men-obligation-b2252376.html.
16 Whitney Wolfe Herd speaking to Bloomberg Television, 'How Bumble Will Use AI to Create Healthier Relationships', YouTube (9 May 2024), https://www.youtube.com/watch?v=zYzuycrGqkI.
17 Daniel Horowitz, 'Tinder (app)', EBSCO Research Starters (2023), https://www.ebsco.com/research-starters/business-and-management/tinder-app.
18 50 million users worldwide: Nick Bilton, 'Tinder, the Fast-Growing Dating App, Taps an Age-Old Truth', *New York Times* (29 Oct. 2014), https://www.nytimes.com/2014/10/30/fashion/tinder-the-fast-growing-dating-app-taps-an-age-old-truth.html?_r=1. Up to a billion swipes daily: Padraig Belton, 'Love and Dating after

the Tinder Revolution', BBC News (13 Feb. 2018), https://www.bbc.co.uk/news/business-42988025.
19   Horowitz, 'Tinder (app)'.
20   Isobel Lewis, 'Tinder Select: New "VIP" Service Allows Users to Message People They're Not Matched with', *Independent* (26 Sep. 2023), https://www.independent.co.uk/life-style/tinder-select-price-app-features-match-b2418674.html.
21   Nayden Tafradzhiyski, 'Tinder Revenue and Usage Statistics (2025)', Business of Apps (updated 25 Feb. 2025), https://www.businessofapps.com/data/tinder-statistics/.
22   Dale Markowitz, 'Hinge's CEO Says a Good Dating App Relies on Vulnerability, Not Algorithms', *Washington Post* (29 Sep. 2017), https://www.washingtonpost.com/news/soloish/wp/2017/09/29/hinges-ceo-says-vulnerability-not-an-algorithm-is-the-key-to-a-good-dating-app/.
23   Mabel Banfield-Nwachi, 'The Price of Love: How Much Does Dating Cost – and Who Pays the Bill?' *The Guardian* (9 Nov. 2024), https://www.theguardian.com/lifeandstyle/2024/nov/09/how-much-does-dating-cost-pay-bill-apps.
24   'Roses', Hinge (n.d.), https://help.hinge.co/hc/en-us/articles/36311177115027-Roses.
25   David Curry, 'Hinge Revenue and Usage Statistics (2025)', Business of Apps (updated 2 Sep. 2025), https://www.businessofapps.com/data/hinge-statistics/.
26   Around 50 million Bumble users: David Curry, 'Bumble Revenue and Usage Statistics (2025)', Business of Apps (updated 2 Sep. 2025), https://www.businessofapps.com/data/bumble-statistics/. Around 3 million paying Bumble subscribers: 'Bumble Inc. Announces Fourth Quarter and Full Year 2024 Results', Business Wire (18 Feb. 2025), https://ir.bumble.com/news/news-details/2025/Bumble-Inc.-Announces-Fourth-Quarter-and-Full-Year-2024-Results/default.aspx.
27   David Curry, 'Dating App Revenue and Usage Statistics (2025)', Business of Apps (6 Jun. 2025), https://www.businessofapps.com/data/dating-app-market/.
28   Tafradzhiyski, 'Tinder Revenue and Usage Statistics (2025)'.
29   Curry, 'Hinge Revenue and Usage Statistics (2025)'.
30   Samantha Subin, 'Bumble IPO: The Female Founder behind the Dating App Making Market History', CNBC (11 Feb. 2021), https://www.cnbc.com/2021/02/11/bumble-ipo-the-woman-behind-dating-app-making-market-history.html.
31   Michael J. Rosenfeld, Reuben J. Thomas and Sonia Hausen, 'Disintermediating Your Friends: How Online Dating in the United States Displaces Other Ways of Meeting', *Proceedings of the National Academy of Sciences*, 116/36 (2019), 17753–58. https://www.pnas.org/doi/full/10.1073/pnas.1908630116.
32   Emily Washburn, 'Most American Couples Meet Online, Survey Shows', *Daily Citizen* (11 Oct. 2024), https://dailycitizen.focusonthefamily.com/most-american-couples-meet-online-survey-shows/.

NOTES

33   Daniel Rosney and Roisin Hastie, 'Dating Apps: Tinder, Chappy and Bumble "Least Preferred" Way to Meet People', BBC Newsbeat (3 Aug. 2018), https://www.bbc.co.uk/news/newsbeat-45007017.

34   Rosney and Hastie, 'Dating Apps'.

35   'Hinge Launches Prompt Feedback to Help Daters Create Unique and Authentic Profiles', Hinge Newsroom (15 Jan. 2025), https://hinge.co/pt-pt/newsroom/prompt-feedback.

36   Elisabeth Timmermans, Elien De Caluwé and Cassandra Alexopoulos, 'Why Are You Cheating on Tinder? Exploring Users' Motives and (Dark) Personality Traits', *Computers in Human Behavior*, 89 (2018), 129–39. https://doi.org/10.1016/j.chb.2018.07.040.

37   'What is Most Compatible?', Hinge Help Center (n.d.), https://help.hinge.co/hc/en-us/articles/360011233073-What-is-Most-Compatible.

38   'What Is Standouts?', Hinge Help Center (n.d.), https://help.hinge.co/hc/en-us/articles/360057625534-What-is-Standouts.

39   'Top Picks', Tinder Help Center (n.d.), https://www.help.tinder.com/hc/en-us/articles/360005039092-Top-Picks.

40   'Benching', 'breadcrumbing' and 'cloaking': Gary W. Lewandowski Jr, '21 Terms That Explain Modern Dating', *Psychology Today* (20 Jan. 2025), https://www.psychologytoday.com/gb/blog/the-psychology-of-relationships/202501/decoding-modern-dating-the-new-lingo-you-need-to-know. 'Orbiting': Lewandowski Jr, '21 Terms'; Jaik Puppyteeth, 'Orbiting Is Just a Form of Ghosting, Get Over It', *VICE* (30 Apr. 2018), https://www.vice.com/en/article/orbiting-is-just-a-form-of-ghosting-get-over-it/. 'Throning': Lucy Mangan, 'Breadcrumbing, Ghosting, Throning: Lucy Mangan Explains Why She's All for Inventing New Words', *Stylist* (n.d.), https://www.stylist.co.uk/people/lucy-mangan/breadcrumbing-ghosting-throning-millenial-dating-terminology-creating-new-words/266572.

41   Rebecca Jennings, 'Stop Canceling Normal People Who Go Viral', *Vox* (21 Jan. 2022), https://www.vox.com/the-goods/22716772/west-elm-caleb-couch-guy-tiktok-cancel.

42   Freya India, 'Can a New Dating App Stop "Ghosting"?', *The Spectator* (2 Mar. 2022), https://www.spectator.co.uk/article/can-ghosting-be-eradicated/.

43   River Page, 'Reviewing Men? There's an App for That', *Free Press* (31 Jul. 2025), https://www.thefp.com/p/the-app-made-to-review-men.

44   theteapartygirls, 'Is He a Red Flag or a Green Flag?! Dare I Say You Must Go to Tea ASAP, Type in Your Man's Name, and See What His "Dating Data" Is?!', Instagram (26 Sep. 2024), https://www.instagram.com/p/DAXTsK-Ppl_/.

45   Dylan Donnelly, 'What Is Tea – the Women-Only App with Millions of Users?', Sky News (31 Jul. 2025), https://news.sky.com/story/what-is-tea-the-women-only-app-with-millions-of-users-13401888.

46   Serena Smith, 'Tea: Inside the New App Where Women Anonymously Review Men', *Dazed* (24 Jul. 2025), https://www.dazeddigital.com/life-culture/article/68302/1/tea-the-new-app-where-women-anonymously-review-men.
47   Tea [homepage], https://www.teaforwomen.com/.
48   Kali (@kalithompson), 'No cuddles', TikTok (17 Dec. 2022), https://www.tiktok.com/@kalithompson/video/7178044359311363333.
49   'Tinder: The App That Helps You Meet People for Sex', *The Guardian* (16 Aug. 2013), https://www.theguardian.com/lifeandstyle/shortcuts/2013/aug/16/tinder-app-meet-people-sex-celebrities.
50   Nancy Jo Sales, 'Tinder and the Dawn of the "Dating Apocalypse"', *Vanity Fair* (6 Aug. 2015), https://www.vanityfair.com/culture/2015/08/tinder-hook-up-culture-end-of-dating.
51   Yana Tallon-Hicks, 'How to Be an Ethical Hookup Partner', *Teen Vogue* (12 Aug. 2019), https://www.teenvogue.com/story/how-to-be-an-ethical-hook-up.
52   Gigi Engle, 'Anal Sex: Safety, How tos, Tips, and More', *Teen Vogue* (12 Nov. 2019), https://www.teenvogue.com/story/anal-sex-what-you-need-to-know.
53   'the most-listened to podcast...': *Call Her Daddy* [podcast], YouTube, https://www.youtube.com/channel/UCyGi3eCuxko37WB6uUr7LjA. 'blow job technique': '3 – The Gluck Gluck 9000', *Call Her Daddy* [podcast] (3 Oct. 2018), https://www.podchaser.com/podcasts/call-her-daddy-709485/episodes/3-the-gluck-gluck-9000-33886838. 'fuck buddy life': '11 – MILF Hunting Season', *Call Her Daddy* [podcast] (21 Nov. 2018), https://www.podchaser.com/podcasts/call-her-daddy-709485/episodes/11-milf-hunting-season-33888583.
54   The respective episodes can be found on various podcast sites, including Podchaser: https://www.podchaser.com/podcasts/call-her-daddy-709485/episodes/welcome-to-slut-camp-40284981 ('38 – Welcome to Slut Camp', 5 Jun. 2019), https://www.podchaser.com/podcasts/call-her-daddy-709485/episodes/2-if-youre-a-5-or-6-die-for-th-33886837 ('2 – If you're a 5 or 6, Die for that D*ck', 3 Oct. 2018), and https://www.podchaser.com/podcasts/call-her-daddy-709485/episodes/31-youre-just-a-hole-38849581 ('31 – You're Just a Hole', 17 Apr. 2019).
55   Hannah Clarke, '"Call Her Daddy" Is Selling $30 T-Shirts That Say "Cheat on Him", and It's Anything but Empowering', Swoon (15 Jul. 2020), https://www.theodysseyonline.com/call-her-daddy-shirts-no-excuse.
56   '50 – Milf Hunter (Guest #1)', *Call Her Daddy* [podcast] (28 Aug. 2019), Podchaser, https://www.podchaser.com/podcasts/call-her-daddy-709485/episodes/milf-hunter-guest-1-44022393.
57   'Word of the Year': 'Rizz Crowned Oxford Word of the Year 2023', Oxford University Press (4 Dec. 2023), https://corp.oup.com/news/rizz-crowned-oxford-word-of-the-year-2023/. 2 billion TikTok views: Krystal Miller, 'Don't Fall for

NOTES

a Situationship', *The Quinnipiac Chronicle* (22 Feb. 2023), https://quchronicle.com/80508/opinion/dont-fall-for-a-situationship/.

58 Myisha Battle, 'Situationships Are the Future of Dating. That's Not a Bad Thing', *Time* (18 Mar. 2023), https://time.com/6263743/situationships-dating-benefits/.

59 Kelly McCarthy, 'Sweethearts Creates Situationship Candy Full of Mixed Messages for Valentine's Day', ABC News (4 Jan. 2024), https://abcnews.go.com/GMA/Food/sweethearts-creates-situationship-candy-full-mixed-messages-valentines/story?id=106095774.

60 Sweethearts Candies, 'Sweethearts Situationships are the perfect gift for anybody out there in a blurry relationship. And we mean anybody', Instagram (8 Jan. 2024), https://www.instagram.com/p/C12d7sxvm1J/.

61 Keiran Southern, 'It's Complicated: How the "Situationship" Went Mainstream', *The Times* (4 Feb. 2024), https://www.thetimes.com/world/article/be-my-convenient-valentine-how-the-situationship-went-mainstream-n2cx23vnk.

62 'TINDER'S YEAR IN SWIPE™ Dating Games are dead in 2022 said Young* Singles in Australia', Tinder Newsroom (28 Nov. 2022), https://au.tinderpressroom.com/Tinders-Year-In-Swipe-2022.

63 'Tinder Introduces Relationship Goals, Because Sharing What You Want Is Sexy', Tinder Newsroom (15 Dec. 2022), https://au.tinderpressroom.com/relationshipgoals.

64 Daniel A. Cox and Kelsey Eyre Hammond, 'Romantic Recession: How Politics, Pessimism, and Anxiety Shape American Courtship', Survey Center on American Life (29 Jan. 2025), https://www.americansurveycenter.org/research/the-state-of-american-romance-how-politics-and-pessimism-influence-dating-experiences/.

65 Cox and Hammond, 'Romantic Recession'.

66 Daniel A. Cox, Kelsey Eyre Hammond and Kyle Gray, 'Generation Z and the Transformation of American Adolescence: How Gen Z's Formative Experiences Shape Its Politics, Priorities, and Future', Survey Center on American Life (9 Nov. 2023), https://www.americansurveycenter.org/research/generation-z-and-the-transformation-of-american-adolescence-how-gen-zs-formative-experiences-shape-its-politics-priorities-and-future/.

67 'BEH4.A Sexual Activity: Percentage of High School Students Who Reported Ever Having Had Sexual Intercourse by Gender, Race and Hispanic Origin, and Grade, Selected Years 1991–2021', Forum on Child and Family Statistics (n.d.), https://www.childstats.gov/americaschildren/tables/beh4a.asp.

68 Grant Bailey and Brad Wilcox, 'The Sex Recession: The Share of Americans Having Regular Sex Keeps Dropping', Institute for Family Studies (30 Aug. 2025), https://ifstudies.org/blog/the-sex-recession-the-share-of-americans-having-regular-sex-keeps-dropping.

69 Dr Justin Lehmiller, 'Gen Z Aren't Having the Sex You Think: Here's Why', Lovehoney (26 Jun. 2022), https://www.lovehoney.com/blog/gen-z-are-having-less-sex-here-is-why.html.

70 2013 figure: 'Pornhub 2013 Year in Review', Pornhub (n.d.), https://www.pornhub.com/insights/pornhub-2013-year-in-review. 2019 figure: 'The 2019 Year in Review', Pornhub (n.d.), https://www.pornhub.com/insights/2019-year-in-review.

71 Around 130 million visits a day: 'The Pornhub Tech Review', Pornhub (n.d.), https://www.pornhub.com/insights/tech-review. Top ten most visited: 'Top Websites in Worldwide (All Industries)', Semrush (Jul. 2025), https://www.semrush.com/trending-websites/global/all/.

72 David Holmes, 'Pornhub Launches "Netflix for Porn" Subscription Service', *The Guardian* (6 Aug. 2015), https://www.theguardian.com/culture/2015/aug/06/pornhub-launches-paid-subscription.

73 Madeleine Morley, 'The UX of Porn Tube Sites Are Designed for the Ultimate Money Shot: How Porn Sites Pioneered Ecommerce Platforms and Got Their Hands All Over Our Hard Data', AIGA Eye on Design (29 Jul. 2022), https://eyeondesign.aiga.org/the-ux-of-porn-tubes-are-designed-for-the-ultimate-money-shot/.

74 Frederick S. Lane III, *Obscene Profits: The Entrepreneurs of Pornography in the Cyber Age* (Routledge, 2000), quoted in Morley, 'The UX of Porn'.

75 Data mining to track users: Patrick Keilty, 'Desire by Design: Pornography as Technology Industry', *Porn Studies*, 5/3 (2018), 338–42. https://doi.org/10.1080/23268743.2018.1483208. Sharing viewing habits: Elena Maris, Timothy Libert and Jennifer Henrichsen, 'Tracking Sex: The Implications of Widespread Sexual Data Leakage and Tracking on Porn Websites', arXiv preprint (July 2019). https://doi.org/10.48550/arXiv.1907.06520.

76 Harriet Grant, '"I Didn't Start Out Wanting to See Kids": Are Porn Algorithms Feeding a Generation of Paedophiles – Or Creating One?', *The Guardian* (5 Apr. 2025), https://www.theguardian.com/society/2025/apr/05/i-didnt-start-out-wanting-to-see-kids-are-porn-algorithms-feeding-a-generation-of-paedophiles-or-creating-one.

77 Nicholas Kristof, 'The Children of Pornhub', *New York Times* (4 Dec. 2020), https://www.nytimes.com/2020/12/04/opinion/sunday/pornhub-rape-trafficking.html.

78 Nicholas Kristof, 'These Internal Documents Show Why We Shouldn't Trust Porn Companies', *New York Times* (10 May 2025), https://www.nytimes.com/2025/05/10/opinion/pornhub-children-documents.html.

79 Fiona Vera-Gray et al, 'Sexual Violence as a Sexual Script in Mainstream Online Pornography', *British Journal of Criminology*, 61/5 (2021), 1243–60. https://doi.org/10.1093/bjc/azab035.

NOTES

80 Michael B. Robb and Supreet Mann, 'Teens and Pornography' [report], Common Sense Media (2023), https://www.commonsensemedia.org/sites/default/files/research/report/2022-teens-and-pornography-final-web.pdf.

81 Shiona McCallum, 'Children as Young as Nine Exposed to Pornography', BBC News (31 Jan. 2023), https://www.bbc.co.uk/news/technology-64451984.

82 PitifulGuardsman, 'When Did You First Get Exposed to Pornography?', Reddit, r/GenZ (27 Oct. 2024), https://www.reddit.com/r/GenZ/comments/1gdo7zj/when_did_you_first_get_exposed_to_pornography/.

83 Cox and Hammond, 'Romantic Recession'.

84 Robb and Mann, 'Teens and Pornography'.

85 '"A Lot of It Is Actually Just Abuse": Young People and Pornography' [information sheet], Children's Commissioner (Jan. 2023), https://assets.childrenscommissioner.gov.uk/wpuploads/2023/01/cc-pornography-and-young-people-information-sheet.pdf.

86 Isabel Hogben, 'I Had a Helicopter Mom. I Found Pornhub Anyway', *The Free Press* (29 Aug. 2023), https://www.thefp.com/p/why-are-our-fourth-graders-on-pornhub.

87 McCallum, 'Children as Young as Nine Exposed to Pornography'.

88 '"A Lot of It Is Actually Just Abuse"', Children's Commissioner.

89 McCallum, 'Children as Young as Nine Exposed to Pornography'.

90 By 1,400%: '2017 Year in Review', Pornhub (n.d.), https://www.pornhub.com/insights/2017-year-in-review. Nearly three in every ten: 'How Many Women Watch Porn?', Fight the New Drug (n.d.), https://fightthenewdrug.org/how-do-men-and-womens-porn-site-searches-differ/.

91 Isabelle Kirk, 'How Often do Britons Watch Porn?', YouGov (1 Jul. 2022), https://yougov.co.uk/society/articles/42945-how-often-do-britons-watch-porn.

92 Eleanor Rose, '"Porn for Women" Searches Up 1,400 Per Cent in a Year, Pornhub Reveals', *Evening Standard* (11 Jan. 2018), https://www.standard.co.uk/news/world/porn-for-women-searches-up-1-400-per-cent-in-a-year-as-websites-hail-2018-the-year-of-the-woman-a3737351.html.

93 'crass': Shirley Halperin, 'Note to Miley Cyrus: Please Stop; Plus Other VMAs Ruminations', *Hollywood Reporter* (26 Aug. 2013), https://www.hollywoodreporter.com/news/music-news/note-miley-cyrus-please-stop-614407/. 'degrading': Sean Michaels, 'Miley Cyrus's VMAs Routine Was "Degrading", Says Backup Dancer', *The Guardian* (14 Oct. 2013), https://www.theguardian.com/culture/2013/oct/14/miley-cyrus-vmas-degrading-for-dancer.

94 B. J. Steiner, 'The Most Awkward Hip-Hop Moments at MTV's 2013 Video Music Awards', *XXL* (26 Aug. 2013), https://www.xxlmag.com/the-most-awkward-hip-hop-moments-at-mtvs-2013-video-music-awards/.

95   'Miley Cyrus Defends Her Performance at MTV VMAs', BBC Newsbeat (4 Sep. 2013), https://www.bbc.co.uk/news/newsbeat-23952940.
96   Lulu Garcia-Navarro, 'Miley Cyrus Told Us to Ask Her Anything', *New York Times* (31 May 2025), https://www.nytimes.com/2025/05/31/magazine/miley-cyrus-interview.html.
97   Erin Lindsay, 'Netflix's "Sex Education" Should Be Required Viewing for Teenagers', *IMAGE* (5 Feb. 2020), https://www.image.ie/editorial/netflix-sex-education-required-viewing-teenagers-177048.
98   Ingeborg van Lotringen, 'Is Instagram Giving You "Porn Face"?', *Cosmopolitan UK* (10 Jul. 2017), https://www.cosmopolitan.com/uk/beauty-hair/a9993367/porn-face-instagram-beauty/.
99   '"A Lot of It Is Actually Just Abuse"', Children's Commissioner.
100 Tamara Cohen, 'Teenagers Exposed to "Horrific" Content Online – and This Survey Reveals the Scale of the Problem', Sky News (19 Mar. 2025), https://news.sky.com/story/teenagers-exposed-to-horrific-content-online-and-this-survey-reveals-the-scale-of-the-problem-13331556.
101 Jeff Horwitz and Katherine Blunt, 'Instagram's Algorithm Delivers Toxic Video Mix to Adults Who Follow Children', *Wall Street Journal* (27 Nov. 2023), https://www.wsj.com/tech/meta-instagram-video-algorithm-children-adult-sexual-content-72874155.
102 Sex videos to minors and promotion of OnlyFans: Rob Barry et al, 'How TikTok Serves Up Sex and Drug Videos to Minors', *Wall Street Journal* (8 Sep. 2021), https://www.wsj.com/articles/tiktok-algorithm-sex-drugs-minors-11631052944; Dan Milmo, 'TikTok "Directs Child Accounts to Pornographic Content within a Few Clicks', *The Guardian* (3 Oct. 2025), https://www.theguardian.com/technology/2025/oct/03/tiktok-child-accounts-pornographic-content-accessible. Twitch exposing children to explicit live streams: Luke Andrews, 'New Twitch Trend That Sees Scantily-Clad "Influencers" Licking Mics and Ears Seductively on the Kid-Friendly Platform', *Daily Mail* (4 Sep. 2023), https://www.dailymail.co.uk/health/article-10735311/children-sexual-content-twitch-warning-parents.html.
103 htaming, 'Anyone wanna try this app and let us know?', Reddit, r/replika (8 Dec. 2022), https://www.reddit.com/r/replika/comments/zg59a1/anyone_wanna_try_this_app_and_let_us_know/.
104 David Ingram, 'Ads for AI Sex Workers Are Flooding Instagram and TikTok', NBC News (1 Sep. 2023), https://www.nbcnews.com/tech/social-media/ai-girlfriend-ads-instagram-tiktok-chat-pics-chatgpt-dose-rcna97547.
105 Josh Pieters, 'I Slept with 100 Men in One Day | Documentary', YouTube (7 Dec. 2024), https://www.youtube.com/watch?v=mFySAhog-MI.
106 Pieters, *I Slept with 100 Men*.

NOTES

107 Claudia Cox, 'Behind-the-Scenes Details of How Lily Phillips Apparently Slept with 1,113 Men in One Go', The Tab (29 Jun. 2025), https://thetab.com/2025/07/01/behind-the-scenes-details-of-how-lily-phillips-apparently-slept-with-1113-men-in-one-go.

108 Alice Giddings, 'Shocking Photo Reveals Aftermath of Bonnie Blue's 1,057 Men in a Day Sex Challenge', *Metro* (13 Jan. 2025, updated 16 Jan. 2025), https://metro.co.uk/2025/01/13/bonnie-blue-sex-1-057-men-a-day-photo-shows-shocking-aftermath-22347344/.

109 Anna Cooban, 'OnlyFans Has Boomed During Lockdown. Users Spent $2.4 Billion on the Adult-Entertainment Site in 2020, and 120 Million People Now Use It', *Business Insider* (27 Apr. 2021), https://www.businessinsider.com/onlyfans-lockdown-boom-transactions-hit-24b-revenue-up-553-2021-4.

110 Kayla Kibbe, 'OnlyFans Traffic Is Up Thanks to a Beyoncé Shoutout', *InsideHook* (4 May 2020), https://www.insidehook.com/culture/beyonce-onlyfans.

111 Joshua Nair, 'Bella Thorne Explained Surprising Reason She Joined OnlyFans after Making "£750,000 in Her First Day"', LADbible (12 Mar. 2025), https://www.ladbible.com/entertainment/celebrity/bella-thorne-money-made-adult-subscription-site-760812-20250312.

112 'Bella Thorne Joins OnlyFans', *Paper* (19 Aug. 2020), https://www.papermag.com/bella-thorne-joins-onlyfans-subscribe#rebelltitem15.

113 Amy Kaufman, 'Bella Thorne Has Made $2 Million on OnlyFans in Less Than a Week. A Movie Is Next', *Los Angeles Times* (25 Aug. 2020), https://www.latimes.com/entertainment-arts/movies/story/2020-08-25/bella-thorne-sean-baker-onlyfans-movie.

114 Amanda Prestigiacomo, 'Demi Lovato Tells Followers To "Be A Sl*t", "Make Porn", "Be Kinky", Promotes Prostitution', Daily Wire (8 Sep. 2021), https://www.dailywire.com/news/demi-lovato-tells-followers-to-be-a-slt-make-porn-be-kinky-promotes-prostitution.

115 On Instagram: Tana Mongeau, 'Why do u do OnlyFans? Good month @ unrulyagency', Instagram (17 Nov. 2020), https://www.instagram.com/p/CHtQwxEBGwX/?hl=en. On Twitter: Tana Mongeau (@tanamongeau), 'onlyfans is fun..... y'all liked what u saw this month... time to step it up ;)', Twitter (9.40 p.m., 17 Nov. 2020) https://x.com/tanamongeau/status/1328815240616714240.

116 Tana Mongeau (@tanamongeau), 'me with everything ur dad bought me on OnlyFans', Twitter (16 Jun. 2021), https://x.com/tanamongeau/status/1404938333709430784.

117 Tana Mongeau (@tanamongeau), 'if ur seeing this – this is a sign to start an onlyfans & make that bread ;)', Twitter (2.13 a.m., 29 Jan. 2021), https://x.com/tanamongeau/status/1354976238524198914.

118 Melissa Copelton, 'Tana Mongeau Gets Real About All Things Dating: Sexuality, Exes, Deal-Breakers and More', *Life & Style* (20 Feb. 2020), https://www.lifeandstylemag.com/posts/tana-mongeau-gets-real-about-all-things-dating-and-sexuality/.
119 blueeyedkaylajade (@blueeyedkaylajade), 'How much money I made today', TikTok (17 Apr. 2024), https://www.tiktok.com/@blueeyedkaylajade/video/7358772151052176647?lang=en.
120 blueeyedkaylajade (@blueeyedkaylajade), 'Im so grumpy today 😊 #storytime #dayinmylife #makemoneyfromhome', TikTok (23 May 2024), https://www.tiktok.com/@blueeyedkaylajade/video/7371978419195710727?lang=en.
121 livedexperienceeducator. 'Recently I shared on my stories that I used to be [a] full service sex worker for two years and I wanted to share how this particular work actually suited my Autism and ADHD', Instagram (23 Oct. 2022), https://www.instagram.com/p/CkCRu8fvKht.
122 'Student Sex Workers', Students' Union UCL (n.d.), https://studentsunionucl.org/advice-and-support/support/student-sex-workers.
123 Gaynor Trueman, Saskia Hagelberg and Teela Sanders, 'Student Sex Work Toolkit for Staff in Higher Education', University of Leicester (n.d.), https://le.ac.uk/-/media/uol/docs/academic-departments/criminology/student-sex-work-toolkit-for-staff-in-he.pdf.
124 Holly Bancroft, 'Durham University Offers Training for Students Working in Sex Industry', *Independent* (12 Nov. 2021), https://www.independent.co.uk/news/uk/home-news/sex-work-durham-university-students-b1956484.html.
125 Noel Titheradge and Rianna Croxford, 'The Children Selling Explicit Videos on OnlyFans', BBC News (27 May 2021), https://www.bbc.co.uk/news/uk-57255983.
126 Thea de Gallier, 'The Hidden Danger of Selling Nudes Online', BBC Three (7 Apr. 2020), https://www.bbc.co.uk/bbcthree/article/5e7dad06-c48d-4509-b3e4-6a7a2783ce30.
127 Meredith Somers, 'Deepfakes, Explained', MIT Management, Sloan School (21 Jul. 2020), https://mitsloan.mit.edu/ideas-made-to-matter/deepfakes-explained.
128 Nicholas Kristof, 'The Online Degradation of Women and Girls That We Meet With a Shrug', *New York Times* (23 Mar. 2024), https://www.nytimes.com/2024/03/23/opinion/deepfake-sex-videos.html.
129 '2023 STATE OF DEEPFAKES', Security Hero (n.d.), https://www.securityhero.io/state-of-deepfakes/.
130 How AI Is Being Abused to Create Child Sexual Abuse Imagery', Internet Watch Foundation (Oct. 2023), https://www.iwf.org.uk/media/q4zll2ya/iwf-ai-csam-report_public-oct23v1.pdf.
131 Matt Burgess, 'Millions of People Are Using Abusive AI "Nudify" Bots on Telegram', *Wired* (15 Oct. 2024), https://www.wired.com/story/ai-deepfake-nudify-bots-telegram/.

NOTES

132 Cyrus Farivar, 'Etsy Has Been Hosting Deepfake Porn Of Celebrities', *Forbes* (20 Dec. 2023), https://www.forbes.com/sites/cyrusfarivar/2023/12/20/etsy-has-been-hosting-deepfake-porn-of-celebrities/.

133 Healing & Growing with Nichole (@mindbodysouls), '#narcissisticrelationship #healingtiktok #traumabond #healingfromnarcissisticrelationship #narcissisticex #healingfromnarcissisticabuse #toxicrelationship #bbreakingupwithanarcissist #lovebombing', TikTok (29 Nov. 2022), https://www.tiktok.com/@mindbodysouls/video/7171248591812562218.

134 all power to the people (@realdocv), 'Unpopular dating opinion: The intense chemistry you feel with someone you just met is a huge red flag. Most likely, they are similar to an early caregiver that neglected you & your subconscious mind is attracted to them to try to fix an old wound', X (4.27 p.m., 13 Dec. 2023), https://x.com/realdocv/status/1734973417387065582.

135 blcksmith, 'siri play truth hurts by lizzo (quote by @dozyhrs, on a mural by @shannnonbaird with @klutchko, @calmmurals, and @rupeezy)', Instagram (26 Aug. 2020), https://www.instagram.com/p/CEXFRS9htmh/.

136 'Red Flag' [search results], TikTok, https://www.tiktok.com/channel/red-flag?lang=en, accessed Jul. 2025.

137 Jenny McCartney, 'Could Andrew Tate Split the Republican Party? Christian Conservatives Despise Him', *UnHerd* (22 Mar. 2025), https://unherd.com/2025/03/could-andrew-tate-split-the-republican-party/.

138 Ewan Somerville and Euan O'Byrne Mulligan, 'UK Prosecutors Say 21 Charges Authorised Against Tate Brothers', BBC News (28 May 2025), https://www.bbc.co.uk/news/articles/ckg41g1140po.

139 *FreshandFit* [podcast], YouTube, https://www.youtube.com/@freshfitmiami.

140 *whatever* [podcast], YouTube, https://www.youtube.com/whatever.

141 whatever Clips, 'DELUSIONAL Girls Rate Themselves A 10 But Brian HUMBLES Them!', YouTube (17 Aug. 2023), https://www.youtube.com/watch?v=EIEes45HbeI; whatever Clips, *FreshandFit*, 'Why FEMINISM Made Women UNDATEABLE and Low Quality!', YouTube (17 Apr. 2025), https://www.youtube.com/watch?v=J-yIlRxo14E&t=1s; *FreshandFit*, 'Lonely Older Woman REALIZED That Feminism BACKFIRED On Her!', *YouTube* (30 Oct. 2024), https://www.youtube.com/watch?v=D9kT5WPh_io.

142 Kiera (@famousblonde), 'taken down at 1mil views, edited so it fits tiktok's approval (this doesn't break any guidelines!!) #fyp #foryou #viral #feminism', TikTok (28 Sep. 2020), https://www.tiktok.com/@famousblonde/video/6877316667072908550?lang=en.

143 Kat Rosenfield, 'Here Come the Female Andrew Tates', *UnHerd* (17 Aug. 2023), https://unherd.com/2023/08/is-this-the-female-andrew-tate/.

144 '30 – Sex Toys & How to Not Catch Feelings', *Call Her Daddy* [podcast] (10 Apr. 2019), Podchaser, https://www.podchaser.com/podcasts/call-her-daddy-709485/episodes/30-sex-toys-how-to-not-catch-f-38660443. Quotes from episode as described by Ana Altchek, 'Opinion | "Call Her Daddy" podcast entertains and degrades', *The Pitt News* (18 Sept. 2019).

145 'These Modern Women': Whatever Podcast Clips, 'These Modern Women Are Insane', YouTube (19 Jun. 2023), https://www.youtube.com/watch?v=xaXuZFkZh-Y. 'Don't Need Men': 'We Don't Need Men (Full Josie Canseco Interview)', *Call Her Daddy* [podcast], YouTube (10 May 2021), https://www.youtube.com/watch?v=5EPG8AxAlRA.

146 '4 SIGNS': esthersarphatie (@sarphatieesther), '4 Signs that your relationship won't last…', TikTok (27 Dec. 2022), https://www.tiktok.com/@sarphatieesther/video/7181803806449995013; '3 BIG SIGNS': vampyangelll (@vampyangelll), '#shouldIbreakup #breakuprecoverytips #breakup #shouldIbreakupwithhim #relationshipproblems #uncoupling #shadowwork #intuitivecoach Should I break up with them, should I break up with him, should I cut them off, cord cutting, relationship advice', TikTok (19 Nov. 2022), https://www.tiktok.com/@vampyangelll/video/7167848069663296811; 'if you get sick': 'Paul Brunson: Women Need to Lower Their Standards! If They Have These 3 Traits, Never Let Them Go!', *Diary of a CEO* [podcast], YouTube (30 Jan. 2025), https://www.youtube.com/watch?v=6ikIGGi859w; 'eventually cheat on you': 'Esther Perel: The 3 Attachment Styles & Why You're Struggling With Love!', *Diary of a CEO* [podcast] (7 Dec. 2023), YouTube video, 2:02:42, https://www.youtube.com/watch?v=nTWXfo7narw.

147 Jason Parham, 'The Real Relationship Hustlers of TikTok', *Wired* (28 Jun. 2024), https://www.wired.com/story/the-real-relationship-hustlers-of-tiktok/.

148 Flirtini Team, 'Love and Likes: Can TikTok Be Trusted for Dating Advice?', *Flirtini* [blog] (17 Jun. 2024), https://www.flirtini.com/blog/love-and-likes-can-tiktok-be-trusted-for-dating-advice.html.

149 Parham, 'The Real Relationship Hustlers of TikTok'.

150 Faith Hill, 'America Is in Its Insecure-Attachment Era', *The Atlantic* (27 Apr. 2023), https://www.theatlantic.com/family/archive/2023/04/insecure-attachment-style-intimacy-decline-isolation/673867/.

151 36,000 weekly visitors: 'r/AnxiousAttachment', Reddit (n.d), https://www.reddit.com/r/AnxiousAttachment/. Almost a billion views: Anna Salleh, Sana Qadar, James Bullen and Rose Kerr, 'Attachment Styles Are All the Rage on TikTok but Can They Really Doom Your Relationship?', ABC News (31 Aug. 2024), https://www.abc.net.au/news/health/2024-09-01/attachment-styles-relationships-social-media-tik-tok-instagram/104279024.

NOTES

152 Reddit user, 'Triggered by partner's instagram use', Reddit, r/AnxiousAttachment (31 May 2024), https://www.reddit.com/r/AnxiousAttachment/comments/1d4r5zx/triggered_by_partners_instagram_use/.

153 Gigi Fong, 'The Results Are In: Situationships Cut Deeper Than Relationships', *HYPEBAE* (6 Sep. 2023), https://hypebae.com/2023/9/gen-z-dating-trends-situationships-eharmony-dating-diaries.

154 Daniel A. Cox, 'Is America Experiencing an Infidelity Epidemic?' [newsletter], Survey Center on American Life (20 Feb. 2025), https://www.americansurveycenter.org/newsletter/is-america-experiencing-an-infidelity-epidemic/.

155 '"A Lot of It Is Actually Just Abuse"', Children's Commissioner.

156 Lower relationship satisfaction: Amanda M. Maddox, Galena K. Rhoades and Howard J. Markman, 'Viewing Sexually-Explicit Materials Alone or Together: Associations with Relationship Quality', *Archives of Sexual Behavior*, 40/2 (2011), 441–448. https://doi.org/10.1007/s10508-009-9585-4. Higher likelihood of cheating: 'What Research Supports the Idea that "Porn Kills Love"?', Fight the New Drug (n.d.), https://fightthenewdrug.org/the-science-how-porn-kills-love/.

157 Press Association, 'Billie Eilish Says Pornography "Destroyed My Brain"', RTÉ (15 Dec. 2021), https://www.rte.ie/entertainment/2021/1215/1266821-billie-eilish-says-pornography-destroyed-my-brain/.

158 anongal774, 'Major fear that my boyfriend will watch porn when i'm not around', Reddit, r/relationshipanxiety (21 May 2020), https://www.reddit.com/r/relationshipanxiety/comments/goobvc/major_fear_that_my_boyfriend_will_watch_porn_when/.

159 brofistnugget, 'I (F 27) am extremely anxious and jealous about the thought of my partner (M 26) watching porn', Reddit, r/relationship_advice (18 Apr. 2024), https://www.reddit.com/r/relationship_advice/comments/1c72648/i_f_27_am_extremely_anxious_and_jealous_about_the/.

160 Myles Bonnar, '"I Thought He Was Going to Tear Chunks out of My Skin"', BBC News (23 Mar. 2020), https://www.bbc.co.uk/news/uk-scotland-51967295.

161 Julie Jargon, 'Teen Girls' Sexy TikTok Videos Take a Mental-Health Toll', *Wall Street Journal* (5 Feb. 2022), https://www.wsj.com/articles/teen-girls-sexy-tiktok-videos-take-a-mental-health-toll-11644016839?mod=newsarchive_trending_now_article_pos5.

162 Kate Gibson, 'Facebook and Instagram Are Steering Child Predators to Kids, New Mexico AG Alleges', CBS News (6 Dec. 2023), https://www.cbsnews.com/news/facebook-instagram-meta-mark-zuckerberg-children-pedophiles-new-mexico-lawsuit/.

163 E. J. Dickson, 'How TikTok Teens Are Ending Up on Pornhub', *Rolling Stone* (24 Sep. 2020), https://www.rollingstone.com/culture/culture-news/tiktok-dance-pornhub-nonconsensual-porn-1064794/.

164 'Meta Boss Mark Zuckerberg Apologises to Families in Fiery US Senate Hearing', BBC News (1 Feb. 2024), https://www.bbc.co.uk/news/technology-68161632.

165 Katie McQue, 'Meta Documents Show 100,000 Children Sexually Harassed Daily on Its Platforms', *The Guardian* (18 Jan. 2024), https://www.theguardian.com/technology/2024/jan/18/instagram-facebook-child-sexual-harassment.

'EMPOWERED'

1 '*Cinderella* (2021): Quotes', IMDb (n.d.), https://www.imdb.com/title/tt10155932/quotes/?item=qt5889692.

2 Lydia – Manifestation Big Sis (@lydiakillion444), 'UNIVERSE SHOW ME #testtheuniverse #howtoquantumjump #quantumjumping #quantumleap #quantumjump #lawofdetachment #lawofdetachmentjourney #lawofattractiontips #lawofdetachmentguide #manifestfast #manifestationhelp #manifestationhack #manifestationmethod #instantresults #manifesteasily #lawofassumption #nevillegoddard', TikTok (12 Dec. 2023), https://www.tiktok.com/@lydiakillion444/video/7311839695346879776.

3 egeceler (@egeceler), 'I AM this song was written to make a manifest video' #@CLATagoo @Ezgi #manifestation #manifest #ritual #keşfet', TikTok (1 May 2024), https://www.tiktok.com/@egeceler/video/7364150042476924166?lang=en.

4 'In U.S., Decline of Christianity Continues at Rapid Pace' [report], Pew Research Center (17 Oct. 2019), https://www.pewresearch.org/religion/2019/10/17/in-u-s-decline-of-christianity-continues-at-rapid-pace/.

5 Daniel A. Cox and Kelsey Eyre Hammond, 'Young Women Are Leaving Church in Unprecedented Numbers', Survey Center on American Life (4 Apr. 2024), https://www.americansurveycenter.org/newsletter/young-women-are-leaving-church-in-unprecedented-numbers/.

6 Ryan Burge, 'Highly Educated Men Are More Likely to Be in Church Than Highly Educated Women', Graphs About Religion (10 Jun. 2024), https://www.graphsaboutreligion.com/p/highly-educated-men-are-more-likely.

7 Cox and Hammond, 'Young Women Are Leaving Church in Unprecedented Numbers'.

8 Rikki Schlott, 'Gen Z "More Spiritual" Than Millennials – Yet More Suspicious of Denominations', *New York Post* (27 May 2023), https://nypost.com/2023/05/27/why-gen-z-is-more-spiritual-and-religious-than-millennials/.

9 Sydney Clarke, 'Gen Z Is Deconstructing Religion and Finding Faith', *VICE* (18 Feb. 2021), https://www.vice.com/en/article/gen-z-is-deconstructing-religion-and-finding-faith/.

10 'Do You Think There Is Any Truth Whatsoever in Astrology and Star Signs?'

NOTES

[survey], YouGov (26 Feb. 2016), https://yougov.co.uk/topics/society/survey-results/daily/2016/02/26/15dco/1, cited in Poppy Sowerby, 'How Astrology Fooled Womankind', *UnHerd* (23 Jul. 2024), https://unherd.com/2024/07/how-astrology-fooled-womankind/.

11 'defining trend': Daisy Jones, 'How Pop Astrology Became the Trend of the 2010s', *VICE* (17 Dec. 2019), https://www.vice.com/en/article/astrology-trend-2010s-co-star-the-pattern/. 'age of uncertainty': Christine Smallwood, 'Astrology in the Age of Uncertainty', *New Yorker* (21 Oct. 2019), https://www.newyorker.com/magazine/2019/10/28/astrology-in-the-age-of-uncertainty.

12 Lara Wildenberg, 'Generation Z Turn to Astrology "to Answer Life's Big Questions"', *The Times* (19 Jan. 2025), https://www.thetimes.com/uk/society/article/generation-z-turn-to-astrology-to-answer-lifes-big-questions-hnc2mjnv8.

13 'Astrology Market Research, 2031' [report], Allied Market Research (n.d.), https://www.alliedmarketresearch.com/astrology-market-A31779.

14 Co-Star app: Co-Star Personalized Astrology [mobile app], Co-Star Astrology Society, https://play.google.com/store/apps/details?id=com.costarastrology. User figures: 'Number of Registered Co-Star Users Worldwide from October 2019 to July 2023', Statista (n.d.), https://www.statista.com/statistics/1451873/costar-registered-users/.

15 Katie Gatens, 'Did They See the Signs? Astrology's Star Is Rising', *Sunday Times* (20 Nov. 2022), https://www.thetimes.com/business-money/technology/article/did-they-see-the-signs-astrologys-star-is-rising-mqwcs57dj.

16 Antonio Pagliarulo, 'Why Paganism and Witchcraft Are Making a Comeback', NBC News (30 Oct. 2022), https://www.nbcnews.com/think/opinion/paganism-witchcraft-are-making-comeback-rcna54444.

17 Lois Heslop, 'The Rise of WitchTok', *The Spectator* (10 Nov. 2021), https://www.spectator.co.uk/article/the-rise-of-witchtok/.

18 'natural born witch': Shayla Belle @shaylapatchkid, 'Take what applies & leave the rest #witchtok #blackwitchtok', TikTok (11 Feb. 2023), https://www.tiktok.com/@shaylapatchkid/video/7198761698981858603?lang=en. Witchy morning routines: Celeste – Mage By Moonlight (@magebymoonlight), 'How I start my day on a witchy and relaxed note: no screentime, meditation in bed, herbal tea, setting an intention, rune casting and offering for my deities, ancestors and spirit guides...', TikTok (22 May 2023), https://www.tiktok.com/@magebymoonlight/video/7236027358866640171?lang=en.

19 r/WitchesVsPatriarchy, GummySearch (n.d.), https://gummysearch.com/r/WitchesVsPatriarchy/.

20 Claire Jones, 'WitchTok: The Witchcraft Videos with Billions of Views', BBC Newsbeat (31 Oct. 2022), https://www.bbc.co.uk/news/newsbeat-63403467.

21   Tara Isabella Burton, 'The Long, Strange History of "Manifesting"', *New York Times* (9 Mar. 2024), https://www.nytimes.com/2024/03/09/opinion/manifesting-spirituality-america-reality.html.
22   'MONEY MANIFESTING COACH DIPLOMA', Soul Awakening Academy (n.d.), https://soulawakeningacademy.co.uk/step/manifesting-abundance/; 'Manifest A Specific Person Workshop', Roxy Talks Courses, https://courses.roxytalks.com/manifest-a-specific-person-workshop.
23   '"Manifest" Is Cambridge Dictionary's Word of the Year 2024', *Cambridge Dictionary* (n.d.), https://www.cambridge.org/news-and-insights/word-of-the-year-2024.
24   Christopher Lasch, *The Culture of Narcissism: American Life in an Age of Diminishing Expectations* (W. W. Norton & Company, 1979).
25   'specific request': Anna Schlinghoff (@annaschlinghoff), 'the universe wants to help you #spiritualpractice #spiritualprayer', TikTok (7 Dec. 2023), https://www.tiktok.com/@annaschlinghoff/video/7309651499129261354. 'greater plan': alesha.soul (@alesha.soul), 'the universe has got you. this is one of my favorite prayers/intentions of all time #prayer #universehasyourback #loa #manifestation', TikTok (16 Dec. 2023), https://www.tiktok.com/@alesha.soul/video/7313217836485266730.
26   Haley Hoffman Smith (@haleyhoffmansmith), 'nighttime affirmation', TikTok (10 Apr. 2023), https://www.tiktok.com/@haleyhoffmansmith/video/7220221857868336426.
27   'Choose Plan', Calm (n.d.), https://www.calm.com/freetrial/plans.
28   'BetterHelp': BetterHelp (@betterhelp), 'Get it off your chest with BetterHelp', Twitter (10.11 p.m., 18 Jan. 2019), https://x.com/betterhelp/status/1086385622737010688. 'no judgement': Mo Heart (@iammoheart), '#ad no judgement no shame. Check out @BetterHelp to get started. #betterhelppartner #betterhelpsponsored', TikTok (22 Jun. 2023), https://www.tiktok.com/@iammoheart/video/7247638190176193835.
29   BetterHelp, 'Real Talk – "Existential"', YouTube (18 Aug. 2022), https://www.youtube.com/watch?v=iRcTwLDT6NI.
30   'all about you': Karin Andrea Stephan, 'AI Mental Health Chatbots: 6 Ways to Elevate Your Wellbeing', *Earkick* [blog] (n.d), https://blog.earkick.com/ai-mental-health-chatbots-6-ways-to-up-wellbeing/. 'full attention': Karin Andrea Stephan, '5 Ways a Personal AI Chatbot Can Support Mental Health', *Earkick* [blog] (n.d.), https://blog.earkick.com/5-ways-personal-ai-chatbots-support-mental-health/.
31   Shannon Whaley, 'Walking Away from What No Longer Serves You', *HuffPost* (16 Aug. 2016, updated 19 Aug. 2016), https://www.huffpost.com/entry/walking-away-from-what-no-longer-serves-you_b_57b35c16e4b04147250fcfdd.

NOTES

32 Richard Pollina, 'University of Cincinnati Student Alleges Professor Failed Her for Using the Term "Biological Women"', *New York Post* (5 Jun. 2023), https://nypost.com/2023/06/05/university-of-cincinnati-student-alleges-professor-failed-her-project-for-using-the-term-biological-women/.

33 Helen Lewis, 'How Social Justice Became a New Religion', *The Atlantic* (18 Aug. 2022), https://www.theatlantic.com/ideas/archive/2022/08/social-justice-new-religion/671172/.

34 'Younger Generations Stand Out on Identity, Acceptance, and Progressive Policies', AP-NORC Center for Public Affairs Research (16 Dec. 2021), https://apnorc.org/projects/younger-generations-stand-out-on-identity-acceptance-and-progressive-policies/.

35 Far outnumber men: 'Global Universities Address Gender Equality, but Gaps Remain to Be Closed', Times Higher Education and UNESCO International Institute for Higher Education in Latin America and the Caribbean (IESALC) (8 Mar. 2022), https://www.timeshighereducation.com/press-releases/global-universities-address-gender-equality-gaps-remain-be-closed. Social sciences and humanities: Sławomir Trusz, 'Why Do Females Choose to Study Humanities or Social Sciences, While Males Prefer Technology or Science? Some Intrapersonal and Interpersonal Predictors', *Social Psychology of Education*, 23 (2020), 615–39. https://doi.org/10.1007/s11218-020-09551-5.

36 Derek Thompson, 'Colleges Have a Guy Problem', *The Atlantic* (14 Sep. 2021), https://www.theatlantic.com/ideas/archive/2021/09/young-men-college-decline-gender-gap-higher-education/620066/.

37 Agreeableness: Christine Anne Andary-Brophy, 'Political Correctness: Social-Fiscal Liberalism and Left-Wing Authoritarianism', master's thesis, University of Toronto, 2015, https://tspace.library.utoronto.ca/bitstream/1807/75755/3/Brophy_Christine_201511_MA_thesis.pdf. Score higher in than men: P. T. Costa Jr, A. Terracciano and R. R. McCrae, 'Gender Differences in Personality Traits across Cultures: Robust and Surprising Findings', *Journal of Personality and Social Psychology*, 81/2 (2001), 322–31. https://doi.org/10.1037/0022-3514.81.2.322. Conformity: Alice H. Eagly and Carole Chrvala, 'Sex Differences in Conformity: Status and Gender Role Interpretations', *Psychology of Women Quarterly*, 10/3 (1986), 203–20. https://doi.org/10.1111/j.1471-6402.1986.tb00747.x.

38 Survey Center Staff, 'The Growing Political Divide Between Young Men and Women', Survey Center on American Life (31 May 2022), https://www.americansurveycenter.org/short-reads/the-growing-political-divide-between-young-men-and-women/.

39 30% of women and 27% of men: Survey Center Staff, 'The Growing Political Divide'. In 24 years of polling: Daniel de Visé, 'Young Women Are Trending Liberal.

Young Men Are Not', *The Hill* (6 Oct. 2022), https://thehill.com/homenews/campaign/3675477-young-women-are-trending-liberal-young-men-are-not/.

40   Daniel A. Cox, Kelsey Eyre Hammond and Kyle Gray, 'Generation Z and the Transformation of American Adolescence: How Gen Z's Formative Experiences Shape Its Politics, Priorities, and Future', Survey Center on American Life, American Enterprise Institute (9 Nov. 2023), https://www.americansurveycenter.org/research/generation-z-and-the-transformation-of-american-adolescence-how-gen-zs-formative-experiences-shape-its-politics-priorities-and-future/.

41   'Young Women's Political Engagement in Elections and Beyond', Center for Information & Research on Civic Learning and Engagement, Tufts University (18 May 2020), https://circle.tufts.edu/latest-research/young-womens-political-engagement-elections-and-beyond.

42   Lydia Saad, Sarah Elizabeth Jones and Sarah Fioroni, 'Exploring Young Women's Leftward Expansion', Gallup (12 Sep. 2024), https://news.gallup.com/poll/649826/exploring-young-women-leftward-expansion.aspx.

43   Ruby Granger, 'Study with Me || 14 Hour Study Day', YouTube (28 Jan. 2017), https://www.youtube.com/watch?v=RH0MT6VPWr0.

44   Ruby Granger, 'Live Reaction to My First ESSAY MARK at UNIVERSITY (I Cried...)', YouTube (1 Dec. 2018), https://www.youtube.com/watch?v=-q8GgvN3Yac.

45   Roger McNamee, 'Sheryl Sandberg Made Facebook into a Giant – but at a Cost to the World', *Time* (2 Jun. 2022), https://time.com/6183520/sheryl-sandberg-facebook-legacy/.

46   Sara Fischer, 'Sheryl Sandberg's Advertising Jackpot', *Axios* (2 Jun. 2022), https://www.axios.com/2022/06/02/sheryl-sandbergs-advertising-jackpot-facebook.

47   Judith Newman, '"Lean In": Five Years Later', *New York Times* (16 Mar. 2018), https://www.nytimes.com/2018/03/16/business/lean-in-five-years-later.html.

48   Sophia Amoruso, *#Girlboss* (Portfolio/Penguin Random House, 2014).

49   Allie Anderson, '"Fertility Perks" in the Workplace Aren't a Feminist Victory', *Glamour* (11 Dec. 2023), https://www.glamourmagazine.co.uk/article/companies-offering-egg-freezing.

50   Charles Gasparino, 'Wall Street "Egging" on Freezing Egg Pregnancy Delays', *New York Post* (22 Apr. 2023), https://nypost.com/2023/04/22/wall-street-egging-on-freezing-egg-pregnancy-delays/.

51   Emily Canal, 'High-Tech Cribs, Breast Milk Delivery, and Traveling Nannies: Just Some of the Perks Companies Are Offering New Parents', *Inc.* (7 Feb. 2019), https://www.inc.com/emily-canal/maternity-perks-benefits-new-parents-snoo-patagonia.html.

52   Robotic cribs: Aaron Mok, 'JPMorgan, Snap, and Other Employers Are Giving $1,700 Snoos to Employees with Newborns as Part of Their Parental Benefits

NOTES

Packages', *Business Insider* (25 Jul. 2023), https://www.businessinsider.com/companies-hulu-snap-jpmorgan-employees-free-snoo-parental-benefit-perk-2023-7. Workplace nurseries: 'The Fortune 100 Companies That Offer On-Site Day Care to Employees', *The Outline* (31 May 2017), https://theoutline.com/post/1610/the-fortune-100-companies-that-offer-on-site-day-care-to-employees.

53 Eugene Kim, 'Yahoo CEO Marissa Mayer Explains How She Worked 130 Hours a Week and Why It Matters', *Business Insider* (4 Aug. 2016), https://www.businessinsider.com/yahoo-ceo-marissa-mayer-on-130-hour-work-weeks-2016-8.

54 James Tapper, 'Quiet Quitting: Why Doing the Bare Minimum at Work Has Gone Global', *The Guardian* (6 Aug. 2022), https://www.theguardian.com/money/2022/aug/06/quiet-quitting-why-doing-the-bare-minimum-at-work-has-gone-global.

55 'soft-girl revolution': Stephanie McNeal, 'Welcome to the Soft-Girl Revolution: How Young Women Are Rejecting Girlboss Culture for a Life of Leisure', *Glamour* (24 Oct. 2023), https://www.glamourmagazine.co.uk/article/soft-girl-revolution-girlboss-culture-opinion. 'decidedly over': Marisa Meltzer, 'Where Have All the Girlbosses Gone?', *Vanity Fair* (6 Sep. 2023), https://www.vanityfair.com/style/2023/09/where-have-all-the-girlbosses-gone.

56 Kimberley Bond, 'What Does the Rise of "Lazy Girl Jobs" Say About Our Attitude Towards Work Right Now?', *Cosmopolitan* (30 May 2024), https://www.cosmopolitan.com/uk/work/careers/a60949199/lazy-girl-jobs/.

57 Monica Ainley, 'I Lived The "Trad Wife" Life for A Week. This Is What It Taught Me', *British Vogue* (24 Feb. 2024), https://www.vogue.co.uk/article/trad-wife-trend.

58 Rory Satran, 'Stay-at-Home Girlfriends Are Having a Moment', *Wall Street Journal* (22 Dec. 2023), https://www.wsj.com/style/fashion/stay-at-home-girlfriends-tiktok-instagram-sahg-b7c20c6a.

59 One example is the 'Ballerina Farm Willa Sourdough Starter' sold by Ballerina Farm, https://ballerinafarm.com/products/ballerina-farm-sourdough-starter-willa.

60 Fortesa Latifi, 'For High School Age TikTok Influencers, Online Fame Can Bring Real-Life Consequences'. *Teen Vogue* (24 Oct. 2024), https://www.teenvogue.com/story/for-high-school-age-tiktok-influencers-online-fame-can-bring-real-life-consequences.

61 Jia Tolentino, 'The Very Unnerving Existence of Teen Boss, a Magazine for Girls', *New Yorker* (27 Mar. 2018), https://www.newyorker.com/books/page-turner/the-very-unnerving-existence-of-teen-boss-a-magazine-for-girls.

62 Rebecca Rubin, '"Cinderella" Trailer: Camila Cabello's Princess Wants Her Own Fashion Empire, Not Prince Charming', *Variety* (3 Aug. 2021), https://variety.com/2021/film/news/cinderella-trailer-camila-cabello-1235033631/.

63   Wage stagnation: Lawrence Mishel, Elise Gould and Josh Bivens, 'Wage Stagnation in Nine Charts', Economic Policy Institute (6 Jan. 2015), https://www.epi.org/publication/charting-wage-stagnation/. Soaring living costs: Rachel Clun, 'Live Reporting: Inflation Reaches Highest Level Since January 2024', BBC News (20 Aug. 2025), https://www.bbc.co.uk/news/live/cp895dyjo46t#:~:text=Inflation%20rose%20to%203.8%25%20in,National%20Statistics%20(ONS)%20show. Soaring house prices: Hal Bundrick, E. Napoletano and Aly J. Yale, 'Why Are Home Prices So High? How Today's Market Impacts Housing Costs', Yahoo! Finance (15 Aug. 2025), https://finance.yahoo.com/personal-finance/mortgages/article/why-are-home-prices-so-high-how-todays-market-impacts-housing-costs-184935828.html.

64   Melissa A. Fabello, PhD (@fyeahmfabello), 'PS: Someone reached out and asked for an example of how you can respond to someone if you don't have the space to support them. I offered this template', Twitter (12.09 a.m., 19 Nov. 2019), https://x.com/fyeahmfabello/status/1196581296564256768?s=20.

65   Bella (@whoslulugirl_2), 'Decided to vlog the whole morning! The cup is so cute!! #stanleyxstarbucks #stanleycup #starbucks #winterpink #stanley #target #vlog', TikTok (3 Jan. 2024), https://www.tiktok.com/@whoslulugirl_2/video/7319896253398060330.

66   'Transform Mobile Shopping With AR at Scale', Snapchat for Business (n.d.), https://forbusiness.snapchat.com/blog/catalog-powered-shopping-lenses.

67   Steffi Cao, 'Here's What I Tried on While Shopping at the Snapchat AR Store', BuzzFeed News (27 Jan. 2023), https://www.buzzfeednews.com/article/stefficao/snapchat-ar-shopping-feature.

68   Dhruv, 'What Is the Amazon Influencer Program?', EyeUniversal (7 Oct. 2024), https://www.eyeuniversal.com/blog/ecommerce/what-is-the-amazon-influencer-program/.

69   'TikTok Is the Platform Where Content and Commerce Converge, Helping Consumers Discover and Make Their Next Purchase', TikTok Newsroom (5 Jul. 2023), https://newsroom.tiktok.com/en-sg/tiktok-is-the-platform-where-content-and-commerce-converge-helping-consumers-discover-and-make-their-next-purchase-sg.

70   Conor Murray, 'Why Are Stanley Cups Trending on TikTok? The Water Bottle Craze Racks up Millions of Views and Lots of Revenue', *Forbes* (3 Jan. 2023), https://www.forbes.com/sites/conormurray/2024/01/03/why-is-tiktok-obsessed-with-stanley-cups-the-water-bottle-craze-racks-up-millions-of-views-and-lots-of-revenue/.

71   Jonelle Awomoyi, 'What Is Behind the TikTok Thirst for Stanley Water Cups?', BBC News (19 Jan. 2024), https://www.bbc.co.uk/news/entertainment-arts-67999424.

72   Rupert Neate, 'Ryan Kaji, 9, Earns $29.5m as This Year's Highest-Paid YouTuber', *The Guardian* (18 Dec. 2020), https://www.theguardian.com/technology/2020/dec/18/ryan-kaji-9-earns-30m-as-this-years-highest-paid-youtuber.

NOTES

73   Ryan's World, 'HUGE EGGS Surprise Toys Challenge with Inflatable Water Slide', YouTube (13 Apr. 2016), https://www.youtube.com/watch?v=jjd-BeTX6U0.

74   'Kids for Sale: Online Advertising and the Manipulation of Children' [report], Global Action Plan (2020), https://www.globalactionplan.org.uk/files/kids_for_sale.pdf.

75   Main source of shopping inspiration: Christoph Kastenholz, 'Gen Z and the Rise of Social Commerce', *Forbes* (17 May 2021), https://www.forbes.com/councils/forbesagencycouncil/2021/05/17/gen-z-and-the-rise-of-social-commerce/. Around 72 million data points: 'Kids for Sale', Global Action Plan.

76   Sophia Trimble, 'How to Nail Tik Tok's Catholic Girl Aesthetic', *Chatty Chums* (24 Oct. 2022), https://www.chattychums.com/articles/lifestyle/how-to-nail-tik-tok's-catholic-girl-aesthetic?srsltid=AfmBOopiZAYrEucL1S2TGe8S79j0JXqStrzOd0APbuzTXRELZFOCZJnP.

77   Ella Jae (@ellaajaee), 'why is this SO HARD HELP #stress #anxiety #ubereats', TikTok (16 Apr. 2023), https://www.tiktok.com/@ellaajaee/video/7222551526655528193.

78   Jeffrey J. Arnett, 'Emerging Adulthood: A Theory of Development from the Late Teens Through the Twenties', *American Psychologist*, 55/5 (2000), 469–80. https://doi.org/10.1037/0003-066X.55.5.469.

79   Daisy Buchanan, '25 Will Never Be the New 18 – So Parents, Don't Infantilise Young Adults', *The Guardian* (24 Sep. 2013), https://www.theguardian.com/commentisfree/2013/sep/24/25-will-never-be-the-new-18.

80   Isabel Atkinson, Bee Boileau and David Sturrock, 'Hotel of Mum and Dad? Co-Residence with Parents Among Those Aged 25–34' [report], Institute for Fiscal Studies (11 Jan. 2025), https://ifs.org.uk/publications/hotel-mum-and-dad-co-residence-parents-among-those-aged-25-34.

81   Nearly half of young adults: Erum Salam, 'Nearly 50% of US Parents Financially Supporting Adult Children, Study Finds', *The Guardian* (12 Mar. 2024), https://www.theguardian.com/us-news/2024/mar/12/parents-adult-children-financial-support. About 18% of Americans: Richard Fry, 'The Shares of Young Adults Living with Parents Vary Widely Across the U.S.', Pew Research Center (17 Apr. 2025), https://www.pewresearch.org/short-reads/2025/04/17/the-shares-of-young-adults-living-with-parents-vary-widely-across-the-us/.

82   Jean M. Twenge and Heejung Park, 'The Decline in Adult Activities Among U.S. Adolescents, 1976–2016', *Child Development*, 90/2 (2019), 638–54. https://doi.org/10.1111/cdev.12930.

83   Jean M. Twenge and Heejung Park, 'Teens Are Growing Up More Slowly Today than They Did in Past Decades' [news release], Society for Research in Child Development (19 Sep. 2017), https://www.eurekalert.org/news-releases/678786.

84   David Brooks, 'Excess Caution Its Own Risk', *Times-Tribune* (9 May 2023), https://www.thetimes-tribune.com/2023/05/09/excess-caution-its-own-risk/.
85   David Brooks, 'What Our Toxic Culture Does to the Young', *New York Times* (4 May 2023), https://www.nytimes.com/2023/05/04/opinion/gen-z-adulthood.html.
86   Jonathan Haidt and Greg Lukianoff, *The Coddling of the American Mind: How Good Intentions and Bad Ideas Are Setting up a Generation for Failure* (Penguin, 2018).
87   Brad Wolverton, 'As Students Struggle with Stress and Depression, Colleges Act As Counselors', *New York Times* (21 Feb. 2019), https://www.nytimes.com/2019/02/21/education/learning/mental-health-counseling-on-campus.html.
88   Walter E. Williams, 'College Lie About Their Worst Practices', *Investor's Business Daily* (17 Aug. 2015), https://www.investors.com/politics/commentary/walter-e-williams-colleges-creating-hostile-environment-for-free-speech/.
89   'heal our inner child': 'Inner Child Work: Understanding Your Childhood to Improve Mental Health', BetterHelp (updated 26 Aug. 2025), https://www.betterhelp.com/advice/therapy/inner-child-what-is-it-what-happened-to-it-and-how-can-i-fix-it/. 'reparent ourselves': Madeline Holcombe, 'It Might Be Time to "Reparent" Yourself. Here's How to Get Started', CNN (29 Apr. 2025), https://edition.cnn.com/2025/04/28/health/reparenting-yourself-how-to-start-wellness. Watch cartoons: Elisabeth Sherman, 'Therapists Explain How Cartoons Affect Your Mental Health', *VICE* (23 Mar. 2017), https://www.vice.com/en/article/therapists-explain-how-cartoons-affect-your-mental-health/. Sleep with stuffed animals: Sarah Gannett, 'The Case for Sleeping with Stuffed Animals as an Adult', *New York Times* (6 Feb. 2024), https://www.nytimes.com/wirecutter/blog/adults-who-sleep-with-stuffed-animals/.
90   Over 20% of plush toys in the US: Madeline Holcombe, 'Adults Can Sleep with Stuffed Animals, Too. It Might Even Be a Good Thing, Experts Say', CNN (30 Mar. 2025), https://edition.cnn.com/2025/03/30/health/adults-sleep-stuffed-animals. Those aged 12 and over: Sarah Whitten, 'Adults Are Buying Toys for Themselves, and It's the Biggest Source of Growth for the Industry', CNBC (19 Dec. 2022), https://www.cnbc.com/2022/12/19/kidults-biggest-sales-driver-toy-industry.html.
91   'Toying with Tradition: Nostalgic Kidults Fuel £1bn Surge as UK Gears up for Record Christmas Sales', Circana (13 Nov. 2024), https://www.circana.com/intelligence/press-releases/2024/toying-with-tradition-nostalgic-kidults-fuel-1bn-surge-as-uk-gears-up-for-record-christmas-sales/.
92   Adult Lego sets: 'Are LEGO® Sets for Adults?', Lego (n.d.), https://www.lego.com/en-gb/categories/adults-welcome. Adult days at Disneyland: 'How Disney Has Grown Its Business by Appealing to Adults', WARC (14 Aug. 2025), https://www.warc.com/content/feed/how-disney-has-grown-its-business-by-appealing-to-adults/en-GB/10877.

NOTES

93 '#adulting' [page], Tiktok (n.d.), https://www.tiktok.com/tag/adulting?lang=en.

94 Freya India, 'What Does Gen Z Have Against Motherhood?', *The Spectator* (15 Feb. 2022), https://www.spectator.co.uk/article/why-are-gen-z-against-motherhood/.

95 zoomie (@zoomie), 'Replying to @mafu Ngongoma the pregnancy nose saga continues', TikTok (26 Mar. 2024), https://www.tiktok.com/@zoomie/video/7350801106319985962.

96 'Yuni's Pros and Cons List of Having Children', *Wixsite* (n.d.), https://yuniquethoughtslist.wixsite.com/yuni-s-pros-and-cons/the-list.

97 Amanda Barroso, Kim Parker and Jesse Bennett, 'As Millennials Near 40, They're Approaching Family Life Differently Than Previous Generations' [report], Pew Research Center (27 May 2020), https://www.pewresearch.org/social-trends/2020/05/27/as-millennials-near-40-theyre-approaching-family-life-differently-than-previous-generations/.

98 James Beal, 'Young Put Off Having Children by Global Fears', *The Times* (26 Jul. 2023), https://www.thetimes.com/uk/healthcare/article/young-put-off-having-children-by-global-fears-z5c2w5f3l.

99 Martin Armstrong, 'Why Americans Don't Want Kids' [chart], Statista (22 Nov. 2021), https://www.statista.com/chart/26231/reasons-for-not-having-kids-united-states/.

100 Carolina Aragão, 'Among Young Adults Without Children, Men Are More Likely Than Women to Say They Want to Be Parents Someday', Pew Research Center (15 Feb. 2024), https://www.pewresearch.org/short-reads/2024/02/15/among-young-adults-without-children-men-are-more-likely-than-women-to-say-they-want-to-be-parents-someday/.

101 Jonathan Haidt, *The Anxious Generation: How the Great Rewiring of Childhood Caused an Epidemic of Mental Illness* (Penguin, 2024).

102 Zach Rausch, 'The Great Deterioration of Local Community Was A Major Driver of the Loss of the Play-Based Childhood', *After Babel* [Substack] (10 Jun. 2024), https://www.afterbabel.com/p/community-based-childhood.

103 Zach Rausch, 'Why Are Religious Teens Happier than Their Secular Peers?', *Boston Globe* (6 Jun. 2024), https://www.bostonglobe.com/2024/06/06/opinion/religious-teens-mental-health/.

104 Giancarlo Lucchetti, Harold G. Koenig and Alessandra Lamas Granero Lucchetti, 'Spirituality, Religiousness, and Mental Health: A Review of the Current Scientific Evidence', *World Journal of Clinical Cases*, 9/26 (2021), 7620–31. https://doi.org/10.12998/wjcc.v9.i26.7620.

105 Joey Marshall, 'Are Religious People Happier, Healthier? Our New Global Study Explores This Question', Pew Research Center (31 Jan. 2019), https://www.pewresearch.org/short-reads/2019/01/31/are-religious-people-happier-healthier-our-new-global-study-explores-this-question/.

106   All data in this paragraph is from Marshall, 'Are Religious People Happier, Healthier?'
107   'Rising School Pressure and Declining Family Support Especially Among Girls, Finds New WHO/Europe Report' [media release], World Health Organization (13 Nov. 2024), https://www.who.int/europe/news/item/13-11-2024-rising-school-pressure-and-declining-family-support-especially-among-girls--finds-new-who-europe-report.
108   Phyllis Ingham, 'Breaking the Silence: Addressing Burnout and Stress in College Healthcare Students and Educators', *ASCLS Today*, 38/5 (2024), https://ascls.org/breaking-the-silence/.
109   Anna Codrea-Rado, 'Do I Have Productivity Dysmorphia?', *Refinery29* (9 Sep. 2021), https://www.refinery29.com/en-gb/2021/09/10640493/what-is-productivity-dysmorphia.
110   David Brooks, 'What Our Toxic Culture Does to the Young', *New York Times* (4 May 2023), https://www.nytimes.com/2023/05/04/opinion/gen-z-adulthood.html.
111   Helen Sweeting, Kate Hunt and Abita Bhaskar, 'Consumerism and Well-being in Early Adolescence', *International Journal of Adolescence and Youth*, 17/3 (2012), 802–20. https://doi.org/10.1080/13676261.2012.685706.
112   'Kids for Sale? Children and Digital Action', Global Action Plan (n.d.), https://www.globalactionplan.org.uk/online-climate/end-surveillance-advertising-to-kids/end-surveillance-advertising-to-kids-faqs, citing Helga Dittmar et al, 'The Relationship Between Materialism and Personal Well-Being: A Meta-Analysis', *Journal of Personality and Social Psychology*, 107/5 (2014), 879–924. https://doi.org/10.1037/a0037409.
113   Jon Haidt, 'Why the Mental Health of Liberal Girls Sank First and Fastest', *After Babel* [Substack] (9 Mar. 2023), https://www.afterbabel.com/p/mental-health-liberal-girls.
114   Conservatives' internal and liberals' external locus of control: Kaye D. Sweetser, 'Partisan Personality: The Psychological Differences Between Democrats and Republicans, and Independents Somewhere in Between', *American Behavioral Scientist*, 58/9 (2014), 1183–94. https://doi.org/10.1177/0002764213506215. Greater likelihood of loneliness, anxiety and depression: Johanna H. M. Hovenkamp-Hermelink et al, 'Differential Associations of Locus of Control with Anxiety, Depression and Life-Events: A Five-Wave, Nine-Year Study to Test Stability and Change', *Journal of Affective Disorders*, 253 (2019), 26–34. https://doi.org/10.1016/j.jad.2019.04.005.
115   Bruce Handy, 'Dystopia Now: Why *The Hunger Games* Still Speaks Volumes About Teens, War, Propaganda, and More', *Vanity Fair* (20 May 2025), https://www.vanityfair.com/hollywood/story/dystopia-now-why-the-hunger-games-still-speaks-volumes-about-teens-war-propaganda-and-more.

NOTES

116 'U.S. Teen Girls Experiencing Increased Sadness and Violence' [press release], Centers for Disease Control and Prevention (13 Feb. 2023), https://www.cdc.gov/media/releases/2023/p0213-yrbs.html.

117 Richard Partington, 'Mental Health Crisis "Means Youth Is No Longer One of Happiest Times of Life"', *The Guardian* (3 Mar. 2025), https://www.theguardian.com/society/2025/mar/03/youth-mental-health-crisis-happiness-un-uk-us-australia.

CONCLUSION

1 Niomi Harris, 'The Unrecognisable Photo That Sparked Molly-Mae's Epic Transformation before TV Fame Resurfaces in Wake of Documentary', *Daily Mail* (17 Jan. 2025), https://www.dailymail.co.uk/tvshowbiz/article-14292133/Molly-Mae-hague-unrecognisable-photo-transformation-TV-fame-documentary.html.

2 Rob Haskell, 'Bella from the Heart: On Health Struggles, Happiness, and Everything in Between', *Vogue* (15 Mar. 2022), https://www.vogue.com/article/bella-hadid-cover-april-2022.

3 Laura Ceci, 'Quarterly Downloads of Facetune 2019–2022, by Region', Statista (4 Mar. 2024), https://www.statista.com/statistics/1351687/downloads-of-facetune-by-region/.

4 Backlash against platforms like BetterHelp: e.g. Ashley Viola, 'BetterHelp Is Bad for Your Mental Health', YouTube (27 Feb. 2024), https://www.youtube.com/watch?v=AAYLHcjXVp0. Young women opening up: e.g. Rikki Schlott, 'Gen Zers Says Antidepressants Have Ruined Their Sex Lives: "I'm Dead Inside"', *New York Post* (25 Feb. 2025), https://nypost.com/2025/02/25/us-news/gen-zers-says-antidepressants-have-ruined-their-sex-lives/.

5 Convinced them they were mentally ill: Zeynab Mohamed, 'Young Women Are Self-Diagnosing Personality Disorders, Thanks To TikTok', *Elle UK* (21 Apr. 2022), https://www.elle.com/uk/life-and-culture/a39573245/young-women-self-diagnose-personality-disorder-tiktok/. Only made things worse: David Cox, '"It Feels like We've Been Lobotomised": The Possible Sexual Consequences of SSRIs', *The Guardian* (2 Mar. 2024), https://www.theguardian.com/society/2024/mar/02/ssri-antidepressants-sexual-dysfunction-side-effects-consequences-libido.

6 Michelle Faverio, Monica Anderson and Eugenie Park, 'Teens, Social Media and Mental Health' [report], Pew Research Center (22 Apr. 2025), https://www.pewresearch.org/internet/2025/04/22/teens-social-media-and-mental-health/.

7 Emma Ayers, 'Gen Z on a "Dopamine Diet" – They're Bringing Back the Flip Phone', *Washington Times* (18 Apr. 2025), https://www.washingtontimes.com/news/2025/apr/18/generation-z-bringing-back-flip-phone-young-people-go-dopamine-diet/.

8   Zach Rausch and Jon Haidt, 'The Youth Rebellion Is Growing', *After Babel* [Substack] (20 May 2024), https://www.afterbabel.com/p/the-youth-rebellion-is-growing.

9   Dan Milmo, 'Gen Z Is Breaking Up with Dating Apps, Ofcom Says', *The Guardian* (28 Nov. 2024), https://www.theguardian.com/lifeandstyle/2024/nov/28/gen-z-breaking-up-with-dating-apps-ofcom.

10 Michelle Goldberg, 'Why Sex-Positive Feminism Is Falling Out of Fashion', *New York Times* (24 Sep. 2021), https://www.nytimes.com/2021/09/24/opinion/sex-positivity-feminism.html; Gaby Hinsliff, '"It Stopped Me Having Sex for a Year": Why Generation Z Is Turning Its Back on Sex-Positive Feminism', *The Guardian* (2 Feb. 2022), https://www.theguardian.com/lifeandstyle/2022/feb/02/it-stopped-me-having-sex-for-a-year-why-generation-z-is-turning-its-back-on-sex-positive-feminism.

11 Madeleine Holden, 'These Gen Z Women Think Sex Positivity Is Overrated', BuzzFeed News (29 Jul. 2021), https://www.buzzfeednews.com/article/madeleineholden/gen-z-sex-positivity.

12 Constance Grady, 'The Return of the Porn Wars: How Today's Fight over Pornography Is Rooted in a 40-Year-Old Feminist Schism', *Vox* (16 May 2023), https://www.vox.com/the-highlight/23699724/pornography-wars-feminism-pornhub-andrea-dworkin-catharine-mackinnon-amia-srinivasan-kelsy-burke.

13 Hinsliff, '"It Stopped Me Having Sex for a Year"'.

14 Erica Pandey, 'Young Men Are Leading a Religious Resurgence', *Axios* (10 May 2025), https://www.axios.com/2025/05/10/religious-young-people-christianity-rise.

15 Gregory A. Smith et al, 'Decline of Christianity in the U.S. Has Slowed, May Have Leveled Off: Findings from the 2023-24 Religious Landscape Study' [report], Pew Research Center (26 Feb. 2025), https://www.pewresearch.org/religion/2025/02/26/decline-of-christianity-in-the-us-has-slowed-may-have-leveled-off/.

16 Hattie Williams, '"Dramatic Growth" in Church Attendance by Young People, Bible Society Research Finds', *Church Times* (8 Apr. 2025), https://www.churchtimes.co.uk/articles/2025/11-april/news/uk/dramatic-growth-in-young-people-attending-church-bible-society-research-finds.

17 Katie O'Connor, 'SAMHSA Survey Shows Four Years of Mental Health, Substance Use Trends', Psychiatry Online (1 Aug. 2025), https://psychiatryonline.org/doi/10.1176/appi.pn.2025.09.9.34.

18 Melissa Jenco, 'CDC: Teens' Mental Health Worse Than a Decade Ago Despite Small Improvements in 2023', *AAP News* (6 Aug. 2024), https://publications.aap.org/aapnews/news/29622/CDC-Teens-mental-health-worse-than-a-decade-ago; 'Youth Risk Behavior Survey Data Summary & Trends Report, 2013–2023', Centers for Disease Control and Prevention (2023), https://www.cdc.gov/yrbs/dstr/pdf/YRBS-2023-Data-Summary-Trend-Report.pdf.

Index

academic pressure 204–205, 222–223
activism, social justice 113–117, 201–202
ADHD 63–65
adulthood, postponement of 216–219
aesthetics 213–214
affirmation 195–196, 198–200
aging, anxieties about 33, 52–53
AI enhancement 25–26
AI therapy 74–75
algorithms
 effect on identity 214–215
 and insecurity 32–34
 and marketing 33–36
Amoruso, Sophia 206
anxiety, social 3, 5, 7, 152–153, 155 (*see also* depression)
Arnett, Jeffrey 216
Ask.fm 111–112
astrology 197–198
attachment issues 63, 184, 188–189
'authentic self' 47–48, 134
autism 63–64, 83

Barbie 77
'Bed Rotting' 143
Bell, Kristin 80–81
BeReal, app 96–97, 130
BetterHelp 67, 69–73
Bine, Anne-Sophie 59
biometric data collection 34–35
Black Lives Matter (BLM) 116–119
BlackBerry Messenger 131
Blanchflower, David 224
Body Dysmorphic Disorder (BDD)
 and filters 50–51
 and suicide risk 49
Botox 33, 42, 52–53
bullying, online 110–113
Bumble, app 146, 161, 164–165, 239

Call Her Daddy, podcast 44, 72, 169, 186–187
Cerebral Inc. 78–80, 82
Character.ai 74, 148
Charles, James 21, 23–25, 38, 44, 48, 108–109
ChatGPT
 as friend 149

ChatGPT (cont.)
  launch of 147
  and mental health
    support 74–75
Cheyenne, Jordan 104
child rearing
  postponement of 206–207
  rejection of 219–220
community, and social
  media 139–142, 144
consumerism 210–215, 234
Cooney, Eugenia 65
cosmetic surgery 42
  BDD 49
  as empowerment 45
  on Instagram 29, 42
  rise in numbers of 52
  as self-care 48
couple influencers 99–103
Cyrus, Miley 175–176

dating 158–161
dating apps 161–167
  backlash against 239
dating influencers 183–188
de Jager, Nikkie 46–48
deepfakes 182–183
depression 3, 7, 223–225, 241
  and algorithms 65
  awareness as sales strategy 67, 70, 73
  causes 77, 86
  divorce 153
  Hers (company) 81
  influencers 73
  Instagram 120

  medication 82
  porn 189, 191
  religion 222
  rising rates of 5, 7, 16, 83
  school-based therapy 87
  on Tumblr 59
Deyes, Alfie 99
divorce 133–136, 153–154
Dobrik, David 100
Done, company 80
Dove, beauty brand 29, 43–44, 51

eating disorders
  divorce 153
  rates 7, 16, 83, 230
  social contagion 84
  statistics 49–50, 59
  TikTok 191
Elomia, chatbot 74
'emerging adulthood' 216
emotions 90–91
empowerment
  divorce as 135
  emotional detachment as 186
  genuine 226, 249
  OnlyFans as 180
  pornography as 175
  as sales strategy 9, 11, 44–45, 48, 55, 210, 225, 229, 233
  sex work as 181–182
  sex-positivity 176
  work as 205–206
estrangement, family 137–138
Euphoria, TV show 157–158, 176

INDEX

Facebook
    activism on 114–116
    advertising 34
    algorithms 32
    AR filters 30
    BDD 49
    child sex abuse 191
    children on 106–107
    'Poke' function 128
    rates of use 123
    redefinition of 'friend' 128
    Stories 95
Facebook Messenger 128–129
Facetune, app 142
    advertising for 44
    AI assistant 148
    body dysmorphia 50
    as community 144
    decline in downloads 238
    as empowerment 48
    fix for insecurities 26
    Instagram Face 40
    launch of 22–23
    mental health 46–47
    statistics 25
    use of 21–23, 47, 142
Facetune2, app 25
Field, Evie Meg 85
Fizz, app 112
Floyd, George 116
Franke, Ruby 120–121
Franke, Shari 120–121
Friend, wearable AI 127–128
friends, close 132–133, 151–152, 250
friends, simulation of, via AI 145–150

Garza, Koti and Haven 43
gender dysphoria, rates of 66, 83, 85–86
George, Alex 75–76

Habboo, Sophie 101
Haidt, Jonathan 132, 142, 217, 221–222, 224
Harmon, Demetrius 67
Harris, Kamala 117
'hashtag activism' 116
hate pages 110
helicopter parenting 217
Hers, company 73, 79–81, 88, 230
Hims, company 79
Hinge, app 115–116, 130, 164–166, 239, 243
hook-ups 166–171

Instagram 22–23
    (see also Facetune, app)
    ad revenue 36
    advertising statistics 213
    algorithms 32, 34
    body image 49, 52
    'Boyfriends of Instagram' 102–103
    bullying 110–112
    child sex abuse 191–192
    data on users 10
    and depression 120
    eating disorders 49
    filters 22–23, 28, 30
    mental health 60
    monthly users worldwide 97
    and pornography 107, 176–177

Instagram (*cont.*)
  regrets about 123
  Shop tab 211
  Stories 95
  temporary ban of filters 29
  use by children 123
Instagram Face 39–40, 42, 177, 215, 238

Jenner, Kendall 66–67
Jenner, Kylie 25, 35, 41–42

Kardashian, Khloé 24, 44–46
Kardashian, Kim 37–40, 43, 46, 161
Kardashian, Kylie 39, 41
Kardashian-Jenner family 38–39
Keech, Daisy 78
Keeping Up with the Kardashians 39, 41, 46
Kopf, Corinna 67
Koshy, Liza 100

Laing, Jamie 101
Lasch, Christopher 199
Lightricks 22, 25, 35, 46
loneliness 150–155
L'Oréal 30
Lovato, Demi 117, 180
Lukianoff, Greg 217

Madonna 45
manifestation 195–196, 198–199
manosphere 185
marriage rates 136–137

medication, mental health
  online sales 78–80
  prescription rates 82
  safety of 77–78
  as self-care 81
  SSRIs 75–77, 88–89
  stigma 76, 81–82
mental health
  apps for 142, 144
  harmed by social media 125–126
  increase in rates of disorder 7, 83–85
  and mental health influencers 67–68
  pushback against overdiagnosis 238
  and self-care 47
  as social media topic 60–62, 67–68
MeToo movement 115–116
Microsoft Messenger 128
misogyny 45, 185–186
Mongeau, Tana 23, 41, 44, 80, 100, 180
Monk, Brooke 119
Mooney, Daniel 29
MSN 128, 130, 141

neurodivergence 63–64
New Age spirituality 197–198

OkCupid 115
online therapy 69–73
OnlyFans 177, 179–182, 209

INDEX

Paul, Jake 100
Perfect365 23, 26, 35
Phillips, Lily 178–179
politics 113–119, 138, 201–203, 221
Pornhub 144, 157–158, 172–175, 191–193, 228, 231, 234
pornography
 (*see also* OnlyFans; Pornhub)
 age at first exposure 9, 171–175, 221
 backlash against 239–240
 damage from 189–193
 deepfakes 182–183
 industry 11, 233
 and self-esteem 189–191
 sexual violence 174–175
 social media platforms 177–178
Post-SSRI Sexual Dysfunction (PSSD) 88
productivity 204–210
prostitution 181–182
Psychologist (chatbot) 74
'Put a Finger Down Challenge" 63–64, 79

quiet quitting 207

Reddit
 AI 147–148
 anonymity 60
 BDD 50
 community 141
 deepfakes 182

pathologizing personality 137, 152
pornography 174, 189–190
PSSD 89
relationships 103, 188–190
skincare 52–53
witchcraft 198
religion
 and activism 201–202
 as aesthetic 214
 decline in 4, 155, 196–198, 215, 221–222, 232
 mimicking of 199–200, 225
 renewed interest in 240
 self as God 200
 and therapy 200
Replika, app 146–148, 177–178, 230, 234

Saccone Joly, Jonathan and Anna 105–106
Sandberg, Sheryl 205–206
Scott, Travis 70
self-care
 beauty routines as 46–47
 change of concept 142–143, 298
 infantilisation 218
 medication as 79, 81
 relationships 137
 as sales strategy 47–48, 55, 79
sex workers 181–182
sexting 160–161, 171
Shrier, Abigail 87
situationships 169–170, 189
Skype 130

Snap Inc. 28
Snapchat
  activism on 114–115
  'Best Friends' feature 131, 159
  body image 49
  bullying 110
  cosmetic surgery 52
  'Friend Solar System' 131
  influencer videos 37–38
  Lens Studio 28
  Lenses 27–28, 30–31, 115
  mental health 60–61
  monthly users worldwide 97
  My AI 147–148
  'My Eyes Only' 160
  pornography 177
  rates of videos per day 95
  regrets about 123
  sexting 160
  Shoppable AR lenses 211
  Snap Map 111, 129
  Snap Scores 159
  'Snapchat dysphoria' 52
  Stories 37, 95–96, 129–130
  Streaks 129, 154
  use of algorithms 32
  vlogging 94
social contagion 84–86
SocialAI, app 145
SSRIs 75–77, 88–89
Star, Jeffree 108–109
suicide 7, 77, 88, 120
  Ask.fm 112
  BDD 49
  divorce 153
  medication 230
  plans 59

  rates 5, 7, 16, 224
  religiosity 222
  suicidal thoughts 77, 88, 120, 122, 241

Talkspace 69, 71, 73
Tate, Andrew 185
Tattle Life 109
Tea, app 166
Teigen, Chrissy 24
therapy, online 69–72
TikTok
  ad revenue 36
  AR filters 28–31
  and BetterHelp 73
  Bold Glamour beauty filter 29
  CommunityToks 139
  data on users 10, 34–35
  dating advice 184, 187–188
  dating influencers 184
  Effect House 28
  and insecurity 35
  inverted filter 50
  mental health 60–62, 68, 86
  mental health influencers 63–66
  monthly users worldwide 97
  as news source 118
  pornography 177–178
  Pride 115
  regrets about 123
  Retouch feature 31
  self-diagnosis 84
  sex workers on 181
  social contagion 84–85
  TikTok Shop 36, 211–212
  toxic family members 137–138

INDEX

transgender 66, 86
use of algorithms 32–33, 65
Tinder 13, 116, 162–165, 168, 170, 192, 227, 239
Tourette's syndrome 84–85
trad wives 207–208, 214
transgender people 66, 86, 106, 118, 122, 201
Trump, Donald J. 115
Tumblr 59–60, 75, 141, 239
Twenge, Jean 132, 150, 217, 224
Twitter. *see* X (formerly Twitter)

vlogging 94
  of children 104–106

Westbrook, Tati 108–109
WhatsApp 10, 95, 129
witchcraft 197–198

Wolfe Herd, Whitney 161–162

X (formerly Twitter) 21, 23, 32, 66, 177, 180, 209, 239

YikYak 112
YouTube
  child abuse 120–122
  child audience 123
  influencer videos 21, 36–43
  launch of 94
  monthly users worldwide 97
  Westbrook-Charles feud 108–109

Zoella (Zoe Sugg) 36–37, 40, 58–59, 99
Zoom 31
Zuckerberg, Mark 149, 191

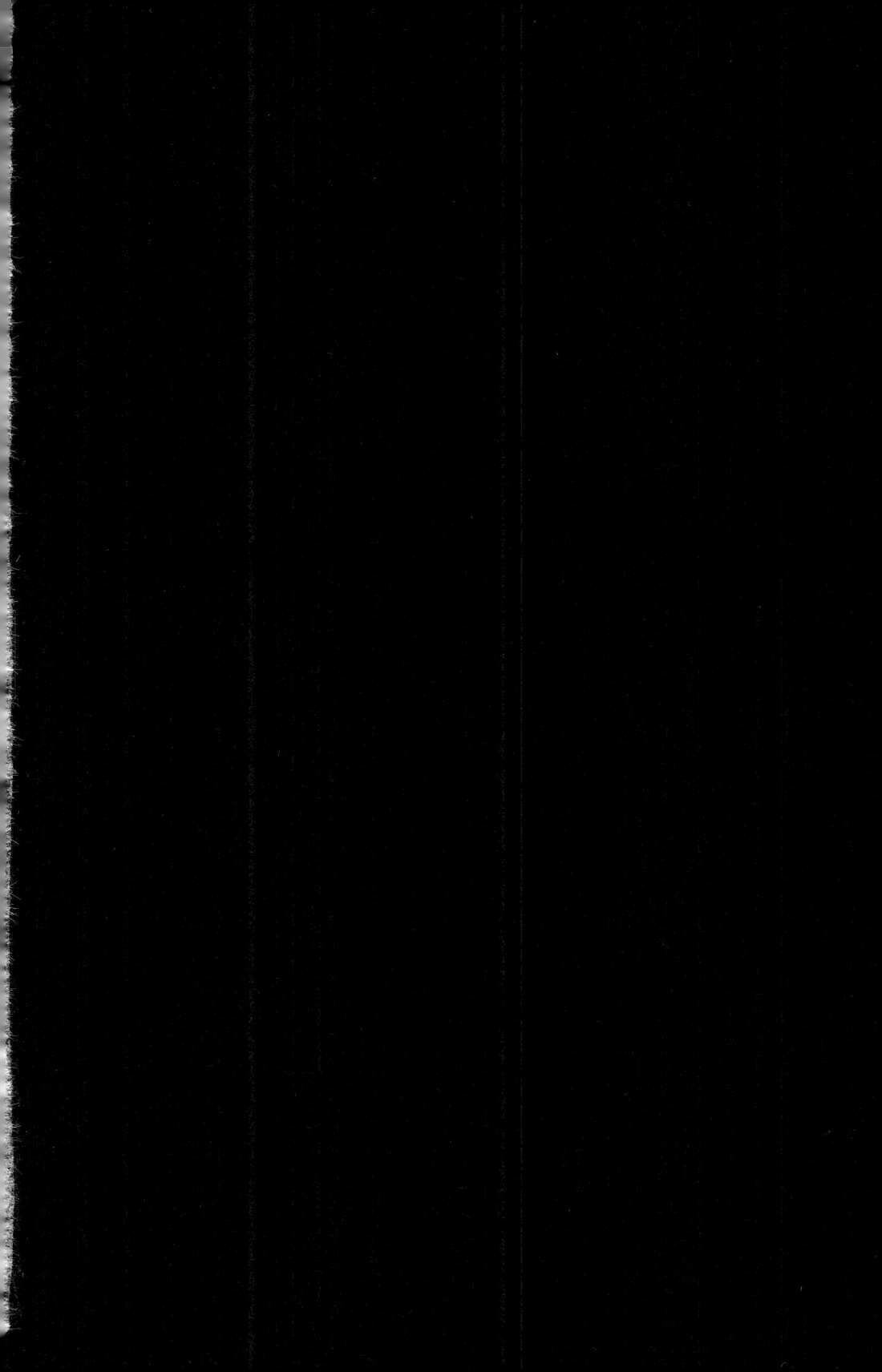